THE AEPCO PROJECT

VOLUME I

Greenlee to Dos Condado Survey

and

Data Recovery of Archaeological Resources

by

Kay Simpson and Deborah A. Westfall

with contributions by:

Jeanette Dickerson

E. Jane Rosenthal

Jon Czaplicki

Gerald K. Kelso

Cultural Resource Management Section
Arizona State Museum
The University of Arizona

May 1978

Archaeological Series No. 117

ABSTRACT

The Arizona Electric Power Cooperative, Inc. contracted with the Cultural Resource Management Section of the Arizona State Museum for an intensive survey of the R-O-W corridor and access roads of a proposed transmission line system in the Safford-Clifton area. Eighty-nine sites were found. Of these, three Mogollon pithouse villages, recommended for nomination to the National Register of Historic Places, were avoided by construction activities. Mitigation was required for a 30 percent sample of the remaining sites. These included surface scatters of tools and lithic debris, two historic trash scatters, and a prehistoric water control system. Research focused on land-use patterns and cultural-historical inferences.

ACKNOWLEDGEMENTS

We wish to thank and acknowledge the many individuals who contributed to this report. We are especially grateful to the sponsor, Arizona Electric Power Cooperative, Inc. Don Powell, Right-of-Way Agent, has been outstanding in his efforts in coordinating archaeological studies with AEPCO's requirements and activities. The Burns and McDonnell Engineering Company, Kansas City, Missouri, is also to be thanked for providing technical assistance to Arizona State Museum survey and monitoring crew members.

Many people in the Safford and Phoenix offices of the Bureau of Land Management provided background information for the project area, assisted in consultations with AEPCO, and assisted in nomination of sites to the National Register of Historic Places. Gay Kinkade of the Safford office deserves special praise.

Very special thanks are due to Dean and Mary Krieg, owners of the Country Manor Motel, Safford, for their cheerful hospitality.

Larry Humphries, BLM soil scientist, Safford District, and Alfred Dewall, USDA soil scientist, Safford District, provided technical assistance and unpublished soil reports. Mr. Humphries took the time to visit our field operation and identify soils at Arizona CC:2:40 and CC:2:44. Identification of lithic material was assisted by Paul Dunlevy, BLM geologist, Safford District, and Robert O'Haire, Arizona Bureau of Mines, University of Arizona.

Appreciation is extended to Emil W. Haury and William J. Robinson for discussing problems of the area's culture-history with us. William Liesenbein and James E. Ayres advised and assisted in identification of historical materials. W. Bruce Masse and R. Gwinn Vivian provided unpublished manuscripts and helpful advice on southwestern water control systems. Emil W. Haury and Gay Kinkade aided in ceramic identification.

The lithic analysis was assisted by Larry Linford, Arizona State Museum, and George Teague, National Park Service. Curtis Schaafsma provided his unpublished analysis of materials from Abiquiu Reservoir, New Mexico as a model for our analysis. Roberta Hagaman wrote the computer program for the lithic analysis and offered valuable comments on our statistical results.

Those involved in producing this report deserve special citation for taking our drafts and translating them into final copy. Virginia Diebold and Sue Brew shared the burden of typing the rough drafts, but Virginia and Barbara Beane had the onerous job of typing final copy. Artifact photographs were taken by Helga Teiwes. Marcia Petta, Kathryn Kamp, and Charles Sternberg drafted contour and feature maps. Ken Rozen and Bonnie Marson illustrated the lithic artifacts. Gayle Hartmann edited the final copy.

Lastly, we would like to thank Jon Czaplicki, Project Director for the data recovery phase; Lynn Teague, Project Director for the survey phase and Head of the Cultural Resource Management Section; and R. Gwinn Vivian, the Principal Investigator of the AEPCO Project. All had the task of reading rough drafts and encouraging us when "the rocks wouldn't cooperate."

TABLE OF CONTENTS

LIST OF FIGURES

LIST OF TABLES

CHAPTER 1

THE AEPCO PROJECT

Introduction

The Arizona Electric Power Cooperative, Inc. (AEPCO), a Rural Electrification Administration generation and transmission cooperative, is adding generating units and associated transmission segments to their present system in southeastern Arizona. On September 24, 1976, AEPCO contracted with the Cultural Resource Management Section of the Arizona State Museum (ASM) to survey and evaluate the cultural resources of the right-of-way (R-O-W) corridor and access roads for the northern portion of this system. Following this survey, recommendations were made by ASM for protection of archaeological resources through a combination of site protection, site monitoring, and partial data recovery on selected sites. These contracts were in accordance with the National Environmental Policy Act of 1969 which states that it is the "continuing responsibility of the Federal Government to use all practical means, consistent with other essential considerations of national policy, to improve and coordinate Federal plans, functions, programs and resources to the end that the nation may...preserve important historic, cultural, and natural aspects of our national heritage." This act provides for archaeological research in areas affected by federal land modification guidelines of Title 36 CFR 800 of the Advisory Council on Historic Preservation pursuant to the National Historic Preservation Act of 1966.

The survey discovered 72 archaeological sites in the R-O-W corridor and 17 sites on access roads. Three of these sites were recommended to the Bureau of Land Management (BLM), the acting Federal agency, for nomination to the National Register of Historic Places. Adverse effects on the other sites, primarily lithic scatters, were mitigated by a program of research and data recovery involving a 30 percent sample of archaeological loci. Research concentrated on developing a program of analysis and interpretation of lithic use area involving non-contemporaneous surface scatters of tools and lithic debris without obvious chronological or cultural indicators. In addition, two historic trash scatters and a prehistoric water control system were investigated.

Location and Boundaries of the Project

AEPCO plans to construct two new generating units at their existing Apache plant site in Cochise County. Related transmission facilities include the building of 105 km of new 230-kV transmission line (the Greenlee-Dos Condado segment), the replacement of 102 km of 115-kV line with 230-kV line (the Dos Condado-Apache segment), the building of two 345-kV lines (the TG&E-Greenlee substation loop and the Vail-Bicknell line), and the building of three new AEPCO substations (the Greenlee, Morenci, and Hackberry substations). This report concerns the survey and data recovery on land affected by the 230-kV line, the TG&E-Greenlee 345-kV loop, and the three substations (Figure 1). The report of the Dos Condado-Apache segment will be presented in Volume II of the AEPCO Project; the Vail-Bicknell line was reported by McClellan (1976). Volume III will contain site descriptions and their location along the transmission line R-O-W corridor.

The first segment of 230-kV transmission line begins at AEPCO's proposed Greenlee Substation, located immediately north of the existing TG&E Reactor Substation, near York in Greenlee County. AEPCO will tap the TG&E 345-kV line and extend a 2.4 km 345-kV "shoofly" line to connect this line to the AEPCO Greenlee Substation. The 230-kV line then exits the Greenlee Substation, extending west-northwest to the AEPCO Morenci 230-kV Substation. This line segment is 15.7 km long. The center line of this corridor crosses a canyonland-mesa system draining south from the Big Lue Mountains into the Gila River.

A 230-kV line then exits north from the Morenci Substation to the Phelps-Dodge Mining Company in Morenci, terminating near existing smelter buildings. This 25.7 km segment crosses ridgelands between the Gila and San Francisco rivers, the San Francisco River, and crosses the tailings pond of the Phelps-Dodge mines.

The second line segment exits from the Morenci Substation and extends southwesterly approximately 40 km to the new Hackberry 230-kV Substation. This segment follows a rather circuitous route due to the extremely rough terrain. The center line extends from the Morenci Substation almost due south for 3.7 km, crossing the Gila River. The line then turns west and southwest through the northern part of the Peloncillo Mountains, then due west for 8.8 km through the Peloncillo foothills. It then extends north-northwest, crossing the Gila River and its floodplain to a point near Head Canyon. There the line turns northwest to the Hackberry Substation crossing Pleistocene terraces and the lower bajada of the Gila Mountains.

From the Hackberry Substation a 230-kV mine service line will extend northwest-north for 12.8 km along the upper bajada of the Gila Mountains, terminating at the Phelps-Dodge Safford mine.

The fourth line segment begins at the Hackberry Substation, extends south for 7.2 km, then turns southwest for 4 km to the existing Dos Condado Substation. This line segment crosses the lower bajada of the Gila Mountains,

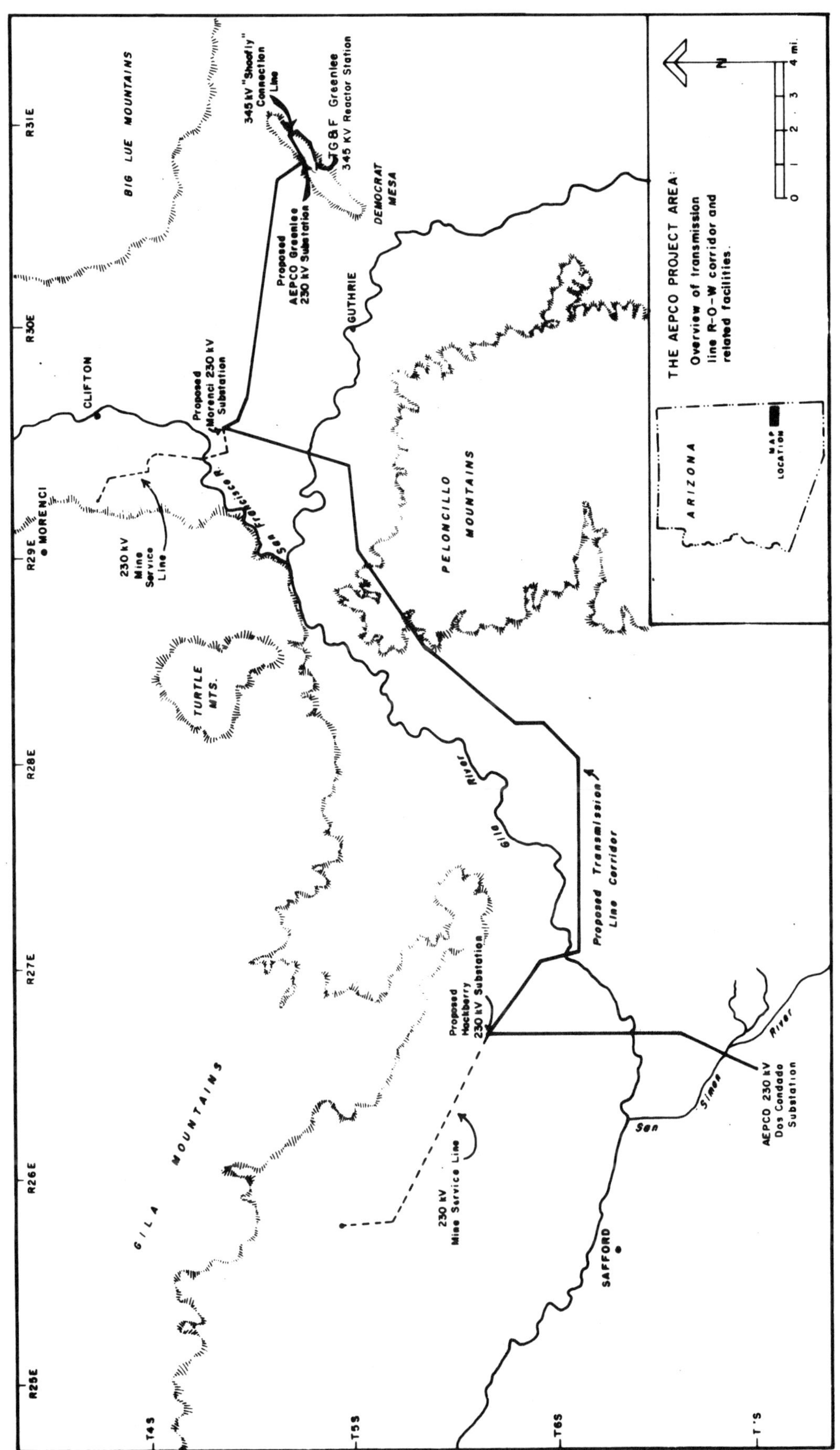

Figure 1. Overview of AEPCO Greenlee-Dos Condado Transmission System.

Pleistocene terraces of the Gila River, the Gila River and its floodplain, and the San Simon River Valley (Burns and McDonnell 1974:A-31-35).

In addition to the original R-O-W corridor, a 2.4 km re-alignment corridor was surveyed when the transmission line was moved to avoid Arizona CC:2:30, a site recommended for nomination to the National Register of Historic Places.

Identification of Impact Areas

The direct impact area of the transmission line is the 30 m wide R-O-W corridor; maximum impact will occur at the tower locations within this corridor. The proposed 230-kV transmission line will be placed on wooden "H" frame structures. The main poles will be 45.7 cm in diameter at the base and set approximately 3 m into the ground. Disturbance will result from erection of poles, backfilling, and surface destruction due to power equipment. Major items of such equipment include:

> ...power auger for drilling pole hoses; air compressor for tamping backfill around structures; vehicle with power-operated boom for lifting structures into place (structures of this type are normally assembled on the ground and then lifted into place with a vehicle-mounted boom); power-operated tensioner for pulling in conductors under tension; lowboy semi-trailers for hauling poles and other materials; and trucks and pickups for hauling tools and personnel (Burns and McDonnell 1974:A-29).

There is considerable variation in span lengths of distance between structures, but the average is approximately 230 m or five structures per kilometer.

The substations average 275 m long by 150 m wide, the entire area to be impacted by construction. Adjacent to such substations are additional impact zones for access, parking areas, and construction. ASM surveyed the substation sites, but because the adjacent impact areas were still in the planning stage, the museum did not survey the latter.

The access roads for construction vehicles are another primary adverse impact on archaeological resources. The survey of the access roads did not occur until after completion of the transmission line R-O-W survey. Due to time limitations and contract stipulations, only proposed access roads were surveyed. Existing roads were not surveyed but were spot-checked, since disturbance had already occurred and future impacts would be minimal. Where terrain permits, AEPCO plans to limit vehicles to the R-O-W corridor in order to confine impacts. Where necessary, AEPCO will put in roads laterally to the corridor. Impacts will include blading, dumping dirt on road sides, and vehicle tracks.

CHAPTER 2

THE PROJECT AREA: BIOPHYSICAL AND CULTURAL BACKGROUND

Environment

Introduction

Subsistence technology and site distribution are profoundly influenced by cultural-environmental interaction. Knowledge of environmental characteristics such as the location of water resources, rock outcrops for tools, exploitable plant and animal resources, and arable lands aids the archaeologist in understanding why sites are located where they are and in evaluating possible site activities. A regional overview of the environmental resources of the project area is presented below.

Physiography: Topography and Mineral Resources

Physiographically the Greenlee-Dos Condado R-O-W corridor is located in the Mountain Region (also known as the Mexican Highland Region) of the Basin and Range Province in southeastern Arizona (Wilson 1962:86). The Mountain Region extends across Arizona in a broad belt trending northwest to southeast though in the project area it trends more nearly north to south. This region includes some of the highest and widest mountain ranges in the province and is characterized by a great number of short, nearly parallel ranges that rarely exceed 80 km in length and 2400 m in elevation. The highest peak is Mt. Graham at 3265 m in the Pinaleño Range just west of the project area.

The ranges generally consist of Paleozoic quartzites, sandstones, and limestones resting on Precambrian schists and granites. In most places these older rocks are covered by Tertiary flows of basalt, rhyolites, and andesites.

Topographically the whole mountain region north of the Gila River near Morenci and Clifton appears as a maze of short ridges, minor plateaus, and peaks. This area is primarily an intricately faulted plateau where the older rocks are covered by heavy flows of basalt. Headwater erosion has been severe; southward flowing streams have eroded deep canyons in the eastern and western parts of the area. The San Francisco River is the major water source with the Blue River and Chase Creek its only important tributaries. The San Francisco River flows in a canyon several hundred meters deep, cut in detrital formations. Country between the San Francisco and Gila rivers consists of gradually rising terraces of detrital material (Lindgren 1905 a,b; Moolick and Durek 1966).

The Gila Mountains are also tilted fault-blocks of volcanic rock. The topography is one of long finger-like mesas and ridges having gently rounded tops and steep sides with ridges ranging from several centimeters to 60 m in height. The bajada and pediment consist of a southwestward dipping, dissected erosional plain. Five geologic terraces have been created by alternate periods of downcutting and stabilization of the Gila River. Eagle and Bonita creeks, northeast of the transmission line, are the only perennial tributaries flowing through the Gila Mountains into the Gila River. Bonita Creek separates the Gila Mountains from the Turtle Mountains (a southeastern extension of the Natanes Rim) (Heindl and McCullough 1961; Robinson and Cook 1966; Arizona Highway Department 1965 a,b; Gelderman 1970:52-53).

The Peloncillo Mountains consist of pumiceous, volcanic cinder deposits (Wilson 1965:26). The R-O-W corridor passes through the Black Hills section of these mountains, an area of basalt flows almost barren of vegetation. The highest peak in this range is Guthrie Mountain at 1370 m.

The corridor also crosses a series of canyons that are dissected pediments of the Big Lue Mountains. These southwest-dipping erosional plains have drainages with steep, almost vertical sides, dropping from a few centimeters to 30 m in places.

The Gila and San Simon river basins lie in a large structural trough flanked by the Gila, Pinaleño, and Peloncillo mountains. The Safford Basin is 13.7 km in length and 2.4 km to 7.2 km wide. The Gila River, known as the "Upper Gila" east of San Carlos Reservoir, enters the valley 27 km above Safford at 792 m above sea level. The gradient is a fairly uniform 3 m to the kilometer. The Gila Valley trough is deeply cut and hemmed by terrace fronts that abruptly rise several hundred meters. Tributary streams have cut laterally into the older valley alluvium, capping lake clays. Alkali flats are present on these terraces (Poulson and Youngs 1938:1-3; Wothke and Yarbrough 1953:5).

The San Simon River is an intermittent stream that flows northwestward in Cochise and Graham counties and discharges into the Gila River near Solomon. Its gradient averages 6 m per kilometer. The lowering of the Gila River twice during the Pleistocene initiated erosion cycles that altered the San Simon valley floor. The old surface of the valley now consists of gravel-capped terrace remnants sloping gently on both sides toward the valley floor. The present steep-walled trench of the San Simon River is a recent creation, in stark contrast to its pre-1890s unchanneled, almost imperceptible bed (Bell 1869:51 in Hastings 1958-1959).

Basalt, rhyolite, and andesite are local raw materials for prehistoric lithic artifacts. "Apache tears" obsidian is found in minute quantities, and cherts, quartzites, jasper, and chalcedony are also available. Gold, silver, and copper deposits have been worked since the mid-1860s by Anglo settlers (Wilson 1965).

These raw materials are found in the project area's igneous mountain ranges or in gravel beds of streams issuing from these areas. Specific geological transects have not been made for this area but the survey team noted unworked "Apache tears" strewn across the area, particularly in the Peloncillo mountains and foothills. The geologic terraces of the Gila and San Simon rivers are cobble-strewn desert pavements affording some workable materials. Only in the material-deficient Gila and San Simon river floodplains and on the silty catchment basins present on the lower bajada of the Gila Mountains would total reliance on stream cobbles or material procured from adjacent areas be necessary.

Climate

The climate of the Safford-Clifton area is arid to semi-arid with great difference depending on elevation. Mt. Graham and the Pinaleño Mountains southwest of Safford have marked effects on the local climate. These mountains block air masses that carry moisture, causing higher temperatures and lower humidity than at comparable elevations on windward sides of the ranges. This entrapment of warm air has permitted a finger of the Sonoran Desert to move up the Safford Basin.

Most precipitation falls in July through September; winter precipitation is greatly reduced by the mountain barriers. Rainfall is about 25.4 cm annually in the Safford area, and 38 cm in the Clifton area. Summer daytime temperatures range in the 30s (C.) (86°F) and winter temperatures fall in the 15-20 degree C. range (59°-68°F) while below-freezing nighttime temperatures are rare. The diurnal temperature range in the Safford Basin is usually large, averaging 16 degrees (C.) (60°F) in winter and 21 degrees (C.) (69°F) in late spring. The Safford Basin's warm temperatures allow a 205-day growing season, ideal for cotton and corn (Poulson and Youngs 1938; Sellers and Hill 1974:160, 522).

Soils

Poulson and Youngs (1938:7-8) have distinguished five major soil types in the study area:

1. Soils south and west of the Gila and San Simon rivers are almost totally granitic.

2. Soils north and east of these two rivers have developed from basalt, andesite, and rhyolite.

3. Unconsolidated salty old lake clays occur as terraces and remnants adjacent to the lower or northeast part of the alluvial valleys.

4. Material of mixed origin has been brought in by the Gila and San Simon rivers. These are the soils of the floodplains and lower terraces.

5. "Made soils" exist in the upper Gila Valley. The soil profile is "artificial" in that it has been deeply covered by silt from irrigation water.

Flora

The project area lies within two life-zones, the Lower Sonoran and the Upper Sonoran (Lowe 1964; Shreve and Wiggins 1964); these gradually merge along the upper Gila River Basin. There are major differences in vegetation within these zones according to elevation and soil types. Vegetation is primarily desertscrub with open stands of microphyllous shrubs and trees with a strong admixture of succulents.

The creosotebush (*Larrea tridenta*) community is present over most of project area. The community is composed mainly of shrubs and dwarf shrubs with creosotebush dominant. Bursage (*Franseria* sp.), a usually common co- or sub-dominant of such communities, is rare, while catclaw (*Acacia greggii*) is especially abundant on the upper bajadas and along stream courses. Ocotillo (*Fouquieria splendens*) becomes a local dominant on the shallow soils of rocky or coarse outwash slopes.

The Gila and San Simon rivers formerly had extensive stretches of marshes, swamps, and floodplains with riparian communities. The Gila River floodplain today is under extensive irrigated cultivation and little remains of the original riparian communities. Thistle, (*Cirsium* sp.), saltbush (*Atriplex* sp.), and cottonwood (*Populus fremonitii*) are the present-day dominant native species, and saltcedar (*Tamarix oentandra*), an introduced species, is now choking channelways of both rivers.

Another important vegetation type is the mesquite bosque that occurs along the rivers and major tributaries (Nichol 1952:223). Originally occurring as dense virgin forests in a land where little usable wood was available, only small bosques now remain after continued timber cutting. However, the "Army of the West" in 1847 reported few mesquite bosques and larger trees along this segment of the Gila; it may be surmised that earlier inhabitants also exploited this resource and rarely allowed maximum growth to occur.

The San Simon Valley was once a lush waist-high grassland. Around the turn of the centry, overgrazing and severe drought exposed the topsoil; subsequent heavy rains washed away part of the exposed topsoil and eroded steep-walled arroyos (Knechtel 1938:188-190; U.S. Department of the Interior

1971). Channeling has also been attributed to a ditch dug by settlers near the mouth of the river (Hastings 1958-1959).

Desert grassland communities of the Upper Sonoran Life-zone occur at approximately 1067-1524 m in elevation. In this area grass communities are much reduced due to the shallow, rocky soils. Prickly pear and cholla (*Opuntia* sp.), pincushion cacti (*Mammillaria* sp.), agave (*Agave* sp.), yucca (*Yucca* sp.), catclaw, and mesquite (*Prosopis juliflora*) are in competition. Sotol (*Dasylirion wheeleri*) is occasionally dominant. Therefore, these are not pure grasslands but mixed grass-scrub communities.

Chaparral occurs only over 1200 m in elevation in the Peloncillo Mountains. Scrub pinyon (*Pinus* sp.), juniper (*Juniperus* sp.), scrub oak (*Quercus* sp.), and sotol are the dominant species, though grasses are fairly extensive.

Fauna

These topographic settings and flora communities have created diverse environments for fauna. Prehistoric populations likely took full advantage of such resources.

Small birds and rodents are the prevalent animal life forms, with deer, fox, and coyote the only large mammals in the area today. The formerly dense vegetation of the Gila River floodplains supported a tremendous quantity and variety of wildlife. The San Simon Valley also supports diverse faunal life; certain amphibian, reptilian, bird, and mammalian species are unique to the region (Quinn and Roney 1973:5).

Corridor Environmental Strata

It is useful to understand what the present environment in the corridor is like, but it must be remembered that what is seen today is probably not what prehistoric inhabitants encountered. The hills have been subjected to overgrazing and creosotebush invasion, as well as disturbances due to mining operations. The Gila River floodplain has been intensively cultivated and leveled and is now covered largely by "made soils." The San Simon Valley has undergone drastic biotic and topographic change within living memory. Therefore, it is with great caution that an archaeologist can make statements concerning prehistoric resource exploitation. The applicability of modern vegetation patterns to the past must be critically evaluated prior to developing hypotheses on prehistoric land-use. Additionally, restrictions of investigations to artifically delineated narrow transects do not provide a true picture of all microenvironments used by prehistoric man in a given region. It is with these problems in mind that the strata discussed below are presented. The problems of dealing with linear transects in an archaeologically sound manner has been discussed by Goodyear (1975a) and is discussed in Chapter 3.

The strata presented below are but the broadest geomorphic patternings observed along the R-O-W corridor. These patterns provided a convenient and useful mechanism for stratification of the AEPCO R-O-W corridor into basic sampling units for testing generalizations on past man-land relationships. A much fuller ecological description of each stratum is presented in Chapter 8. The information given below is condensed from the U.S. Soil Conservation Service (1973 a,b).

1. Gila River Floodplain. The nearly level to gently sloping floodplain and alluvial fans of the Gila River comprise this stratum. Soils are deep, medium to moderately coarse-textured loams and sandy loams. Elevation ranges from 945 to 1097 m; average annual precipitation is 20 to 35.5 cm; frost-free period ranges from 200 to 230 days; annual mean temperature is 14 to 18 degrees C. (57 to 64 degrees F). Present vegetation on areas not in cropland consists of mesquite, catclaw, creosotebush, saltbush, various cacti and cottonwood, willow and tamarisk trees along the stream channel (Figure 2).

2. San Simon River Valley. Low terraces with rounded ridges are characteristic of the San Simon Valley. Soils are deep, gravelly, moderately coarse to moderately fine-textured loams and sandy loams. Elevation ranges from 823 to 975 m; average annual precipitation from 20 to 30.5 cm; frost-free period ranges from 150 to 230 days; and annual mean temperature from 14 to 17.9 degrees C. (57.2 to 64.4 degrees F). Present vegetation on terraces includes creosotebush, cholla, mesquite and annual grasses after rainy periods; floodplain vegetation is similar to the Gila River floodplain (Figure 3).

3. Gila River Pleistocene Terraces and Lower Bajada of Gila Mountains. This zone includes the high terraces and valley slopes that occur above the Gila River bottomlands. The terraces are dissected and drained by washes that flow into the Gila River. These washes have cut deep canyons with steep side slopes. Soils are both deep and shallow, gravelly, fine to medium textured sandy loams. Elevation ranges from 853 to 1554 m; average annual precipitation from 25.4 to 35.5 cm; frost-free period ranges from 150 to 230 days; and annual mean temperature is 14 to 17.9 degrees C (57.2 to 64.4 degrees F). Present vegetation consists of creosotebush, whitethorn and catclaw acacia, and mesquite (Figure 4).

4. Upper Bajada of Gila Mountains. This includes the gently rolling low mountainous slopes of the basaltic Gila Mountians. Soils are shallow, fine and moderately fine textured clayey loams containing gravels and cobbles. Elevation ranges from 1067 to 2042 m; average annual precipitation from 30.5 to 45.7 cm; frost-free period from 150 to 200 days; and annual mean temperature from 14 to 17.9 degrees C (57.2 to 64.4 degrees F). Present vegetation on south-facing slopes includes ocotillo, cacti, and snakeweed (Figure 5).

5. Peloncillo Mountain Foothills. These foothills consist of steep to very steep, deeply dissected old terrace fronts adjacent to the Gila River floodplain and bottoms. Soils are deep and shallow, gravelly, medium

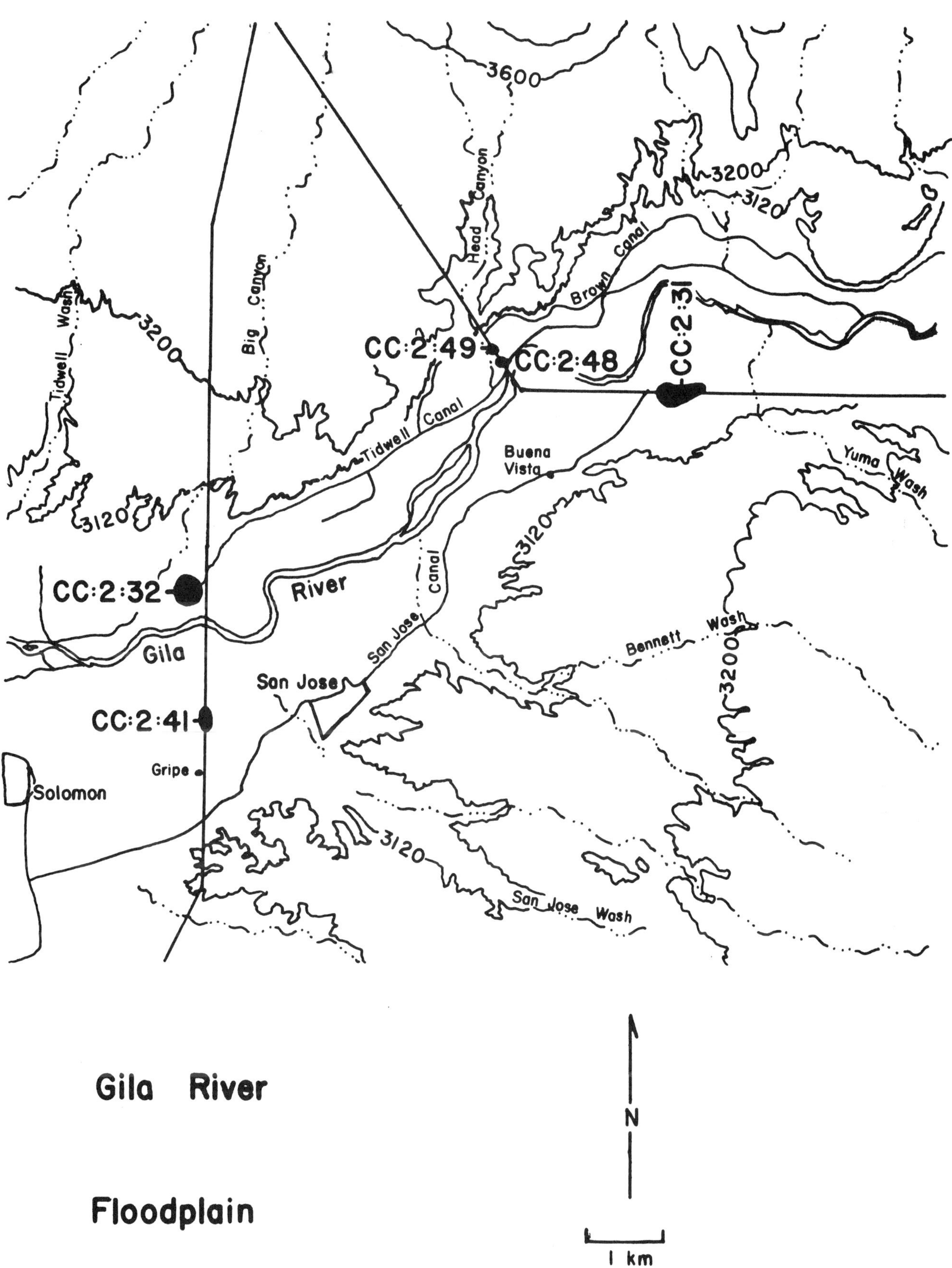

Figure 2. Stratum 1: Topographic Stratum and Archaeological Sites

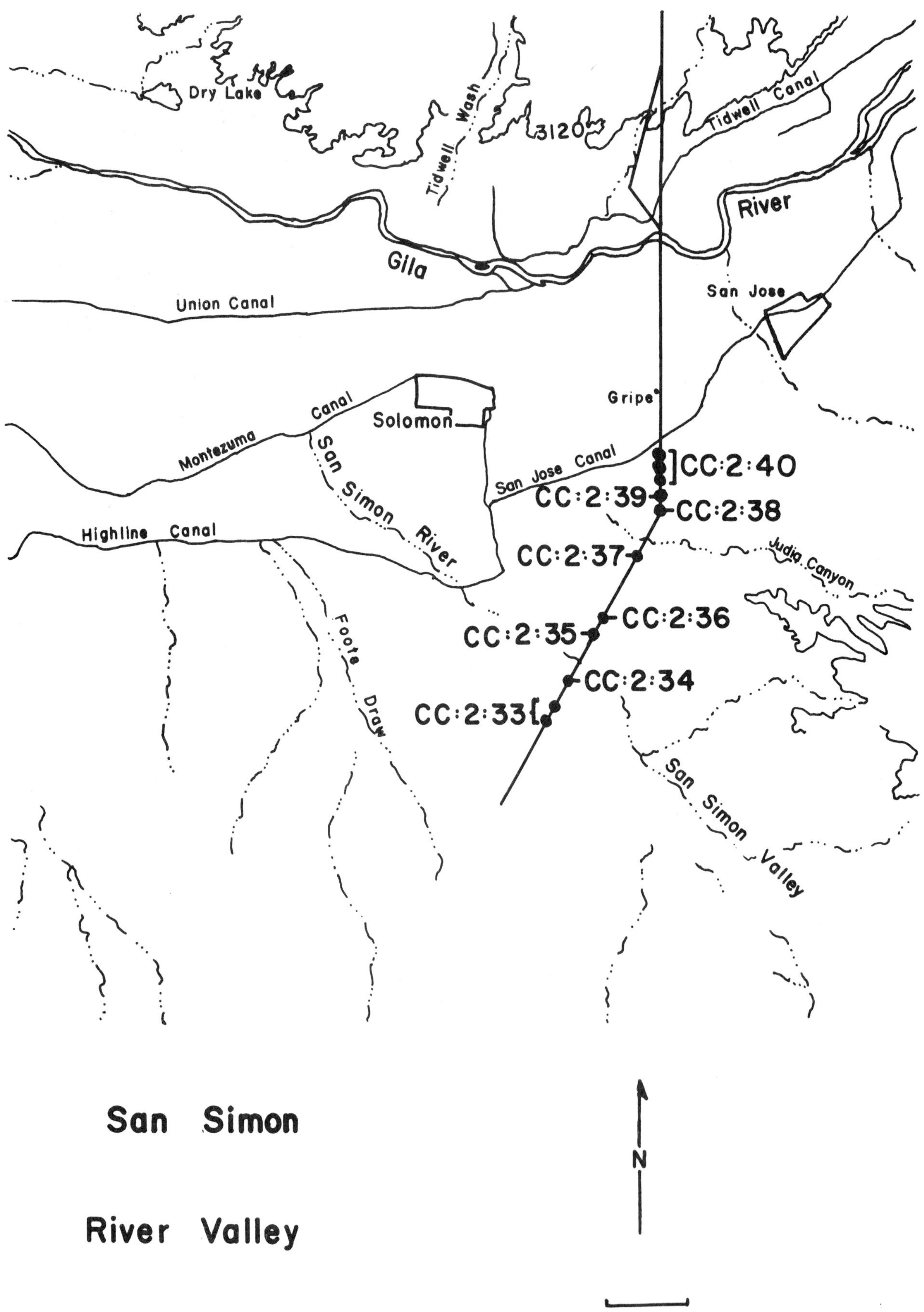

Figure 3. Stratum 2: Topographic Stratum and Archaeological Sites

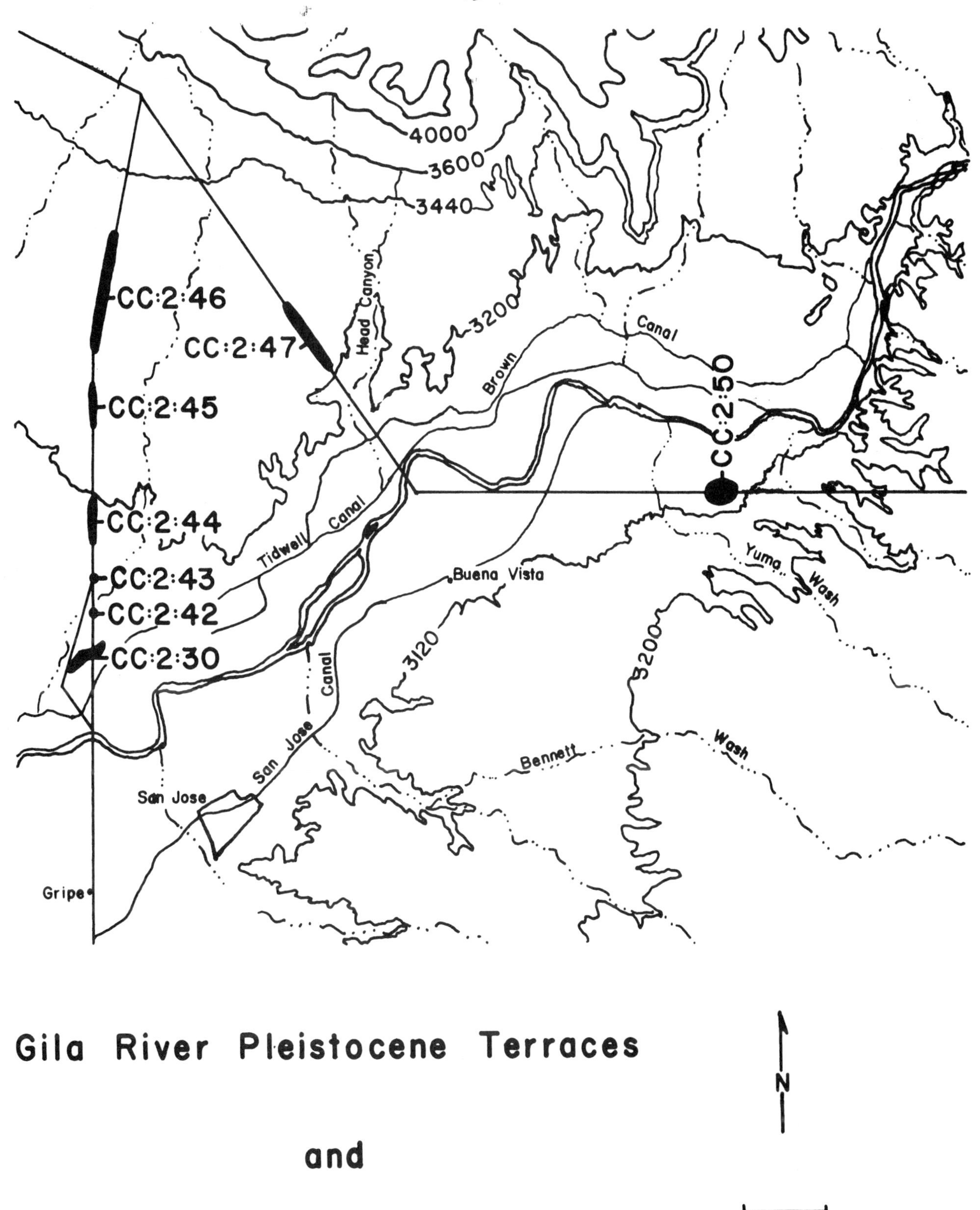

Figure 4. Stratum 3: Topographic Stratum and Archaeological Sites

Figure 5. Stratum 4: Topographic Stratum and Archaeological Sites

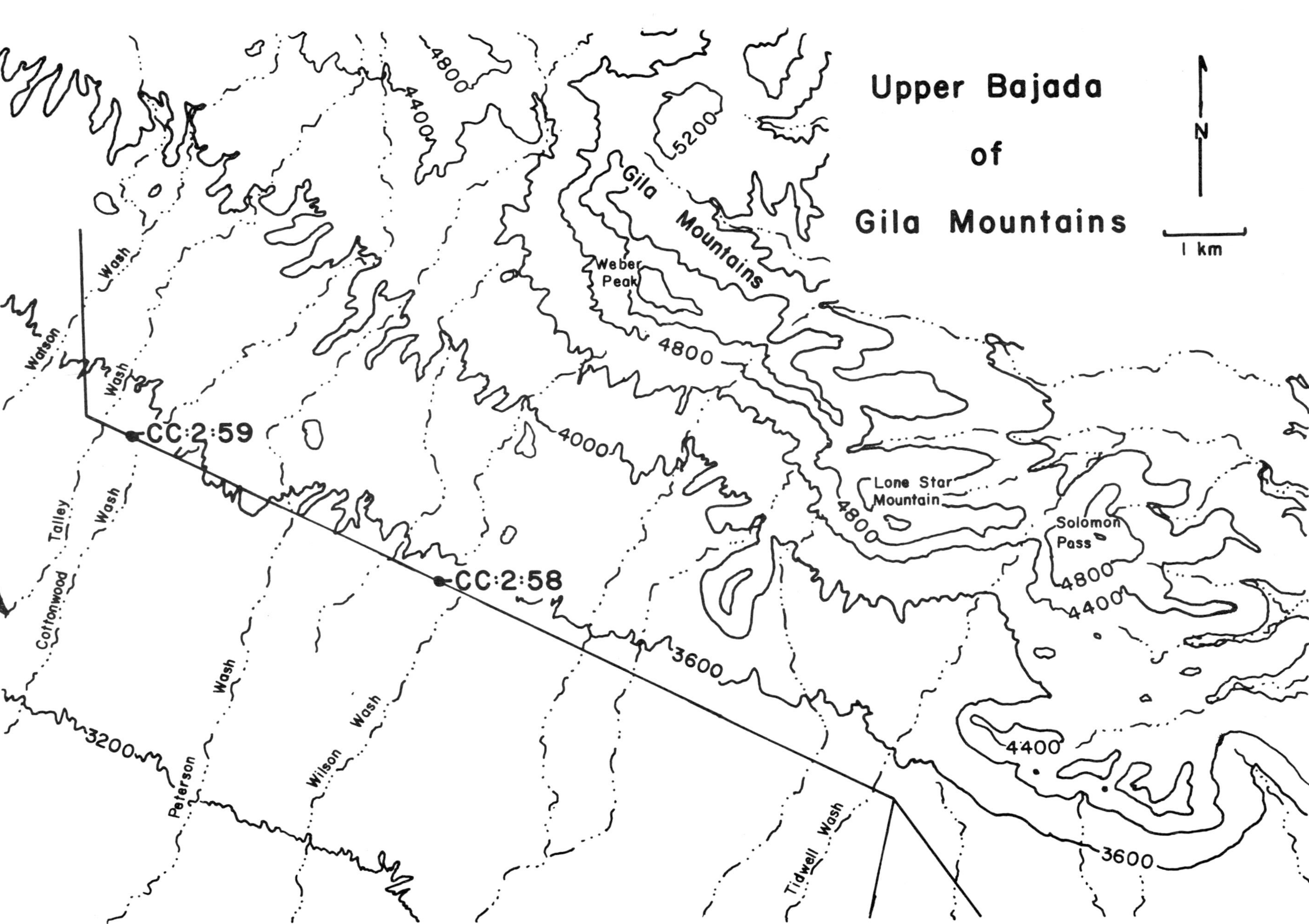

to coarse textured sandy loams and loams. These soils overlie conglomerate rock, siltstone and limestone. Ridgetop remnants range from a few meters to a few hundred meters wide and from 1 to 4 km long. Elevation ranges from 853 to 1524 m; average annual precipitation from 25.4 to 40.64 cm; frost-free period ranges from 155 to 220 days; and annual mean temperature from 14 to 17.9 degrees C (57.2 to 64.4 degrees F). Present vegetation is a sparse cover of mesquite, creosotebush, catclaw and whitethorn acacia, and cacti with a scattering of grasses (Figure 6).

6. Peloncillo Mountains. The Peloncillo Mountains consist of steep to very steep basalt hills and low mountains. The northeastern pediment is greatly dissected by deep washes that flow into the Gila River. The area is characterized by the smooth appearance of the topography and a surface cover of basalt cobbles and gravel. Rock outcrops and talus are common. Soils are shallow, fine and moderately fine textured clayey loams containing gravel and cobbles. Elevation ranges between 1067 to 2042 m; average annual precipitation from 30.5 to 45.7 cm; frost-free period ranges from 150 to 200 days; annual mean temperature from 14 to 17.9 degrees C (57.2 to 64.4 degrees F). Present vegetation consists mainly of tobosa, beargrass, and grama grasses. Mormon tea, juniper and pinyon grow on north facing slopes; ocotillo, cacti, and snakeweed on south facing slopes (Figure 7).

7. Gila River Terraces. This zone includes steep to very steep, deeply dissected old terrace fronts adjacent to the Gila River floodplain and bottoms. Soils are deep and shallow, gravelly, medium to coarse textured eroded loams. Elevation ranges from 1067 to 1676 m; average annual precipitation from 25.4 to 35.5 cm; frost-free periods range from 155 to 228 days; and annual mean temperature from 14 to 17.9 degrees C (57.2 to 64.4 degrees F). Present vegetation consists of a sparse cover of creosotebush, catclaw and whitethorn acacia, mesquite, cacti, and some grasses.

8. San Francisco River Terraces. This zone is very similar to Zone 7; however, the ridges are steeper, narrower, and slightly higher in elevation than those along the Gila River. Grasses were observed to be more common and creosotebush less common than in the former zone. Ocotillo is often dominant on rocky slopes (Figure 8).

9. Big Lue-Gila River Canyonlands. This zone is also very similar to Zone 7, but here the land is more nearly flat and dissected by a few large canyons instead of many washes. The resulting topography is smoother without the extensive ridge systems of Zone 7. Vegetation is sparser than along the Gila River terraces (Figure 9).

10. Democrat Mesa. A short section of the corridor crosses the high terraces and valley slopes above the Gila River bottomlands and below the Big Lue Mountains. Soils are both deep and shallow, gravelly, fine to medium textured sandy loams overlying an accumulated lime hardpan. Elevation ranges from 853 to 1463 m; average annual precipitation from 25.4 to 35.5 cm; frost-free period ranges from 200 to 275 days; and annual mean temperature from 14

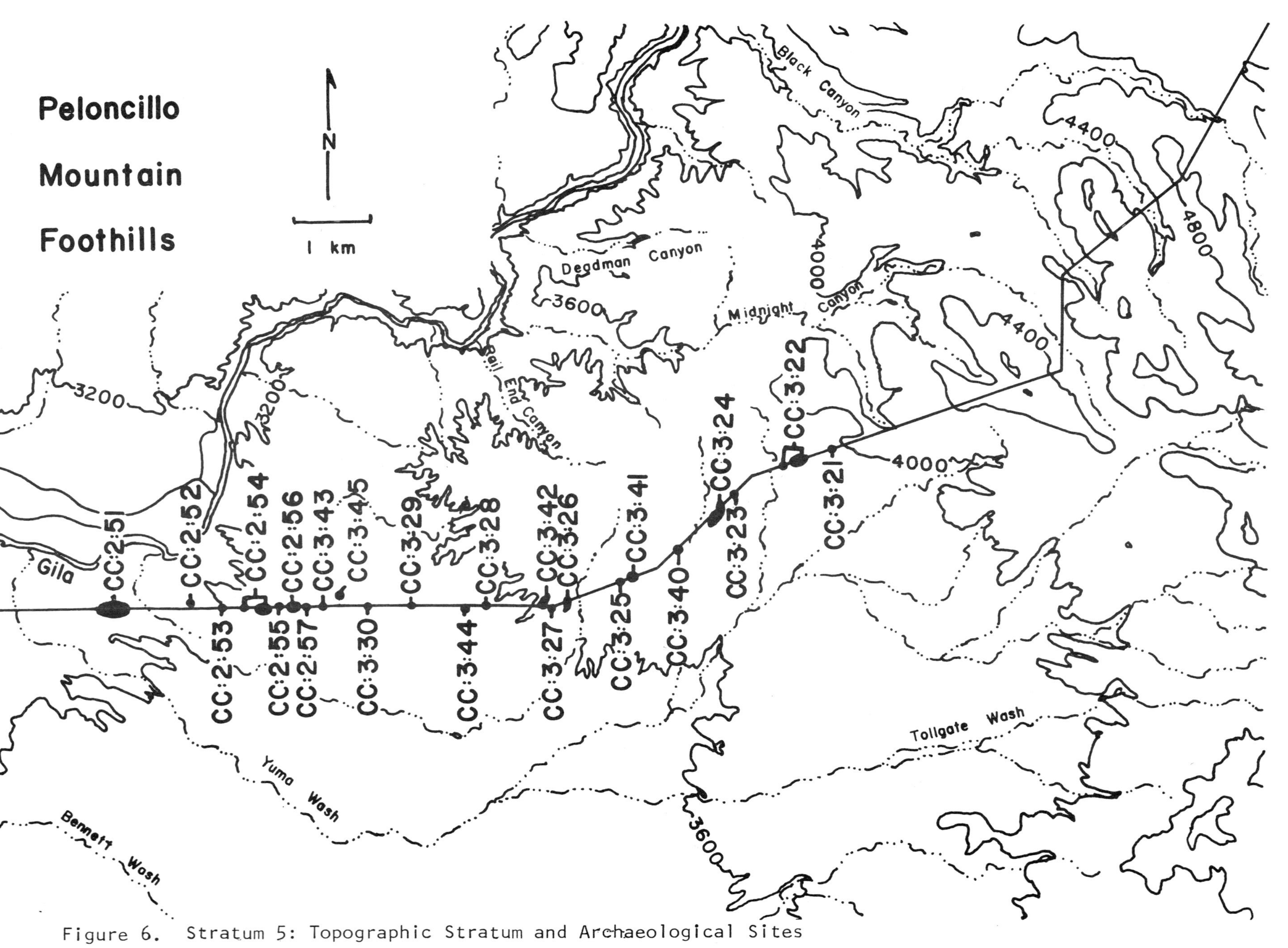

Figure 6. Stratum 5: Topographic Stratum and Archaeological Sites

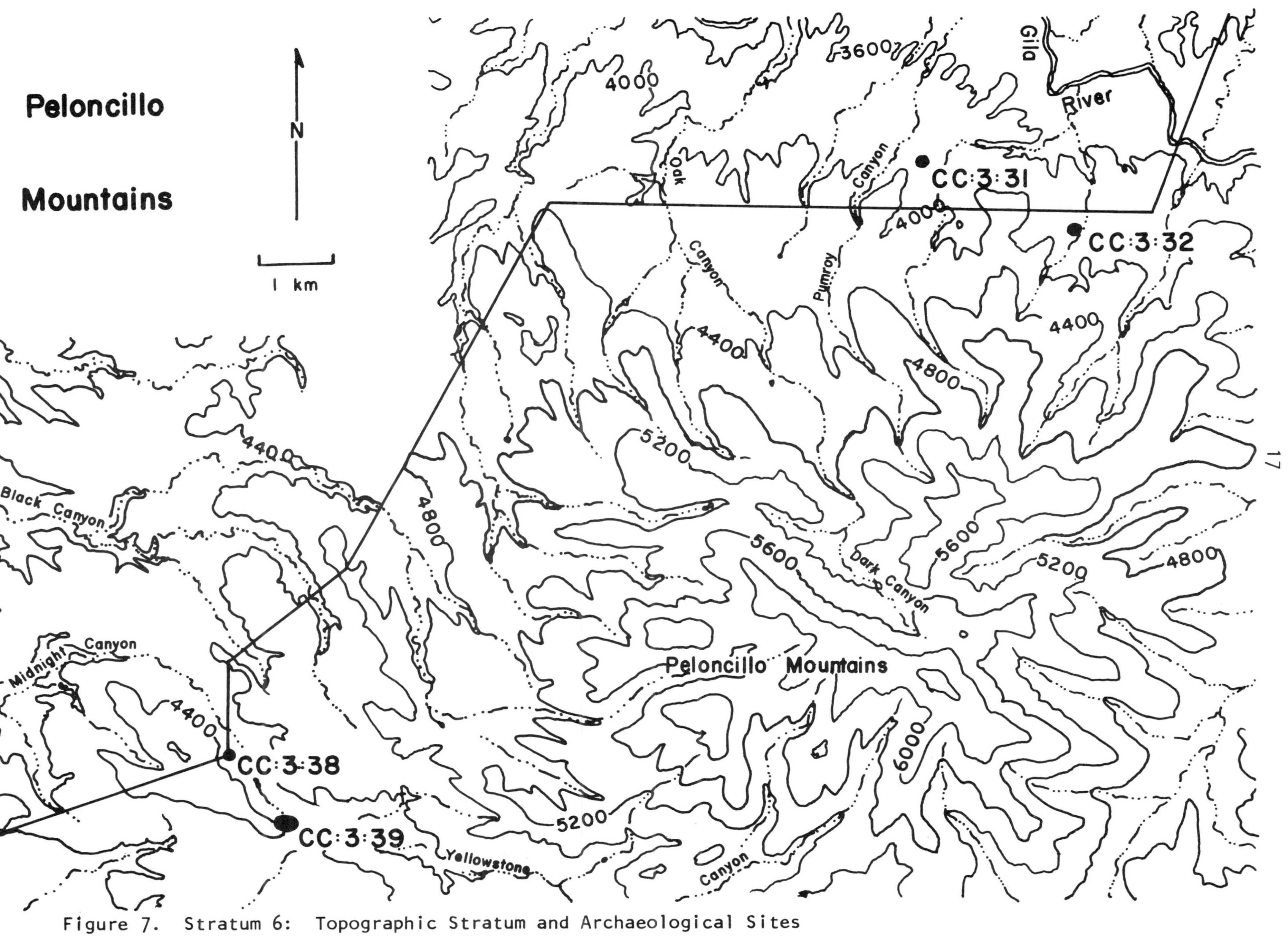

Figure 7. Stratum 6: Topographic Stratum and Archaeological Sites

Figure 8. Stratum 7: Topographic Stratum and Archaeological Sites

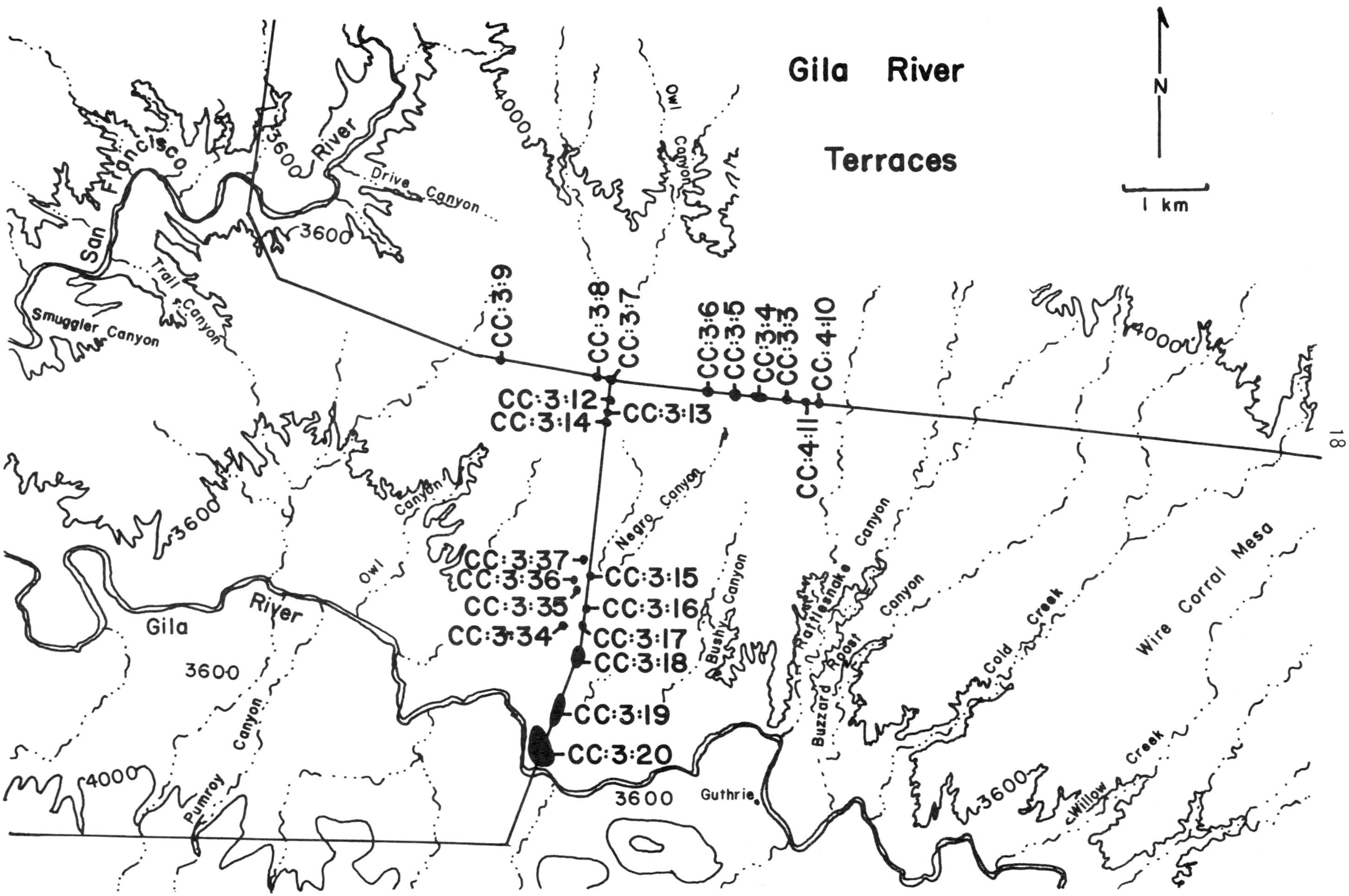

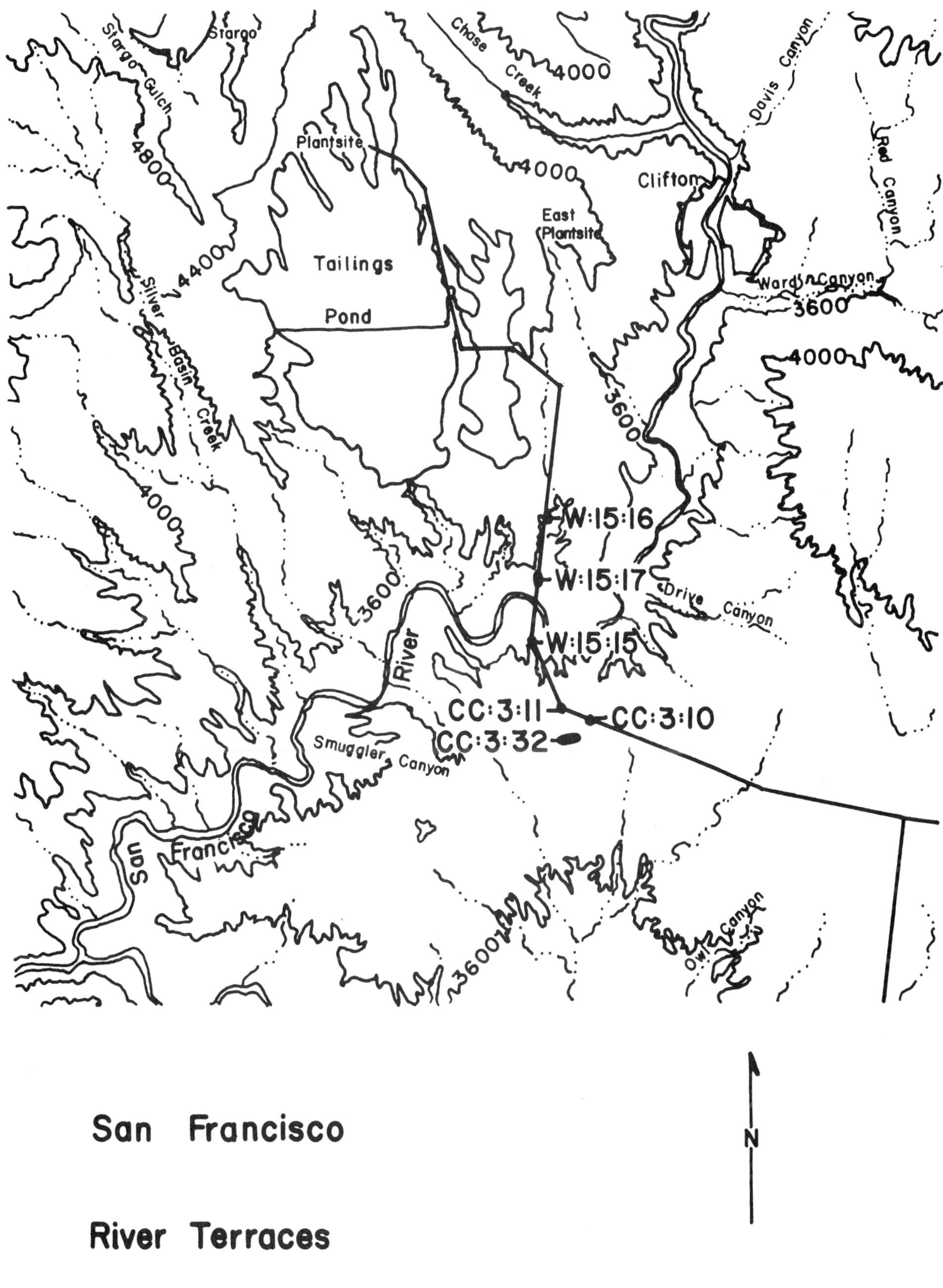

Figure 9. Stratum 8: Topographic Stratum and Archaeological Sites

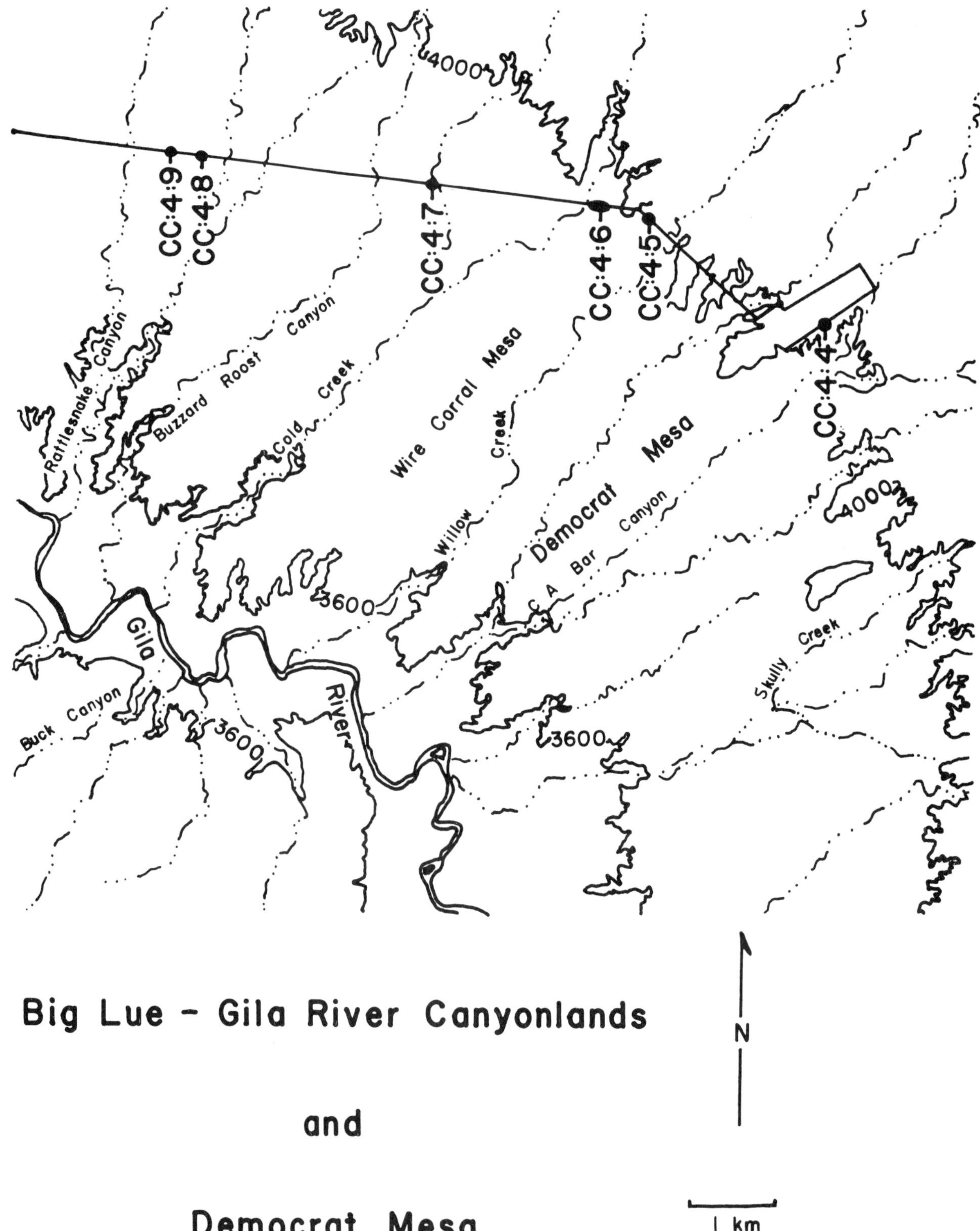

Figure 10. Strata 9/10: Topographic Strata and Archaeological Sites

to 19 degrees C (57.2 to 66.6 degrees F). Present vegetation consists of creosotebush, whitethorn and catclaw acacia, mesquite, and annual grasses (Figure 10).

Archaeology

Introduction

A mixture of major Southwestern traditions (Hohokam, Anazazi, Salado, Mogollon) have been found in the region. However, as the systematic work undertaken in the area has been limited there is much confusion as to the cultural identification and age of materials previously collected and little understanding of cultural process.

The following sections discuss the previous archaeological research in the area and review the known culture history of the Safford-Clifton area.

History of Archaeological Research

Prior to 1959, no site in the study area had been professionally excavated and reported. There were, however, several early reports and cursory descriptions of sites in the Safford Valley (Emory 1848; Bandelier 1892; Fewkes 1904; Hough 1907; Sauer and Brand 1930). The major site noted was Buena Vista (also known as Pueblo Viejo or the Curtis Ranch site). This Hohokam-Salado site with Mogollon affinities was partially excavated in 1931 by Oscar Tatman; a brief summary of excavation results was written by Morris (1932). In 1926 the Gila Ranch Ruin near Bylas was excavated by Byron Cummings; however, no report of this excavation was ever published.

The first extensive survey of the Clifton area was in 1947 by the Peabody Upper Gila Expedition. Danson (1957) recorded several Mogollon sites along the Gila, Blue, and San Francisco rivers; also in 1947 Wendorf recorded villages and an artifact scatter with possible pithouses. Little subsequent work has been done in the Clifton area.

Tuohy (1960) conducted an extensive survey of Gila River channel lands. He identified 39 sites in the Safford Valley, and tested five of these. Most of these sites were dated by ceramics to AD 1000-1450. Upon Tuohy's recommendation two of these sites, Arizona V:16:8 and V:16:10, were further excavated in 1963 by William Wasley and Alfred Johnson of the ASM. Their preliminary report dated these two pueblos to the 12th century, classifying them as a local variant of the Western Pueblo culture (Johnson 1965; Johnson and Wasley 1966).

Salado polychrome ceramics have been found on terraces above the Gila River and on sites downstream from Safford. Brown (1973) surveyed 11 sites in the Safford Valley, most of them previously known, and excavated the

Methodist Church site. His research concentrated on the nature and extent of the Salado occupation in the valley and on the distribution of intrusive Maverick Mountain wares.

There have been three recent ASM projects in the Safford-Clifton area. Doyel (1972) conducted an archaeological survey of the TG&E San Juan-Vail power transmission line, a section of which passed through the San Simon Valley, the Whitlock Mountains, and the Peloncillo Mountains. A rock shelter, a lithic scatter, and a village site were found, the latter belonging to the San Simon branch of the Mogollon.

Kinkade (1975) surveyed two washes southeast of Safford, Foote Wash and No Name Wash, which were to be affected by a floodwater control project. Twenty-one activity loci were recorded, of which all but one were lithic scatters situated on terrace tops or upper slopes. The settlement pattern appeared to be one of temporary camps with associated chipping stations and lithic scatters. The one ceramic site had redwares and red-on-brown wares dating from AD 900-1250. Fitting (1977) carried out a data recovery program on these sites that entailed controlled surface collection and test excavations.

Gilman and Sherman (1975) surveyed the floodplain and first and second terraces north of the Gila River in a study area 16 km north of Safford. Five sites were located: Arizona CC:1:17 consists of 10 linear rock alignments; CC:1:2 consists of an unusually extensive system of gridded gardens; CC:1:19 is a large pueblo site dated by ceramics to AD 900-1375; CC:1:18 is a historic CCC water control system, and CC:1:20 is a petroglyph site.

Regional Culture History

The American southwest is a region where many distinctive prehistoric cultures existed during a long span of time. In southeastern Arizona, elements of Cochise, Hohokam, Mogollon and Salado have been identified, of which the Cochise culture has been the focus of much research.

Cochise. The earliest archaeological manifestation in this vicinity is the Cochise culture, one of several Desert Archaic traditions of the arid Southwest. The lower San Simon Valley has yielded much of our information on the Cochise culture (Sayles and Antevs 1941; Sayles 1945). Sites there are located in valley bottomlands (Sayles and Antevs 1941), terraces and pediments above the floodplains (Whalen 1975), and mountainous areas (Martin and others 1952; Dick 1965). Though specific Cochise sites have not been identified in the Safford-Gila Valley it has been suggested as the northern boundary of the culture (Sayles 1945).

Four stages based on changes in artifact types have been proposed: the Sulphur Spring stage (8000-5000 BC); Cazador (5000-4000 BC); Chiricahua (4000-2056 BC); and the San Pedro stage (1350 BC-AD 100).

The traditional view holds that during the first stage people were predominantly plant gatherers, an assumption based on a predominance of grinding and chopping tools from these early sites and lack of projectile points that would indicate hunting. Faunal remains found among the material culture assemblage include bones of extinct camel, mammoth, dire wolf and horse.

The Cazador stage was defined after investigations at the Double Adobe type site in the lower Sulphur Spring Valley (Whalen 1971:68). Based on differences in material culture assemblages it was suggested that the Cazador was a distinct transitional stage between the Sulphur Spring and Chiricahua stages. Artifacts found in the Cazador stratigraphic level included biface blades, leaf-shaped projectile points, bone implements and milling stones. The critical feature is the occurrence of projectile points, which were absent in the preceding Sulphur Spring stage. Whalen (1971:81), in a review of the data, points out that artifacts of the Sulphur Spring and Cazador stage occur in the same stratigraphic and geological beds. He notes that although projectile points were absent in the Sulphur Spring stage, nevertheless the occurrence of scraping and cutting tools with burned and splintered bone indicates some participation in hunting. Therefore, Whalen suggests that the Sulphur Spring and Cazador actually belong to one stage; Sulphur Spring representing the gathering and processing aspect and the Cazador representing the hunting facet.

The Chiricahua stage is represented by a trend toward larger grinding stones, biface percussion-flaked tools and pressure-flaked points. The Chiricahua period is a critical one, for during this time corn and squashes were introduced from Mexico, and beans arrived some time later during the San Pedro phase (Whalen 1971:91). The San Pedro stage is characterized by the appearance of pithouses and a dominance of pressure-flaked implements in the tool kit. Increased sedentism and use of floral resources is indicated for the San Pedro phase. Martin and Plog (1973:277) have surmised that the San Pedro stage probably had at least the beginnings of rudimentary agriculture, but Whalen (1973:91) believes that the Cochise people did not take full advantage of agriculture during this time. Pollen and floral remains from the Cochise levels at Ventana Cave (Haury 1950) and San Pedro stage sites in the San Pedro drainage (Whalen 1971) indicate an emphasis on wild biotic resources. He suggests that agriculture did not effectively diffuse in the Southwest until around the time of Christ when population pressures created a demand for alternative food resources.

In summation, the Cochise culture was originally defined on the basis of changes in the artifact assemblage. The data indicated an early emphasis on plant gathering that was gradually replaced by a dominance of hunting-related activities. Other research, however (Irwin-Williams 1967; Whalen 1971; Windmiller 1973; Quinn and Roney 1973) indicates a more mixed, seasonally exploited subsistence base, utilizing wild resources as they were available.

The Cochise culture as a recognizable hunting and gathering tradition terminated around AD 100 with the introduction of agriculture and pottery. Some researchers believe the Mogollon evolved from the early Cochise culture base, however, this hypothesis has yet to be substantiated.

Mogollon. The Safford-Clifton area lies primarily in the recognized Mogollon cultural sphere, although some Hohokam and Salado influences are also evident.

The Mogollon were originally defined as a puebloan people who inhabited the mountain and mountain-lowland transition zones of east-central Arizona and western New Mexico (Wheat 1955). Mogollon culture history lacks a synthesis at the current movement, since research has focused primarily on single site analysis and deriving explanations for variations within the basic Mogollon cultural pattern as evidenced at these sites. Consequently, several branches or sub-groups of Mogollon, are currently recognized in different geographical areas but their relationship to each other are by no means clearly defined. Some of these branches are: Mimbres, in the Mimbres Valley of New Mexico; San Simon in the San Simon Valley in the area of Safford and Willcox, Arizona; Forestdale and Point of Pines near Showlow, Arizona; Pinelawn in the Reserve area of western New Mexico; and the Little Colorado branch sites occur in that particular drainage of east-central Arizona (Wheat 1955). The San Simon and Mimbres branches are both in the project area and only these two will be discussed as relevant cultural-historical problems for the study area.

The San Simon branch as defined by Sayles (1945) was based on investigations at two sites in the San Simon Valley: San Simon Village and Cave Creek Village. The established cultural sequence is as follows: Peñasco phase (300 BC-AD 100), Dos Cabezas phase (AD 100-400), Pinaleño phase (AD 400-650), Galiuro phase (AD 650-850), Cerros phase (AD 850-950), and Encinas phase (950-1200?). The San Simon Village and Cave Creek Village sites show a direct superposition of Peñasco phase pottery on the earlier non-ceramic San Pedro Cochise horizon. Throughout the sequence there is trend from the oval/circular Peñasco pit houses towards the rectangular Encinas pit house type. Aboveground pueblo architecture has not been found at San Simon branch sites, although rock-lined and masonry-lined rooms do occur. Pottery types recognized for the San Simon branch are Dos Cabezas Red-on-brown, Pinaleño Red-on-brown, Galiuro Red-on-brown, Cerros Red-on-white, and Encinas Red-on-brown, each of which corresponds to the respective phase designation of the San Simon branch. The dominant plainware is Alma Plain.

A post-Peñasco trend is towards increasing contact with other cultural groups and by the Encinas phase many Hohokam traits are present. Mimbres branch Mogollon elements also occur at San Simon branch sites during the Dos Cabezas and Encinas phases; San Francisco Red is intrusive as well as the distinctive Mimbres Black-on-white pottery.

Classic Mimbres sites have also been found in the old Hot Springs area 11.2 km south of Safford. These tiny pueblos are the farthest downstream Mimbres sites known (Sauer and Brand 1930:428-29). On the terraces above the Gila River, Tularosa phase black-on-white pottery known from the Reserve area of New Mexico occurs, and small pueblos with about a dozen rooms have been found in association with mountain redwares dating to around AD 1200.

By the 14th century much of the Mogollon area was abandoned while the remaining inhabited portion showed a strong mixture of Mogollon-Hohokam or Mogollon-Anasazi characteristics (McGregor 1965). These influences were already appearing in the Mogollon area by AD 1000. Johnson (1965) interprets this as the disappearance of the Mogollon and the emergence of the "Western Pueblo Culture," a syncretism of the three co-traditions. The Bylas sites, Arizona V:16:8 and V:16:10, have been tentatively identified as variants of this culture (Johnson and Wasley 1966).

<u>Hohokam</u>. The Hohokam culture, partially contemporaneous with the Mogollon, developed west of the study area. Safford has long been viewed as the easternmost extent of the Riverine Hohokam (Gladwin and Gladwin 1935; Haury 1976). Hohokam occupation in the area is recorded only in the Gila floodplain and is thought to be of the Colonial-Classic periods (AD 700-1400) (Tuohy 1960). The Hohokam had considerable effect on local Mogollon peoples; late phases in the Safford area exhibit both Hohokam and Mogollon elements (Sayles 1945).

The following traits characterize Riverine Hohokam material culture: permanent habitation sites, wattle and daub construction, platform mounds, ball courts, large-scale irrigation systems, primarily agricultural subsistence, cremation of the dead, red-on-buff pottery, smudged redwares, full troughed metates, and a great array of projectile points but a few formal chopping, scraping, or cutting tools (Haury 1950:547, Debowski and others 1976:23).

During the Civano phase of the Classic period, there was a trend towards greater elaboration in architecture and a ceramic assemblage characterized by a shift from the red-on-buff pottery to Salado polychromes.

<u>Salado</u>. The Safford Valley has many cultural remains identified as Salado. The Salado complex is a difficult cultural entity to define but the traditional definition includes the following cultural traits: polychrome, black-on-white, polished redware, and corrugated plainware ceramics; puebloan architecture associated with coursed masonry or solid adobe, cliff dwellings, compounds or defense walls; storage pits; sheet rubbish deposition instead of trash mounds; and primary inhumation of the dead (Gladwin 1957:264; Weaver 1976:19). The heartland appears to be the Roosevelt and Tonto Basin region with heavy occupation in Canyon and Cibecue Creeks, the upper Salt River Valley and the Safford Valley. The primary diagnostic trait is a distinctive ceramic assemblage--Pinto, Tonto, and Gila Polychromes. The Salado appeared

as a distinct entity by AD 1100 in the mountainous country north of the middle Salt River Valley. By AD 1300 characteristic Salado stylistic traits had appeared in widespread areas of the Southwest.

Much research has concentrated on what constitutes the Salado and its derivations. Opinions have fallen into five main camps (Lindsay and Jennings 1968:4; DiPeso 1974):

1. Western Pueblo: a mixture of Anasazi and Mogollon
2. Mogollon (including Casas Grandes)
3. An indigenous population similar to Sinagua
4. An indigenous population with influences from the Little Colorado cultural tradition
5. An outpost for Casas Grandes based puchteca.

Salado polychromes have been found on terraces above the Gila River, mainly on sites downstream from Safford. Salado in the Safford area differs from Tonto Basin Salado by the presence of Point of Pines-Reserve ceramic types, the absence of compund architecture, and the absence of late northern tradewares (Brown 1974).

Brown's (1973) research on the Salado occupation in the Safford Valley concentrated on the distribution of Maverick Mountain wares. These wares represent an intrusive element in the Point of Pines region from the Kayenta area of northeast Arizona around AD 1275-1325 (Haury 1958). The presence of Maverick Mountain wares in the Safford Valley has led to speculations that this was a refuge area for Kayenta immigrants after they left Point of Pines (Wasley 1962:392). A cache of ceremonial items including a Maverick Mountain polychrome jar was found on Bonita Creek, northeast of Safford and 51.5 km south of Point of Pines. Another such vessel has been found in the vicinity of Bylas.

Some of the current thinking on Salado relates it more closely to Casas Grandes, the large, late prehistoric community in Chihuahua, Mexico. As LeBlanc and Nelson (1976:78) comment, "The founding of Casas Grandes at about AD 1150 certainly had enormous effects on much of the Southwest." Gila Polychrome, the hallmark of Salado culture, may have its origin at Casas Grandes (DiPeso 1976), and the dense population of the Safford Valley by AD 1300 may have been related to an exodus from the Casas Grandes area (LeBlanc and Nelson 1976:78).

Apache. The culture history of the study area during the period AD 1400-1600 is unknown. The Apache were late migrants to the Southwest; the date of their arrival is disputed, but Wilcox (1973) suggests that there is little evidence for a pre-Spanish entry into the Southwest. The Apache of southeastern Arizona did not come into contact with the Spanish until after AD 1680; Anglo expansion and subsequent warfare did not begin until the 1700s. Not until this time were Apachean subgroups recognized. The Western Apache ranged from the present Arizona-New Mexico border west to the San Pedro River Valley and thus commanded the main corridors into Mexico. These they raided with virtual impunity.

The Apache were primarily hunters and gatherers though the Western Apache did practice some agriculture. Raiding was also of economic importance (Basso 1971:16). The Apache moved about seasonally, occupying short-term camps. Consequently, Apache sites are characterized by an absence of architecture and a sparsity of artifacts and are often recognized solely on the basis of historic trade goods. Two blue glass trade beads were found at Arizona V:15:4 and V:16:1 indicating Apache use (Tuohy 1960:13) but other material remains point to a 14th or 15th century Salado site.

Euro-American Period. There is little documentary history of the project area in the 16th and 17th centuries. The only Spanish explorer to pass through the upper Gila River area was Coronado in 1540. His army marched from a point near modern Benson, Arizona, northeast to the foot of Eagle Pass, the opening between the Pinaleño and Santa Teresa mountains. Here was "Chichilticale," which may be one of the pueblo ruins located today on the 76 Ranch.

Coronado was disappointed to find that the pueblo had been destroyed, and a nomadic Gila River tribe was living in isolated huts among the ruins. Coronado then crossed an uninhabited wilderness from Chichilticale to about the present location of Bylas, and then across the mountains of eastern Arizona to the Little Colorado River (Wagoner 1975:50-56). There were other Spanish military expeditions in this area, primarily to subdue the Apaches, but these are poorly documented.

In the early 19th century, the upper Gila was explored by American mountain men who rarely recorded their journeys in great detail (Pattie 1930). During this time, relations with the Apache were fairly tranquil. But in 1833, after a series of disputes with the Spanish, the Apache of eastern Arizona and western New Mexico followed their plunder trails into Sonora. A major route was the Chiricahua Trail used by the Chiricahua, Mimbreño, Mogollonero, Tonto and other Apache bands. From the Gila River the trail paralleled the San Simon River to the Chihuahua-Sonora boundary line. Due to Apache incursions, Mexican settlement in southeast Arizona was minimal (Wagoner 1975:239).

In 1847 the "Army of the West", commanded by General Stephen Kearny, was organized to take New Mexico and California from Mexico. At Santa Fe, the army was divided into four parts. One part, called the Mormon Battalion and led by Lt. Colonel Phillip St. George Cooke, was ordered to open a wagon road to California. This battalion passed through the upper Gila River drainage (Faulk 1973:19). The report of this reconnaissance is the earliest extensive description of the study area (Emory 1848). The army reported the Safford Basin as being uninhabited by either Mexican or sedentary Indians. However, Mexicans were permanent inhabitants of the valley in the 1850s and 1860s (Poulson and Youngs 1938:3).

After the Gadsden Purchase was ratified in June of 1854, Anglo-Apache relations deteriorated rapidly. During the 1860s the upper Gila River was the scene of heavy fighting between Apache and Anglos. In the 1870s an intensive Anglo invasion of the original San Carlos Apache Reservation occurred. Large pieces of the reservation were taken for copper mining in the Clifton-Morenci area, and Mormon farmers pushed into the rich agricultural district of Safford. The new farmers appropriated Gila River water to such an extent that San Carlos irrigation suffered. During the Geronimo Wars, Mormon farmers were often harassed by Apache passing through the Gila River corridor on their raiding expeditions into Mexico (Williams 1937; Spicer 1962:229-61; Myrick 1975:79).

Mining of gold at Morenci began in 1870, but it was not until copper increased in value and the installation of the first railroad in 1882 that Morenci began serious production. The first important railroad line was the Arizona and New Mexico, built from the Southern Pacific main line originating in Lordsburg, New Mexico. Around Clifton several narrow-gauge mining railroads were built. One of these was the Morenci Southern Railroad (1901-1922), an affiliated line of El Paso and Southwestern Railroad (Myrick 1966). This abandoned railroad lies adjacent to the transmission line corridor near Arizona CC:3:20.

Summary

Previous research in the Safford area suggests a complex culture history that is unquestionably in need of further study and interpretation. The mixture of traits characteristic of several major cultural traditions, typical of the area throughout the prehistoric occupation, is difficult to interpret. Large-scale population movement is frequently suggested as the cause of stylistic transitions and changes in settlement type and distribution. Alternative explanations deserve, however, careful consideration. These include the consequences of developing trade and communication networks, as well as the responses of resident populations to environmental pressures or long-term internal cultural trends. Also, care should be taken, particularly in a relatively little studied area such as this, not to misinterpret the significance of isolated or infrequent occurrences of non-indigenous elements. The assessment of significance presented in Chapter 3 will deal in more detail with these problems.

CHAPTER 3

THE SURVEY

Operational Survey

The approach of the survey was exploratory in nature, the primary focus being identification and evaluation of cultural resources within the transmission line corridor. Contractual obligations included an inventory of archaeological resources to be affected by the proposed construction, an assessment of their scientific, historic, social, and monetary significance (Scovill and others 1972; Moratto 1975) and an estimate of data recovery costs.

A secondary goal was to formulate future research objectives for the project area. Information from the survey can contribute to projections of site distributions and density on a regional basis.

Theoretical Orientation

Survey approaches are determined by the problems an archaeologist hopes to solve. However, in contract archaeology the survey line is determined by the company contracting for research. By establishing an artificially-bound universe, such transects limit the type of research that can be done.

Such transects are usually inadequate in determining statistically reliable variability in space. Samples cannot be collected within natural parameters or within discrete cultural divisions. Therefore, the transect cannot be used as a statistically reliable representation of micro-environments, exploitative activities, or settlement patterns. It has been noted by previous researchers that transects tend to overrepresent activities oriented towards river terraces and mountain passes as these are the easiest places for construction (Doyel 1972; Goodyear 1975a). The transect surveyed here tended to overrepresent ridge tops.

Traditional research has concentrated on single site analysis and cultural-ecological analysis. Research is focused on intra-site variability because complete access to the site surface is available. Information on surface contextual distribution can be quickly observed.

As transects usually cross several physiographic units, research can begin with a set of environmental observations potentially relevant to past man-land relationships. Hopefully, an intensive ecological analysis of site function and location will lead to the discovery of regional regularities (Goodyear 1975a). Utilization of subsistence models derived from ethnographic data can also be used to infer the past effective environment of an area. In the absence of botanical and faunal evidence, archaeologists often assume that the present environment of an area is similar to that of the late prehistoric populations (Debowski and others 1976:48).

Advance planning is needed before either the material culture or the physical environment is sampled. The former requires intra-site surface sampling such as that used by Redman and Watson (1970). The latter may require techniques such as those used in quantitative plant ecology. Such research also entails critical evaluations concerning the applicability of modern vegetative patterns to past patterns. Modern man has extensively disrupted natural vegetative patterns, and it must be assumed that prehistoric man did likewise, though on a more limited basis. Modern grazing practices have altered the rangeland vegetation on the terrace systems of the valley, while both modern and prehistoric peoples have disrupted the natural environment of the floodplains through agricultural practices.

Initial Survey Research Goals

Since the AEPCO Greenlee-Dos Condado survey was contracted on an emergency basis, and since existing data on the area were insufficient for definition of detailed research problems, the first survey objective was acquisition of very basic data concerning cultural resources that lay within the transmission line corridor. The primary hypothesis to be tested was that the major Southwestern prehistoric groups in this intercultural area can be correlated with specific subsistence activities as well as material culture patterns. Correlative hypotheses were: (1) that different cultural groups will be practicing the same subsistence activities; (2) that different cultural groups will be practicing different subsistence activities; and (3) that a single cultural group will be practicing different subsistence activities. Research focused on definition of intra-site activities more than on intense analysis of cultural-environmental interrelationships. A major focus concerned agricultural water control systems.

The presence of substantial agricultural features in the upper Gila Valley suggested that this Safford-Clifton transect was likely to yield data on prehistoric water control systems. There is no one-to-one correspondence between water control systems and culture areas; that is, there is no unique Mogollon or Anasazi system. However, it may be assumed that a variety of water control techniques were available to prehistoric populations. In looking at an intercultural area it may be possible to examine selective pressures operating on the types of water control systems chosen. Also water control systems often reflect cultural choices as well as economic necessity. For example, canal irrigation was feasible at Point of Pines but was never practiced (Woodbury 1961). In an intercultural situation specific groups may be exploiting specific resources; thus cultural boundaries may be reflected ecologically.

These initial research goals proved to be of limited utility since water control systems were found on few sites. After completion of the survey, these research goals were not abandoned but were restricted to sites for which they were applicable while new research goals generated by the survey data were pursued.

Logistics and Methods

Logistics. Logistics of the AEPCO Greenlee-Dos Condado survey were largely based on guidelines established by the Cultural Resource Management Section of the Arizona State Museum. The approach was a two-phase mitigation program (Canouts and others 1972:40-41; Raab 1973:1; Vivian and Thompson 1973:1). Phase I included preparation of a research design for an archaeological survey and implementation of this design by initiating field operations. Phase II included a synthetic interpretative report on field operations, description of resources, recommendation of significant resources for nomination to the National Register of Historic Places and proposal for mitigation of adverse effects of construction.

The primary concern of the Phase I survey was the fulfillment of contract obligations to AEPCO. This included the location and mapping of all archaeological resources in the transmission line corridor and in buffer zones around high impact areas. The goal of this research was to maximize the recovery of scientific and cultural information.

The Phase I survey lasted from October 12, 1976, to December 15, 1976, a total of 164 field and research man-days. The field team consisted of Kay Simpson (Field Supervisor), Carol Coe, Stephen Lensink, Carole McClellan, and Kathleen Quinn. Lynn Teague was Project Director. Research and write-up of the Phase I survey data began December 2, 1976, and terminated February 11, 1977, for a total of 156 man-days. Participants were Kay Simpson, Carol Coe, and Carole McClellan. The survey of access roads began January 20, 1977, and terminated February 24, 1977. The access road field team consisted of Carol Coe (Field Supervisor) and Anne Rieger. Write-up participants were Kay Simpson (Project Supervisor) and Kathy Kamp. Jon Czaplicki was Project Director.

Seventy-two archaeological sites were recorded during Phase I; several of these were later combined under one ASM site number. In addition, 159 isolated artifact loci were recorded. Seventeen new sites were located on the access road survey. One site, Arizona W:15:17, was recorded in the data recovery phase but was not included in mitigation proposals because it was located outside the R-O-W corridor.

Methods. The AEPCO Greenlee-Dos Condado survey was essentially an inventory survey. The primary objective was to locate, identify, record, and evaluate all archaeologically significant resources in the proposed corridor.

The field survey was conducted on foot. The centerline of the corridor was marked for the archaeological survey crew by AEPCO linemen, and we gratefully acknowledge this assistance. It would have been virtually impossible to stay within the narrow corridor in rugged terrain without extensive use of surveying instruments. By marking the corridor for us, AEPCO provided a quick and efficient survey route. The survey crew can state with a high degree of confidence the accuracy of the location of all recorded sites.

The crew walked the 30 m wide corridor four abreast at 25-foot intervals. Crew members rarely had to zig-zag to cover the survey area. One vehicle was left at a point the crew considered it was able to cover in a day's walk. A second vehicle was then driven to the point where the previous day's survey had ended. Daily coverage averaged 2.8 km per day, though it varied from 2.4 km to 8 km per day. Coverage depended on terrain, weather, access roads and number, size, and complexity of archaeological resources. Site recording averaged one-half hour for "short-form" sites and 1.5 hours for "long-form" sites. However, complex sites such as Arizona CC:2:30 took as long as 8 hours to record.

The access road corridor was 4.5 m in width. Only proposed access roads were examined by ASM for archaeological resources; existing dirt roads were not surveyed though some proposed blade cuts on these roads were spot checked. The access routes were determined and flagged by Burns & McDonnell Engineering Co. except for the segment crossing the Peloncillo Mountains which was done by BLM personnel. When an archaeological site was found an attempt was made by both engineering crews to re-align the access roads to avoid the site if such re-alignment was also feasible in terms of construction and environmental impacts.

<u>Site Recognition</u>. The fundamental units identified at the survey level of investigation are termed sites. Sites can be defined as any place, of any size, where there are found traces of human occupation or activity (Hole and Heizer 1965:59). Three minimal criteria were used to define an archaeological site (Arizona State Museum 1976:4; Debowski and others 1976: 53): (1) it must have definable limits in time and space; (2) it must contain more than one definable locus of past human activity; and (3) it must have more than one single occurrence of activity at any one locus.

One previous ASM criterion for site recognition was discarded as being impractical: it must have density of more than five artifacts per square meter. The majority of sites in the Safford-Clifton area have extremely low artifact densities. Because this type of site is so prevalent, its exclusion would limit site investigation to one type of settlement or use pattern--the Gila floodplain villages and water control systems. Instead the survey recognized that these low density lithic scatters were definable loci present in large, diffuse lithic use areas. Such lithic scatters were often continuous over large areas; because of time and contract limitations their natural site boundaries outside the R-O-W were not defined. Many of these loci were finally combined under one ASM site designation during later stages of analysis and fieldwork.

The standard ASM site survey form was used to record multi-component or multi-feature sites. This form was designed to answer the following questions (Canouts 1975:vii):

1. The cultural and temporal affiliation of the site
2. The past activities represented at the site
3. The nature of site deposits (stratified or surface)
4. The degree to which past human activities could be determined to have affected the environmental setting
5. The degree and nature of post-occupation site disturbance
6. The eligibility of the site for inclusion in the National Register of Historic Places
7. The relationship of the site to others in the region.

A number of sites encountered on the survey lacked the density and/or complexity that would warrant recording on the detailed ASM site survey form. Such sites were small surface sherd and lithic scatters and chipping stations. These single component, single feature sites were recorded on a short form developed for the survey (Figure 11).

Some subjectivity entered into judgments as to whether to record a site on the long form, short form, or as an isolated feature or artifact. Generally, long-form sites were often judged by a greater amount of material as well as complexity. Short-form sites were generally small sparse lithic scatters, usually with fewer than 100 observable artifacts. Isolated artifacts and features were indicated by an "X" on aerial maps with pertinent information recorded on the map and in field journals. Such cultural remains were generally isolated lithic flakes, tools, projectile points, and rock piles. Site disturbance was also used as a guide. Sherd scatters noted in the Gila River floodplain may in fact be part of large multi-component and multi-feature sites, but there was usually no way to assess the site due to coverage by crops or destruction by plowing. Such sites were recorded on the short form.

Once a site was recognized it was given a survey field number: AEPCO 1, AEPCO 2, and so forth. Right-of-way corridor sites were numbered from 1 to 100 consecutively; access road sites were numbered from 101 to 200. Site information was then recorded on either the long or short form. The location of each site was plotted on 15 minutes USGS quadrangle maps and on 200-foot horizontal scale aerial maps of the corridor supplied by AEPCO. Site maps were drawn directly on these aerials.

All crew members participated in site recording. Each site's field number was recorded on a wooden stake left at the site. Site boundaries, if known, were flagged with blue tape. When the site continued many hundreds of meters outside of the 30 m corridor, lateral boundaries were flagged only to a 15 m buffer zone on each side of the corridor. AEPCO did not contract for recording and mapping of sites or site boundaries outside the R-O-W corridor, but it was always noted when site boundaries did extend outside the corridor, and artificial and natural site boundaries were carefully distinguished on

OTHER MAP REFERENCE

____

____

____

Limited Activity Area

Recorded by____

Date____

Project___________________________________Site Field Number__________________

Photographs: B/W No(s):_______________ Color No(s)___________________________

State____________________________ County______________________________

Map Quad Name and Series____

T__________ R__________ Sec.__________,__________ $\frac{1}{4}$ of the__________ $\frac{1}{4}$.

UTM Zone_______________ Easting_______________ Northing_______________

Description of how to get to the site:

Elevation:____________________________ Dimensions of site____________________

Vegetation:

Topography:

Components:

Material Culture:

Disturbance:

Comments:

Figure 11. AEPCO Site Survey Short Form

site maps. Crew members acquired information on natural site boundaries needed for nomination to the National Register of Historic Places on sites that the BLM indicated they would consider eligible.

Site Collections. It is the policy of the Arizona State Museum not to make surface collections of artifacts on an initial survey. Many Southwestern desert sites tend to be shallow and often have a "fragile pattern" (Hayden 1965) type of artifact distribution. Thus, indiscriminate collecting could literally remove the site. However, as the cultural affiliations of the project area were so diverse and the crew members were not familiar with all ceramic and lithic types and regional varieties, samples of diagnostic artifacts were occasionally collected. No formal sampling design was used for such collections. The location of all artifacts removed from a site was plotted on the site maps to preserve surface context for future investigations.

Archaeological Resources

The survey crew located and recorded 72 sites within the transmission line corridor. Sites were found along all segments of the 105 km corridor except for the 19 km segment in the Peloncillo Mountains and its northeastern pediment, for a total site density of 0.68 sites per linear kilometer. Both prehistoric and historic sites were discovered. These have been divided into five types according to size and the types of activities apparent at each. All sites recorded in the R-O-W survey are listed in Table 1 and are presented in order by environmental stratum. Sites recorded in the access road survey and construction monitoring phases are listed in Table 2.

Historic Sites

Evidence of historic Anglo activity was found, particularly along the Morenci Substation-Morenci Mines route. These were turn of the century encampments related to mining or railroad activities, and isolated artifacts consisted of pre-1930s glass, mining claims, and depression-era Civilian Conservation Corps (CCC) terraces. The latter two were not recorded as site features but as site disturbances. Only one totally historic site was recorded, Arizona CC:3:7. It consisted of trash heaps of pre-World War I materials.

Prehistoric Sites

Habitation Sites. These are areas characterized by evidence of permanent settlement over a long period of time with a diversity of activities carried out at the location. Habitation sites were defined by evidence of house structures and variety of artifacts.

Three sites were recorded as habitation sites: Arizona CC:2:30, a pithouse village, Arizona CC:2:31, a floodplain village with cobble structures; and Arizona CC:3:32, a three component village with pithouses, cobble structures,

Table 1. Archaeological Resources
AEPCO Greenlee-Dos Condado R-O-W Corridor

Site Number	Field Designation	Stratum	Landform	Type of Boundary	Site Dimensions (in meters)	Site Type	Grinding Implements	Lithic Artifacts			Ceramics		Features			Historic Artifacts		
								Flakes	Cores	Tools	Plain	Decorated	Chipping Stations	Rock Piles	Rock Align-ments	Glass	Metal	Ceramics
CC:2:31	56	1	floodplain	arbitrary	400 x 500	habitation	X	X	X	CT	X	X		X	X	X	X	X
CC:2:32	79	1	floodplain; ridges	natural	260 x 410	habitation		X	X	UTF	X	X			X	X	X	X
CC:2:41	46	1	floodplain	arbitrary	36 x 60	habitation	X	X	X	PT	X	X						
CC:2:48	54	1	floodplain	arbitrary	122 x 60	habitation	X	X	X		X	X						
CC:2:49	55	1	floodplain	arbitrary	114 x 60	habitation	X	X	X		X	X						
CC:2:33	36	2	terrace edge	natural	52 x 30	lithic scatter	X	X	X				X	X				
CC:2:33	37	2	terrace edge	natural	47 x 45	lithic scatter		X	X									
CC:2:34	38	2	floodplain	natural	75 x 17	" "	X	X	X									
CC:2:35	39	2	flat terrace	arbitrary	125 x 60	" "		X	X	UTF			X	2				
CC:2:36	40	2	flat terrace	natural	10 x 7	" "		X	X					X				
CC:2:37	41	2	flat terrace	arbitrary	88 x 60	" "		X		UTF				X				
CC:2:38	42	2	flat terrace	natural	47 x 35	" "		X	X				X					
CC:2:39	78	2	flat terrace	natural	30 x 30	" "		X	X	CH								
CC:2:40	43	2	flat terrace	arbitrary	64 x 60	" "		X	X	CH	X							

Table 1 (cont). Archaeological Resources
AEPCO Greenlee-Dos Condado R-O-W Corridor

Site Number	Field Designation	Stratum	Landform	Type of Boundary	Site Dimensions (in meters)	Site Type	Grinding Implements	Lithic Artifacts			Ceramics		Features			Historic Artifacts		
								Flakes	Cores	Tools	Plain	Decorated	Chipping Stations	Rock Piles	Rock Alignments	Glass	Metal	Ceramics
CC:2:40	44	2	terrace edge	arbitrary	103 x 60	Lithic Scatter		X	X				X		3			
CC:2:40	45	2	terrace edge	arbitrary	31 x 60	" "		X	X				X		X			
CC:2:30	47	3	terrace remnant	natural	500 x 180	Habitation	X	X	X	CH,B,Hoe	X	X		X	X			
CC:2:42	48	3	terrace remnant	natural	112 x 53	Lithic Scatter	X	X	X				2		2			
CC:2:43	49	3	terrace edge	arbitrary	100 x 60	" "		X	X	CH,CT			X					
CC:2:44	50	3	catchment basin	arbitrary	650 x 60	" "		X	X	CH,Core tool								
CC:2:45	51	3	catchment basin	arbitrary	430 x 60	" "		X	X	CH,CT,SC				X				
CC:2:46	52	3	catchment basin	arbitrary	1223 x 60	" "		X	X	CH,CT			X					
CC:2:47	53	3	catchment basin, terrace edge	arbitrary	830 x 60	" "	X	X	X	CH,CT,UTF			X	X	X			
CC:2:50	57	3	catchment basin	natural	345 x 215	" "		X	X	CH,CT		X		X	X			
CC:2:58	76	4	ridge	natural	62 x 30	" "		X		UTF								
CC:2:59	77	4	ridge	arbitrary	100 x 60	" "		X	X				3					

Table 1 (cont). Archaeological Resources
AEPCO Greenlee-Dos Condado R-O-W Corridor

Site Number	Field Designation	Stratum	Landform	Type of Boundary	Site Dimensions (in meters)	Site Type	Grinding Implements	Lithic Artifacts			Ceramics		Features			Historic Artifacts		
								Flakes	Cores	Tools	Plain	Decorated	Chipping Stations	Rock Piles	Rock Alignments	Glass	Metal	Ceramics
CC:2:58	76	4	ridge	natural	62 x 30	Lithic Scatter		X		UTF								
CC:2:59	77	4	ridge	arbitrary	100 x 60	" "		X	X				3					
CC:2:51	58	5	ridge	arbitrary	390 x 60	" "		X	X	CH,CT,UTF				X	X			
CC:2:52	59	5	ridge	arbitrary	190 x 57	" "		X	X				X	5				
CC:2:53	60	5	ridge	natural	127 x 30	" "		X	X									
CC:2:54	61	5	ridge	arbitrary	35 x 74	" "		X	X									
CC:2:54	62	5	ridge	arbitrary	168 x 60	" "		X	X	CH			X					
CC:2:55	63	5	wash	natural	3 x 3	Lithic Manufacturing Loci		X	X				X					
CC:2:56	64	5	ridge	arbitrary	143 x 213	Lithic Scatter		X	X				X					
CC:2:57	65	5	ridge	natural	113 x 46	" "		X	X	CH								
CC:3:30	66	5	ridge	natural	35 x 15	" "		X										
CC:3:29	67	5	wash	natural	10 x 4	Lithic Manufacturing Loci		X	X				X					
CC:3:28	68	5	ridge	arbitrary	155 x 26	Lithic Scatter		X	X	CH,UTF				X	X			

Table 1 (cont). Archaeological Resources
AEPCO Greenlee-Dos Condado R-O-W Corridor

Site Number	Field Designation	Stratum	Landform	Type of Boundary	Site Dimensions (in meters)	Site Type	Grinding Implements	Lithic Artifacts			Ceramics		Features			Historic Artifacts		
								Flakes	Cores	Tools	Plain	Decorated	Chipping Stations	Rock Piles	Rock Align-ments	Glass	Metal	Ceramics
CC:3:27	68	5	ridge	arbitrary	155 x 26	Lithic Scatter		X	X	CH,UTF				X	X			
CC:3:27	69	5	ridge	natural	26 x 77	Lithic Manufact-uring Loci		X	X				3					
CC:3:26	70	5	ridge	arbitrary		Lithic Scatter		X	X						2			
CC:3:25	71	5	ridge	natural	35 x 111	" "		X	X	UTF			2					
CC:3:24	72	5	ridge	natural	280 x 53	" "		X	X				3					
CC:3:23	73	5	ridge	natural	4 x 4	Lithic Manufact-uring Loci		X	X				X		X			
CC:3:22	74	5	ridge	natural	5 x 5	Lithic Manufact-uring Loci		X	X				X					
CC:3:21	75	5	mountain saddle	natural	1 x 1	Lithic Manufact-uring Loci		X	X				X					
CC:3:12	1	7	ridge	natural	66 x 29	Lithic Scatter		X	X									
CC:3:13	12	7	ridge	natural	9 x 5.5	Lithic Manufact-uring Loci		X	X				X					
CC:3:14	13	7	ridge	natural	3 x 3	Lithic Scatter		X		UTF								

Table 1 (cont) Archaeological Resources
AEPCO Greenlee-Dos Condado R-O-W Corridor

Site Number	Field Designation	Stratum	Landform	Type of Boundary	Site Dimensions (in meters)	Site Type	Grinding Implements	Lithic Artifacts			Ceramics		Features			Historic Artifacts		
								Flakes	Cores	Tools	Plain	Decorated	Chipping Stations	Rock Piles	Rock Alignments	Glass	Metal	Ceramics
CC:3:15	6	7	ridge	natural	20 x 32	Lithic Scatter	H	X	X					X				
CC:3:16	14	7	ridge	arbitrary	55 x 91	" "	X	X										
CC:3:17	9	7	ridge	natural	114 x 72	" "		X	X				X					
CC:3:18	10	7	ridge	natural	260 x 125	" "		X	X				2	2				
CC:3:19	16	7	hilltop	arbitrary	380 x 60	" "		X	X					9	?			
CC:4:10	22	7	ridge	natural	17 x 50	" "		X	X									
CC:4:11	23	7	ridge	natural	54 x 20	" "		X	X				X					
CC:3:3	24	7	ridge	arbitrary	22 x 24	" "		X	X	Knife								
CC:3:4	25	7	ridge	natural	75 x 60	" "		X	X					2	1			
CC:3:5	26	7	ridge	natural	38 x 56	" "		X										
CC:3:6	27	7	ridge	natural	20 x 14	" "		X										
CC:3:8	28	7	ridge	natural	65 x 25	" "	H	X	X									
CC:3:7	29	7	ridge	natural	210 x 110	Historic										X	X	X
CC:3:9	30	7	ridge	natural	28 x 14	Lithic Scatter			X					X	?	X		

Table 1 (cont). Archaeological Resources
AEPCO Greenlee-Dos Condado R-O-W Corridor

Site Number	Field Designation	Stratum	Landform	Type of Boundary	Site Dimensions (in meters)	Site Type	Grinding Implements	Lithic Artifacts			Ceramics		Features			Historic Artifacts		
								Flakes	Cores	Tools	Plain	Decorated	Chipping Stations	Rock Piles	Rock Alignments	Glass	Metal	Ceramics
CC:3:10	31	8	ridge	natural	20 x 18	Lithic Scatter		X	X				X					
CC:3:11	32	8	ridge	natural	42 x 28	Lithic Scatter		X	X	UTF								
W:15:15	33	8	ridge	natural	64 x 39	" "		X	X				4					
W:15:16	34	8	ridge	arbitrary	42 x 28	" "		X	X									
W:15:17	35	8	ridge	natural	37.5 x 1275	" "		X	X	S				X	X		X	
CC:4:5	17	9	flat terrace	arbitrary	40 x 68	Lithic Scatter		X	X	B, preform			X	5				
CC:4:6	18	9	flat terrace	arbitrary	120 x 60	" "		X		PT,SC					X			
CC:4:7	19	9	flat terrace	natural	62 x 35	" "		X		UTF, PT						X		
CC:4:8	20	9	flat terrace	natural	65 x 50	" "		X										
CC:4:9	21	9	flat terrace	arbitrary	97 x 70	" "		X	X	UTF								
CC:4:4	15	10	mesa slope	arbitrary	34 x 54	Lithic Scatter		X	X									

KEY: UTF = Utilized Flake CH = Chopper PT = Point H = Hammerstone
CT = Cobble Tool SC = Scraper B = Biface

Table 2. Archaeological Resources
AEPCO Greenlee-Dos Condado Access Road Corridors

Site Number	Field Designation	Stratum	Landform	Type of Boundary	Site Dimensions (in meters)	Site Type	Grinding Implements	Lithic Artifacts			Ceramics		Features			Historic Artifacts		
								Flakes	Cores	Tools	Plain	Decorated	Chipping Stations	Rock Piles	Rock Alignments	Glass	Metal	Ceramics
CC:3:31	101	6	terrace	arbitrary	145 x 85	Lithic Scatter		X	X	UTF								
CC:3:32	102	6	mountain saddle	natural	145 x 120	Lithic Quarry		X	X	UTF, CH								
CC:3:33	103	8	ridge	natural	182 x 84	Lithic Scatter	X	X	X	CH, CT					3			
CC:3:20	104	7	terrace	natural	416 x 280	Lithic Scatter; Historic	H,X	X	X	CH, Point, UTF			X	X	X	X	X	
CC:3:34	105	7	ridge	arbitrary	175 x 5	Lithic Scatter		X	X				X					
CC:3:35	106	7	ridge	natural	20 x 26	Lithic Scatter; Quarry (?)		X	X									
CC:3:36	107	7	ridge	natural	71 x 23	Lithic Scatter		X	X		X			X				
CC:3:37	108	7	ridge	natural	45 x 15	Lithic Scatter		X							X			
CC:3:38	109	6	terrace	natural	190 x 220	Lithic Scatter; Quarry (?)	X	X	X	RTF, Core Tools, AP			X					
CC:3:39	110	6	terrace	arbitrary	195 x 95	Lithic Scatter		X	X	UTF			3		3	X		X
CC:3:23	111	5	hillslope	arbitrary	260 x 60	Lithic Manufacturing Loci		X	X	UTF, CT			5					
CC:3:40	112	5	slope	natural	0.86 x 0.86	Lithic Manufacturing Loci		X	X				1					

Table 2 (cont). Archaeological Resources
AEPCO Greenlee-Dos Condado Access Road Corridors

Site Number	Field Designation	Stratum	Landform	Type of Boundary	Site Dimensions (in meters)	Site Type	Grinding Implements	Lithic Artifacts			Ceramics		Features			Historic Artifacts		
								Flakes	Cores	Tools	Plain	Decorated	Chipping Stations	Rock Piles	Rock Alignments	Glass	Metal	Ceramics
CC:3:41	113	5	ridge	natural	13,500 m^2	Lithic Scatter	H	X	X	UTF, CH			1	1	1			
CC:3:42	114	5	ridge	natural	8,225 m^2	Lithic Scatter		X	X	CT, CH				1	4			
CC:3:43	115	5	hillslope	natural	4 x 2	Lithic Manufacturing Loci		X	X				1					
CC:3:44	116	5	ridge	natural	120 x 40	Lithic Scatter		X	X				1	2				
CC:3:45	117	5	ridge	natural	648 x 343	Lithic Scatter		X	X									

KEY:
- UTF = Utilized Flake
- CT = Cobble Tool
- CH = Chopper
- SC = Scraper
- PT = Point
- B = Biface
- H = Hammerstone
- RTF = Retouched Flake
- AP = Archaic Point

and historic structures. Three sherd scatters in the Gila River floodplain, Arizona CC:2:41, 48, and 49, may have been habitation sites but are so disturbed that it is difficult to assess them.

Lithic Scatters. These scatters of stone tools and debitage are often thought to be areas of limited activity and periodic, usually seasonal, occupation. Artifacts are generally uniform and appear to be related to food procuring and processing activities. Chipping stations and rock piles are the only features; plainware ceramics and ground stone artifacts are rarely present. It is believed that if the sites had been located via an areal survey instead of a linear survey, many of them would have formed concentrations within large "use areas" (Doyel 1972:27). A use area is defined as the presence of isolated artifacts or very low-density scatters throughout a locality.

Arizona CC:2:40 is unique among the surveyed sites in that it is a large sherd and lithic scatter with water control features.

Lithic Manufacturing Loci. These are sites that exhibit the remains of specific lithic activity, such as chipping stations where flakes were obtained for stone tools. Chipping stations usually consist of a core and two or more flakes and, like the lithic scatters, are probably features within a larger lithic use area.

Isolated Activity Loci. Cultural materials in isolated context were encountered in every segment of the line; however, the density was extremely low in the Peloncillo Mountains where no sites were encountered along the transmission line R-O-W corridor. Such artifacts and features were generally lithic flakes or tools, rock piles, or historic "pot breaks." No prehistoric "pot breaks" were observed. Refer to Volume III for a list of isolated activity loci.

Significance of the Archaeological Resources

The concept of archaeological significance involves considerations of both research and resource management problems. Four categories of significance have been defined by Moratto (1975). His categories have been used as guidelines for assessing the significance of the archaeological resources found on the initial survey of the Greenlee-Dos Condado transmission line corridor.

Legal Significance

The federal government has established one important measure of significance. According to Federal Regulation 36 CFR 800.10 page 3369, any site which has in the past added to our knowledge of prehistory or history or is potentially capable of doing so may qualify for nomination to the National Register of Historic Places (Federal Register, Vol. 39, No. 18, Part III).

Historic Significance

Scovill, Gordon, and Anderson (1972:20) have assessed the historic value of archaeological resources:

> Cultural resources are historically significant if they provide a typical or well-preserved example of a prehistoric culture, historic tribe, period of time, or category of human activity. Archaeological remains are historically significant if they can be associated with a specific individual event or aspect of history.

Historic archaeological sites are often ignored as archaeological resources. But history is more than written records, and archaeology can supplement written sources by providing information through material culture analysis.

Scientific Significance

Cultural resources are significant when they offer the potential to contribute information regarding prehistoric behavior. If this information can aid in explaining differences and similarities between various cultural groups and the reasons for variation, then they are scientifically significant (Scovill, Gordon, and Anderson 1972:20). In this light, <u>every</u> archaeological entity is significant, not simply because it is unique and non-renewable, but because it forms part of a sample or data base necessary for testing anthropological generalizations. The assessment of scientific worth is dependent upon such factors as:

> ...(1) the relative abundance of the resources to be affected; (2) the degree to which specific resources and situations are confined to the project area; (3) the cultural and environmental relationship of the archaeology of the project or program area to the surrounding culture province or provinces; (4) the variety of evidence for human activities and their environmental surroundings that is confined in the project or program area; (5) the range of research topics to which the resources may contribute; and (6) specific deficiencies in current knowledge that study of these resources may correct (Scovill, Gordon, and Anderson 1972:21).

The Scientific and Historic Significance of the Greenlee-Dos Condado Resources

The study area is one of intercultural contact among several major prehistoric Southwestern traditions. Such an area offers an excellent opportunity to study processes of culture change through time. The area lacks a detailed cultural-historical framework, and while it is generally recognized that a strictly historical paradigm is inadequate for modern research, all studies of cultural process rest on control of culture history. It is unknown if different groups inhabited the region at different time periods or if there were contemporary occupations. Therefore, it is imperative that current knowledge of the area's culture history be expanded. A review of previous archaeology stresses the need for information on site activity specialization. Large habitation sites are known as well as areas of lithic exploitation and water control networks. Further work is needed to define the cultural-environmental relationships in order to obtain a clearer idea of subsistence activities.

The archaeological potential of this region is still excellent although sites are rapidly disappearing. Previous excavations and surveys have indicated close relationships between the Safford Valley and the Point of Pines-Natanes Mountains to the north, Mimbres branch Mogollon to the northeast, San Simon branch Mogollon to the south, and Hohokam to the west. The exact nature of the relationship among groups in this and other areas cannot be established without more controlled research in the Safford Valley-Clifton foothills region. In the valley land leveling, plowing, and channel improvement have destroyed most of the large habitation sites. Arizona CC:2:31 and 32 are almost unique in the valley in having only minimal disturbance. Sites on the first terraces of the river systems and within the foothills of the various local mountain ranges are more protected. These latter sites are rarely reported to archaeological agencies and generally have gone unnoticed in previous research designs.

Several important cultural-historical questions remain unanswered and are cited here as examples of the archaeological significance of the region. The Gila River drainage is a logical place for Cochise cultural material to be located, but no evidence of this pre-agricultural period has been identified in the area. The verification of the absence or rarity of early hunters and gatherers would be a useful research problem. Determination of what environmental or cultural factors might have discouraged such settlement would be especially illuminating (Teague 1974:25).

Another critical research problem is the inter-relationships of the San Simon and Mimbres branches of the Mogollon. Was there indigenous development of one or both in the Gila River drainage? If not, population movements must be investigated. During this time period there was contact not only between these two branches but between them and the Hohokam to the west. What was the nature of this contact? Was it trade, population movements, or co-existence? Archaeological research in the Southwest has focused upon heartland areas of major cultural groups, while little is known of processes and interactions in peripheral areas. The Safford-Clifton region could provide data for such a research focus.

A third problem area would be a better definition of the Salado culture itself. Most of our cultural-historical information is on the Safford Valley Salado period. But this information is inconsistent and minimally published. The relationship between the Tonto Basin homeland and areas such as the Safford Valley region is unknown. Is there more than one ceramic complex of which one or all are Salado? Is the Safford region peripheral to the primary

Salado region? Is the Safford area a region of Salado colonization? Do Salado ceramic styles represent population movements, trade, or stimulus-diffusion of design styles? What is the relationship of Salado to the earlier or contemporary Mogollon?

Finally, there is no archaeological or historical information for the period between the Salado occupation and settlement of the area by Apaches and Europeans. Research on this time gap, particularly on the entrance of Athabascan peoples into the area, would be valuable not only from a cultural-historical standpoint but would also provide information on culture change, stability, abandonment, and interaction between groups.

Cultural-historical questions are not the only possible research orientation in the project area. Research could also be focused on understanding the non-diagnostic lithic scatters that are so common. Localized studies of resource exploitation may be the key to understanding such sites. Identification of site activities will aid in the understanding of regional settlement patterns and interactions. If the cultural affiliation of these sites can be identified then it will be possible to make statements concerning cultural processes through time, but defining temporal attributes and sequences at sites is crucial to such studies. Analyses of lithic artifacts focusing on stage of manufacture, evidence of use, and function will be used to understand site specialization, while analyses of technological tradition will be used to identify cultural affiliation. The sites discovered on the initial survey are ideally suited to such research problems.

Recommendations for Nomination to the National Register of Historic Places

According to Federal Regulation 36 CFR 800 any site that has in the past added to our knowledge of prehistory or history or is potentially capable of doing so in the future may qualify for nomination to the National Register of Historic Places. The following sites are considered to possess such qualifications and are recommended to be nominated to the register: Arizona CC:2:30, 31 and 32. No other sites are recommended for nomination to the register. It is recommended that AEPCO construction plans be modified to avoid cultural remains only at Arizona CC:2:30, 31, and 32. Stipulations were drawn up for monitoring construction activities at all other sites.

Recommendations for Research and Data Recovery

This section presents ASM's recommendations for the management of the cultural resources located within the AEPCO Greenlee-Dos Condado transmission line corridor. The results of a 100 percent archaeological survey of the corridor and access roads indicate that 89 historic and prehistoric sites would be destroyed or severely affected by the AEPCO project.

The effects on cultural resources due to the construction of the AEPCO power line include indirect and long-term effects as well as the more obvious direct, short-term ones. Indirect impacts are usually defined as adverse effects on sites adjacent to the R-O-W and include construction activity and opening of the area to vandalism. The options available in dealing with the loss of cultural resources are: (1) site protection through avoidance of the cultural resources, and (2) adequate data recovery of cultural resources (Debowski and others 1976:176).

Site Protection

Three sites located within the R-O-W corridor are recommended for nomination to the National Register of Historic Places. As these sites are not duplicated in kind within the corridor their destruction would be a serious loss to the archaeology of the region. Due to site size and complexity, data recovery costs would be quite high, and ASM, in consultation with AEPCO, recommends avoidance of the following sites:

Arizona CC:2:30: pithouse village. AEPCO has agreed to realign that section of the transmission line in order to completely bypass this site.

Arizona CC:2:31: pithouse village. AEPCO has agreed to restrict construction activities to existing disturbed areas located on the site.

Arizona CC:2:32: pithouse village. AEPCO has agreed to restrict construction activities to existing disturbed areas located on the site.

Site Monitoring

Survey conditions were very poor along the section of the corridor within the Gila River floodplain, with the land in field crops or dense with riparian vegetation. The surveyors were able to check for evidence of sites only in cleared fields and since these fields have been subjected to severe land alteration methods, lack of surface indications does not automatically mean lack of deposition. For this reason ASM suggests monitoring by appropriate archaeological personnel while towers M-27 to M-118 and L-117 to L-124 are being installed.

Many of the sites found on the access road survey were protected by avoidance. As many of the re-aligned access roads lie adjacent to sites or transact light density site perimeters, ASM recommends an archaeological monitor be present during the construction of these roads.

Site Sampling and Data Recovery

Total data recovery is rarely recogized as feasible. For example, Canouts (1975:161) states:

> Total data recovery (100 percent recovery of all relevant information from all impacted resources in the project area) is neither feasible nor actually achievable and represents a less than equal alternative to site protection. The knowledge that further developments in archaeological method, technique and theory will increase the potential for deriving data from undisturbed sites argues for the protection of sites whenever possible. Total data recovery is also unfeasible from the point of diminishing information returns. Costs involved in total data recovery...would represent the expenditure that is neither justifiable nor necessary. Furthermore, the time required to implement programs for carrying out total data study would be impractical...

As total data recovery was not recommended, a program of partial data recovery was initiated. A sample of all recorded sites in the R-O-W corridor was selected for controlled surface collection and detailed mapping of features and artifact scatters. Test excavations were conducted to ascertain if there was deposition.

Sampling procedures combined two common archaeological procedures: probability and judgment sampling. Judgment sampling is the "conscious selection of units to investigate based on what the researcher considers to be the most productive or most representative samples" (Redman 1975:149). Probability sampling draws samples using rigorous mathematical theory.

Common criteria for dividing sites into strata, or groups of similar sites, can be based on (1) chronological periods, (2) topographic or biotic zones, or (3) site types. Since little information was available on chronology, a combination of the second and third criteria were used. Each stratum could then be sampled with equal intensity or could be differentially sampled according to the archaeologists' prior knowledge.

The primary criterion used to determine site membership in a stratum was topographic zone location. This was initially based on the surveyors' observations that sites in similar topographic settings tended to be very similar, while differing between topographic zones. When necessary, these groupings were further stratified by site type. Therefore, research was begun with a set of environmental observations potentially relevant to past man-land relationships.

The following list is of topographic strata and site types occurring within the strata from which a sample population was drawn. Following the stratum type is the number of sites in the stratum and, in parentheses, the percentage of all sites this number represents. Stratum 6 (Peloncillo Mountains) has been omitted because no archaeological resources were found on the survey. Stratum 10 (Democrat Mesa) has been combined with adjacent Stratum 9 (Big Lue-Gila River Canyonlands) due to the scarcity of archaeological resources in the former.

Stratum 1:	Gila River floodplain - 5 (6.94%)
Sites:	Habitation - 5
Stratum 2:	San Simon Valley - 11 (15.28%)
Sites:	Lithic scatters - 11
Stratum 3:	Gila River Pleistocene terraces and lower bajada of Gila Mountains - 8 (11.11%)
Sites:	Habitation - 1
Sites:	Lithic scatters - 7
Stratum 4:	Upper bajada of Gila Mountains - (2.78%)
Sites:	Lithic scatters - 2
Stratum 5:	Peloncillo Mountain foothills - 18 (25.00%)
Sites:	Lithic scatters - 12
Sites:	Lithic manufacturing loci - 6
Stratum 7:	Gila River terraces - 17 (23.61%)
Sites	Lithic scatters - 15
Sites:	Lithic manufacturing loci - 1
Sites:	Historic site - 1
Stratum 8:	San Francisco River terraces - 5 (6.94%)
Sites:	Lithic scatters - 5
Stratum 9/10:	Big Lue canyonlands - Democrat Mesa - 6 (8.33%)
Sites:	Lithic scatters - 6

The AEPCO R-O-W corridor transected most major physiographic zones in the upper Gila Valley: the Peloncillo Mountains; geologic terraces descending from the Gila, Peloncillo, and Big Lue Mountains; the San Simon River and adjacent terraces; the San Francisco River and adjacent terraces; several major tributary canyons of the Gila River; and the Gila River floodplain, twice south of the Gila Box where the river flows through a wide fertile valley, and once north of the Box where the river descends through a narrow canyon. Zones in this region that were not transected by the R-O-W corridor were the Gila Mountains and major tributary rivers such as Bonita Creek and the Blue River.

The AEPCO line did tend to overrepresent ridgetops and flat geologic terraces; therefore, sites occurring on these landforms are probably also overrepresented. River terraces and floodplains were avoided by AEPCO when possible because of construction problems associated with river flow and problems in acquiring rights-of-way across valuable agricultural land. Thus, river terraces and floodplains were underrepresented in the physiographic sample. Because of this, few habitation sites were discovered as such sites tend to occur on or adjacent to the Gila floodplain or along major tributary rivers of the Gila. Stratum 1 (Gila River floodplain) was later omitted from the data recovery program because its three habitation sites were protected by avoidance and the three recorded sherd and lithic scatters have been largely destroyed by modern cultivation.

Selection of sites to be investigated was not done by any statistical means, as the total number of sites within each stratum was too small to warrant complex sampling procedures. The artifical boundaries of the R-O-W corridor would also promote statistical distortion. Instead, a sample of sites to be investigated was drawn in such a way as to insure a reasonable representation within strata and to insure that sites selected had qualities relevant to project objectives. For example, sites with extensive disturbance were generally not selected.

Sample size is of extreme importance when the number of cases is less than 100, as it was with the AEPCO population. Cowgill (1975:263) has observed that "unless the sampling fraction is more than 20 percent of the total population, the proportion of the population included in the sample is of negligible importance." The sample of sites to be further investigated was drawn from the strata in such a way that a minimum of 30 percent of the total number of recorded sites would be studied. This sample size was chosen because it was felt that less than 30 percent would be inadequate while more than 30 percent would not be justified by cost in comparison to information gained.

It should be reiterated that the sampling population is the total number of sites found along the AEPCO R-O-W corridor <u>minus</u> the sites AEPCO avoided. It is not a sample of all site types known to exist in the project transect, especially as habitation sites were excluded from the sample. However, in spite of the many criticisms leveled at linear surveys and their inherent biases (Goodyear 1975a), it is felt that the AEPCO R-O-W corridor transected most major environmental zones and most site types existing in the area and the survey observed a full range of cultural resources present in the Safford-Clifton area. The data recovery program tried to minimize the loss of information that would result from destruction of the archaeological sites by protecting major sites and mapping and collecting a reasonable percentage of the minor sites.

Sites selected from within the R-O-W corridor in each stratum for data recovery were:

<u>Stratum 1</u>
All sites avoided

<u>Stratum 2</u>
Total number of sites: 11
Sites selected for data recovery: AEPCO 36 (Arizona CC:2:33)
AEPCO 38 (Arizona CC:2:34)
AEPCO 44 (Arizona CC:2:40)
Percentage of sites to be investigated: 27.27%.

Stratum 3
Total number of sites: 8
Sites selected for data recovery: AEPCO 49 (Arizona CC:2:43)
AEPCO 50 (Arizona CC:2:44)
AEPCO 52 (Arizona CC:2:46)
Percentage of sites to be investigated: 37.50%.

Stratum 4
Total number of sites: 2
Sites selected for data recovery: AEPCO 76 (Arizona CC:3:58)
Percentage of sites to be investigated: 50%.

Stratum 5
Total number of sites: 18
Sites selected for data recovery: AEPCO 58 (Arizona CC:2:51)
AEPCO 64 (Arizona CC:2:56)
AEPCO 70 (Arizona CC:3:26)
AEPCO 72 (Arizona CC:3:24)
AEPCO 74 (Arizona CC:3:22)
Percentage of sites to be investigated: 27.77%.

Stratum 6
No sites recorded

Stratum 7
Total number of sites: 17
Sites selected for data recovery: AEPCO 9 (Arizona CC:3:17)
AEPCO 10 (Arizona CC:3:18)
AEPCO 16 (Arizona CC:3:19)
AEPCO 25 (Arizona CC:3:4)
AEPCO 29 (Arizona CC:3:7)
Percentage of sites to be investigated: 29.41%.

Stratum 8
Total number of sites: 5
Sites selected for data recovery: AEPCO 33 (Arizona W:15:15)
AEPCO 35 (Arizona W:15:17)
Percentage of sites to be investigated: 40%.

Stratum 9/10
Total number of sites: 6
Sites selected for data recovery: AEPCO 17 (Arizona CC:4:5)
AEPCO 18 (Arizona CC:4:6)
Percentage of sites to be investigated: 33.3%

The access road survey was conducted during the writing of the survey report and consequently, sites located were not included in the original site population. Several of these access road sites were then added to the data recovery program. The primary criterion for selection was amount of potential dangers. If an access road transected a major portion of a site it was considered for data recovery. But if an access road completely avoided a site or crossed a site at its periphery, the site was not selected for further research. For example, no sites from Stratum 6 (Peloncillo Mountains) were selected because the engineering team planned all access roads to avoid sites. Some access roads were re-routed to follow the R-O-W in an attempt to confine construction impacts to a single corridor; however, it was more feasible to carry out data recovery on several of the sites within the access road R-O-W, rather than re-route the road around a site.

In order not to increase AEPCO's expenses nor to enlarge the sample size unreasonably, only six out of 17 access road sites were chosen for further data recovery procedures. These were:

Stratum 5: AEPCO 68 (Arizona CC:3:28)
AEPCO 116 (Arizona CC:3:44)
AEPCO 111 (Arizona CC:3:22)
AEPCO 61 (Arizona CC:2:54)
AEPCO 62 (Arizona CC:2:54)

Stratum 7: AEPCO 104 (Arizona CC:3:20)

During the data recovery phase, fieldwork was initiated on three sites adjacent to two of the originally selected 21 sites. This was done because the proximity of the sites suggested they should be studied as a unit.

Stratum 2: APECO 37 (Arizona CC:2:33)
AEPCO 43 and 45 (Arizona CC:2:40)

Thus, the final percentages of all sites investigated in each stratum were:

Stratum 1: 0.00%
Stratum 2: 54.55%
Stratum 3: 37.50%
Stratum 4: 50.00%
Stratum 5: 40.00%
Stratum 6: 0.00%
Stratum 7: 27.27%
Stratum 8: 33.33%
Stratum 9/10: 33.33%

In summary, 30 (33.70 percent) of the 89 sites discovered during all phases of survey were investigated in the data recovery program.

Research Design

The most significant archaeological sites found in the project area were protected by avoidance. The remaining cultural resources consisted primarily of light-to-moderate density lithic scatters. Previous research designs in the area have concentrated on large habitation sites and have ignored smaller activity areas. These small sites, which seem to be insignificant when viewed as isolated entities, become important when studied as a pattern of use. Research objectives for this project, therefore, involved collecting two basic kinds of archaeological information from these small sites: chronological and functional. Many of the small sites cannot be placed in any cultural-historical context, nor is it likely that they can ever be. However, it was thought the larger lithic scatters might yield such information.

A research design to define relationships between sites and resources had been devised for the Foote Wash-No Name Wash project; this was near the AEPCO project area and similar in archaeological manifestations (Teague 1975). This design, with some modifications, was adopted here.

The major hypothesis proposed in the Foote Wash research design was that prehistorically, the natural resources of the area were "exploited by short-term procurement and processing activities which are components of a larger system of subsistence-related behavior" (Teague 1975:7). Corollary hypotheses were derived from this major hypothesis and are presented below; test implications consisting of data to support the hypotheses follow each corollary. Null alternatives of all hypotheses are implied.

I. Sites represent procurement of stone cores for use elsewhere in tool manufacture.

Assumptions: Raw material split or quartered at the site. Some test flaking carried out to determine stone suitability.

Test Implications: Presence of split raw materials, relatively few cores, small number of flakes, with the majority being cortical. Few or no tools.

II. Sites represent procurement of stone flakes for use elsewhere in tool manufacture.

Assumptions: Cores produced and large cortical and primary flakes struck off at the site. Flakes transported elsewhere.

Test Implications: Presence of worked raw materials, relatively numerous cores, relatively numerous flakes, with few being cortical. Few or no tools.

III. Sites represent processing of stone to form tool blanks that are transported elsewhere for finishing into bifacial tools.

Assumptions: Tool blanks manufactured at site for transport.

Test Implications: Presence of a broad spectrum of lithic debris, including some biface thinning flakes and broken or discarded biface tool blanks. Few or no tools.

IV. Sites represent procurement and processing of stone into finished tools.

Assumptions: Tool kits refurbished during seasonal rounds.

Test Implications: (a) Presence of a broad spectrum of lithic debris, including broken or discarded tool blanks and finished tools; few or no utilized tools. (b) Presence of small amounts of locally-occurring stone with evidence of flake removal; few or no utilized tools.

V. Sites represent plant processing stations.

Assumptions: Stone procured and processed in small amounts at the place of use. Plants processed at site.

Test Implications: Presence of specialized cutting and grinding tools with evidence of use (modern resources include saltbush, cactus fruit, etc.).

VI. Sites represent plant storage stations.

Assumptions: Plants collected and stored at central facilities, either long-term or short-term storage.

Test Implications: Presence of economic plant remains in cobble cists.

VII. Sites represent roasting stations.

Assumptions: Food processed and cooked on site. Rock piles are stones used for roasting pits or hearths.

Test Implications: Excavation will reveal ash, burnt bone, and/or pollen adjacent to rock piles.

VIII. The pattern of site usage identified in Hypotheses I through VII reflects a subsistence strategy characterized by broad-based seasonal exploitation of non-domestic resources. (Diagnostic artifact analysis will be used to arrange the pattern of site usage through time.)

Assumptions: Sites served the needs of a population adapted to seasonal hunting and gathering. Tools were made and used in the procurement area. Short-term camps were occupied and storage facilities were constructed.

Test Implications: (a) Site types will reflect density of exploitation.
(b) Short-term but intensively occupied campsites will exist.
(c) Storage facilities will exist.
(d) Lithic procurement sites will be of the types described in Hypothesis IV.

IX. The pattern of site usage identified in Hypotheses I-VIII reflects specific resource exploitation as an adjunct to a domestic resource subsistence strategy.

Assumptions: Sites reflect the activities of people who used the procurement area as a storehouse of needed materials and foods that were not available at the base camp or village. Raw materials or economic plants were gathered and transported from the procurement area.

Test Implications: (a) Site types will lack diversity.
(b) Campsites will be nonexistent or ephemeral if present.
(c) Lithic procurement sites will be as described in Hypotheses I-III.

X. Small-scale runoff horticulture was carried out.

Assumptions: Runoff control devices were constructed to provide water for small-scale cultivation.

Test Implications: Presence of check dams, terraces, or other features related to cultivation and water control.

XI. Sites were used as habitation areas.

Assumptions: Cleared rock-lined areas functioned as habitation units or activity areas.

Test Implications: (a) Presence of structures beneath cleared areas.
(b) Presence of tool kits within areas.

These research goals are quite different from the initial survey goals. The initial goals were based on the expectations of a larger number of water control networks associated with habitation sites than were found. Since lithic scatters were the most abundant type of site located on the survey, the goals of the data recovery phase were modified to focus on these sites.

CHAPTER 4

THE DATA RECOVERY PROJECT

Fieldwork was initiated February 28, 1977, and terminated April 15, 1977. Two field crews completed data recovery on 26 sites in addition to mapping and testing two sites recommended for nomination to the National Register of Historic Places. The field crews consisted of Kay Simpson (Project Supervisor); Deborah Westfall (Assistant Supervisor); Bonnie Dement, Linda Gregonis, David Groenfeldt, and Linda Popelish (Crew Members); Jeanette Dickerson (Lab Supervisor) and Deborah Confer (Lab Assistant). Jon Czaplicki was Project Director.

Research Orientation

The goal of the data recovery was to mitigate adverse effects of construction activities on the fragile archaeological resources by attempting to define the nature and function of the many small lithic sites in the R-O-W corridor. Data recovery procedures included detailed site mapping, surface collection of artifacts, test excavations to ascertain cultural deposition, and excavation of features.

Ideally the intersite sample should have been randomized and regionally oriented to insure that unknown factors were not skewing the sample. But an arbitrary sample boundary limited the sample universe to the proposed R-O-W. Because of the large size of most sites, site boundaries rarely fell totally within the impact area. It was hoped that problems of skewed intrasite sampling would be compensated for by the relative homogeneity of sites.

The fundamental units of analysis were artifact concentrations within the R-O-W, not the entire site. Boundaries of many sites extended for an indeterminate distance beyond the R-O-W and to locate them would have involved a massive areal survey.

Site numbers used during the data recovery phase were the field numbers originally assigned by the survey team, for example AEPCO 29. During the report phase of the project formal ASM numbers were assigned, for example AEPCO 29 became Arizona CC:3:7. In several cases more than one site as recorded in the field received a simple ASM number, for example AEPCO 61 and 62 became Arizona CC:2:54. In these cases field numbers were retained as locus designations.

Field Methods

A grid, usually consisting of 5 m squares and labeled by letters on one axis and numbers on the second axis, was staked out over each site within the R-O-W. A minimum of 50 percent of these grid squares was collected, though on some sites--particularly widely dispersed lithic scatters--all grid squares were collected. On a few sites the grid was extended outside of the R-O-W in order to allow sampling of artifact concentrations. On small, contained sites all artifacts were located, mapped, and collected individually. Specific procedures are discussed in the individual site descriptions.

A contour map was drawn using a plane table and alidade; contours, elevations, features, and grids of artifacts were mapped. If the site was part of a continuous lithic scatter, only the section of the site in the R-O-W was mapped. The contour maps included the location of all archaeological features within and adjacent to the R-O-W, as well as existing and proposed tower locations.

All cultural features within the R-O-W were plotted on the contour map and then photographed. These included clusters of lithic material cobble clusters, rock piles and rock alignments. Features outside the R-O-W were investigated only if this was necessary to fully understand the site. Features in the R-O-W were recorded and excavated as a unit. All dirt from tested features was screened through a one-quarter-inch mesh. Additionally, areas of lithic concentration were tested for possible deposition. Generally, topsoil was always screened while subsoil was screened every fourth load. Subsurface artifacts were rarely encountered. Pollen samples were collected from inside and outside the gridded garden borders on Arizona CC:2:40 and from a pit on Arizona CC:2:51. A standard one liter soil sample was taken from each provenience.

A field laboratory was located at the Safford District BLM office. All material was washed, labeled, and processed, and analysis was begun on the chipped stone. Feedback during analysis between lab and field personnel allowed for the immediate correction of problems. For example, the sample of artifacts collected at Arizona CC:2:43 was considered insufficent for statistical purposes by the laboratory team. The field team then set up a second grid system and collected a second sample of artifacts.

CHAPTER 5

HISTORIC SITES AND HISTORICAL BACKGROUND

Introduction

This chapter and subsequent chapters examine the material culture. The sites are discussed by type and within site type by environmental stratum Two historic sites, Arizona CC:3:7 and Arizona CC:3:20 (Component A), were investigated in the course of archaeological research in the project area. Both are situated alongside railroad grades south of the present day mining towns of Clifton and Morenci and, as such, represent activities associated with the railroads that served these towns in historical times. A detailed description of the sites is given and how archaeological investigations were carried out at each site. This is followed by description and analysis of the recovered materials, which in turn are interpreted against the historical background of the Clifton-Morenci district.

Site Descriptions

Arizona CC:3:7

Elevation: 1147-1152 m
Physiographic Zone: Gila River terraces
Site Size: 210 m N/S by 110 m E/W
Field Designation: AEPCO 29

The site is situated on the east slope of a low, gently sloping ridge with a small drainage running east-west along the southern edge of the site area. A Southern Pacific Railroad grade circles around the base of the ridge in a NW/SE direction, and a dirt road cuts through the eastern quarter of the site (Figure 12). The Peloncillo Mountains are 4.8 km to the south; the Turtle Mountains are 16 km to the west; and the Gila River flows 4.8 km to the south. On-site vegetation consists of creosotebush, snakeweed, *Aplopappus*, yucca, barrel cactus, Engelmann prickly pear, and grasses, all sparsely distributed over the site area with a greater density of creosotebush growing in the drainage.

Upon initial observation it was assumed that the historic trash might in some way be associated with railroad construction or maintenance. The trash was mainly concentrated in the area bisected by the drainage west of the

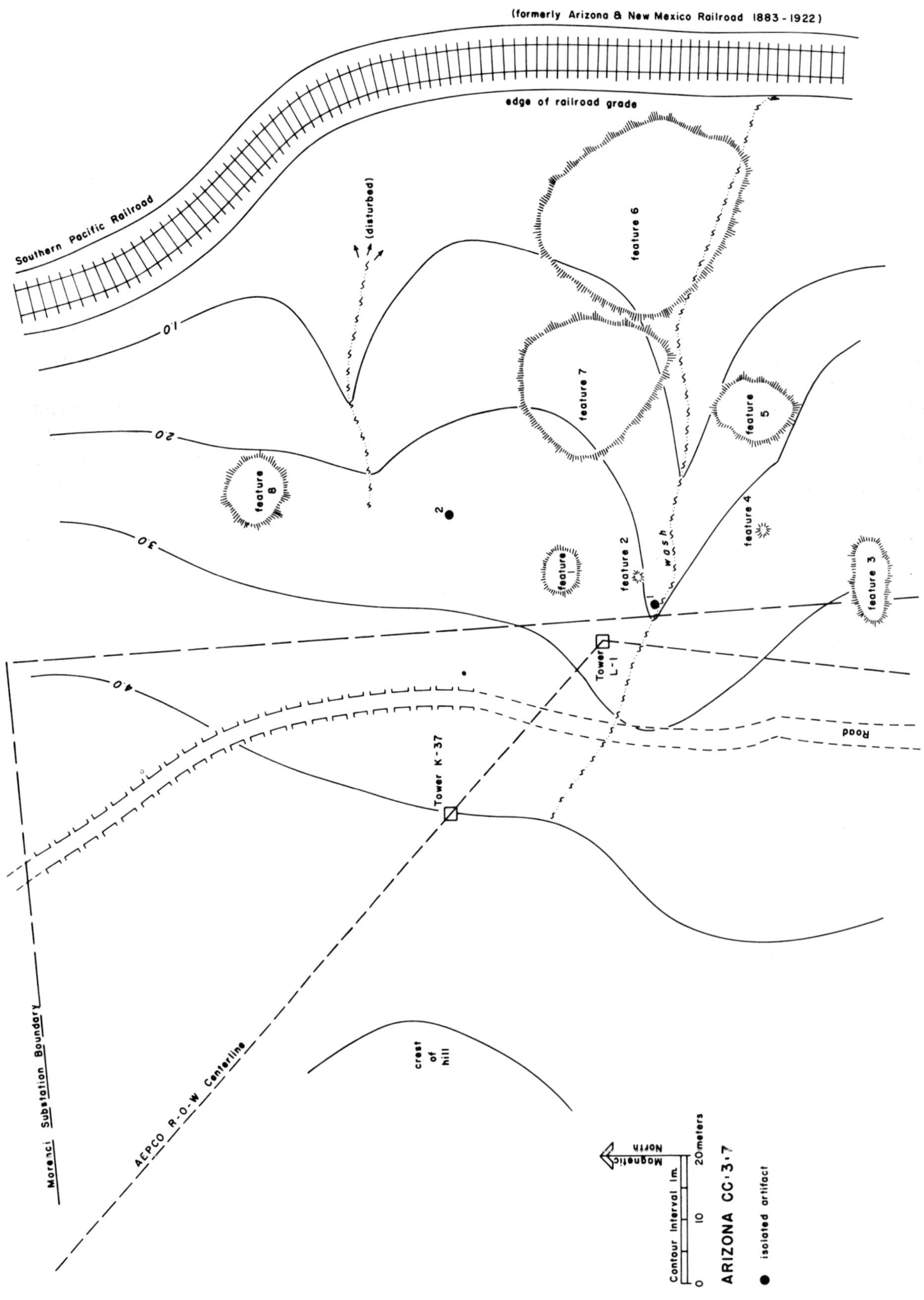

Figure 12. Arizona CC:3:7, site map.

railroad grade; consequently material had eroded downslope. In addition, areas of trash concentration were present in relatively undisturbed context on either side of the drainage. Artifact collection was concentrated in these undisturbed areas in order to maintain primary depositional context, with a few isolated, diagnostic items recovered from the drainage proper. No mounding nor depth of trash was present. Neither was there any evidence of a camp, such as campfire rings, tent platforms, or latrines. This would be expected if a crew of railroad workers had been at the spot for any length of time. The site most likely represented a short-term trash dump used while the railroad was operating.

The dominant materials present were large numbers of hole-in-top tin food cans in varying sizes, followed by beverage bottles, miscellaneous metal items, oil cans, and a few ceramics. In addition, one isolated prehistoric non-utilized lithic flake of siliceous material was located. Due to the impracticality of collecting the entire deposit of tin cans which numbered more than 100, it was decided to collect cans that were representative of size and method of manufacture from each discrete concentration. All glass bottle and jar fragments that had some diagnostic attribute (for example, type of finish, base mark, embossed lettering, sun-colored glass) were collected, as well as all ceramics and odd items.

Twelve surface collections were made from all the recognizable trash deposits, and their specific locations indicated on the general site map (Figure 12). Description, analysis, and conclusions as to cultural attributes of these materials is combined with the discussion of the material culture from the historic component (Component A) of site Arizona CC:3:20, located 4.4 km south of Arizona CC:3:7.

Arizona CC:3:20 (Component A)

Elevation: 1049 - 1073 m
Physiographic Zone: Gila River terraces
Site Size: 160 m N/S by 180 m E/W
Field Designation: AEPCO 104

This is a two component site, of which only the historic component (Component A) will be discussed here. The description of the prehistoric Component B will be found in Chapter 8.

Arizona CC:3:20 (Figure 13) is situated on a unique land form: a high, wide relatively flat triangular-shaped terrace on the north side of the Gila River. The river loops around the terrace on the east, south, and west sides (Figure 86, Chapter 8). The river here flows through a wide, deep gorge, and steep drainages on the east and west sides of the terrace open out into the gorge. To the north are high, dissected hills and ridges supporting a dense creosotebush cover. The terrace supports a relatively sparse vegetation cover consisting of creosotebush, snakeweed, whitethorn acacia, and yucca. The creosotebush is especially dense along the eastern edge of the terrace where it drops down into a deep arroyo.

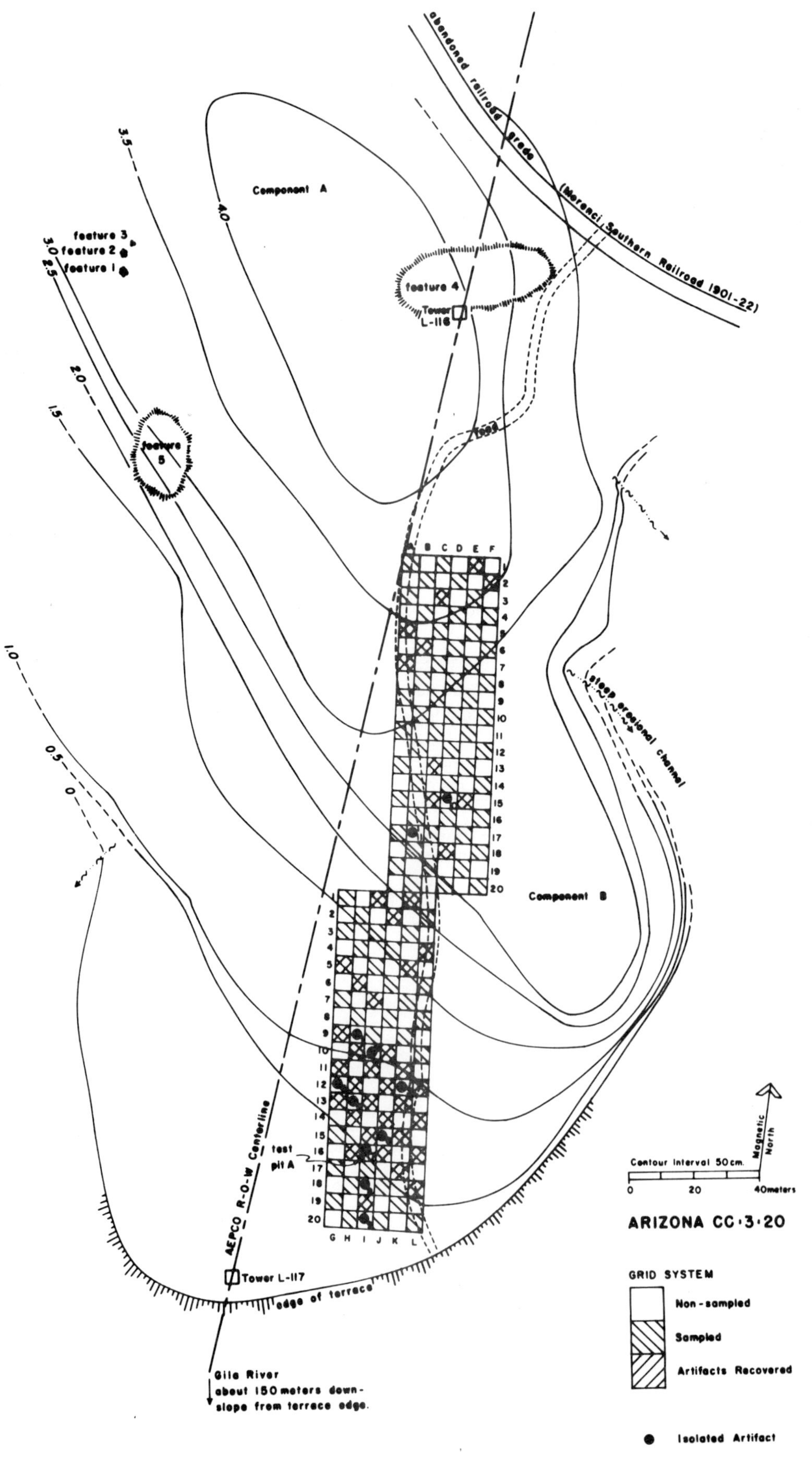

Figure 13. Arizona CC:3:20, Component A, site map.

The central portion of the terrace is dish-shaped, containing aeolian deposited sandy soil with few gravels and cobbles. The eastern and western edges are littered with cobbles and boulders and the northern extent becomes increasingly rocky as the terrace slopes up into the ridges. At the interface of the ridge base and terrace, an abandoned narrow gauge railroad grade runs in a WNW/ESE direction.

Description of the Features. Five features occur in the northern portion of the site in probable association with the railroad grade.

Feature 1 (Figure 14 and Figure 87, Chapter 8)

This a C-shaped, coursed cobble alignment with the open end at the north side.

Dimensions: Exterior N-S: 1.60 m
E-W: 2.17 m
Interior N-S: 1.70 m
E-W: 0.94 m
Maximum height: 0.28 m

Construction: The feature was constructed by laying one course of boulders in a C-shaped arrangement, then a second course was laid atop this row on the south side only. The boulders are of vesicular basalt, fine-grained basalt, and granite. No mortar was used.

Feature 1 was tested by excavating a 1 m wide trench from east to west for a length of 2.5 m through the center of the feature. Excavation was carried out in arbitrary 5 cm levels until natural stratigraphy could be determined. The surface fill, Level 1, consisted of 5 to 6 cm of dry, aeolian-deposited sand containing no cultural materials. Level 2, on which the base of the first course of rocks rested was similarly wind-deposited soil. It was, however, more compacted and contained charcoal flecks, although no burning was indicated. Cultural material was absent at this level also. Directly below Level 2, at a depth of 12 cm below the present ground surface, sterile substrate was encountered. This consisted of reddish sandy clay intermixed with alluvial gravels. Excavation of the trench ended at this level.

Feature 2 (Figure 15 and Figure 87, Chapter 8)

This is a circular rock feature located 6.0 m north of Feature 1.

Dimensions: Exterior N-S: 1.69 m
E-W: 2.23 m
Interior N-S: 0.85 m
E-W: 1.13 m
Maximum height: 0.28 m

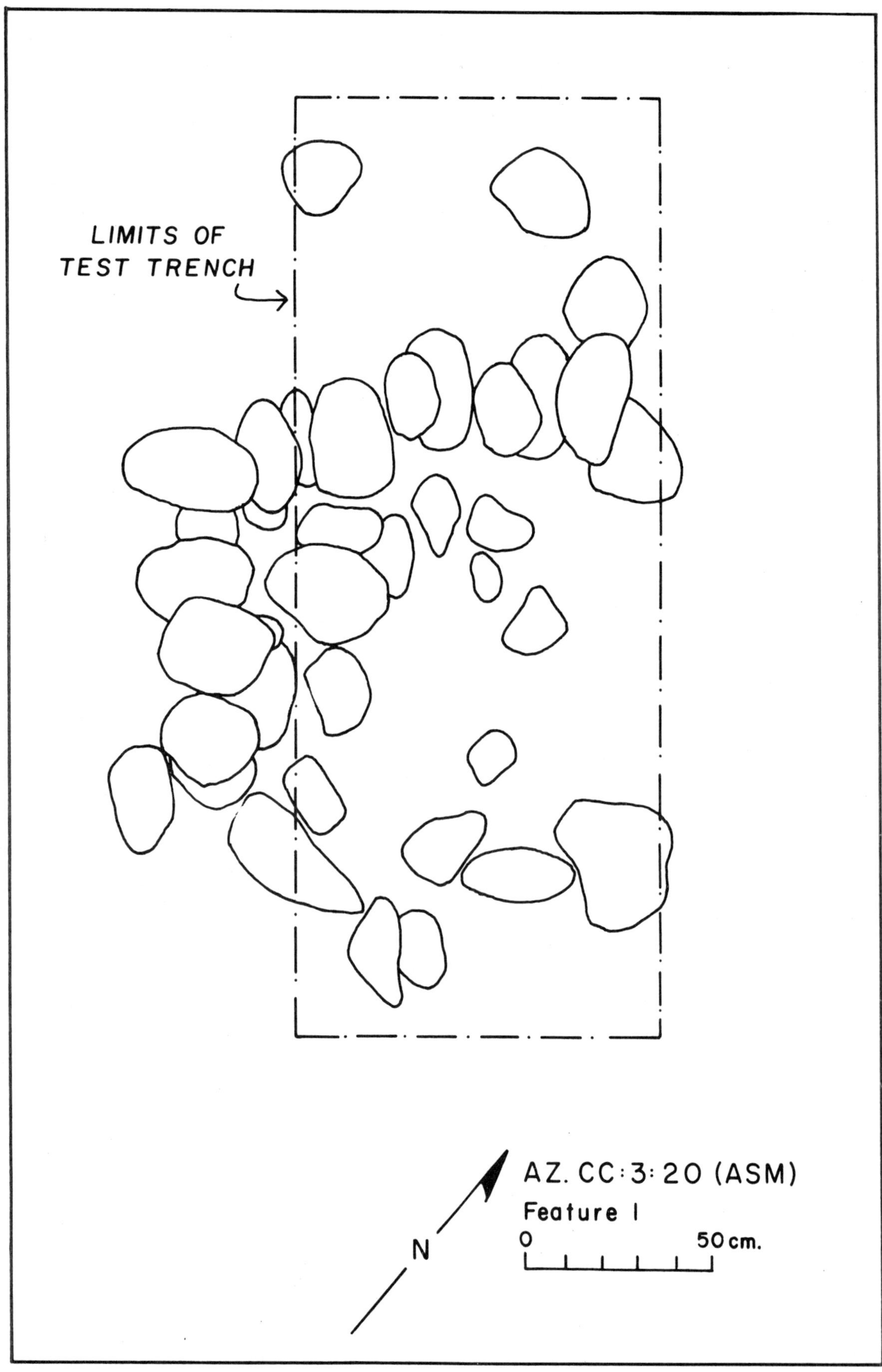

Figure 14. Arizona CC:3:20, Component A, Feature 1

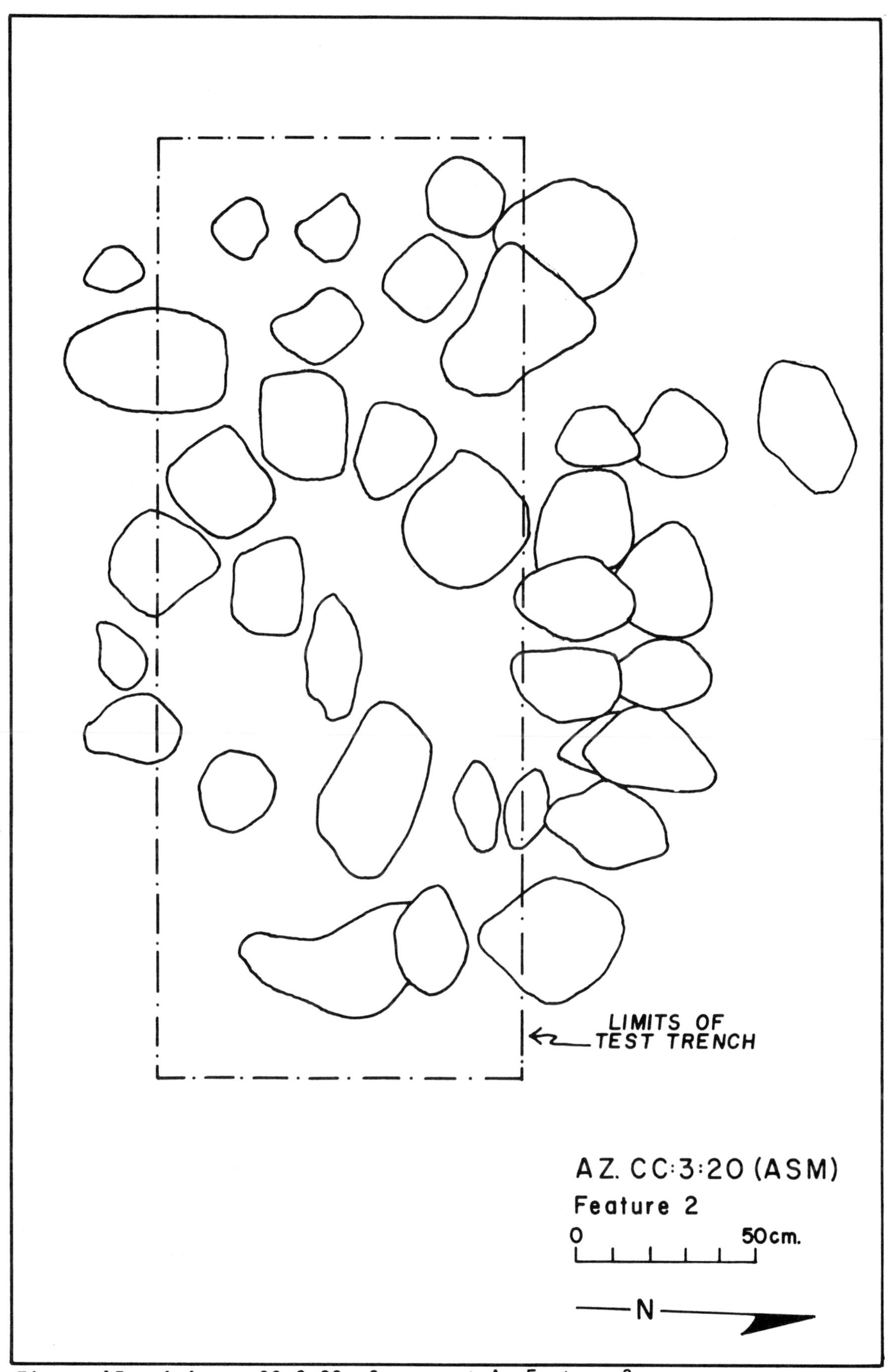

Figure 15. Arizona CC:3:20, Component A, Feature 2

Construction: Feature 2 was constructed by laying one course of small boulders in a circular formation on the ground surface. The boulders are vesicular basalt, fine-grained basalt, and conglomerate. A second partial course was laid on the north side. At the west end is a second, outlying course, which may be fallen rocks of a former second upper course.

Feature 2 was tested in a manner similar to Feature 1. A 1 meter wide trench was excavated for a total length of 2.5 m north-south through the center of the feature. The fill was identical to that encountered in Feature 1, that is, a layer of aeolian sand overlying a more compacted subsurface sandy soil layer. Sterile substrate was reached at a depth of 13 cm below the present ground surface. A corroded hole-in-top tin can was recovered from the uppermost level.

Feature 3

This small rock pile is located 3 m northeast of Feature 2. It was constructed by simply piling seven small irregular boulders of vesicular basalt and granite in a roughly circular formation on the surface. It measures 0.94 m north-south by 0.84 m east-west, and averages 0.18 m high.

Feature 4

This historic trash deposit is in a severely eroded area 40 m south of the old railroad grade. The cultural deposition consists of a widely dispersed scatter of rusted, metal objects including hole-in-top tin cans, railroad spikes, oil cans, and purple glass. The entire scatter measures 14.5 m north-south by 46 m east-west. At the east end of the scatter, on a small, cleared rise of land, are several irregular arrangements of small boulders set on the surface. These occur in groups of three to five boulders, some singular, set into no discernible pattern, and with no deposition present. A collection was made of all diagnostic materials within the general scatter.

Feature 5

This is a historic trash scatter, with a few recent items (for example, aluminum-topped tin cans, plastic shotgun shells), located at the west edge of the terrace 60 m south of Feature 1. The materials present consisted of white earthenware fragments, purple glass, fragments of beverage bottles, tops of hole-in-top tin cans, pieces of metal straps, and two pairs of shoes. The deposit occurs only on the surface, covering an area 23.5 m north-south by 15.2 m east-west. All materials, except for obviously recent trash, were collected.

Historical Background

The two separate collections of historical remains from Arizona CC:3:7 and Arizona CC:3:20, while small and superficial, are significant in that they are remains of a colorful and important time in Arizona history, that of the development of mining in southeastern Arizona and the history of the railroad. The majority of the collected materials date from 1880 to about 1915-20. In order to provide a background for the discussion of the historical collections,°a brief history of the Clifton-Morenci district where mining and the railroad were interdependent is presented.

Copper ore was first discovered in what is now Morenci by a Civil War soldier named Henry Clifton in 1864 who, with several other soldiers, placed a few claims in the area (Tuck 1963:17). At the close of the Civil War, Robert Metcalf came to what is now Silver City, New Mexico (then called San Vincente), attracted by the silver ore in the area and hoping to make his fortune. His efforts proved unproductive, as the silver strike was beginning to play out, and he and several other prospectors headed for Arizona in search of gold. Instead, they found a rich deposit of copper, marked by Henry Clifton, who,by this time, had disappeared. Metcalf began mining operations here and established the beginnings of the town of Clifton. His mine eventually came to be known as the Longfellow Mine and is known today as the Morenci open-pit mine. The date for this founding is still disputed; Tuck (1963:17) gives a date of 1872, while Avery (1942) cites a probable date of 1869.

In the meantime, in Silver City, Henry Lesinsky (also spelled Lezinsky) had opened a general store with his brother and uncle in 1868 to supply the miners of the area. Avery (1942) records:

> A matter of months later, Robert Metcalf walked into the store with a sack of ore, looking for Lesinsky who became known as an expert. The ore was about 50 percent copper and copper was worth 25 cents a pound in the east. Lesinsky saw this as an opportunity to make the fortune he had failed to find in Australia and Nevada.

In 1870, Lesinsky and his partners purchased the claims from Metcalf for the Clifton district and organized the Francisco Mining Company. In 1870 or 1873 (again, the dates are conflicting), Lesinsky built a one-ton smelter on Chase Creek that was later moved to the San Francisco River. In 1874, Lesinsky took over the Longfellow Mine and organized the Longfellow Copper Company. Metcalf retained the Metcalf Hill properties, north of Clifton in Chase Creek Canyon.

That same year, Avery (1942) reports:

> John and William Church drove up to Joy's Camp at the junction of Chase Creek and the San Francisco River in an old prairie schooner. They optioned the claims which had been located by the soldiers, the Arizona Centeral, Copper Mountain, Montezuma, and Yankie. They formed the Detroit Copper Mining Company. Articles of incorporation were filed January 14, 1875.

Thus, by 1875, there were two independently operating copper companies at the two settlements: the Lesinskys' Longfellow Copper Company of Clifton, operating at the Longfellow Mine, and the Churches at Joy's Camp. Granger (1960:169) records that Church re-named Joy's Camp after Morenci, Michigan, his old home town.

During the period 1878-79 a narrow-gauge (20 inch) railroad was built by Lesinsky to transport ore from the mines in Arizona (Avery 1942; Tuck 1963) and was called the Coronado Railroad (Myrick 1968:12). In the beginning, the cars were pulled up the Longfellow Incline from the mine to the smelter by mules, after which the mules were loaded onto a platform car at the rear of the train, which coasted back down to the mine (Avery 1942). Later, a locomotive was acquired to replace mule power.

Having come to the subject of railroads, attention should be focused on the development of the railroad in Arizona, particularly the Southern Pacific. Myrick (1975) has written a thorough and fascinating study of the railroads of southern Arizona. A summary of his study (Myrick 1968) is presented below.

Railroad transport was a critical factor in the development of mining and mining towns in southeastern Arizona, as well as opening up the West for settlement and expansion. Due to the rapidly developing agricultural industry in southern California, a desperate need of rail transport for a variety of products arose, and pressure mounted to build a transcontinental railroad through the southern part of the United States. Thus, Southern Pacific began to build eastward from Los Angeles to Arizona. In 1877, the railroad crossed the Colorado River at Yuma, then was built through Casa Grande, Tucson, and finally reached Deming, New Mexico in 1880. The Southern Pacific passed through Lordsburg, New Mexico and was, at this point, only 112.6 km away from Clifton. By 1883, the railroad had been built through El Paso and then to New Orleans, thus completing the famed Sunset Route and the third transcontinental railroad in the country (the first two being the Union Pacific-Central Pacific and the Southern Pacific-Santa Fe).

In 1881, the Detroit Copper Mining Company was enountering financial difficultites, with the upshot being that William Church went east to New York to obtain financial backing. There, he went to W.E. Dodge, partner in Phelps Dodge and Company, a firm known as "general merchants" that was organized in 1834. As a result of this meeting they called in a metallurgical engineer named Dr. James Douglas who recognized the value of Church's holdings, and advised Phelps Dodge to purchase interest in the Detroit Copper Mining Company (Avery 1942; Cleland 1952). It was the company's first involvement in copper mining and was a significant event, for Phelps Dodge eventually became one of the country's three largest producers of copper and one of the major economic forces in Arizona. Douglas is a well-known historical figure, responsible in a large part for the development of mining towns such as Bisbee, Ajo, and Douglas, in addition to Clifton and Morenci.

From this point, the copper mining industry entered into a period of rapid growth and development with a concomitant increase in the growth of towns and railroad service. In 1882 the Lesinskys and Metcalf sold the Longfellow Mine and the Metcalf properties to a group from Edinburgh, Scotland. This group reorganized and formed the Arizona Copper Company, Ltd., and immediately began building a narrow-gauge railroad from Clifton to Lordsburg, New Mexico. Completed in 1884, it was called the Arizona and New Mexico Railroad, and served both the Detroit Copper Mining Company and the Arizona

Copper Company. After this important line was completed, several small, narrow-gauge railroads were built in and around the Clifton-Morenci district (Figure 16). Of special note was the Morenci Southern Railroad. Myrick (1968:23-24) dates the operation of this line between 1901-22 and writes:

> In 1901 the Detroit Copper Company opened its Morenci Southern Railroad, famous for its four loops as it wound down the canyon. In 1909 another narrow-gauge was built when the Shannon Copper Company, tired of paying the ore rates charged by the Coronado Railroad, built its own Shannon-Arizona Railroad. A fourth short line in the area was the Clifton and Northern Railway. All these railroads are gone, except parts of the Morenci Southern and Shannon-Arizona, which make up the Phelps Dodge industrial railroad between Morenci and the Southern Pacific at Clifton.

One small community along the Arizona and New Mexico Railroad was the small settlement of Guthrie at the Gila River crossing 94.9 km north of Lordsburg. The significance of Guthrie lies in the fact that the Morenci Southern at one time extended from Guthrie to Morenci (Figure 17). Guthrie appears to have functioned primarily as a transfer point from the Arizona and New Mexico Railroad to the Morenci Southern, and was probably established in 1901 for that purpose. Granger (1960:167) writes:

> In 1883 when the Arizona Copper Company built the railroad to the mines at Clifton, it bought the interest of two brothers named J. Duncan Smith and Guthrie Smith. The small railroad location is said to have been named for Sheriff Guthrie Smith. According to another story it is possible that the location was named for a settler called Guthrie, who first lived north of the present Duncan on the river and later established the community on the railroad.

Another source (O'Neill 1973) writes:

> On the Gila River and southerly from Clifton lies Guthrie. This was never a big settlement but at one time was the transfer point from the Arizona and New Mexico Railroad to the Morenci Southern. Here, all materials for Morenci as well as passengers were transferred from the standard gauge railroad to the narrow gauge for the last section of the trip to Morenci.

Apparently, the Morenci Southern from Guthrie to Morenci was built for the purpose of transporting foods from the Southern Pacific directly to Morenci since the Southern Pacific ended at Clifton.

Clason's Industrial Map of Arizona for 1908 indicates three railroads in the Clifton-Morenci district (Figure 17). As the line comes in from Lordsburg, New Mexico, it is labeled "Arizona and New Mexico Ry." When it reaches Guthrie, it forks, one fork leading to Clifton and named "Arizona Copper Co. Ry." The other fork leads to Morenci and the lettering reads "Morenci SR."

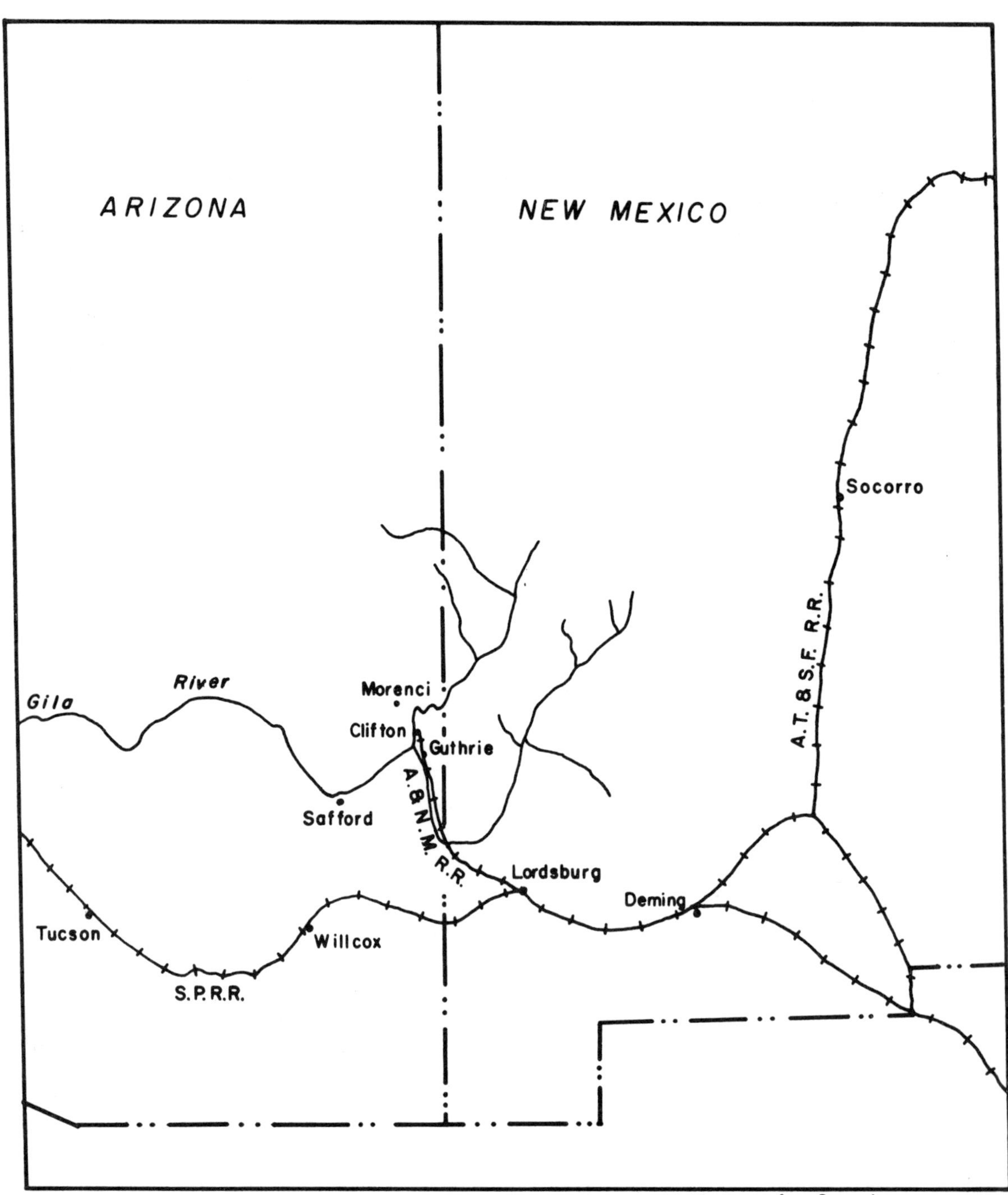

Figure 16. Map Illustrating Railroad Routes and Towns in Southern Arizona and New Mexico, in 1886. (After Gray, 1886)

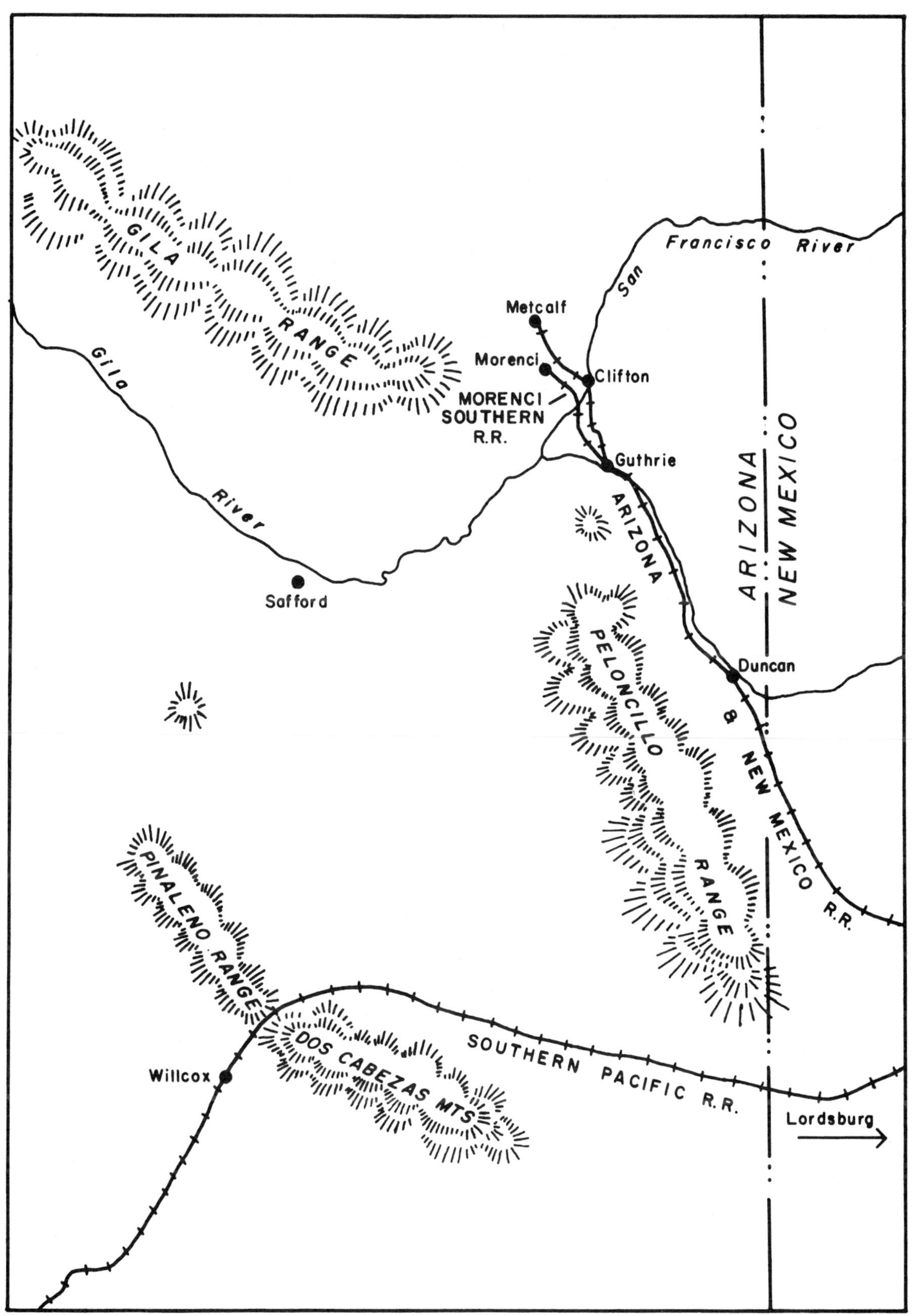

Figure 17. Detail of Arizona and New Mexico Railroad, the Morenci Southern, and Southern Pacific. (After Clason's Industrial Map of Arizona, 1908)

Obviously, this must be a former grade of the partially abandoned Morenci Southern Railroad, and must be the grade whose remnants were recorded near Arizona CC:3:20.

In 1901 the Arizona and New Mexico Railroad was widened. In 1922, the railroad was transferred to the El Paso and Southwestern Railroad, an affiliate of the Southern Pacific, and two years later the Southern Pacific took it over entirely. This is the present-day Southern Pacific Railroad that passes by Arizona CC:3:7. It was probably around this time (1922-24) that Guthrie was abandoned, along with the narrow-gauge Morenci Southern Railroad. Granger (1960:167) notes that the Guthrie post office was discontinued in 1922.

In 1887, Phelps Dodge purchased controlling interest in the Detroit Copper Mining Company. Thus, Phelps Dodge and the Arizona Copper Company were the two major companies operating in the Clifton-Morenci district until 1921, when Phelps Dodge purchased the Arizona Copper Company and consolidated all the major properties under its ownership. In 1937 the Morenci open-pit mine was begun, which now occupies the site of the former mountain where Henry Clifton placed his first claims.

Analysis of Cultural Remains

Analysis is focused here on manufacturers of the glass, metal, ceramic, and wood items represented in the AEPCO collections. Information about manufacturers is recorded primarily to help date sites. It must be emphasized that the dates given in the cited sources are those of a firm's existence, not the years a particular maker's mark was used. It should be noted that the invention of a new form of container does not mean the old form was automatically discarded. Old forms may persist for a decade or two until complete takeover by a new form. This cautionary note must be borne in mind when assigning end-dates for a particular mode of manufacture.

Historic sites can also be dated by examining the color of glass (Hunt 1959; Munsey 1970) and the type of tin cans present (Hunt 1959). Glass at historic sites is sometimes purple or aqua in color, a condition resulting from the oxidation of manganese by prolonged exposure to sunlight. Manganese was added to glass as a decolorizing agent from around 1880 until 1915, when Germany (the major supplier of manganese), curtailed its distribution. Selenium was then used as a decolorizer until 1930; since that time arsenic has been used. Selenium has the effect of turning clear glass amber upon exposure to sunlight (Munsey 1970:55).

Metal products, especially tin cans, can also be dated. A common form of the tin can in the 19th century was the soldered, hole-in-top can, a type that was manufactured in the U.S. from about 1821 until the 1920s. The tin can is further discussed later in this chapter under the section on metal artifacts.

All of the glass artifacts recovered from both Arizona CC:3:7 and Arizona CC:3:20 were in fragmentary condition. All fragments having an identifying mark, even if only partial, were collected. When an obvious "bottle smash" was found, all the pieces were collected. Isolated, plain pieces of glass were collected if they had some diagnostic attribute such as purple or amber color. Plain, clear glass bits were recorded, but not collected.

Special recognition is due Bill Liesenbein, of the Tucson Urban Renewal Project (TUR), ASM, for his assistance in identifying the historic materials. Fortunately, we were able to match fragments of embossed labeling with complete examples from the TUR collections, enabling positive identification of nearly all the AEPCO materials. Liesenbein's wide scope of knowledge regarding sources also contributed to the rapid analysis of the material.

Arizona CC:3:7

Glass Artifacts. The majority of glass artifacts collected from the site were fragments of Budweiser beer bottles concentrated in Feature 5. A total of nine bases, eight finishes, and 17 body fragments with portions of embossed labeling were recovered. In addition, 19 fragments of plain glass, resembling the glass of the known Budweiser bottles, were collected. At the very least, nine bottles were represented, on the basis of the number of bases. The eight finishes were of the "beer" or brandy type (Herskovitz 1975:12, Figure 3C), in which the method of closure was a cork stopper anchored with wire. This type of closure persisted until the 1890s when it was supplanted by metal crown cap closure (Munsey 1970:105). The necks of these bottles are characteristically bulbous and, together with the body fragments, suggest a shape typical of one quart beer bottles made for export.

Comparison of the embossed glass fragments with a complete Budweiser bottle from the TUR collection revealed that the entire label reads: "CARL CONRAD & CO'S / ORIGINAL / BUDWEISER / U.S. PATENT No. 6376." All the bases are embossed "CC&Co." and two examples have the letters "E" and "F" beneath "CC&Co.", respectively.

The history of the Budweiser brewing company has been well-documented by Krebs (1953). Budweiser beer was developed by Carl Conrad of St. Louis, who learned to make, pasteurize, and bottle beer in his home town of Budweis, Germany. Returning to the U.S. in 1876, Conrad contracted with Anheuser Busch Brewing Associates to brew and bottle his formula, and this date marks the initial use of "CC&Co." on the bases of his beer bottles. The patent number 6376 as seen on the label is dated 1877. According to Toulouse (1971), Conrad went bankrupt in 1883 and sold his interest to Anheuser Busch, the heaviest creditor. Toulouse states (1971:118):

> The title of the brand "Budweiser" passed to Anheuser Busch at the time of settling the accounts and was officially transferred in 1891. For many years the Busch label carried the wording "Anheuser Busch Brewing Association" along with the phrase "as brewed especially for C. Conrad & Co."

Thus, the Budweiser beer bottles recovered from Arizona CC:3:7 date between 1876-1883.

Two amber beer finishes with long bulbous necks were found in Feature 1, and like the Budweiser bottles, are of one quart capacity. Absence of their bases does not permit identification of the maker.

Three circular bases of amber beverage bottles bearing embossed labeling on the base were recovered from Features 1, 3, and 7. On two examples, the labeling reads "C V No 1 /MILW" encircling the numbers "9" and "10", respectively. The third is a fragmentary base embossed "...C V Co N° 2...". According to Toulouse (1971) and Noyes (1962), this is the mark of the Chase Valley Glass Co., Milwaukee, Wisconsin. In 1880, Enoch Chase announced his intention of building a glass factory to produce bottles for local breweries. He established the Chase Valley Glass Co. No. 1, probably on his farm in 1880, then moved down the road to establish Company No. 2, which functioned from 1880 to 1881. In 1881, the Chase Valley Glass Co. underwent reorganization and became the Wisconsin Glass Co. There followed several reorganizations and name changes until the firm finally dissolved as a result of Prohibition in 1921 (Noyes 1962:2-7).

One base of an amber beverage bottle from Feature 1 had the following embossings: "M G C°". with a cross above and the number "4" below. This is the mark of the Modes Glass Co., Cicero, Indiana, which operated from 1895 to 1904. Toulouse (1971:360) remarks:

> Modes made beer bottles and beverage bottles at most of the companies with which he was associated...but those under his own name were confined to the nine year period of the Modes Glass Co...There is a strong possibility that his Cicero factory started before 1895, and possibly in the mid-1880s. Beer bottles with "MGCo" made in circa-1800s techniques of a crude finishing have been found in a camp in Arizona known to have been occupied <u>only</u> in the 1880s, and along with beer bottles marked for companies that were in business only in that decade. 1895 is the date of reference in the National Bottler's Gazette.

A second amber glass beverage bottle base was collected from Feature 1, with the base embossed: "F.H.G.W." with the number "6" below. There are two opinions for this mark. Herskovitz (1975:18) reports:

> The mark FHGW is the subject of some speculation. It has been identified by Toulouse (1972:202) as Frederick Hampson Glass Works, Lancastershire, England. He has dated the specimens he has seen as ca. 1880 to 1900, certainly not earlier than 1870, on the basis of the manufacturing technology they exhibit. Jones (1968:17) attributes the mark to F. Hitchins Glass Works, the successor to the Lockport Glass Works, New York. Hitchins bought out the other three original partners of Lockport sometime between 1850 and 1860 and ran the company until 1872 when it was purchased by Alonzo J. Mansfield (McKearin and McKearin 1941:194).

Two basal fragments, one beer finish, and four body fragments of two large, dark amber glass beverage bottles were collected from Feature 5, of which only one base has a mark: "1", which is untraceable. Liesenbein (personal communication) suggests this may be an imported beer bottle.

Feature 3 yielded two aqua-colored soda bottle fragments, which probably represent two bottles. One fragment is embossed "...SON..."; this could be part of a label that once included the word "Tucson", although this is a very tenuous identification. The remaining two fragments are embossed "...BETT" and "...(?)0." These may be a portion of the common name Corbett, since this name was found on metal bottle caps found at Fort Bowie, near the Arizona-New Mexico border. Herskovitz (1975:151) reports,

> Three metal caps bearing the name of "John Corbett, Deming, N.M." were recovered. In 1881 John Corbett moved to Deming from Socorro, New Mexico and opened a bottling firm as he had in Socorro. Corbett joined the Bank of Deming when it was organized in 1892, although it is not clear whether he was still in the bottling business (Deming Headlight, May 24, 1918). Labels on several bottles...indicate he was in the soft drink bottling business.

Given the pre-1881 date of Corbett's bottling firm in Socorro, New Mexico, the AEPCO example could be one of his bottles, with the "0" on one fragment being the last letter in "Socorro". Time did not permit further investigation into the soda bottle industry of New Mexico to further substantiate the assumption that this bottle was, in fact, produced by James Corbett in Socorro.

One fragment of an aqua, paneled bitters bottle was recovered from Feature 7, embossed "...BITTERS." Comparison with an example from the TUR collection indicates this is a portion of a bottle that contained a product called "BAJA CALIFORNIA DAMIANA BITTERS," produced by Lewis Hess of California in 1876 (Wilson 1969:24). It was not made in Baja California, rather it is descriptive of damiana, a plant that grows in Baja California. Herskovitz (1975:33) cites an entry in the patent for Damiana Bitters describing its contents:

> A composition beverage, consisting of the following ingredients, viz. tincture or fluid extract orange peel, tincture or fluid extract cardamon-seed, tincture or fluid extract damiana bitters, whiskey or proof spirits and water, substantially as described.

Bartholomew (1970:35) includes an illustration of an advertisement that appeared in the 1911 Los Angeles Times, which described the properties of this patent medicine:

For Health and Strength

DAMIANA BITTERS

A wonderful invigorating and nervine.
A powerful aphrodisiac and special tonic
for both sexes. For sale at drugstores and
liquor.

F S Brune, Agts.
325 Mission St., San Francisco, Cal.

Another medicine bottle, this one a druggist's bottle, is represented by a basal fragment of a square, purple glass bottle. It was recovered from Feature 1. The base is embossed "W T & Co." the mark for Whitall, Tatum and Co., of Millville, New Jersey, which used this mark during the period 1857 to 1938 (Toulouse 1971:545). One portion of the side of the bottle reads: "...& CO / ...S". Comparison with the TUR collection enabled us to match this fragment to a bottle used by a local Tucson druggist named Fred Fleishman. The complete label of the TUR example reads: "FRED FLEISHMAN & CO / DRUGGISTS / TUCSON." In a reference supplied by Liesenbein, early Tucson newspapers indicate Fred Fleishman advertised his business from 1881 to 1892. Devner (1968:35) states:

> The Fred Fleishman Drug Store was a going concern before 1881, but did not locate in Tucson until that time. A picture of Tucson in the 1890s shows this store at its former location of Congress and Main streets. It was still doing business there in 1908, but sometime shortly after that Fleishman sold out to the Ryan-Evans chain of Rexall drug stores. I have found ads in our local newspapers for the old store, one for 1895 announcing that F. Fleishman dealt in mining and assaying chemicals, drugs, medicines, and mineral water supplies.

The last example of an identifiable glass bottles from this site is the oval base of a small, purple glass bottle from Feature 1. Embossed on the base is "C". Toulouse (1971:99) states, "Ware so marked was made by Cunningham and Co., Pittsburgh, 1879-1909, but this has not been documented." He goes on to say that this mark occurs on the bottoms of general ware made with the techniques common to the 1880s.

In addition to the diagnostic materials described above, plain fragments of glass bottles were also recovered from all locales. These include two finishes (one prescription and one whiskey) and 23 body fragments of purple glass; two bases and 47 body fragments of aqua glass, the latter probably being fragments of beer or soda bottles. Little can be said of these other than that they date between about 1880-1916.

<u>Ceramic Artifacts</u>. Ceramics at Arizona CC:3:7 were rare and represent isolated occurrences within the general refuse deposit. Collected from Feature 7 was an interesting specimen of British brown saltglazed stoneware. It is the lower half of an ink bottle with an imprinted typescript label reading: "VITREOUS STONE BOTTLE / J. BOURNE & SON / PATENTEES / DENBY POTTERS / NEAR DERBY." Beneath this is the legend: "P. & J. ARNOLD / LONDON." Jewitt (1970) gives a concise account of Joseph Bourne and the history of the Denby Potters, founded in 1850, and which functions to this day. The peculiar virtue of Bourne's success was his well-made stoneware vessels. Jewitt (1970:173) states:

> Arnold's is best known to the collector of ink bottles, particularly the pottery or "stone" bottles, in which was shipped both normal inks and the special duplicating inks used in making pressed copies of letters before the typewriter carbon came into use.

Feature 4 yielded a partial, small, white ironstone saucer, a fragment of which bears the imprinted name "MEAKIN" in underglaze. Liesenbein (personal communication) suggests that this may be a product of J. & G. Meakin of Hanley, England. Originally founded in 1845 by James Meakin, it was taken over by his sons James Jr. and George in 1851. They specialized in the manufacture of ironstone tableware much of it for export to the United States (Fontana and Greenleaf 1962: 95). The Meakins used several different marks on their pottery from the company's beginning up to the present time. Since no fragments were recovered bearing an illustrated mark, no more can be said about the period of manufacture of the imprinted fragment.

Metal Artifacts. The majority of metal items consisted of round tin food cans. These numbered over 100 and were concentrated in Features 6 and 7 and an isolated area, Feature 8. With a few exceptions, nearly all were hole-in-top cans. The exceptions were a few open-top beverage cans. The cans range in size from 11.4 cm high and 7.5 cm in diameter to 17.2 cm high and 15.0 cm in diameter.

The invention of the tin can was very important in the history of food preservation. It permitted a reliable source of sustenance during long absences from a permanent food source. There is a wealth of information available on the development of tin cans and the canning industry, even to the sizes and capacities of cans in use during specific time periods in American history (U.S. Bureau of the Census 1924).

A Frenchman, Nicholas Appert is credited with the discovery of the art of canning in 1810 stimulated by the offer of a reward to invent a means of preserving food for Napoleon Bonaparte's armed forces. In that same year, Peter Durand of Britain obtained a patent and began production of tin cans and tinned foods for both Britain and America. Ezra Daggett was the first canner in the United States; although it is not known when he began his canning operations, he was shipping goods to South America as early as 1821 (Cruess 1948).

In the beginning, tin cans were largely made by hand. Fontana and Greenleaf (1962:68) describe the process thus:

> The can...was laboriously cut from tin plated sheet iron by hand or foot-powered scissors; the body formed around a cylinder and the seam soldered...A hole was left in the top through which food was forced. A smaller cap was finally soldered in place after filling. ...A pinhole in the cap allowed gases to vent. One last drop of solder completed the job. This type of can became known to the trade as the "hole-in-top" or "hole-and-cap." This method of closure, with small variations, persisted until the 1900s.

This was an extremely slow process. One expert tinker could produce 60 cans per day and the average was probably less (Cruess 1948:36).

Efforts continued to be directed toward improving tin cans, particularly to develop machinery to produce cans. In 1897, in New York City, Charles Ams and Julius Brenzinger developed the "open top" or "sanitary" can, the form we know today. This method allowed sealing the top and bottom by means of crimping. In 1908, G.W. Cobb formed the Sanitary Can Company, using Ams' machinery to produce open-top cans. By 1922 this can had become the most widely accepted container for preserved goods, supplanting the old hole-in-top can. A diagnostic feature of this type of can is the lapped and locked seam on the side, whereas the hole-in-top can had a lapped and soldered side seam (Fontana and Greenleaf 1962:72). The collection of hole-in-top tin cans from Arizona CC:3:7 indicates the site's primary use during the turn of the century; the presence of a few open-top beverage cans are later occurrences.

Feature 7 also yielded four miscellaneous tin can lids. One was a flat, rectangular lid measuring 5.5 by 4.3 cm; this could be the lid of a meat can, since these were usually in a form based on the square or trapezoid (Fontana and Greenleaf 1962:76). No bodies of square, rectangular, or trapezoidal cans were found, however. A second lid is circular with punctures and a notched wheel on the top, which probably functioned as a shaker for spices. A third lid is circular, with a circular, capped spout in the center. The fourth example is an unusual one. It is a large, circular lid, 12.3 cm in diameter, with a wire loop near the edge, and a triangular flap at the opposite edge with the apex at the center. It had been removed from the can body by cutting one-half inch below the rim of the lid. Davis (1967:Plate 157) illustrates an early (1824) example of a tin meat can with a similar type of lid that has a "lifting ring." The label on the can reads: "Cut round on the top near to the outer edge with a chisel and hammer." This type of opening and the lifting ring resembles that on the AEPCO example. It is not known if this type of closure was used only for preserved meat tins, but may indicate what the AEPCO tin once contained.

Feature 2 included a rectangular metal canister with an oval opening in the top, resembling a tea or cocoa tin. It featured a single lapped and soldered side seam. Partially crushed and distorted, it measures 14.0 cm long, 11.4 cm wide, and 10.8 cm high.

Feature 8 also yielded a cluster of large fragmentary cans and lids. The lids are impressed with concentric circles and the letters "C P W", in addition to other lettering too obscured by corrosion to be read. In addition, two horseshoes were collected from this feature.

Arizona CC:3:20 (Component A)

Glass Artifacts. In contrast to Arizona CC:3:7 glass was not plentiful at Arizona CC:3:20, and was restricted to Feature 5. Nine fragments of an aqua, paneled, patent medicine bottle were recovered, with two fragments exhibiting embossed lettering: "...LOW... / MAS..." According to an illustration in Wilson (1971:19) this could be a portion of a bottle containing either

Ayer's Cherry Pectoral (about 1894) or Ayer's Compound Extract of Sarsaparilla (about 1890). The complete labeling on one panel of the illustrated examples reads: "LOWELL / MASS. U.S.A."

Ayer's Cherry Pectoral was a fairly potent mixture and the company's first bottled product, dating from about 1874. According to Wilson (1971:19):

> Each bottle supposedly contained: acetate of morphis...3 gr., tincture of bloodroot...2 dr., wines of antimony...3 dr. and ipecac...3 dr. plus syrup of wild cherry...3 oz. mix with alcohol and water.

Its curative properties were reported to be especially beneficial for various respiratory and consumptive disorders.

Ayer's Compound Extract of Sarsaparilla contained the following ingredients as of 1890: "fluid extracts of sarsaparilla, stillingia, yellow dock, mayapple, plus iodide of potassium and iron--sweetened with white sugar." This was considered an expensive formula and in later years there were cheaper substitutes made for the Ayer's (Wilson 1971:19). A turn of the century advertisement describes Ayer's Sarsaparilla as essentially a universal cure-all.

Eight fragments of an aqua beverage bottle, including a round base fragment were recovered. The base is embossed: "...A B G..." Comparison with a complete example from the TUR collection indicates this is a beer bottle made by the Adolphus Busch Glass Mfg. Co. in Bellville, Illinois. The dates given for this particular mark, which in complete form reads "A B G Co," are 1886 to 1907.

Also recovered from Feature 5 were fragments of a brown glass beverage bottle; fragments of a dark green, unmarked champagne bottle; fragments of a paneled purple glass bottle with a prescription finish; and a basal fragment of a purple glass bowl. None of these had any identifying marks.

Ceramic Artifacts. The ceramics recovered from Feature 5 are stoneware, specifically white ironstone and "Bristol stoneware" (Liesenbein, personal communication). Fontana and Greenleaf describe the great popularity of ironstone, a common ware found throughout the Old West:

> ...ironstone china (is) a popular nineteenth century ware which is opaque despite its name. Ironstone, also known as white granite china, was developed and patented in 1813 by C.J. Mason and Company of Lane Delph, England.
>
> Shortly after the mid-1800s, ironstone, because it was relatively inexpensive compared to porcelain and because of its durability, began to be exported by England in huge quantities all over the world. Here was a ware that met the requirements of the western frontiers: it was cheap; it could withstand the rigors of overland hauling by wagon or train; it was reasonably handsome and "respectable" (1962:92).

Within the general ironstone sherd collection of Feature 5, at least two large serving bowls ("nappies"), two small bowls, and one plate were represented. Seventy-one small miscellaneous fragments were also recovered, and are believed to be portions of small bowls. An example of nappies is illustrated in the Butler Brothers Grocer's Catalogue of 1915. Three basic styles are shown: plain, plain with a scalloped rim, and a fluted body with a scalloped rim. Of the AEPCO examples, one is plain with a scalloped rim; the other has a fluted body. The two small bowls had an impressed floral design on the exterior. One plate sherd carried the mark of the D.E. McNichol Pottery Co. of Liverpool, Ohio. Stout (1923:76) states that this pottery company was incorporated in 1892, and was still in existence in 1921. Barber (1970:110) states that one of its products was "white granite" ware, which is another name for white ironstone.

Bristol stoneware is represented by two fragments of two separate objects. One appears to be a fragment of a crockery jar; the second may be a lid to a jar.

Metal and Wood Artifacts. The history of the tin can has already been discussed in the section dealing with the collections from Arizona CC:3:7 and need not be repeated here. Eleven round tin food cans were recovered from Arizona CC:3:20; one from Feature 2, two from Feature 5, and eight from Feature 4. The cans range in size from 11.43 cm in height by 7.62 cm in diameter to 17.14 cm in height by 14.6 cm in diameter. In addition, five lids were recovered averaging 8.41 cm in diameter. All examples are hole-in-top cans, with single lapped and soldered side seams (where present).

Two sardine cans were recovered from Feature 4. Both are rectangular with rounded corners, measure 10.16 by 12.7 cm, and have a single lapped and soldered side seam. The tops of both are too corroded to determine the method of opening, but one is pried back. Both examples exhibit a depressed ring on both the top and bottom. This latter feature was invented in 1884 in order to avoid the venting of cans. Previous cans were flat, and a long process was involved in properly packing and sterilizing the cans. By depressing the top the head space was limited and the air could be driven out of the can as the soldering iron followed around the edge making the closure (Bitting 1937: 823).

The remaining metal artifacts are miscellaneous items related to industrial and domestic activities. From Feature 4 the following items were collected: a railroad fishplate (used for joining rails together); an oil can lid with the letters "C P W"; a metal serving spoon; two railroad spikes; and a metal bowl. Feature 5 yielded three rectangular tin can lids, a washer, and one railroad spike.

A pair of men's boots and women's slippers were recorded in Feature 5. Isolated Artifact No. 8 on the southern part of the terrace consisted of a metal faucet head, an unidentified cranking mechanism, and a portion of a latched and hinged wooden box. Isolated Artifact No. 7 is a fragment of a hand-carved wooden panel with a paper label depicting a village scene.

Significance of Cultural Remains

The significance of the historical collections from Arizona CC:3:7 and Arizona CC:3:20 lies in their chronological and cultural-historical attributes.

The tin cans represent a fairly long time span, from about 1820 to 1922, but the glass artifacts allow for more precise temporal assignment to the period 1880 to 1910-15. This would correlate with the construction and maintenance of the Arizona and New Mexico Railroad (later Southern Pacific) during 1883-1922. Due to the lack of permanent or semi-permanent features at Arizona CC:3:7, it was originally hypothesized that the site represented a dump for refuse brought in from elsewhere. The shallow nature of the deposit indicates limited, short-term usage only, although the differences between Features 6 and 7 (tin cans) and Features 1, 3, 4, 5, and 7 (glass and ceramics) appear to indicate separate depositions.

How the trash came to be deposited in this particular locale, far away from any settlement was not immediately evident. It is unlikely that refuse would be hauled to the site from either Guthrie or Clifton. Thus, the deposit had to be associated with railroad activities. James E. Ayres (personal communication) suggests the possibility that it may have been refuse from a movable camp associated with railroad track maintenance. For this activity, "work trains" would move down the line carrying groups of men who repaired ties, rails, bridges, trestles, and performed general all-around maintenance duties. Such crews lived in cars on the train itself rather than establishing camps on the land. This would explain the absence of domestic features at the site. The large deposits of tin food cans indicate some reliance on preserved foods, although the proportion in comparison with perishable foods cannot be determined. Budweiser beer bottles and probable whiskey bottles point to occasions of recreation; Damiana Bitters was available for relieving illnesses. The presence of a bottle from Fred Fleishman's Tucson drugstore indicates Tucson as a possible supply source, and the possible Corbett's soda bottle from Socorro, New Mexico may indicate supplies from there by way of Lordsburg. Ink, of course, was a necessary commodity and is indicative of a wide range of additional items such as paper and pens brought to the towns for carrying out business and personal transactions. That life in early Arizona was not so devoid of small luxuries is borne out by the presence of white English iron-stone. Taken as a whole, the refuse at Arizona CC:3:7 is representative of basic commodities that served everyday needs.

The cultural features and materials at Arizona CC:3:20 reflect a more complex situation than that present at Arizona CC:3:7. At least two separate components are evident in addition to the remnants of the Morenci Southern Railroad. The tin food cans encountered in Feature 4, while very sparse, are contemporaneous with those found at Arizona CC:3:7. Additionally, the presence of railroad spikes, a railroad fishplate, and odd scraps of metal point to association with the railroad grade. They presumably could be related either to the construction or the abandonment and dismantling of the Morenci Southern during the period 1901-22. The deteriorated condition of the cans in contrast to the well-preserved examples at Arizona CC:3:7 would seem to argue for the earlier period. Assuming the refuse deposit reflects a similar situation as at Arizona CC:3:7, this site also may be the remains of a temporary camp of railroad workers. Since so little refuse was present, it is likely the labor crew either lived on the train, or was transported to work sites on a daily basis from a settlement elsewhere.

The remains of Feature 5, including white ironstone, articles of clothing, and permanent stone features reflect more domestic activities and could be a temporary camp. Its association with the railroad is a tenuous one, despite possible temporal contemporaneity. If a railroad crew did camp here at one time, it must have been a small number of people. The presence of both men's and women's rubber soled shoes, however, and the small number of stone features seem to indicate a small family camp. Again, the materials at Arizona CC:3:20 are commonplace objects, typical of western frontier life.

The real significance of products just discussed lies in the fact that they are indicators of trends and changes in American industrial and economic history. Historical remains are significant if they can be associated with a specific individual event or aspect of history (Scovill and others 1972:20). The AEPCO historical remains are important when considered against the background of the later part of the 1800s, which was a period of tremendous economic development in Arizona.

CHAPTER 6

HABITATION SITES

Introduction

Six habitation sites were encountered along the transmission line R-O-W corridor. All are situated proximal to the Gila River near Safford. Mitigation of the three habitation sites recommended for nomination to the National Register of Historic Places involved avoidance of the site and monitoring of construction activities. Archaeological investigations were restricted to mapping and recording features and minimal collection of diagnostic cultural material.

Arizona CC:2:30, CC:2:31, and CC:2:32 are pit house villages exhibiting great complexity in artifact assemblage and architecture. Since investigations were restricted to surficial observations, this report lacks a complete data base from which to draw conclusions regarding the full range of functional and cultural aspects of the sites. What can be determined from the available evidence, however, is that these three sites exhibit characteristics of the Point of Pines-Reserve Mimbres and San Simon branches of the Mogollon (Wheat 1955), with minor indications of Hohokam and Salado influence. Aspects of Mogollon, Hohokam, and Salado presence in the Safford Basin were discussed in Chapter 2. What follows is a site-by-site description of recorded features and collections. Ceramic collections are analyzed and described in greater detail in Appendix II.

Site Descriptions

Arizona CC:2:30

Elevation: 942 m
Site Size: 500 m NE/SW by 180 m NW/SE
Physiographic Location: Stratum 3
Field Designation: AEPCO 47

This is a large pit house village situated on a high terrace remnant 0.9 km north of the Gila River (Figure 22). The general site area conforms to the top and upper slopes of a high, narrow, flat-topped ridge overlooking Big Canyon which drains into the Gila River from the north. Ridge fingers extend outwards from the main terrace mass to the northeast, south, west and southwest. Soils in this area are of the Continental-Pinaleño complex (Gelderman 1970: 14), consisting of well-drained gravelly sandy loams supporting a vegetative cover of creosotebush, catclaw, whitethorn, snakeweed, ocotillo, cholla, and annual weeds and grasses. On-site vegetation consists of creosotebush (dominant), ocotillo, hedgehog, barrel cactus, prickly pear, and mammillaria.

Four "pot holes" were noticed but the site has not been extensively damaged by vandals. A road on the south side of the lower slopes has crossed the edge of the site. Seventy features were found (Figure 18). Fifty of these are circular depressed areas situated across the ridgetop and south-southwest slope. Variation in the dimensions and depth of the features indicates possible different functional or cultural attributes: habitation, storage, task-specific activity areas, and possible agricultural plots. The depressions on the east end of the site are very shallow and have associated ceramics. Most are 4 by 5 m in diameter; larger depressions are present on the northeast ridge near the rock alignments and possible terraces. At least three small circular stone features (Features 32, 65, and 69 are present). Features 33 and 49 are two short alignments of stone, and there are many other short alignments, usually occurring on or near flat cleared areas. Features 47 and 60 are two low (25-35 m high) rock walls constructed by neatly piling basaltic rocks and stream-rolled cobbles to form linear alignments (Figure 20). No coursing or mortar is evident. Feature 47 runs across the flat top of the ridge for a distance of 45 m, then downslope to abut Feature 60. Feature 60 then continues down the ridge slope for a total distance of 120 m. On the south-southwest slope below Feature 60 are several cleared areas (Figure 21). Above Features 47 and 60 along the ridgetop are depressions and more cleared areas. These features could possibly be functionally related to the linear alignments (for example, areas cleared for agricultural plots) if Features 47 and 60 are considered as water control devices. This subject is discussed in greater detail in Chapter 7.

No concentrations of artifactual material were noted at Arizona CC:2:30. The surface is littered with a scatter of sherds and lithic debitage with several tools present. These include a chopper, a stone hoe, bifacially retouched tools, fragments of ground stone, and utilized lithic flakes. No chipping stations or projectile points were found and few cortical flakes and cores were observed. This is in contrast to other lithic use areas in the vicinity. The observed ceramics are almost entirely plain brown and plain redwares which may be locally produced. These were mainly coarse sand-tempered wares with some mica, and several had smudged and polished interiors. Red-on-brown sherds indicative of the San Simon branch Mogollon were observed on the surface and one Mimbres Black-on-white worked sherd was collected.

Investigations at Arizona CC:2:30, while restricted to surface observations, nevertheless reveal a site of some complexity. The available evidence indicates affinities with the Mogollon, specifically the San Simon branch and Point of Pines-Reserve branches. The high density of features present at this site is unusual, since the typical Mogollon village pattern tends toward dispersed, randomly located pit houses (Wheat 1955: 35). Granted, a fair number of the cleared areas designated as features may be small agricultural plots, particularly those on the slopes. Only a thorough investigation can determine the true functional and cultural attributes of the site.

Arizona CC:2:31

<u>Elevation:</u> 928-937 m
<u>Site Size:</u> 400 m N/S by 500 m E/W (minimum; true boundaries not defined)

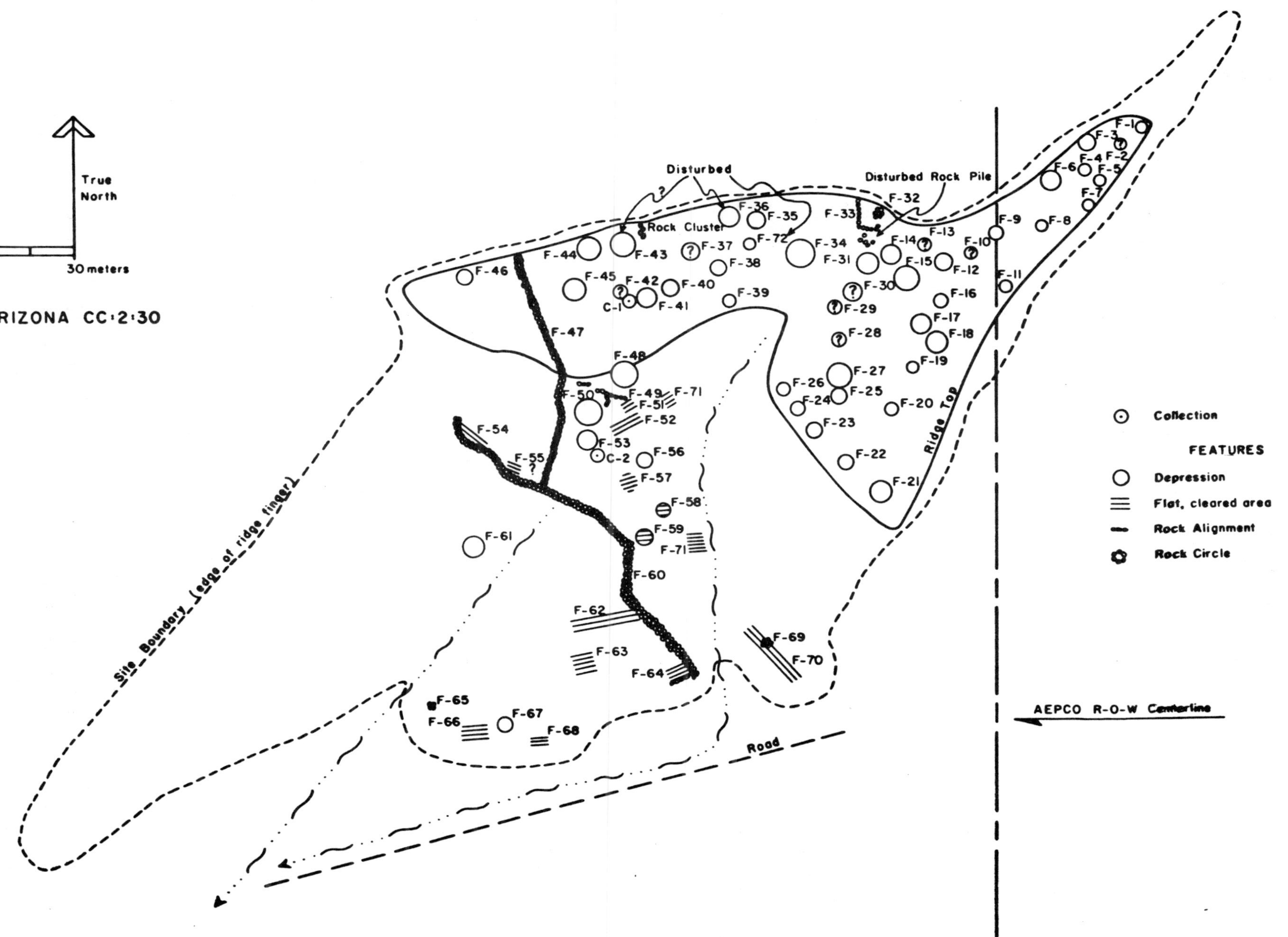

Figure 18. Arizona CC:2:30, site map

Physiographic Location: Stratum 1
Field Designation: AEPCO 56

This large habitation site (Figure 19) is situated on a gently southeastward rising river terrace on the south side of the Gila River floodplain. The Gila River flows 0.32 km to the west-northwest. The topography and vegetation to the north, northwest, and southwest of the site have been altered by modern cultivation activities. The site covers a large portion of the river terrace. Observable on the surface were lithic hammerstones, choppers, cores, utilized and non-utilized flakes of basalt (dominant), chert, chalcedony, and rhyolite. Ground stone fragments included basin and slab metates and manos. Sherds on the surface include plainwares, redwares, and corrugated and decorated ceramics.

The western boundary of the site is marked by a short steep slope, at the base of which is the present-day San Jose Canal. The eastern boundary was not defined, since this portion of the site is a large lithic scatter that blends into a broad, widely dispersed lithic "use area" in the Peloncillo Mountains foothills. The northeast and southwest boundaries were not defined, since the site extends well beyond the R-O-W corridor in both directions. At the very least, features occur as far south as 180 m from the R-O-W centerline and 220 m to the north. Buena Vista, a pueblo site partially excavated in 1931 (Brown 1973: 82) lies approximately 0.8 km to the southeast.

The soils in the area belong to the Grabe-Gila-Anthony association and the site area itself is characterized by Arizo gravelly sandy loam (Gelderman 1970: 9). Saltbush is the dominant vegetation on the river terrace, followed by creosotebush and annual weeds and grasses. Pencil cholla, hedgehog cactus, and yucca occur in scattered numbers. The west edge of the site is dominated by a mesquite bosque encircling the base of the river terrace, a result of recent land modification. Cottonwoods also grow along the San Jose Canal and the Gila River. Disturbance and vandalism at this site have been fairly extensive, obscuring several cultural features.

Investigations at Arizona CC:2:31 included testing at proposed tower location L-117 and locating, defining, and mapping cultural features to assess the site's significance for the National Register of Historic Places. The testing crew consisted of Jon S. Czaplicki (Supervisor), Deborah Westfall, Carol Coe, and Anne Rieger.

Two trenches were laid out on both sides of the tower location stakes. Each trench was oriented north-south and was divided into six, 1 m squares. Squares 1, 3, and 5 of Trench D and Squares 2 and 5 of Trench A were excavated in 15 cm levels. All fill was hand-screened with a one-quarter inch mesh screen. A datum point was established at the southeast corner of Trench D. Datum height is 20 cm above the surface and all measurements of depth given below for Trench D are taken from this elevation.

Trench D contained occasional flakes and unmodified rock, the latter evidently not culturally deposited. In Square D-5 at the 49-60 cm level several possible ground stone fragments and 11 lithic flakes were encountered, and at the 60-80 cm level occasional flecks of charcoal were noted but no

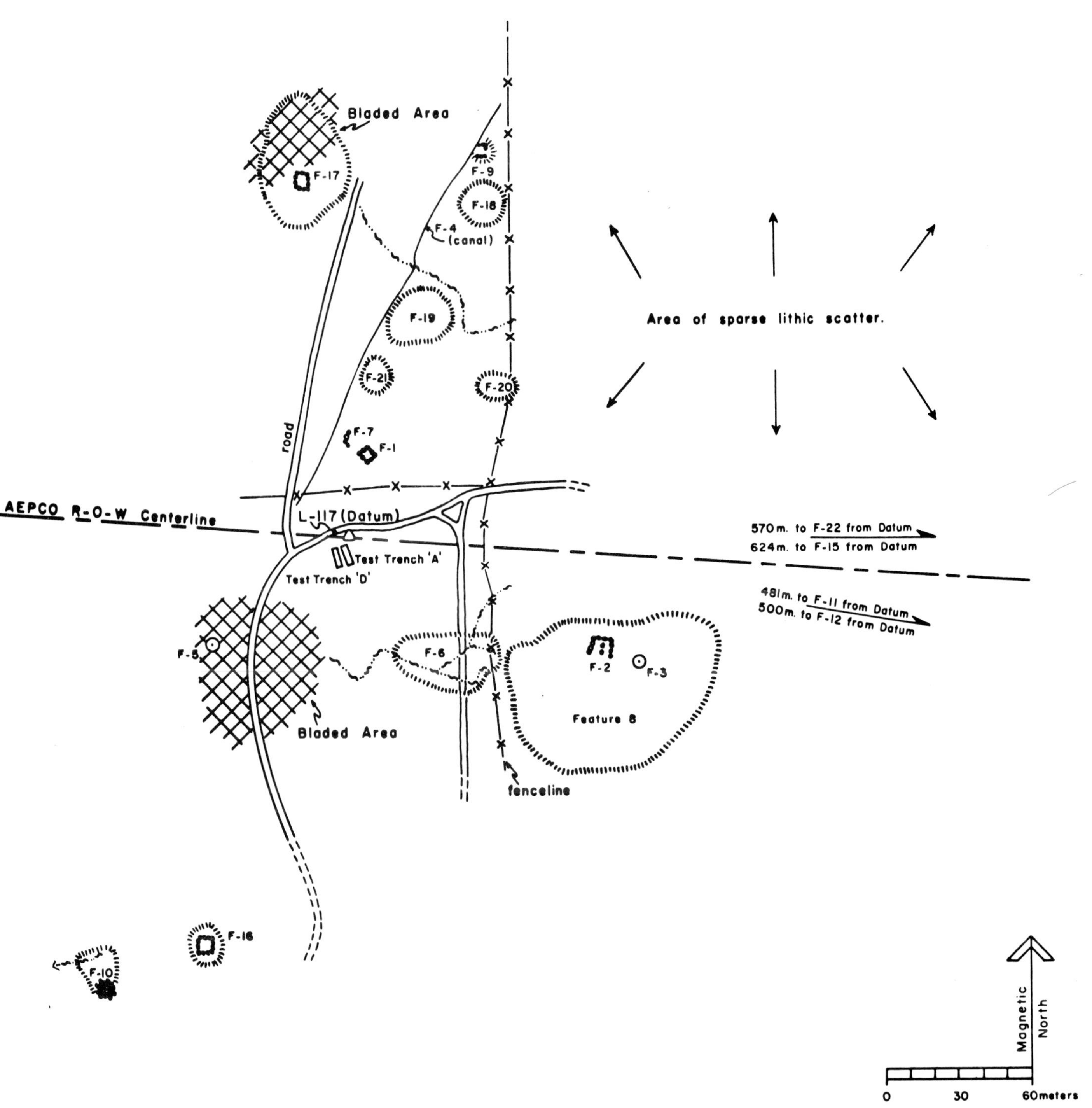

Figure 19. Arizona CC:2:31, site map

Figure 20. Arizona CC:2:30, rock wall alignment.

Figure 21. Arizona CC:2:30, terraces.

Figure 22. Arizona CC:2:30 and CC:2:42, geologic terrace remnant.

Figure 23. Arizona CC:2:31, rock alignment.

definite ash lenses or indications of a fire pit or hearth were encountered. From 80-90 cm no charcoal flecks were seen and only five flakes were recovered. Excavation was stopped at 95 cm in D-5, the deepest level in Trench D.

Trench A revealed the same kinds of materials as Trench D. The datum was 15 cm above the surface and all measurements given below are taken from this elevation. From the surface to 60 cm (51-60 cm) in Square 2, numerous flakes and several cores were found. In succeeding levels less and less artifactual material was recovered; however, at 94 cm a piece of ground stone was found. Charcoal flakes were encountered at 78.5 cm and extended down to about 90 cm. As with the squares in Trench D, the charcoal was very thinly scattered throughout the soil and no ash or charcoal lenses were encountered. There were several pieces of broken, burnt basaltic stone strewn randomly throughout the 70-90 cm levels. Several small pieces of unidentified bone (rodent?) were also found at the 80-90 cm level, but more than likely are intrusive and not culturally deposited. No artifacts were found at this level. At a depth of 120 cm only one flake had been recovered and excavation was terminated.

Each trench was mapped and then backfilled. There were no definable soil profiles or cultural features noted except in Square D-1, which contained what appeared to be a thin stratum of water-laid gravel deposited in an east-west direction; this may be an old drainage channel.

The purpose of testing AEPCO tower location L-117 was to determine what, if any, archaeological resources were present and whether or not tower construction would have an adverse effect on such resources. Tower construction will consist of drilling two holes, approximatey 1 m by 7 m, several meters apart for tower poles. Since the tower location is immediately adjacent to an existing dirt road, damage to the surrounding surface by equipment will be minimal. As cultural remains on the surface at tower L-117 consisted of occasional pieces of flaked stone, damage to the immediate surface area would not significantly destroy information relating to the site. Prior to testing it was felt that cultural remains would be located close to the surface, if indeed they were present beneath the surface. This proved to be the general case but sparse cultural debris were located up to 84 cm beneath the surface. The presence of charcoal in Squares D-5 and A-5 has questionable significance. It was very thinly distributed in the soil and the flecks were not larger than 1 or 2 mm. No lenses or other areas of concentration were noted, and it is felt that the charcoal may be the result of a brush or grass fire some time in the past. Similar charcoal deposits were noted in a bladed road cut 20 to 30 m west of tower L-117 at what appeared to be a similar depth.

The cultural remains found at tower L-117 apparently represent a sparse lithic scatter without any indications of structures or other features. No pottery or diagnostic stone artifacts were discovered which could help in determining cultural affiliation. More than likely, the material is associated with the surface remains of Arizona CC:2:31 and may represent a sparse trash scatter. Excavation elsewhere on the site would probably reveal significant subsurface cultural debris; however, at tower L-117 the density of subsurface cultural material was very low. It is considered highly unlikely that tower construction would have any adverse effect on remaining cultural resources or to the integrity of Arizona CC:2:31 as a whole.

Prior to mapping the site, a brief reconnaissance was made to relocate cultural features recorded during the survey. Two features were discovered to have been recently severely vandalized. A general collection was made of ceramics from the vandalized areas in an attempt to salvage some information. Additionally, small collections of ceramics from specific features were made to determine more precisely the cultural affinities of the site. It must be emphasized that not all cultural features were located at Arizona CC:2:31, particularly to the north and south of the site, since the survey and mapping crews were restricted to the transmission line R-O-W corridor. In this instance, however, the crew went a short distance beyond the R-O-W boundaries in order to assess site complexity, although lack of time prevented complete assessment of cultural features.

Description of the Features.

Feature 1

Dimensions: 6 m N/S by 5 m E/W

Located in the central portion of the site, this feature is a rectangular basaltic cobble outline with a dense sherd concentration within and around the exterior of the feature. It is probably a structure with associated trash.

Feature 2

Dimensions: 7 m N/S by 9 m E/W

This is a partially collapsed and eroded rectangular outline of basaltic cobbles, probably indicative of another structure, with associated sherds and lithics on the surrounding surface.

Feature 3

Dimensions: 3 m in diameter

This is a rather amorphous circular pile of basaltic rocks situated 15 m southeast of Feature 2 and may represent a storage feature associated with Feature 2.

Feature 4

This is a possible canal running northeast-southwest through the site. It is basically a shallow, silted narrow trough that roughly parallels the conformation of the edge of the river terrace, and parallels the present San Jose Canal. From its location near proposed tower L-117 northwards this channel has been altered by natural erosional processes so that it becomes difficult to define. At the southernmost extent all traces have been destroyed by road blading. This feature was not followed northwards to determine its extent beyond the R-O-W boundaries. Sherds and lithics are present within the channel, but these have apparently eroded in from the widespread surface trash.

Feature 5

This feature is located in an area that has been heavily bladed and bulldozed, with tall piles of dirt obscuring the original ground surface. The type of feature cannot be determined, although evidence for one was demonstrated by the presence of sherds, lithics, and areas of charcoal exposed in the blade cut. The ceramics collected from the disturbed area include: Tularosa Black-on-white, St. John's Polychrome and Pinedale Black-on-red (Table 3).

Feature 6
Dimensions: 25 m N/S by 40 m E/W

This is a large multiple activity area containing numerous manos, trough metate fragments, lithic tools and debitage, and dense sherd concentrations. Time did not permit identification of specific activity loci within the general area, but the density of material and the few depressed areas suggest pit houses. A good deal of material has eroded into a deep arroyo bisecting Feature 6, and some of this may be originating from Feature 8, a sherd and lithic concentration directly east. Feature 6 and Feature 8 may actually be one component, but were arbitrarily separated for ease in recording. Table 3 illustrates the types of ceramics collected from Feature 6. Generally, surface sherds are representative of the Mimbres branch Mogollon, with a few possibly locally produced types also present.

Feature 7
Dimensions: 6 m N/S by 4 m E/W

This is a partially eroded rectangular alignment of basaltic cobbles immediately northwest of Feature 1 and may also be a possible structure.

Feature 8
Dimensions: Approximately 65 m N/S by 85 m E/W

This feature consists of a dispersed sherd and lithic scatter with some ground stone distributed around Feature 2 and Feature 3. Due to a similarity to Feature 6 in artifact assemblage, Feature 8 may actually be an extension of the former, although this is a tentative conclusion.

Feature 9
Dimensions: 5.1 m N/S by 6 m E/W

This feature is a roughly square concentration of large stream rolled cobbles, slightly set into the surface. It is situated on the east bank of an eroded channel (Feature 4). Several of the cobbles are placed in alignment on the slope of the bank. Their non-eroded condition and the different composition of the stone (as opposed to the vesicular basalt used in other features) suggest this to be a recent feature. Sherds do occur within and around the feature, but their association appears fortuitous.

Feature 10
Dimensions: Structure: 5.1 m N/S by 6 m E/W
Trash area: 13.9 m N/S by 15 m E/W

This feature is situated in the southern portion of the site on the edge of the river terrace. It is a circular depression approximately 1 m in diameter, lined by and filled with over 75 vesicular basalt cobbles. Surrounding the feature and eroding down the terrace slope is a dense concentration of sherds and lithics.

Feature 11

This is a small sherd concentration at the eastern extreme of the site. A single Gila Polychrome sherd was collected.

Feature 12

This is a small amorphous concentration of rocks and lithics situated 20 m south of Feature 11.

Feature 13

This is a historic trash area, containing prehistoric sherds mixed in with the historic material. This feature was recorded but not mapped on the survey and could not be relocated by the mapping crew.

Feature 14

This feature was not mapped on the survey and could not be relocated. It consisted of a stone feature that contained some polychrome sherds.

Feature 15

This is a stone circle that could not be relocated.

Feature 16
Dimensions: Structure: 5.9 m N/S by 6.2 m E/W
Trash area: 14.3 m N/S by 10.8 m E/W

This feature is a large rectangular structure outlined by basaltic cobbles with a surrounding trash deposit of sherds and lithics. Some mounding of trash is evident east and south of the structure. Feature 16 had recently been heavily vandalized. A collection was made from a pile of sherds that had been left behind. These were analyzed and tabulated as to type and are presented in Table 3.

Feature 17
Dimensions: Structure: 5.6 m N/S by 6.7 m E/W
Trash area: 4.15 m N/S by 25 m E/W (disturbed)

This feature is a rectangular cobble structure situated on the west edge of the river terrace. A fairly dense sherd and lithic concentration radiates outward from the structure. The precise boundaries of the trash scatter could not be defined due to extensive blading of the area and rampant vandalism. A sample of sherds was recovered from the back dirt within the potted interior of the structure, and the various types of ceramics are tabulated in Table 3. A wide variety of ceramic types are present, the majority of which are Mogollon, with some Hohokam types also occurring.

Feature 18
Dimensions: 17 m N/S by 22.3 m E/W

This is a sherd and lithic concentration within the general trash scatter of the site.

Feature 19
Dimensions: 21 m N/S by 23 m E/W

This feature is a sherd and lithic concentration within the general surface refuse scatter on the site.

Feature 20
Dimensions: 9.6 m N/S by 15.6 m E/W

This is a general sherd and lithic concentration with ground stone artifacts and may represent a task-specific activity area.

Feature 21
Dimensions: 15.4 m N/S by 10.3 m E/W

This feature is a sherd and lithic concentration.

Feature 22

This feature could not be relocated and mapped due to lack of time. Its location was interpolated from site survey data and plotted onto the base map. The survey data describes Feature 22 as a possible stone alignment.

To summarize the information gained from limited surface observation, Arizona CC:2:31 is a complex site exhibiting traits that affiliate it with the Mogollon of the point of Pines-Reserve area and the San Simon branch during the time period A.D. 900-1000. The site exhibits the typical Mogollon pit house village layout, that of dispersed randomly located features. The absence of pueblo architecture at this site seems to indicate that occupation terminated around A.D. 1000, but this assumption may be modified when Arizona CC:2:31 is examined with respect to its possible relation to pueblo sites in the vicinity, such as Buena Vista (Brown 1973). That is, it has yet to be determined if Arizona CC:2:31 is an earlier pre-pueblo pit house village or a contemporaneous outlying village of Buena Vista. It is not unusual for Mogollon pit house architecture to be retained alongside pueblo architecture. Excavations in the Point of Pines area indicate that the pit house village pattern maintained itself alongside the pueblo pattern into the 13th century (Wendorf 1950: 146).

Randomly placed rectangular, cobble outlined pit houses are not a common aspect of Mogollon architecture. Pit houses of the San Simon branch utilized no stone in their construction and those of the Reserve-Mimbres area are either unlined or masonry-lined. Features 1, 2, 16, and 17 are only cobble outlines on the surface, with no coursing or masonry evident. Rectangular pit houses with rocks placed around the edge of the pit on the surface have been reported at Nantack Village in the Point of Pines region (Breternitz 1959: 6, 15) where they were assumed to be the basal support for jacal walls. Breternitz (1959: 22) suggests this rock base may represent a transition from semisubterranean pit houses to surface masonry dwellings. The latter architectural style begins around A.D. 1000 in the Point of Pines region. The dates derived from the ceramics at Arizona CC:2:31 allow for placement within this transitional time period, but only excavation can determine the true temporal aspects of these features.

Table 3. Ceramic Types at Arizona CC:2:30, CC:2:31, CC:2:32

	MOGOLLON																		HOHOKAM			ANASAZI					OTHER			
	Reserve-Mimbres-Point-of-Pines												San Simon		Safford Basin															
	Reserve Smudged	San Francisco Red	Mimbres Bold Face B/W	Pine Flat Neck Corr.	Reserve Red	Reserve B/W	Reserve Plain Corr.	Tularosa Patterned Corr.	Reserve Plain Corr. Smudged	Mimbres B/W	Tularosa B/W	San Carlos R/Brn	Galiuro R/Brn	Encinas R/Brn	Sacaton R/Bf. Safford Var.	Tucson B/R	Tucson Poly.	Brown Plainware	Gila Plain	Santa Cruz R/Bf.	Gila Poly.	Snowflake B/W	Puerco B/R	St. John's B/R	St. John's Poly.	Pinedale B/R	Playas Red Incised	Uniden. Red Ware	Uniden. Corr.	Uniden. Plainware
AZ CC:2:30																														
Surface										X								X												
AZ CC:2:31																														
Gen. Surface	X				X		X		X	X	X				X		X	X	X			X	X	X	X		X			X
Feature 5											X														X	X				X
Feature 6	X				X		X	X		X	X				X			X	X											
Feature 11																					X									
Feature 16	X		X		X		X		X	X		X						X	X							X		X	X	
Feature 17	X		X	X	X	X	X		X	X				X	X	X	X	X	X											X
AZ CC:2:32																														
Gen. Surface					X					X																		X		
Feature 1			X		X																									
N. of Hwy.	X	X	X											X						X										
S. of Hwy.			X		X					X			X	X				X												

That more than one cultural component is present at Arizona CC:2:31 is evident; temporal components are more difficult to identify on the basis of surface observations alone. The presence of late tradewares (Gila Polychrome, St. John's Polychrome, Pinedale Black-on-red) indicate a later component but the significance of this is uncertain.

Arizona CC:2:31 is but one site of many in the general area along the Gila River near Safford. As such, it can best be understood when viewed as one component within a regional cultural pattern.

Arizona CC:2:32

<u>Elevation:</u> 920-921 m
<u>Site Size:</u> 260 m N/S by 410 m E/W
<u>Physiographic Location:</u> Stratum 1 and Stratum 2 transition
<u>Field Designation:</u> AEPCO 79

Arizona CC:2:32 is a pit house village located in a physiographic zone interface: Stratum 1 and Stratum 2. This site was discovered as a result of re-aligning the R-O-W corridor to avoid Arizona CC:2:30 (Figures 24 and 28). For ease in recording, the site was arbitrarily divided into northern and southern sections, demarcated by a light-duty paved road that bisects the site from northeast to southwest. The southern part of the site is situated on a low fan-shaped river terrace 0.16 km north of the Gila River (Stratum 1). From this terrace the land rises steadily northward in elevation to a low ridge, which is part of a system of east-west trending ridges at the base of the Gila Mountains (Stratum 2). Soils represented in the site area are Arizo gravelly sandy loams which are typical of river terraces in the Gila River Valley. The northern half of the site represents the Continental-Pinaleño complex, also a gravelly sandy loam (Gelderman 1970: 9, 14). The surface is composed largely of alluvial cobbles and gravels. The Arizo series supports a vegetation consisting of creosotebush, mesquite, annual weeds and grasses, and some cactus. Wolfberry, snakeweed, mesquite, cholla, and creosotebush grow in Continental-Pinaleño complex soils. The entire vegetation pattern of the southern half has been disrupted by recent historic occupation; at present only creosotebush and saltbush grow on the flat terrace area, and a dense mesquite bosque encircles the base of the terrace slope. The upper ridge slopes support a vegetation cover of creosotebush (dominant), ocotillo, pencil cholla, and hedgehog cactus.

Surface disturbance at this site is extensive. An abandoned adobe house, latrine, and corrals occupy the southeastern quadrant of the site and most of the southern half is crisscrossed by dirt roads and bulldozed areas. The highway bisecting the site has exposed cross-sections of pit houses and cultural deposits in the upper terrace profile.

The entire site area is littered with a sparse to medium-dense scatter of lithic material, ground stone, and sherds. Concentrations within the scatter are not readily apparent in the southern portion of the site due to surface disturbance, but there are a few scattered low mounds that may indicate cultural deposits. Concentrations of cultural material are evident, however, on the north part of the site, where they appear to be associated with areas that have been cleared of rocks. Thirteen features were located and recorded at Arizona CC:2:32 (Figure 25).

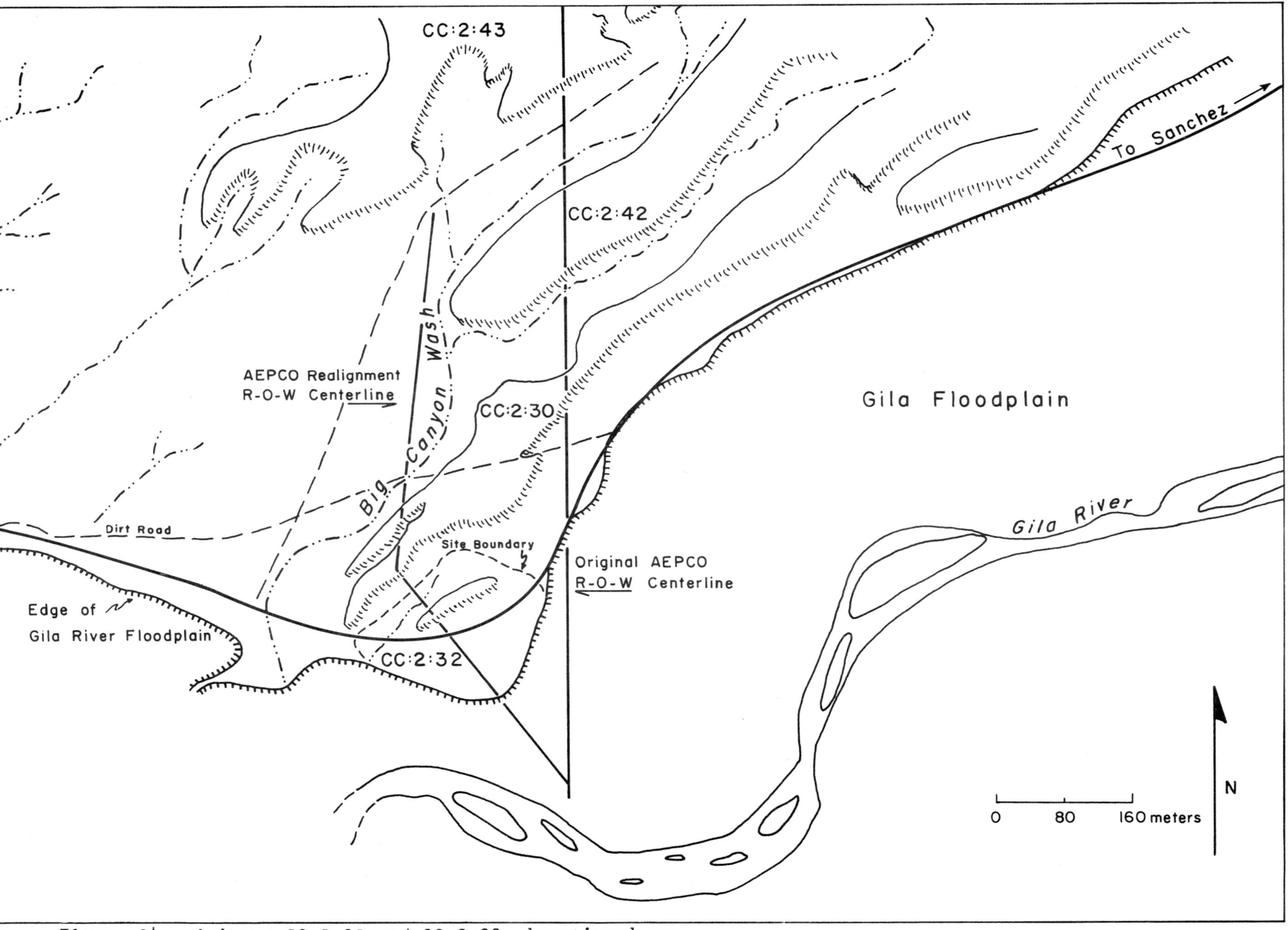

Figure 24. Arizona CC:2:30 and CC:2:32, locational map

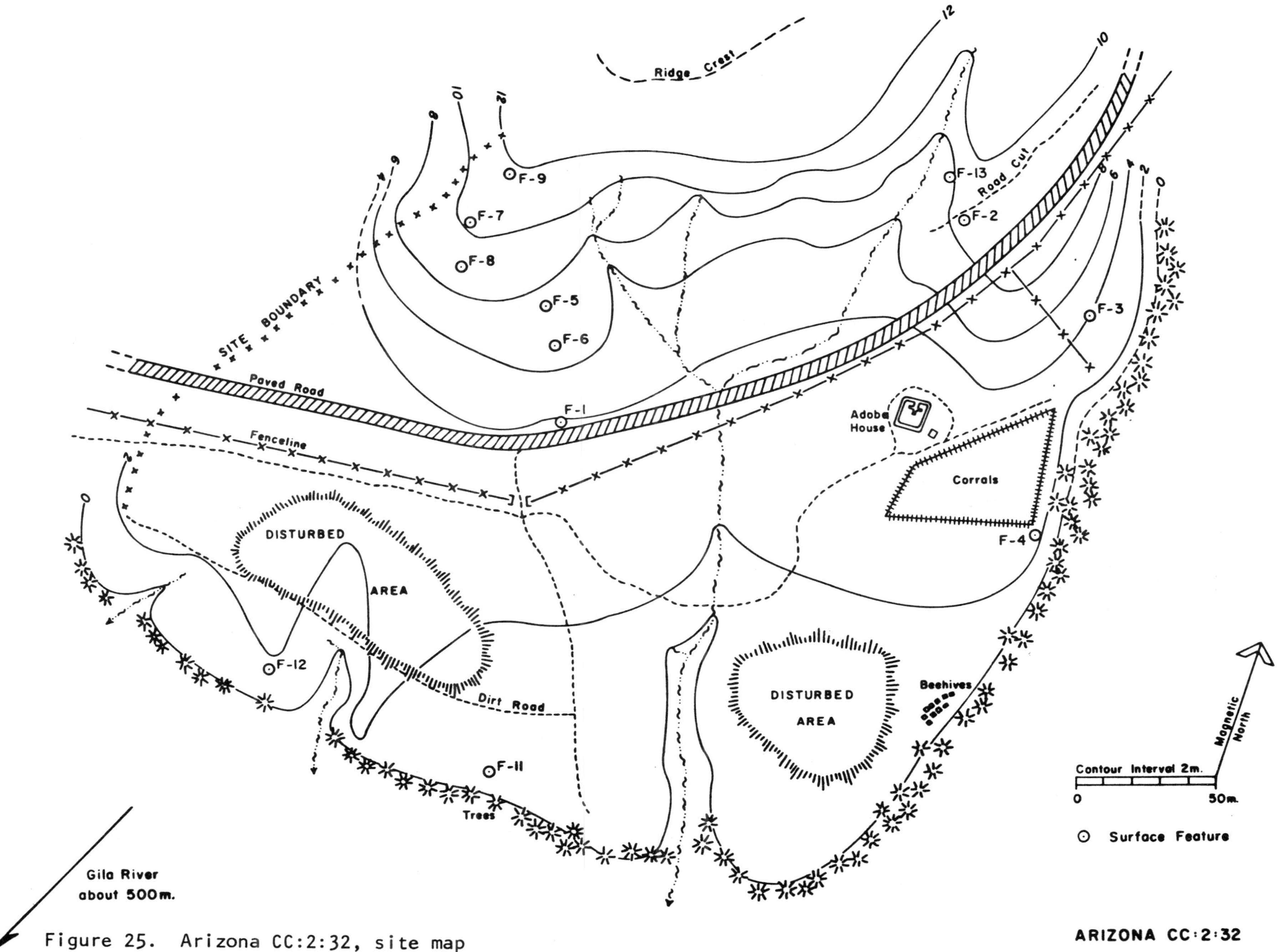

Figure 25. Arizona CC:2:32, site map

Description of the Feature.

Feature 1
Dimensions: 3.4 m E/W

This is a pit house that had been sliced through by a paved highway, and was exposed in the profile as an ashy deposit. No prepared floor is evident, and cultural material is sparse.

Feature 2
Dimensions: 0.63 in diameter

This is an irregular cobble feature also exposed in the road cut, 0.76 m below the present ground surface. The fill of the feature is ashy soil, and few sherds were evident eroding from beneath the feature.

Feature 3
Dimensions: 4 m NW/SE by 4.5 m NE/SW

This is an alignment consisting of two rows of cobbles laid at right angles to each other (Figures 26 and 29) and may represent remnants of a possible structure near the edge of the river terrace.

Feature 4 (Figure 27)
Dimensions: 4.8 m N/S by 3.6 m E/W

This feature is a roughly rectangular, amorphous alignment of cobbles that may represent a cobble feature similar to Feature 3.

Feature 5
Dimensions: 5 m N/S by 5 m E/W

This is a flat cleared area on the lower slopes of the ridge, north of the highway cut. Lithic materials occur around this cleared area, but none is present within the feature.

Feature 6 (Figure 30)
Dimensions: 6 m N/S by 8 m E/W

This feature is a flat cleared area on the lower slopes of the ridge north of the highway cut, downslope from Feature 5. A cobble cluster is at the south edge of the feature and measures 1.46 m N/S by 1.9 m E/W. It is composed of vesicular basalt and granitic cobbles. Additionally, five mano fragments and several lithic artifacts occur in the cluster. The area surrounding Feature 6 is a scatter of sherds and lithics, indicating a possible activity area.

Feature 7
Dimensions: 6 m N/S by 8 m E/W

This is a flat cleared area adjacent to a general trash area of lithic debitage and metate fragments.

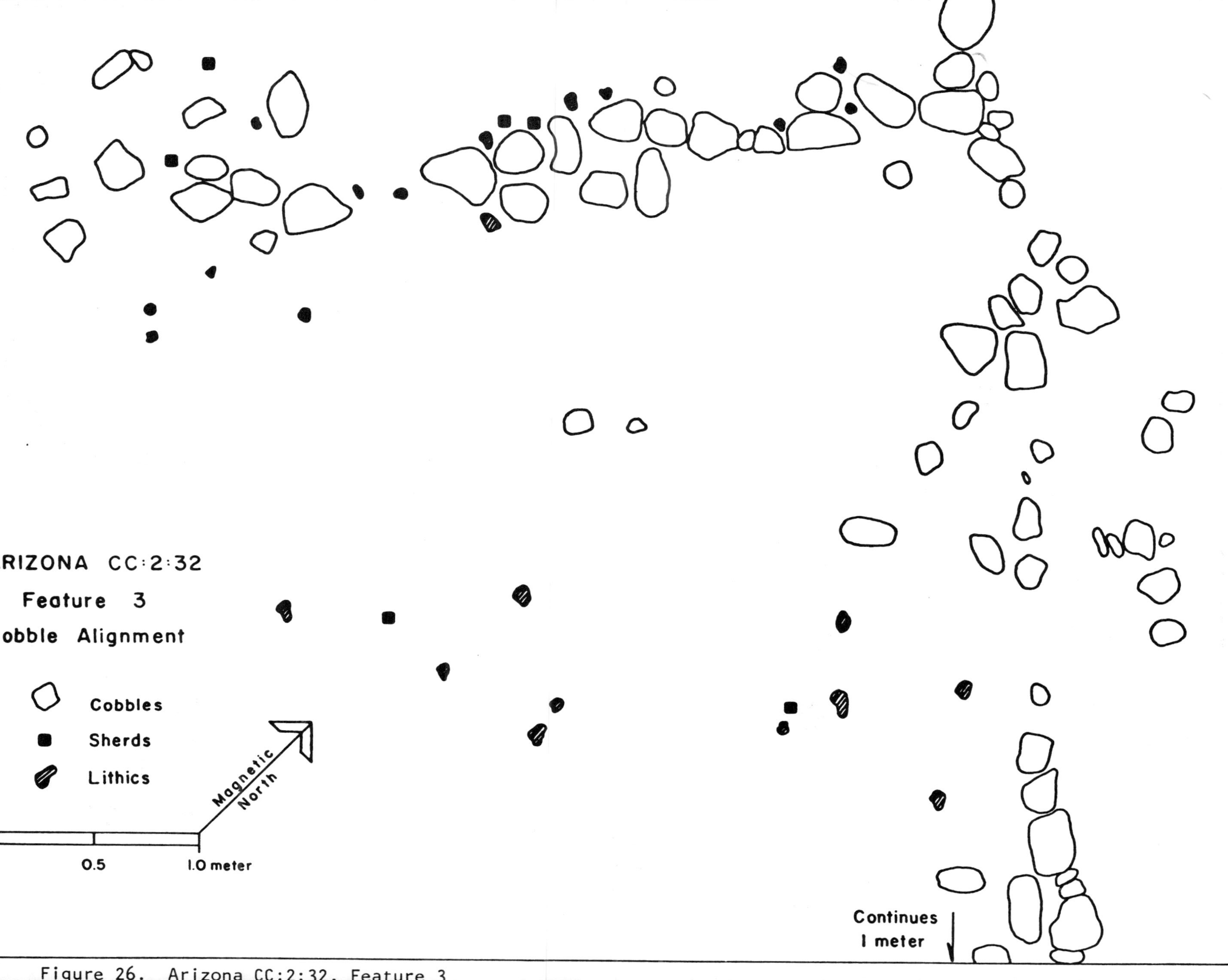

Figure 26. Arizona CC:2:32, Feature 3

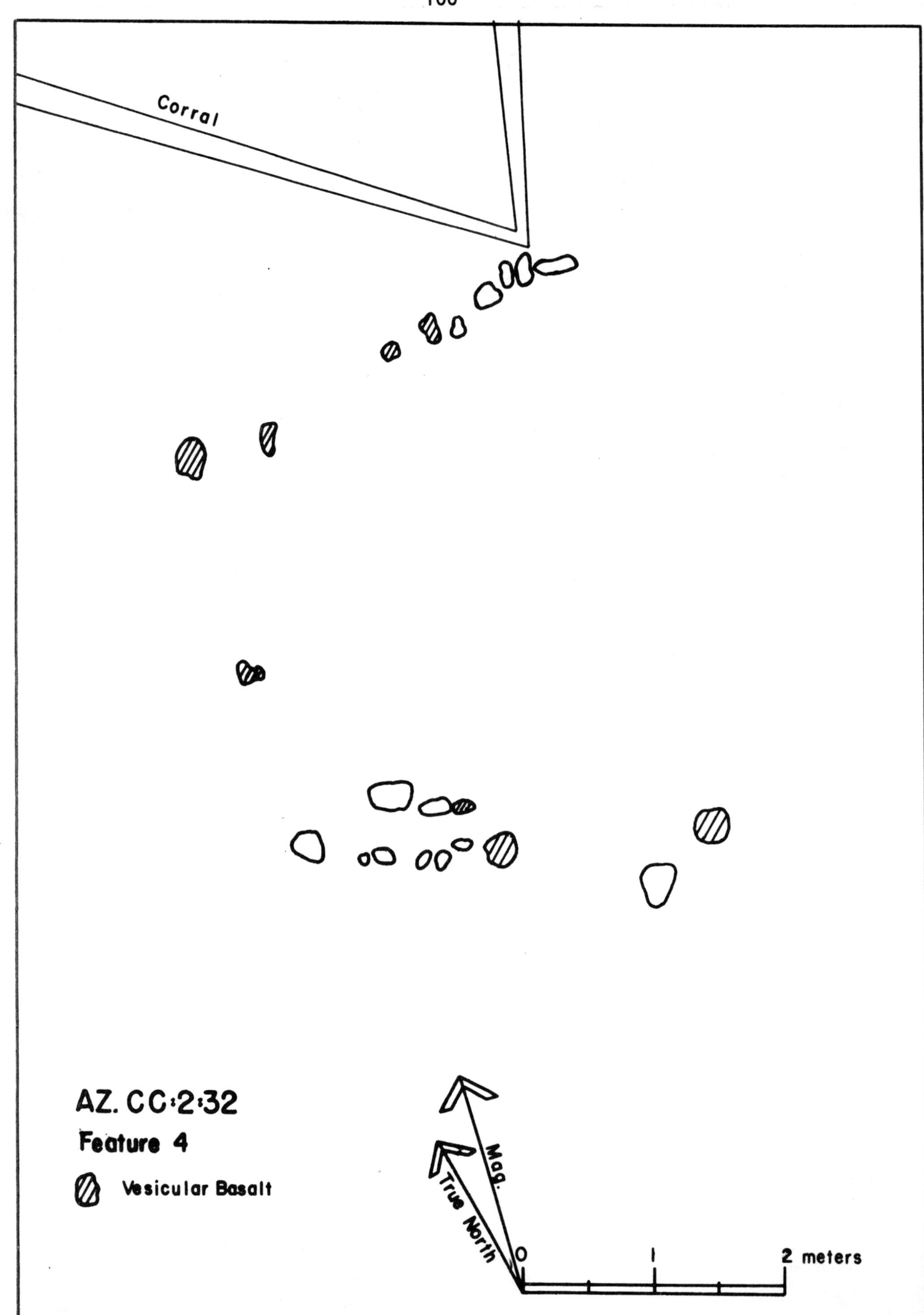

Figure 27. Arizona CC:2:32, Feature 4

Figure 28. Arizona CC:2:32, overview.

Figure 29. Arizona CC:2:32, Feature 3, rock alignment.

Figure 30. Arizona CC:2:32, Feature 6, cobble cluster.

Figure 31. Arizona CC:2:32, Feature 9, cleared depression.

Feature 8
Dimensions: 6 m N/S by 7 m E/W

This feature is a flat cleared area surrounded by a lithic scatter.

Feature 9 (Figure 31)
Dimensions: 6 m N/S by 7 m E/W

This is a flat cleared area similar to Feature 8 and is also ringed by a scatter of lithic flakes.

Feature 10

This is a probable historic feature on the opposite north site of the ridge crest resting on a bed of decomposed clayey shale. It is an arrangement of small cobbles in a rectangle with additional small cobbles laid out in a cellular arrangement within the rectangle. The chronological and cultural affiliation of the feature are unknown.

Feature 11
Dimensions: 5 m diameter

This is a cleared area in a depression. It is south of the highway cut near the west edge of the site.

Feature 12
Dimensions: 5 m diameter

This feature is similar to Feature 11 in that it is another depressed cleared area.

Feature 13

This is a historic trash deposit probably associated wtih the historic adobe house and corral. Material includes purple glass, old Mason jars, earthenware, and hole-in-top cans.

Several collections of sherds were taken from the surface of the site to aid in identifying cultural affinities. These are tabulated in Table 3. Generally, the ceramic picture at Arizona CC:2:32 is earlier than that present at Arizona CC:2:31. Among the ceramics are Mimbres Bold Face Black-on-white, Mimbres Black-on-white, San Francisco Red, and Reserve Red. The San Simon branch Mogollon is represented by Encinas Red-on-brown. One sherd of Santa Cruz Red-on-buff was collected. Plainware sherds are primarily locally produced; they have coarse sand/quartz temper and are brown in color.

On the basis of surface ceramics, Arizona CC:2:32 appears to be chronologically earlier than the other two investigated habitation sites, Arizona CC:2:30 and CC:2:31. Mimbres Bold Face Black-on-white and Galiuro Red-on-brown at Arizona CC:2:32 suggest a pre-A.D. 900 initial occupation date. Village layout at this site conforms to the typical Mogollon pattern of dispersed randomly placed features, as was evident at Arizona CC:2:30 and CC:2:31. The lack of domestic stone architecture at CC:2:32 is an additional feature setting this site apart from the other two habitation sites. Whether this is a cultural or chronological aspect has yet to be determined. For example, the San Simon branch Mogollon used no stone in pit house architecture (Sayles 1945: 30); in the Mimbres branch stone architecture begins around A.D. 850-900 (Haury 1936: 62). Again, only further research can allow a more complete definition of attributes at Arizona CC:2:32.

Arizona CC:2:41, CC:2:48, CC:2:49

These three sites were recorded on the survey and are believed to be the remains of habitation sites. All have been heavily plowed and were only recognized by the presence of sherds, lithics, and ground stone. Cultivation and irrigation have eradicated all indications of surface features, but the density and horizontal distribution of cultural material in the plow zone suggests that in certain places multiple activities were carried out at one time.

Summary

A complete study of the cultural resources at the AEPCO habitation sites must await future research into these sites. For the present, the foregoing description of cultural traits and features must suffice.

The significance of the sites lies in their potential for yielding valuable information about the prehistory of the Safford Basin. The area has long been recognized as an area of cultural mixing and blending, situated as it is at the interface of Mogollon, Hohokam, and Salado cultural spheres. While Mogollon traits are dominant at the three pit house villages none is "pure" Mogollon in character. Too little is known about the sites to determine if they are a local manifestation of processes that led to the development of the Western Pueblo cultural pattern, as has been described for other sites in the vicinity (Johnson and Wasley 1966). Hohokam and southern Mogollon influence is strongly evident at the AEPCO sites over any distinctive Western Pueblo traits. Arizona CC:2:31, for example, exhibits a mixture of Mogollon traits from both the Mimbres and San Simon branch Mogollon, with a small number of Hohokam elements.

One problem in the Safford Basin concerns the degree of participation of Hohokam traits in the San Simon branch during the later period. There is a good deal of indecision as to whether Hohokam or Mogollon people or a local indigenous group was producing Red-on-brown pottery (Tuthill 1950). Red-on-brown pottery is typical of Tucson Basin archaeology, where it is believed to have been made by Hohokam groups inhabiting the area. Red-on-brown pottery made in the mountainous New Mexico Mogollon area is certainly Mogollon in character. DiPeso (1956) feels that the Ootam produced this pottery, at least in southeastern Arizona. Complicating the issue is that micaceous Gila Basin Red-on-buff type pottery is sometimes found in association with Red-on-brown pottery, as is typical black-on-white Mimbres pottery. The question is, are the Red-on-brown ceramics at Arizona CC:2:31 made by Hohokam, San Simon branch Mogollon or a local group? This question leads directly into the problem of more adequately defining the nature and extent of the San Simon branch, which is described only in very general terms (Sayles 1945) and somewhat inconclusively so. In essence, the entire scheme of cultural development in all branches within the Mogollon cultural sphere needs to be more precisely defined, especially the relationship of one branch to another, before any general statement can be made regarding the cultural processes at the AEPCO habitation sites.

CHAPTER 7

WATER CONTROL SYSTEMS

A water control system is a feature or combination of features that provide water for farming or domestic use (Vivian 1974: 94). By not limiting food production areas to the lower elevations where floodwater or canals can be used, such systems permit maximization of potentially arable land and expansion of farming alternatives (Canouts 1975: 82).

Water control features were found on Arizona CC:2:30, 31, and 40. The first two sites are pit house villages that have been discussed in Chapter 6. Arizona CC:2:40 consists of a system of water control features in association with a sherd and lithic scatter.

Water Control Features

Terminology used to refer to water control features has been adapted from Vivian (1974), Masse (1974), and Woodbury (1961). Features found on project sites include:

1. Gridded Gardens (waffle gardens, bordered gardens, grid borders, ridged fields, terrace plots): Small garden areas enclosed by low stone or earthen borders. Generally restricted to flat or gently sloping terrace tops, there can be great variation in size, but usually plots average from 3 to 5 m^2. Such plots can utilize either surface runoff or, if gravel-mulched, direct precipitation. Some of the most spectacular gridded gardens in the Southwest are at Arizona CC:1:2 near Pima, Arizona. Here on the first geologic terrace system north of the Gila River, (a location comparable to Arizona CC:2:40) is a complex field system covering over 150 acres (Stewart 1940: 217; Gilman and Sherman 1975).

2. Check Dams: Linear arrangements of cobble walls, unshaped boulders or mounded earth perpendicular to small drainages used to retain soil and moisture.

3. Contour Terraces (linear borders, terraces): Low walls of cobbles or boulders built across hillsides, talus slopes, or small knolls. Woodbury (1961: 12-13) delineated three functions for contour terraces: as a check against erosion; to slow runoff allowing the ground to soak up more moisture; to clear long strips of land for cultivation.

4. <u>Channelling Borders:</u> Anomalous stone alignments located within or upslope from rock piles or gridded garden plots. One kind of alignment is a linear row of cobbles running perpendicularly through slope contours instead of paralleling contours as contour terraces do. The function appears to be one of channelling runoff to lower elevations, or preventing runoff from spreading outside field boundaries. In the San Pedro Valley these features occur on flat terrace tops guiding runoff to lower fields containing rock piles and check dams (Masse 1974: 15).

5. <u>Rock Piles:</u> These are composed of unmodified cobbles apparently gathered to clear land for agriculture. They average 1 m in diameter and 0.5 m in height. Evenari and others' (1971: 126-47) classic study of "stone mounds" on hill slopes in the Negev Desert indicated that these rock piles were not the result of clearing land for gardens, but that the cleared areas surrounding the rock piles augmented runoff for use by fields in lower elevations.

6. <u>Rock Alignments:</u> Linear rock features composed of uncemented surface cobbles that often accompany rock piles (Canouts 1975: 83).

7. <u>Cleared Areas:</u> Plots or areas on a site where large cobbles and boulders have been removed presumably for <u>in situ</u> agriculture. The Negev study found that clearing cobbles from the ground surface produces a significant increase in runoff. As with rock piles, the problem of interpretation lies in whether the feature was created for an end in itself or whether its purpose was to facilitate another system elsewhere.

8. <u>Wind Breaks:</u> Linear alignments of unshaped cobbles placed perpendicular to the direction of the prevailing winds (Hack 1942: 33; Masse 1974: 30). Such alignments allegedly protected crops from wind by either holding down brush or by acting as a wind break; They work best in areas of blowing sand. Their distribution is confined mainly to the plateau areas of northern Arizona, but it may be that many unidentified rock alignments in other parts of the state are wind breaks.

9. <u>Reservoir (tank):</u> A feature designed for the collection and storage of water, which may be spring fed or filled by runoff. Often stone-lined, they average 30 by 40 m for small ones as found in the Orme Reservoir area (Canouts 1975: 251) to 300 by 200 m for larger reservoirs as found in the northern Rio Grande River area (Ellis 1970: 4).

10. <u>Canal (ditch):</u> Any cut in the earth designed to carry water. Vivian (1974: 97) distinguishes between canals and ditches, the former being greater than 1 m in width and depth and the latter being less. This arbitrary distinction does not seem useful when the full system is not known.

Vivian (1974: 102) has divided water control systems into "conservation systems" and "diversion systems." The former is used in areas dependent on rainfall and runoff; examples are contour terraces and check dams. The latter collects water in one area, which is transported by ditch or canal to another area.

Diversion Systems

These have been amply attested to for the Safford area in prehistoric and historic times; indeed many prehistoric canals were supposedly re-used by early Mormon farmers (Williams 1937). However, few prehistoric canals in the floodplain have been identified due to modern disturbances.

One canal has been tentatively identified at Arizona CC:2:31. The primary reason for designating Feature 4 a possible canal lies in its morphological attributes and the direction of its course. All other erosional channels present on the site are either deeply cut arroyos or areas of sheetwash erosion trending in an east-west direction, whereas Feature 4 crosscuts these erosional vectors. Whether this feature is prehistoric or historic remains to be determined.

Conservation Systems

These features were found at Arizona CC:2:30 and 40. It is difficult to understand the need for elaborate water control systems on terrace tops when the vast, fertile Gila River floodplain was available. It may be that people desired and needed several options for agricultural systems particularly in dealing with problems of scheduling, control, and distribution. By diversifying systems the liklihood of failure by over-reliance on one system is reduced. Some field systems may have been alternatives in terms of seasons, fallowing, or crop types. Also the smaller systems may have fed into the larger floodplain systems. Floodplain villages that presumably had fields fairly close are near the terrace-top gridded gardens of both Arizona CC:1:2 and CC:2:40. Excess runoff could have been diverted from the terrace-tops onto the fields below.

As Vivian (1974: 103) points out, conservation systems do not require extensive management or maintenance, and proportioning and distributing water is of less consequence than that demanded in diversion systems. Also problems of increased erosion and salinization of the soil are not present. On the western slopes of Arizona CC:2:30, a Mogollon pit house village, lie a series of silty, cleared areas with borders of unshaped cobbles that appear to be contour terrace plots. The terraces do not encircle the slope in an unbroken line but occur intermittently. Some are flat, cleared areas, while others appear to be slightly depressed. A long stone alignment running roughly north-south on the western edge of the terrace-top may be a channelling border. This low stone wall is upslope from the terrace plots and may serve to guide runoff to the lower fields. A large 8 by 9 m unlined depression adjacent to the channelling border may be a small reservoir. If so, then this reservoir is much smaller and less elaborate than most reported examples.

Site Description

Arizona CC:2:40

Elevation: 940-945m

Site Size: 305 m by 180 m
Field Designation: AEPCO 43-44-45

The site is located on the slightly dissected, flat, first geologic terrace of the Gila Basin. Judia Canyon is 0.5 km to the south; the Gila River is 2.4 km to the north-northwest and the San Simon River is 2.4 km to the south-southwest. Vegetation includes creosotebush, purple prickly pear, cholla, and whitethorn acacia.

The ground surface is gravelly with few cobbles; soils, as identified by Larry Humphries of the BLM soil sciences staff, are Tres Hermanos clay loams. These soils have severe limitations that reduce the choice of crops and require special conservation practices for farming, or both. While erosion hazard is not high, control of runoff and erosion is still needed. The soild are well suited to surface irrigation, but canals cannot be constructed because a very gravelly material exists below a depth of about 70 cm. Crop rotation and fertilization are needed for modern crop production; without it the land needs to lie fallow for long periods. Small grains and shallow-rooted crops such as corn and cotton are the main modern crops for these soils (Cox 1973: 36-37, 46-50).

The site consists of an agricultural system of the type known as waffle gardens or gridded gardens and an associated sherd and lithic scatter (Figure 45, Chapter 8). The site was originally mapped on survey as three separate sites, AEPCO 43, 44, and 45. These numbers have been retained as loci numbers. All artifacts on the three loci were bagged, mapped by point provenience, and collected.

At Locus 43, the southern most locus (Figures 32 and 45) artifact density was extremely light, consisting of four "Brown plainware" jar body sherds (Appendix II) and fifteen lithic pieces. A test trench near the sherd collection area was excavated to a depth of 20 cm; no cultural materials were found below the surface. No features were observed at this locus.

Locus 44 consists of one large roughly rectangular, isolated plot and two rock alignments (Figure 33). The locus appears to be primarily a cleared area between the other loci. The area around the isolated plot has been deliberately cleared of all large stones; presumably the unmodified cobbles now lining the plot are these same stones (Figure 37). Few other material remains were present. Feature 13 and 14 (Figure 34) are rows of cobbles 9.3 m apart.

A 0.75 by 0.75 m test pit was sunk in the middle of the grid plot. Pollen samples were taken from the surface, and from arbitrary levels at 10 and 20 cm. The surface layer is very gravelly though the plot is not a gravel-mulched border garden (Vivian 1974: 97). Underneath, the soil is very stony with little soil. A test pit was also sunk inside Feature 2 to a depth of 20 cm. No cultural materials or soil differentiation were present.

Locus 45 (Figure 40) consists of contiguous grid plots, a check dam (Feature 4) a cleared area (Feature 6), rock piles (Features 2-3, 7-12) and a sherd and lithic scatter. Locus 45 is on the terrace edge overlooking the

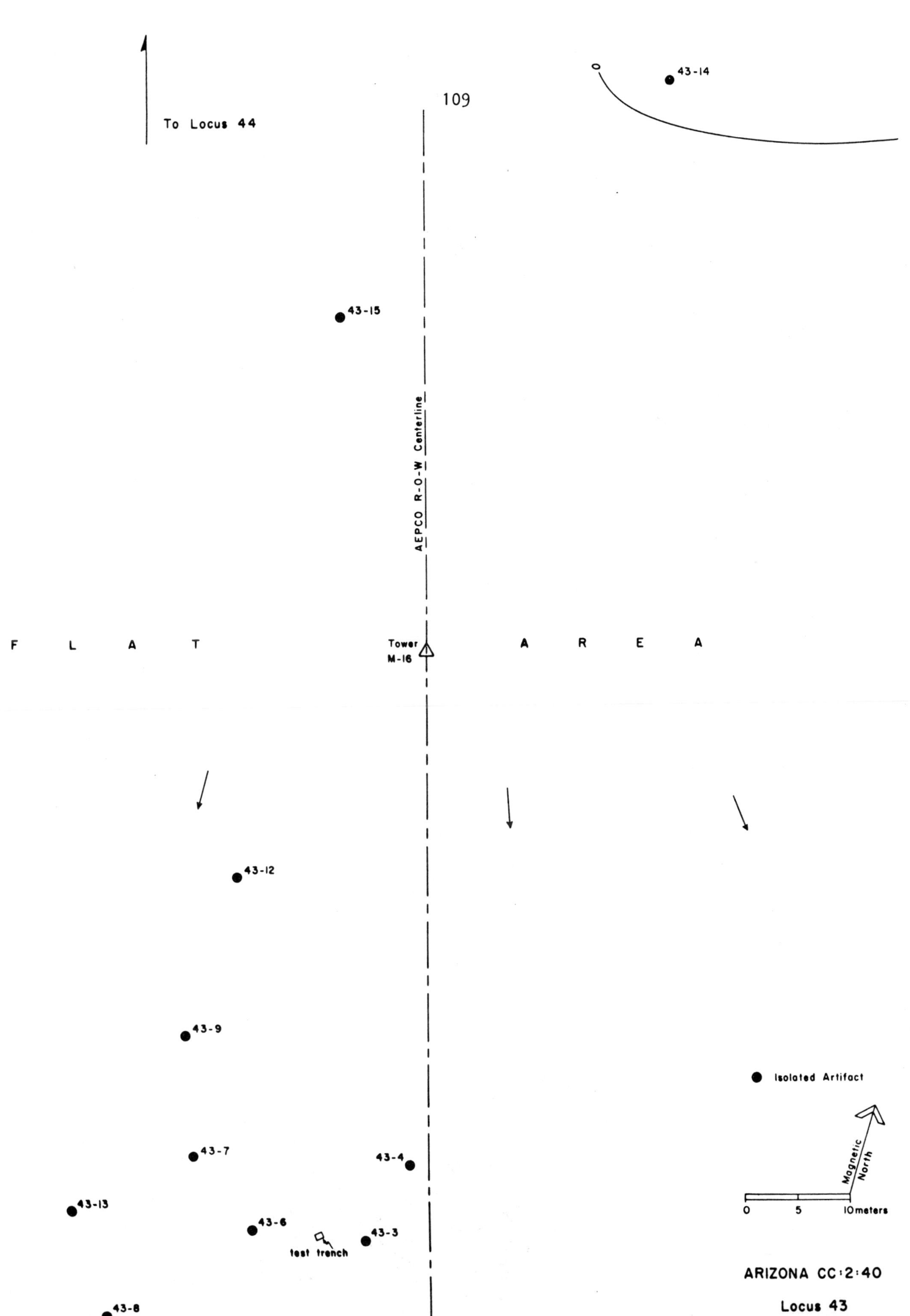

Figure 32. Arizona CC:2:40, Locus 43

Figure 33. Arizona CC:2:40, Locus 44/45

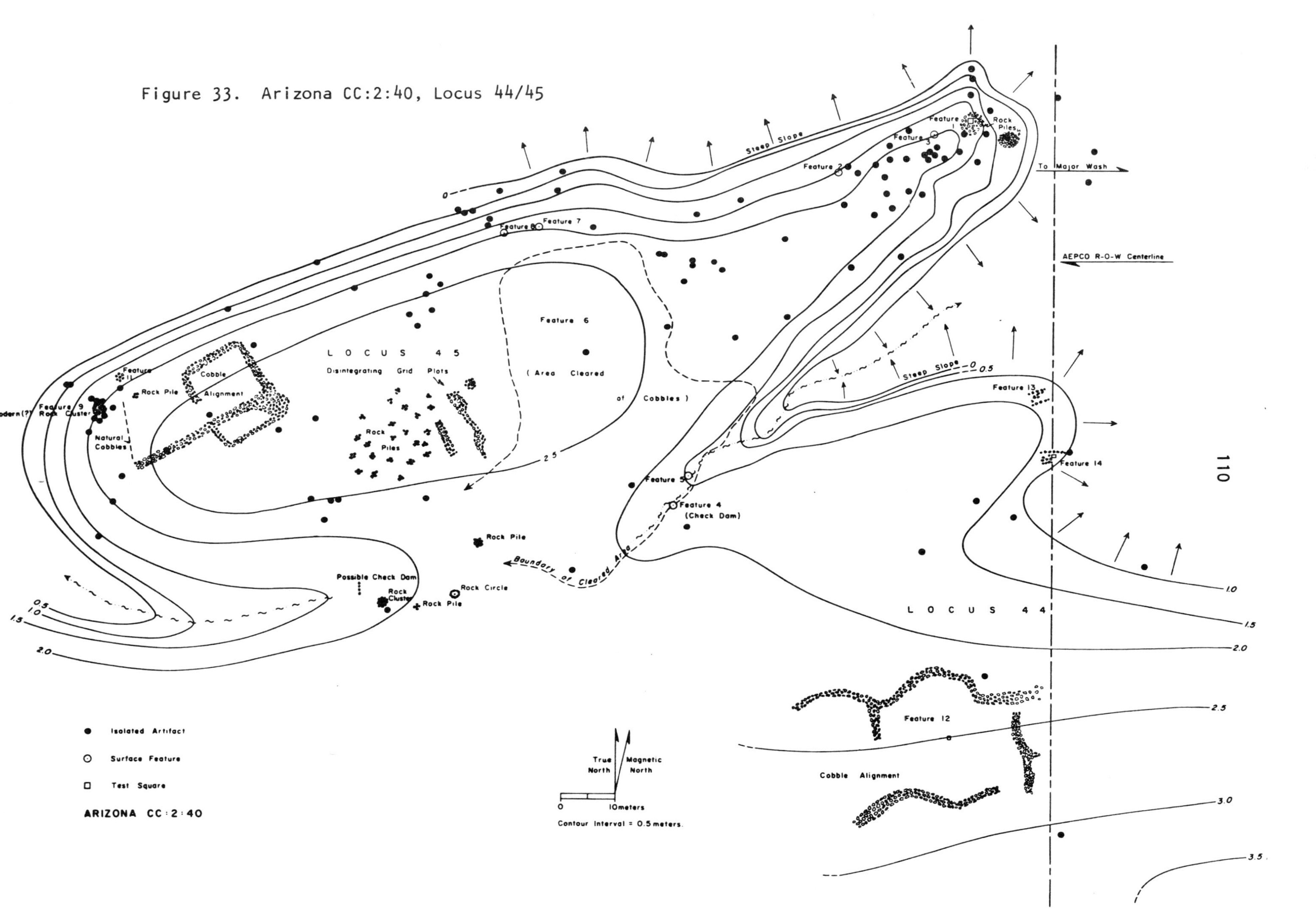

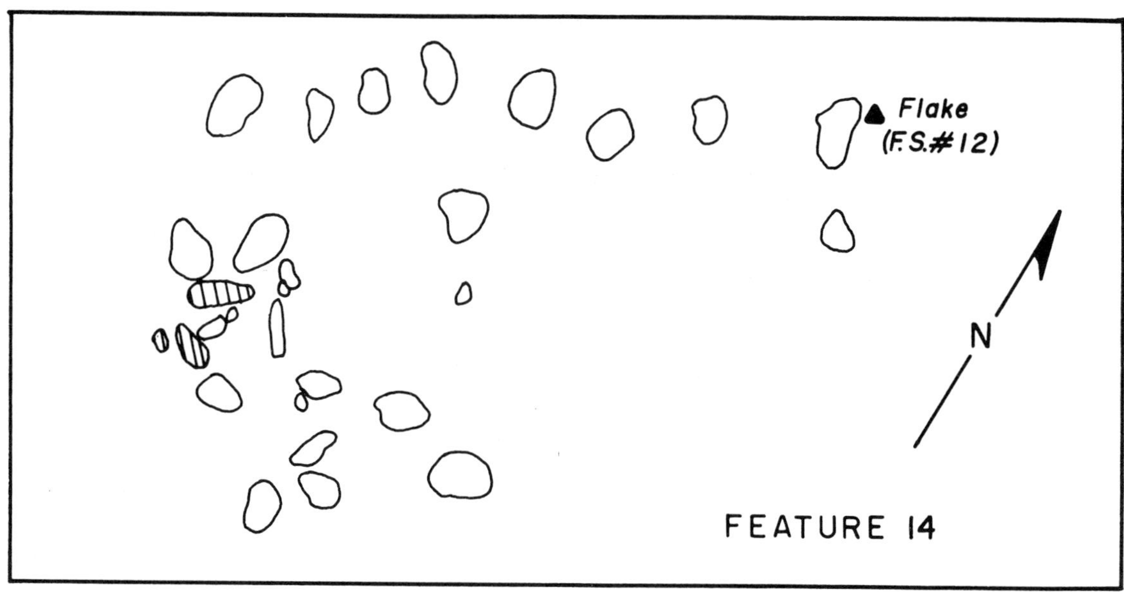

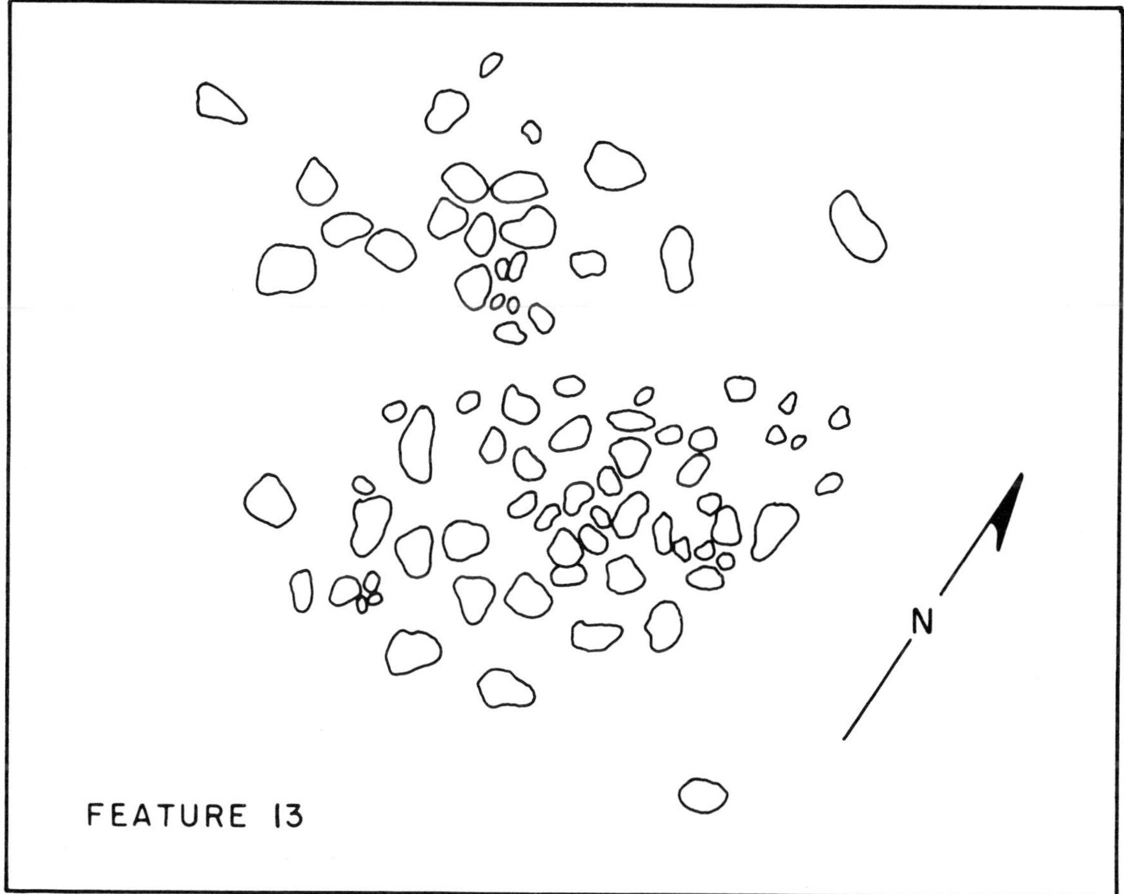

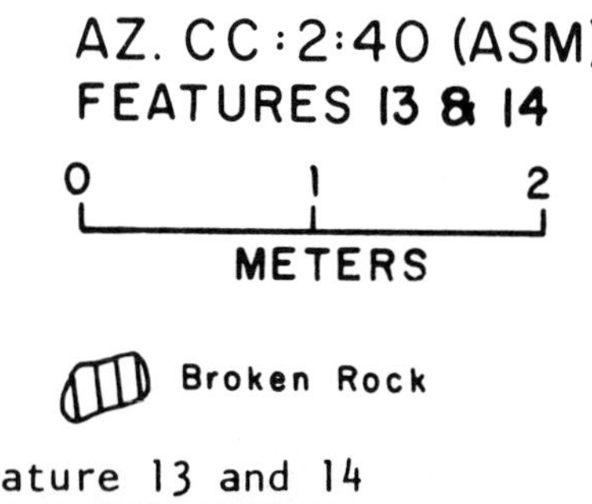

Figure 34. Arizona CC:2:40, Locus 44, Feature 13 and 14

Gila River floodplain. On its slopes are a series of terrace steps that were examined for contour terraces. Regularly spaced stones or low stone walls were not observed, suggesting this is a feature of the natural slope of the hill.

Feature 4, a check dam (Figure 35), was built across an intermittent drainage dividing loci 44 and 45. This is not a low stone wall as the term sometimes implies but an open-ended rectangle of stones laid across the drainage apparently to impede water and soil runoff. Feature 5 is a possible check dam 7.5 m west of Feature 4.

Separating the grid plots from the sherd and lithic scatter is Feature 6, a large area cleared of stones without obvious agricultural features. The area had been deliberately cleared of stones, but whether this was done as an end in itself or merely to acquire stones for the grids is unknown (Figure 38).

The grids presently consist of one large, relatively undisturbed rectangular plot and a series of stone piles that appear to be disintegrated grid corners (Figure 39). Many of the smaller rock piles on the terrace edge may be part of the disintegrated grid system.

A series of cobble clusters and rock piles line the terrace edge on Locus 45. Feature 12 is a cobble cluster on the northeast side of the terrace edge (Figure 36). As both sherds and lithics were found scattered adjacent to and among the rocks, this cluster is believed to be definitely prehistoric. Two (occasionally three) cobble courses are present. Maximum height of the rock pile is 25 cm and the average rock size in the pile is 20 by 30 by 20 cm. The cobbles in the surrounding area are generally smaller, around 15 cm in length. This eastern terrace edge is very rocky in comparison to the cleared area, Feature 6, and appears to be natural desert pavement.

A test pit was excavated in Feature 12. Surface rocks were removed and the ground surface trowelled. One secondary flake was recovered from the first 5 cm below the surface. Between 5 and 25 cm below the surface the soil is loose and very rocky with caliche beginning to appear in the northeast corner. At 30 cm below surface a caliche hardpan is present across the entire trench. No stratigraphy, ash, charcoal, or stained soil were encountered.

Dimensions for other rock piles along the terrace edge are:

Feature 2: 0.50 m N/S by 0.40 m E/W
Feature 3: 1.70 m N/S by 1.20 m E/W
Feature 7: 1.02 m N/S by 1.70 m E/W
Feature 8: 1.50 m N/S by 1.20 m E/W

These features consist of piles of small and medium-sized cobbled one to two courses high. No deposition is present around the bottom stones. Because of their regularity along the terrace edge these piles were thought to be remains of recent fence markers. One small rock pile, unlike the others in size or composition, had a wooden stake and wire still inserted in it. However, several of the piles were associated with lithics and were in alignment with the garden grid corners.

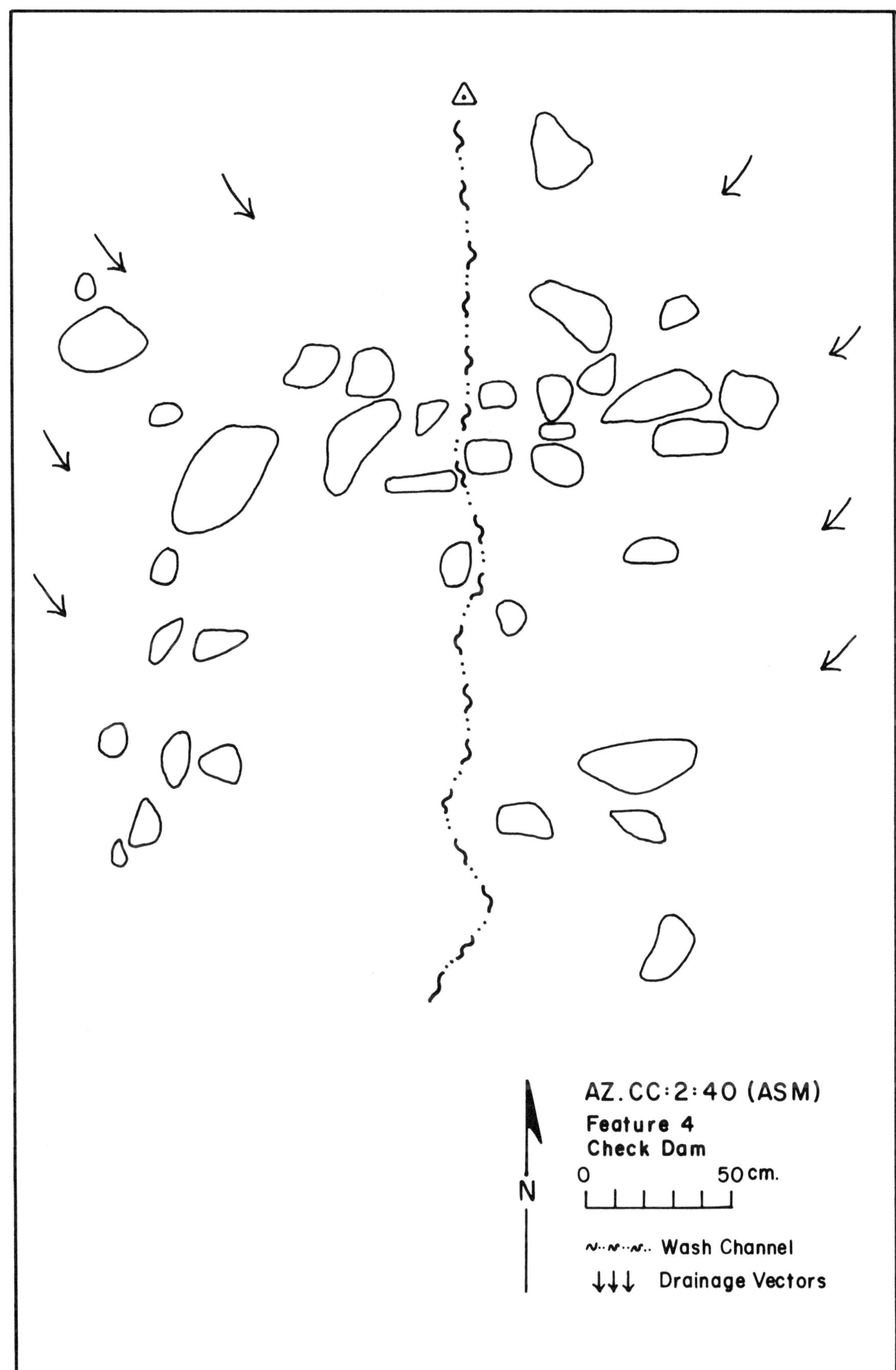

Figure 35. Arizona CC:2:40, Locus 45, Feature 4

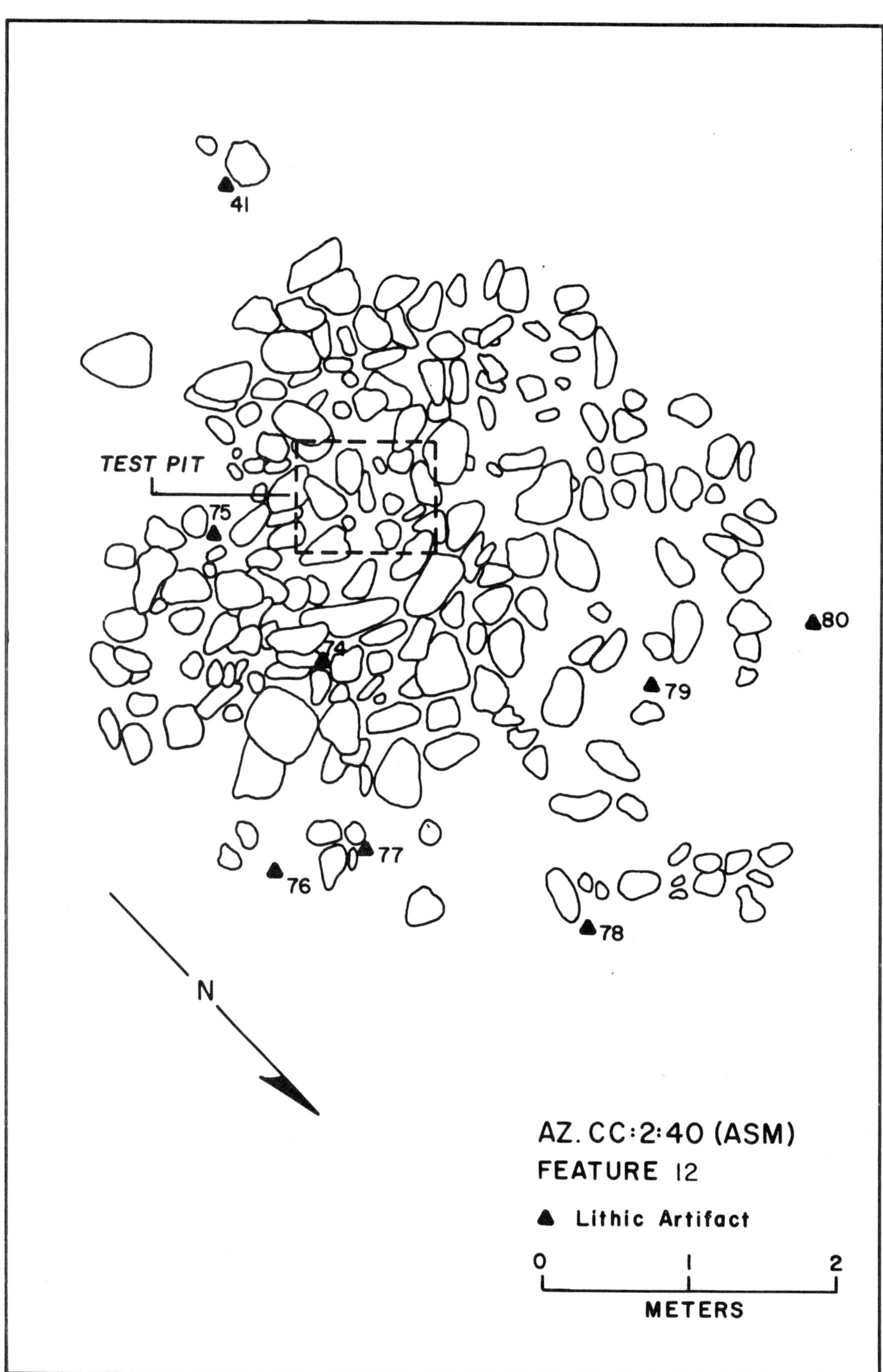

Figure 36. Arizona CC:2:40, Locus 45, Feature 12

Figure 37. Arizona CC:2:40, Locus 44, grid plot.

Figure 38. Arizona CC:2:40, Locus 45, Feature 6.

Figure 39. Arizona CC:2:40, Locus 45, overview

Figure 40. Arizona CC:2:40, Locus 45, overview.

Analysis and Discussion

The problem of whether specific water control systems can be associated with specific prehistoric groups still remains to be resolved. While the Safford Basin's unique intercultural situation is ideal for research into correlation of water control systems, cultural choices, and economic necessities, reliable date are just not present to test such hypotheses. The many village sites and their cultural identifications have been poorly investigated; to date no site in the valley has been properly excavated and published. A more glaring deficit for research into this problem has been a lack of regional orientation. Unfortunately, power line transects are the least efficient method of exploring intra-stratum regional problems. A transect through the valley and terrace systems may not reveal reliable samples of the many cultural and subsistence systems operating in the basin through time. The AEPCO project was fortunate in that this transect crossed three prominent villages and a gridded garden system. We are also grateful that AEPCO protected these resources for future research.

Cultural affiliation of water control features is primarily based on ceramics found on these features or at the sites in which they are located. It can also be based on inferences derived from their proximity to habitation sites of known cultural affiliation. Many of the water control systems found in the Orme Reservoir area were dated in this way (Canouts 1975: 284). Most ceramics found in field systems are plainwares, as is expected, since these are common utility wares. Because the plainwares in the Safford Basin are so poorly known, the problem of ascertaining cultural affiliation is made more difficult.

A significant amount of lithic material was present in the rock pile areas of Locus 45. Little or no material was found in the garden plots and the cleared areas. This phenomenon is also reported for other agricultural areas. All 36 agricultural fields in the Buttes Reservoir area (Debowski and other 1976: 91) contained lithic scatters composed mostly of flakes, cores, hammerstones, choppers, and some knives and projectile points. Grinding and milling implements occurred on less than half of these sites; hearths were present on only nine sites. Cores, hammerstones, utilized flakes, "hoes," and other tools were found at Peppersauce Wash sites (Masse, in preparation; Masse 1974: 29). Masse (in preparation) has postulated that these objects represent an "agricultural field tool kit." Local raw material was used to manufacture tools for use in planting, clearing brush and weeds, and in harvesting.

At Arizona CC:2:40 fragments of a Tularosa Fillet Rim jar and a "Brown plainware" vessel were found within Locus 45. These were undoubtedly used for storage or collection. Dates for the Tularosa Fillet Rim jar are A.D. 1100-1300 (Appendix II). No hearths were found and neither did any sherds show evidence of being used as cooking vessels.

The chipped stone collection from Arizona CC:2:40 totaled 207 artifacts, consisting of 70 cores, 131 flakes, 4 unifaces, 2 bifaces, and 1 tabular knife. As is typical for sites in this stratum, basalt was the dominant material (43 percent), but a variety of other material was also used: rhyolite (20 percent), silicates (19 percent), quartzite (9 percent), obsidian (3 percent), and unidentified types (6 percent). As at other sites in this stratum, material types tended to be spread among artifact types, although reduction of basalt and rhyolite to produce tools appears to be a primary activity.

Uni-directional cores were the dominant core type (73 percent), while bi-directional cores constituted 19 percent, and multi-directional cores 9 percent. Flakes were evenly distributed as to stage of flake reduction. Twenty-five percent were primary flakes, 34 percent secondary flakes, 35 percent tertiary flakes, and 6 percent shatter. One aspect that stands out is that silicate flakes constitute 23 percent of the flake count, contrasted with a low percentage of silicate cores (6 percent of the core total). Additionally, the majority of silicate debitage consisted of small tertiary flakes. This could indicate tool finishing or resharpening, with a preference for siliceous materials. This is further borne out by the presence of four chert unifaces found at the site.

Four unifaces, one silicate biface, one obsidian biface, four utilized flakes, two utilized cores, and a tabular knife constitute the tool assemblage at this site, the largest collection of all sites in Stratum 2. Three flakes were utilized on lateral edges and one on the perimeter; three unifaces demonstrated use on lateral edges and one evidenced wear on the perimeter. The single tabular knife (Figure 41) was heavily striated along one used edge. The mean edge angle on utilized pieces was 62 degrees and light microflaking was present in the form of round and trapezoidal bifacial scars. These attributes taken together may indicate a range of activities probably associated with food gathering.

Summary

Essentially, the chipped stone assemblage does not differ significantly from the assemblages at Arizona CC:2:33 and CC:2:34, except that tool finishing and use are more readily apparent. A specific agricultural tool kit cannot be documented for this site, due to the smallness of the sample. The absence of ground stone argues against the hypothesis that plant processing was occurring on the site. However, the presence of two vessels is possible evidence that plants may have been gathered at the gridded gardens for processing elsewhere.

The Tularosa Fillet Rim jar sherds suggest a date between A.D. 1100-1300 and a cultural affiliation with the Point of Pines Mogollon tradition. The "Brown plainware" is comparable to the local plainwares observed on floodplain villages.

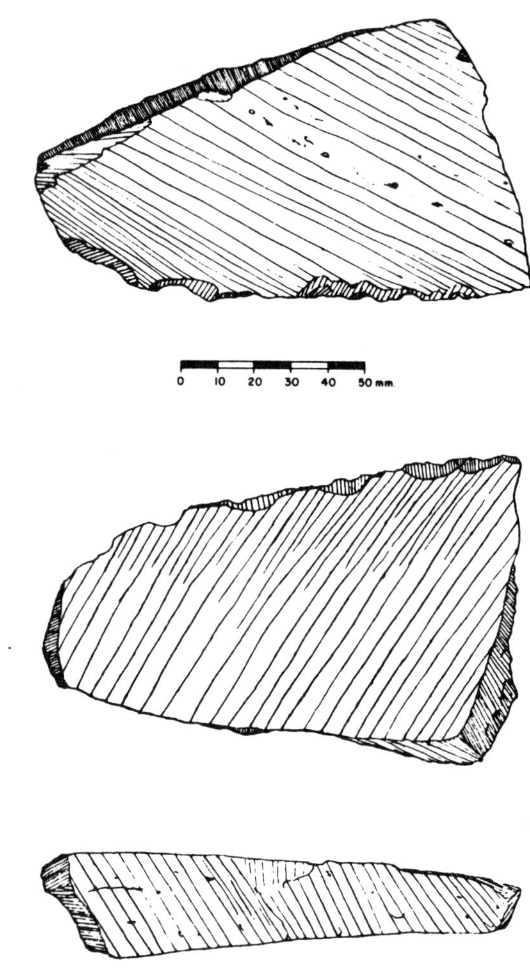

Figure 41. Arizona CC:2:40, tabular knife

CHAPTER 8

LITHIC SCATTERS AND LITHIC MANUFACTURING LOCI

by

Kay Simpson, E. Jane Rosenthal, Deborah A. Westfall, and J. L. Dickerson

Introduction

The majority of sites included in the data recovery program were locations within lithic "use areas" involving surface scatters of tools and debris but without obvious chronological or cultural indicators. Twenty-nine sites were initially selected through a judgmental sampling design formulated to select sites in areas of homogenous lithic use most likely to yield useful information. These sites were then stratified by environmental stratum.

As stated previously, it was hoped that analysis of tools and debitage at project sites would aid in identification of site activities and that these in turn could be correlated to regional settlement patterns and interactions. Analysis of lithic artifacts as to material, stage of manufacture, evidence of use, and function could aid in understanding site specialization, while analysis of technological tradition could be used to identify cultural affiliation.

Prior to describing data recovery procedures and analyzing material culture assemblages, some definition of procedures, terms, and problems is in order. Appendix I presents a tabulation and analysis of the relative frequencies of lithic artifacts present at each site and describes the methodology of the lithic analysis and computer program. The summaries of the material culture for each site in the following text are derived from these data and the reader is urged to refer to Appendix I for clarification and understanding of the terms employed.

One problem inherent in any research project, especially a linear transect, is that of bias. Since the material culture at the majority of investigated AEPCO sites was almost entirely chipped stone, it was logical to develop an analysis program oriented to understanding lithic industries and their relation to prehistoric resource exploitation. Since the AEPCO transmission line corridor transected several physiographic zones, and since time was limited, the lithic analysis was oriented primarily to understanding lithic technologies at the most general level for each physiographic stratum. Implicit in this orientation was the hypothesis that different strata would exhibit different lithic technologies. A corollary to this hypothesis was that different subsistence strategies among strata would be reflected in the lithic assemblages. Of course, also to be considered was the hypothesis that lithic technologies would be the same across physiographic strata. This approach created problems in determining intra-stratum variables, since the final computer analysis provided information of a very general nature. Time was not available to isolate discrete site-specific lithic attributes in order to more fully understand the function of individual sites within each stratum. Consequently, summaries of material culture and postulations as to site function that follow are somewhat generalized.

A problem that arose during site-specific functional analysis was the determination of tool function. There is no single methodology that is generally accepted; rather one must incorporate various aspects of several methodologies to arrive at a workable analysis. Studies of edge angle dimensions on utilized tools (Wilmsen 1970) and studies of use-wear patterns (Tringham and others 1974) were considered in the AEPCO lithic analysis. Neither of these analysis methods has been thoroughly tested; therefore, results must not be taken as conclusive. It is, however, an on-going concern of archaeology to continually test and evaluate such analytical models and the AEPCO lithic analysis addressed itself to this concern. Wilmsen (1970) postulates that different tasks can be inferred from different edge angle values. Thus, low edge angles may be related to cutting activities, and steep edge angles may indicate scraping activities. Correlative to these attributes are salient use-wear patterns that form on a working edge when the tool is applied to items of different textures and hardness. Jelinek (1976: 28) points out that the edge angle recorded by Wilmsen were taken on the "spine-plane angle" rather than on the actual utilized bit of an artifact. He remarks that

> In particular...the major flat surface of retouch was used to determine the angle when the actual bit of the tool had quite a different angle.

The argument here is whether a particular edge angle bears any correlation to overall flake size and shape. Wilmsen found none, but Jelinek suggests that there appears to be a possible correlation of steepness of edges and relative thickness with respect to length and width. Measurements on a spine-plane angle would seem to relate more to flake proportions (tool manufacture) than to function (use and discard). However, a problem with recording edge angles on utilized bits that the edge may no longer be functionally useful, and therefore, the dimension may not be a valid indication of use selectivity. Rather, the spine plane angle would appear to be the significant attribute of a flake selected for use. Although Wilmsen's study was the original impetus for conducting a use-wear analysis on the AEPCO tools, it was decided to test an observation made by Tringham and others (1974: 180) regarding microflaking on utilized edges:

> The micromorphology of the scarring...remains task specific and is not affected by changes in the spine-plane angle. In general, it may be said that an edge with a more acute spine-plane angle is likely to be much more heavily damaged than one with a more obtuse angle performing the same task.

Thus, following Tringham, the AEPCO lithic use-wear analysis emphasized recording of attributes such as microscar shape, degree of damage, and length of utilized edges (Appendix I). The microwear study conducted by Tringham and others is designed to identify the materials on which the tools were used. For example, scraping on bone produces a series of step fractures, while cutting meat produces a different series of microflake scars. The results of this study are provocative, but its results must be applied with caution to other lithic industries. For example, flint was used in these experiments and it is likely that different materials may yield different microflake shapes and patterns.

In summary, the AEPCO lithic use-wear analysis focused on determining attributes restricted to the utilized portion of an artifact. Edge angles were measured on the actual utilized bit and therefore cannot be evaluated using Wilmsen's criteria, although pertinent observations on varying angles were recorded. The small sample size and lack of time to conduct additional computer analyses did not enable us to carry the use-wear analysis to a final conclusion. Indeed, any conclusions on tool function should be accompanied by replication experiments in stone tool manufacture and use, since a great many variables affect the final appearance of a tool. These include type of material (coarse-textured vs. cryptocrystalline), length of use, intensity of use, and type of material worked. Since this was not done, the AEPCO lithic analysis can only record specific attributes for eventual comparative studies. For the present, the function of specific sites and tool assemblages of the AEPCO project can only be postulated.

In the text that follows, sites are described, data recovery procedures are outlined, and a general description and brief summary of each site's artifact collection is presented. The final section of this chapter summarizes the results of the inter-stratum lithic analysis. Research objectives, oriented to defining inter-stratum relationships or differences, are discussed. These are explored by comparing raw material types and tool and debitage types among sites. Finally, general conclusions are drawn regarding lithic technology in the project area.

Site Descriptions

Stratum 1: Gila River Floodplain

As noted previously, this stratum was eliminated from the sample since all recorded sites were avoided by AEPCO.

Stratum 2: San Simon River Valley

The San Simon River Valley stratum encompasses the lower geologic terraces south of the Gila River and the San Simon River floodplain. The San Simon cuts through the second youngest terrace system of the Safford area. These ground surfaces are probably of late Pleistocene or early Holocene age. For 32.2 km south of the Gila River the valley's ground surface is greatly dissected due to the lowering of the Gila River Valley during late geologic time (Schwennesen 1917; Gelderman 1970: 53; Fitting 1977: 7). The ground surface is now composed of barren, gravelly, or cobbley Tres Hermanos soils.

As has been stated in Chapter 2, the modern vegetative cover of the Safford area bears little resemblance to that of the past. The San Simon Valley system is one of the most heavily disturbed vegetation and channelling systems in southeastern Arizona. Hypotheses on prehistoric plant collection based on contemporary vegetation cover such as Goodyear 1975b would be inappropriate here. However, inferential statements concerning floral and faunal resources, based primarily on soils of the study area, are appropriate in that research is directed towards exploring an area's potential.

The stream channel has undergone severe erosion since 1905. Prior to that time the San Simon River was an insignificant and poorly defined stream bed. Around 1867 American cattlemen first grazed herds in the valley. The period 1870-1889 was one of the driest periods of comparable lengths since 1650. This lack of precipitation and extensive overgrazing seems to have contributed to the susceptibility of the alluvial valley to erosion during the major floods of 1905-1917 (Lapham and Neill 1904: 1050; Olmstead 1919: 79; Stockton and Fritts 1968: 20-21; Burkham 1972: 12-13).

Present day vegetation of the San Simon Valley is dominated by creosotebush; few other plants exist on the valley terraces. In the washes and on the terrace slopes cholla, acacia, mesquite, Santa Rita prickly pear, _Aplopappus_, snakeweed, and grasses occur. The "vast grasslands" present in the last century during seasons with adequate precipitation have been totally eradicated. Mesquite bosques are still present in the San Simon channel, but saltcedar is dominant.

Three sites in this environmental stratum were selected for further research: Arizona CC:2:33, 34, and 40, the gridded garden complex (Figure 40). The first two will be discussed in this section while the third was discussed in Chapter 7. The survey team observed that sites in this stratum differed from those in other strata in the following ways: there was less variety in raw material available on the ground surface, though stream cobbles were present in nearby channels; lithics were of a wide variety of material; ground stone and ceramics were occasionally present; and there were unusual stone alignments on one site, later assessed to be a gridded garden complex.

Arizona CC:2:33

Elevation: 935-939 m
Site Size: 170 m N/S by 35 m E/W
Field Designation: AEPCO 36 and 37

The centerline transected the ridge upon which the site is located at two points with a ridge saddle separating the two loci. When natural site boundaries were determined in the data recovery phase, the two loci (AEPCO 36 and 37) were combined as one site.

The site is located on a dissected ridgetop 0.6 km south-southwest of the San Simon channel, 2.4 km before the river enters the Gila River foodplain (Figure 46). A sparse vegetative cover of creosotebush, an invader species, is present. Ground surface is very stony with naturally fractured rock in abundance. The Pinaleño series soils are very susceptible to erosion and the plant community is subject to rapid deterioration wtih overuse (Gelderman 1970: 20).

Due to the unevenness of the ridgetop, the low density of material, and the compactness of the site, a standard grid collection was not made. All artifact and feature proveniences were pinpointed on the contour map (Figure 42). All observed cultural materials were collected within the natural boundary of the site.

Two cobble features were present. Feature 1, a cobble circle on the southeast side of the site was not tested. This circle, composed of ten haphazardly placed stones, was outside the site limits as defined by artifacts and may be a marker associated with a jeep trail south of the site. No ashes or cultural debris were observed within or around the stones. Feature 2, located on the north side of the site, consisted of a circle of large stones measuring 50 cm in diameter and was tested for deposition. Surface stones were removed and a 1 by 1 m test square was trowelled down to a depth of 10 cm. No artifacts were observed nor were ashes, bones, or pit outlines encountered.

Seventy-one chipped stone artifacts were recovered from this site. The assemblage consists of 28 cores, 39 flakes, and 4 bifaces. Rhyolite is the dominant material type represented in the assemblage (36.6 percent), but is closely followed by silicates (23.9 percent) and basalt (23.9 percent). Quartzite (5.6 percent) and other unidentified types (9.9 percent) constitute the remainder. This variety may be correlated with the availability of raw material in nearby drainages.

Uni-directional cores constitute the dominant core type (79 percent of the core total). Bi-directional cores are also present (18 percent), and one multi-directional core is present. Platform preparation is evident on 88 percent of the cores. There is no one-to-one correlation of a dominant core type to a favored material type; a variety of material was utilized for uni-directional cores.

Flakes constitute 55 percent of the total artifact collection. Of the total flake count primary flakes account for 38.4 percent, secondary flakes for 56.4 percent and tertiary flakes for 5.1 percent. Again, as with the cores, a variety of material is represented within the flake assemblage. The close core-to-flake ratio may indicate on-site reduction of cores for flake procurement. The high frequency of secondary flakes is suggestive of primary flake reduction and manufacture of flake tool blanks into preforms. Tool finishing and refurbishing was a minor occurrence, indicated by a low frequency of tertiary flakes.

The tool assemblage consists of two utilized flakes, two utilized cores, and four bifaces. The bifaces are all of rhyolite and may be knife or projectile point preforms. The utilized flakes are primary flakes, one showing use on the distal end, the other on a lateral edge. The mean edge angle on utilized pieces from the AEPCO 36 collection ranges from 64 to 68

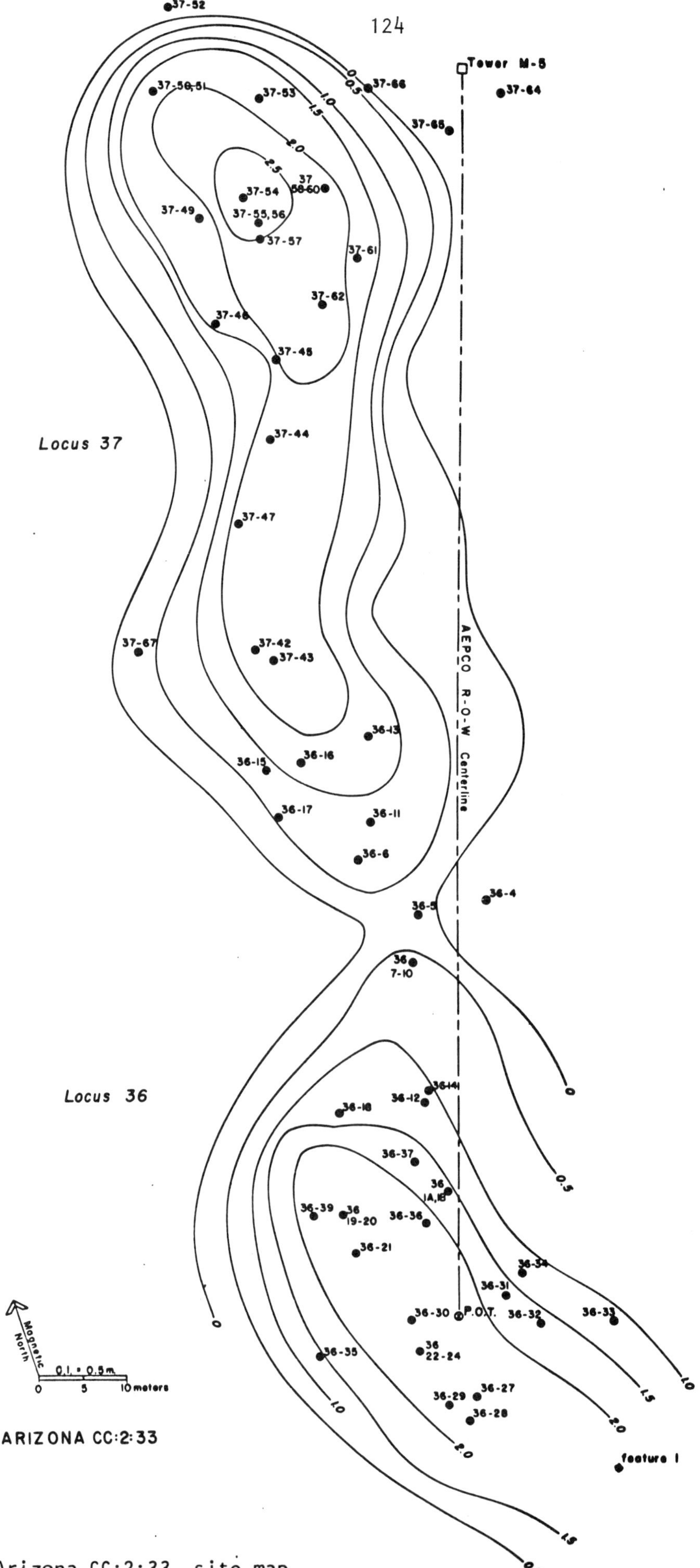

Figure 42. Arizona CC:2:33, site map

degrees with a mean of 65.7 degrees. A single utilized piece from AEPCO 37 has an edge angle of 81 degrees. These dimensions suggest that a fairly steep working edge was a constant attribute of tools used at this site. Another interpretation may be that these edge angle values are the wear angles of discarded tools, in which case, it is expected that they would be steep. Microflaking on one utilized flake appears as heavy scarring and may indicate intensive use. The occurrence of a lithic manufacturing sequence of core reduction, flake procurement, and subsequent use of flakes to accomplish tasks infers a possible complete tool kit was in use to produce tools for carrying out site activitis.

Two pieces of a basalt pestle-like tool were found. No grinding striations were evident, but the surface was polished. The function of this artifact is unknown.

Arizona CC:2:34

Elevation: 916 m
Site Size: 123 m NW/SE by 30 m NE/SW (concentration)
Field Designation: AEPCO 38

This site is located on the heavily silted open floodplain of the San Simon River. The present channel is 213 m to the north-northeast of the site. On-site vegetation includes mesquite bosques and desert saltbush, while Tamarisk lines the San Simon channel. The ground surface is quite flat, the only relief being the 60 to 90 cm high clumps of wind deposited sand at the base of the mesquite. Deep, nearly level, loamy Gila-Glendale soils occur; both are excellent irrigation crop soils.

The survey crew thought the natural boundaries of the site had been located, but during the data recovery phase it was discovered that the site continued eastward for at least 100 m. This continuation consisted of a very sparse scatter of cores and flakes without any observed concentrations.

Artifacts were pinpointed on the site map and then individually bagged and collected. As there was little appreciable contour relief on the floodplain, artifact locations are shown in relation to the bosques in Figure 43. Gully banks and mesquite bosque humps were checked to see if artifacts were eroding out of buried surfaces, but artifacts were found only on the surface; none was even partially buried (Figure 44).

Five test pits were opened to check for deposition. Test Pit 1 was opened where several slab metates were found; Test Pit 2 was near the only sherd found on the site; Test Pit 3 was on a mesquite bosque and was dug to check for buried surfaces; Test Pit 4 was near an artifact concentration; and Test Pit 5 was picked at random in an area without surface artifacts. The soil in all test units consisted entirely of alluvium; no artifacts or cultural layers were encountered.

Forty-five artifacts were collected from the site. The collection is evenly divided between 23 cores and 22 flakes. The site is singular in that no silicate artifacts were found. Basalt was the dominant utilized material (60 percent), followed by rhyolite (9 percent), quartz (4.4 percent), obsidian (4.4 percent), and unidentified types comprising the remaining 22.2 percent.

Several core types are present. Uni-directional cores predominate at 70 percent, bi-directional cores constitute 26 percent of the assemblage, and multi-directional cores comprise the remaining 4 percent. A dominance of basalt flakes (45 percent) correlates with a dominance of basalt cores (75 percent). The stage of manufacture of flakes is fairly evenly distributed among 31.8 percent primary flakes, 22.7 percent secondary flakes, 31.8 percent shatter. Clearly, primary core reduction and possible tool production from basalt is indicated as a dominant lithic industry. No formal chipped stone tools were found. Two cores exhibit utilization but it cannot be ascertained if core reduction was carried out for the purpose of creating core tools.

Two items of ground stone were collected at the site. One is a complete rectangular grinding slab that was unifacially ground in the center; a rotary motion is indicated. The second item is a fragment of a small andesite grinding slab. It is uncertain if the ground stone and chipped stone are contemporaneous, but if they are they may be the remains of a small wild food processing kit.

One bowl body sherd was found in isolated context. It is shown in Figure 43 as 38-17 and apparently washed in from upstream. The sherd was classified as an unidentified smudged plainware of unknown cultural affiliation.

Stratum 3: Gila River Pleistocene Terraces and Lower Bajada of Gila Mountains

Sites occur on the high terraces north of the Gila River and south of the Gila Mountains. The terraces are dissected and drained by washes flowing into the Gila River. Big Canyon and Head Canyon, the major drainages in the stratum, are deep canyons with steep side slopes. The ascent from the Gila River bottomland to the Hackberry substation crosses three geologic terraces.

Creosotebush is the dominant floral species with wolfberry, whitethorn and catclaw acacia, cacti, and Mormon tea also occurring. On the upper terraces wolfberry and paloverde are more common than creosotebush. Annual grasses and weeds grow after rainy periods.

Eight archaeolgoical sites were found in this stratum. All but one are lithic scatters, the exception being a pit house village, Arizona CC:2:30, located on the southern rim of the first terrace (Chapter 6). The three sites chosen for further investigation presented an interesting set of problems: they are all low density, widely dispersed lithic scatters associated with or located near a natural catchment basin; notable is the number of cores and core and pebble tools relative to the number of flakes.

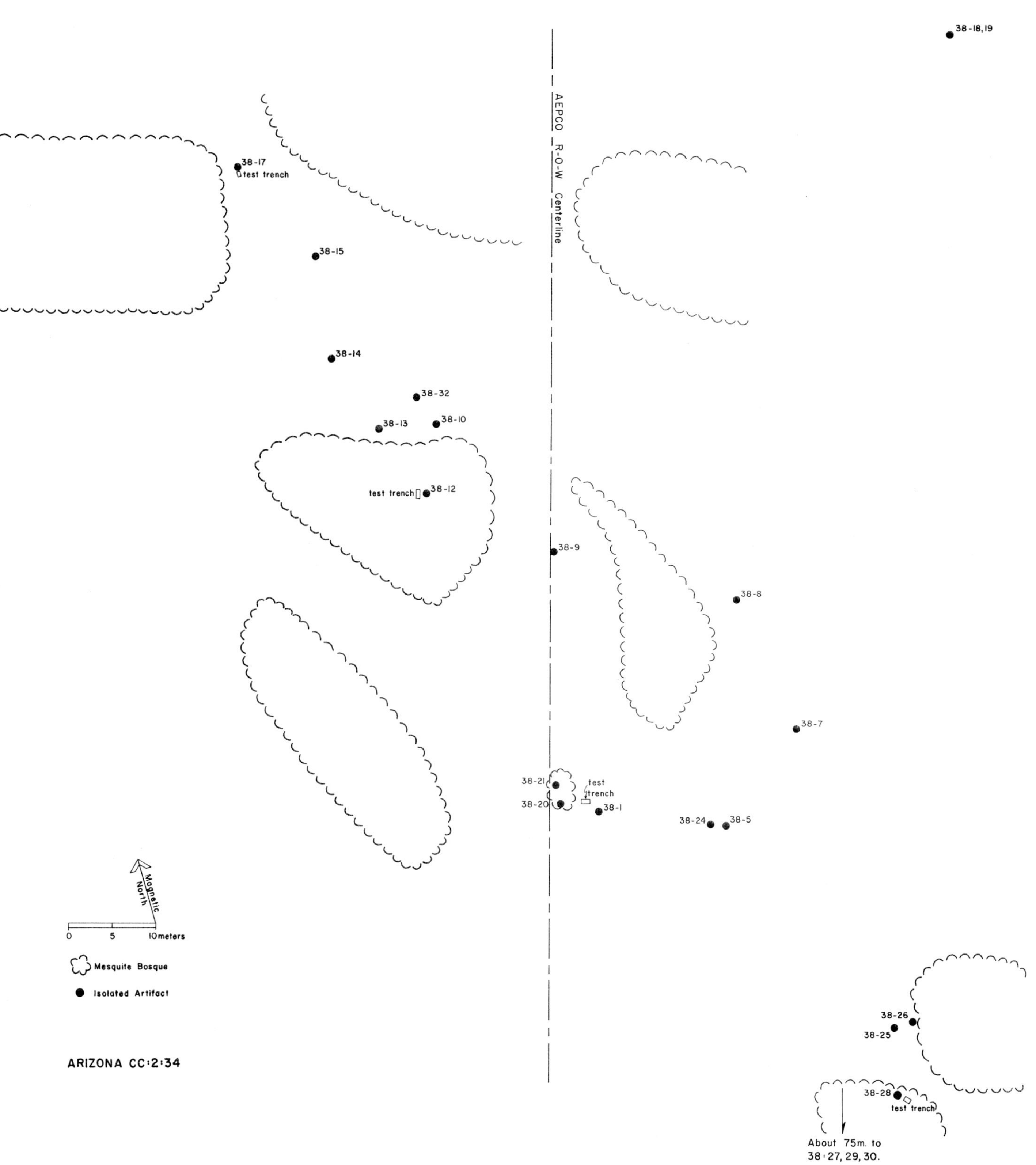

Figure 43. Arizona CC:2:34, site map

Figure 44. Arizona CC:2:34, San Simon River Channel.

Figure 45. Arizona CC:2:40, Locus 43.

Figure 46. Arizona CC:2:33, looking north towards San Simon Channel.

Figure 47. Arizona CC:2:44, showing creosotebush ring.

Figure 48. Arizona CC:2:46, Feature 2, rock pile.

Figure 49. Arizona CC:2:46, creosotebush ring.

Figure 50. Arizona CC:2:43, general overview.

The land surface is of primary interest to an understanding of the sites. These catchment basins were originally assessed as possible playas or alkali flats. Larry Humphries of the Safford District BLM soil sciences staff has identified these catchment basins as remnant tobosa grasslands. He surmised that the basins were probably once a marshy area though they were never lakes. The basins' soils (Artesia series) contain sodium calcinate and exhibit slow permeability; therefore, they tend to pond water. The atea is now overgrazed and most of the tobosa is gone, replaced by creosotebush. The area is believed to have once been a grassland where water collected in the rainy season and where small mammals, especially rodents, were probably plentiful.

On the rim edges Tres Hermanos series soils are present. These soils have quite variable characteristics depending upon slope and water availability. Creosote, the dominant vegetation, is an indicator of overgrazing. Climax potential vegetation consists of 55 percent tobosa grass, burrograss, three-awn, and broom snakeweed and 45 percent black gramma, blue gramma, alkali sacaton, and bush mulhey (Cox 1973: 54).

Tres Hermanos and Artesia soils formedin old alluvium from igneous rocks and are thus quite alkaline. They are unlikely to produce economic plants, now or in the recent past. However, both have high potential for wildlife providing excellent habitats for antelope and good to fair habitats for pheasant, dove, and quail. They are poor habitats for other game species such as deer, duck, or turkey (Cox 1973: 60).

Arizona CC:2:43

Elevation: 971 m
Site Size: 130 m NW/SE by 290 m NE/SW
Field Designation: AEPCO 49

The site is located on the rim of the lower bajada on the oldest geologic terrace system of the Gila Mountains, overlooking Big Canyon to the south. The site surface is very gravelly, in some places consisting of a desert pavement (Figure 50). Vegetation includes creosotebush and hedgehog cactus; Tres Hermanos soils are present.

The site maps (Figures 51 and 52) show both an "original" and a "re-alignment" R-O-W transecting the site. When AEPCO re-aligned the centerline in order to avoid Arizona CC:2:32, the new centerline transected the site on its northern and western boundaries (Figure 53). Initially 30 m southeast-northwest by 90 m northeast-southwest was laid along the re-alignment centerline sectioned into 5 m^2 plots and every other grid square was surface collected. Eighteen isolated artifact locations were also collected. However, it was discovered that this area of the site yielded an insufficient artifact sample. Two more grid square columns, one 25 m east-west by 80 m north-south on the original R-O-W, and one 15 m north-south by 80 m east-west along the rim edge lateral to the two R-O-W corridors where an artifact concentration was located, were laid out and every 5 m^2 grids were collected for a total of 4425 m^2 investigated. This is approximately 13 percent of the total site. Forty-four percent of all squares investigated yielded artifacts.

A rock pile on the rim edge was the only feature on the site. No chipping stations were observed.

Collections from this site yielded 214 chipped stone artifacts: 29 cores, 182 flakes and pieces of shatter, and 3 unifaces. Materials represented in the lithic industry were fairly evenly divided among basalt (33.7 percent), rhyolite (29 percent), and silicates (25.7 percent), with quartzite, obsidian, and unidentified types constituting the remainder. Co-occurring with the even distribution of basalt, rhyolite, and silicates was a nearly one-to-one correlation of cores to flakes. The abundance of basalt and rhyolite may be attributed to their occurrence in the immediate vicinity of the site.

Uni-directional cores are the dominant core type, comprising 62 percent of the core total, with bi-directional cores representing 21 percent and multi-directional cores 17 percent.

Of the total 182 flakes, primary flakes comprise only 10.4 percent, secondary flakes 29.1 percent, tertiary flakes 42.3 percent, and shatter 18.1 percent. The low core to flake ratio (1:6), low primary flake count, and dominance of secondary and tertiary flakes suggest that core reduction was not a primary activity; rather the lithic industry appears to emphasize on-site flake reduction into preforms or tools. That tool re-sharpening also may have taken place is borne out by the dominance of tertiary flakes in the flake total.

The tool assemblage is comprised of three unifaces (two of silicate, one of rhyolite), one utilized flake, and five utilized cores. Two of the unifaces exhibited wear on lateral edges, the third was used on the distal end. The single flake was utilized on a lateral edge. Data are not available to determine the function of the utilized cores. Edge angles on utilized pieces ranged from 50 to 81 degrees, with a mean of 64 degrees. Microflaking was present as round and trapezoidal bifacial scars. These dimensions suggest a relatively steep working edge was favored for scraping activities, with more use of formal tools rather than flakes for carrying out tasks such as woodworking or preparing fiber.

Arizona CC:2:44

Elevation: 971-975 m
Site Size: 650 m (along the R-O-W) by 60 m (arbitrary boundary)
Field Designation: AEPCO 50

The site is located on the lower bajada of the Gila Mountains, 2 km north of the Gila River. It is in a catchment basin ringed by creosotebush (Figure 47) and is almost devoid of surface vegetation except for a tobosa grassland remnant. This latter area is a slight rise with thick grass, wolfberry, and prickly pear cactus. No creosotebush is present. Many deep cattle hoofprints on the rise indicated it was quite boggy after a rain. The basin showed no other evidence of water entrapment. Artesia series soils are present.

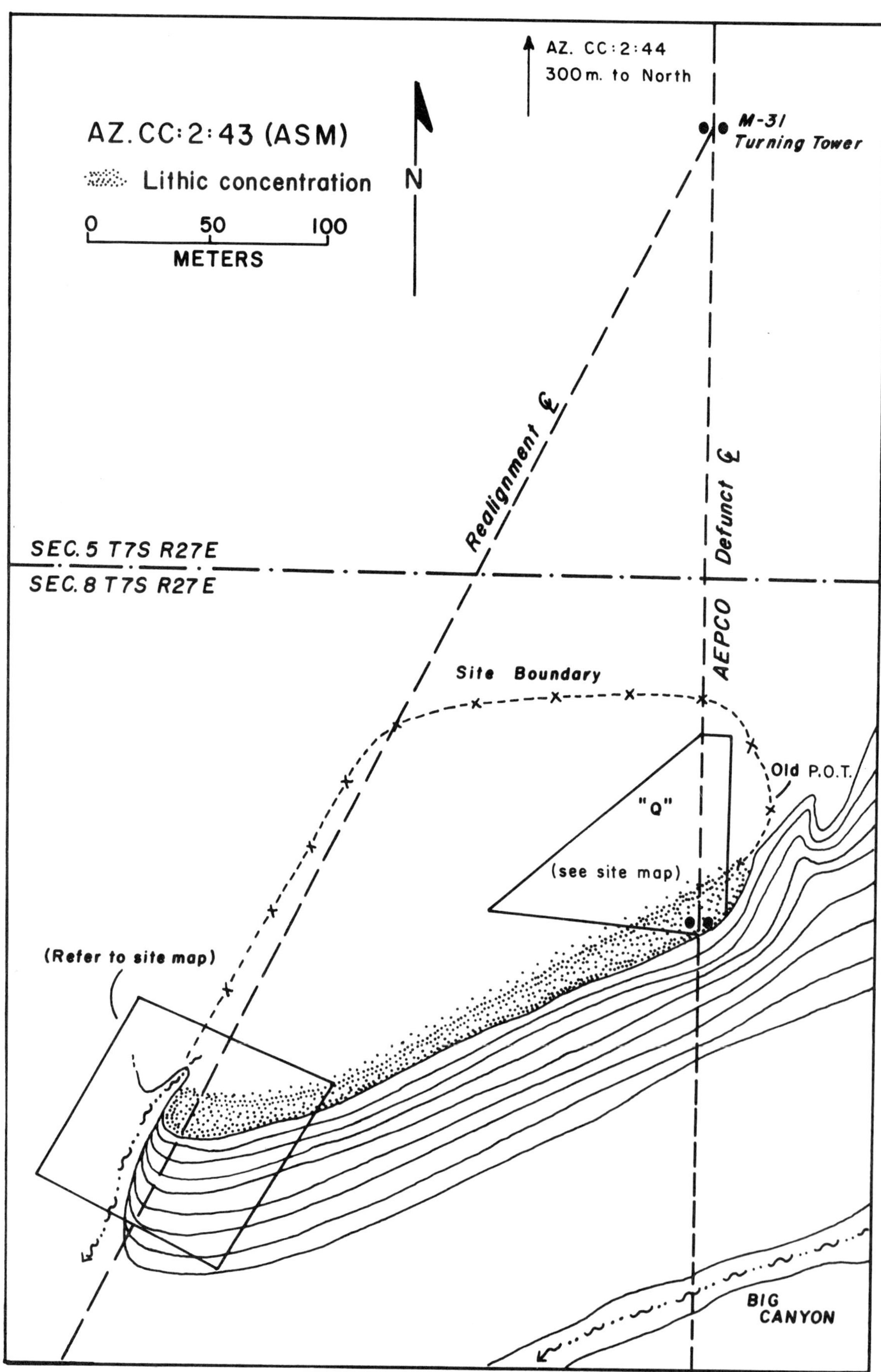

Figure 51. Arizona CC:2:43, Re-alignment centerline

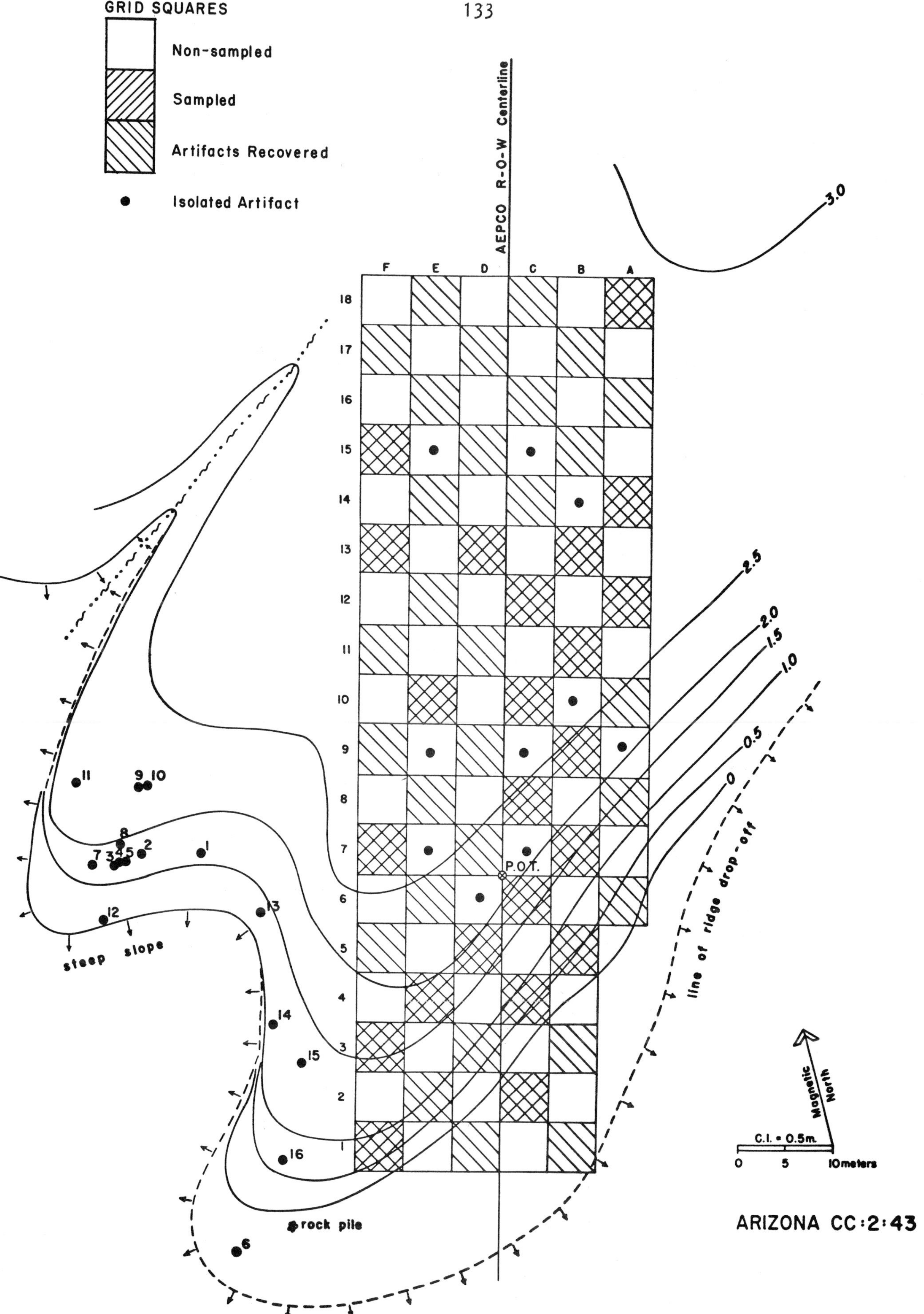

Figure 52. Arizona CC:2:43, Original centerline

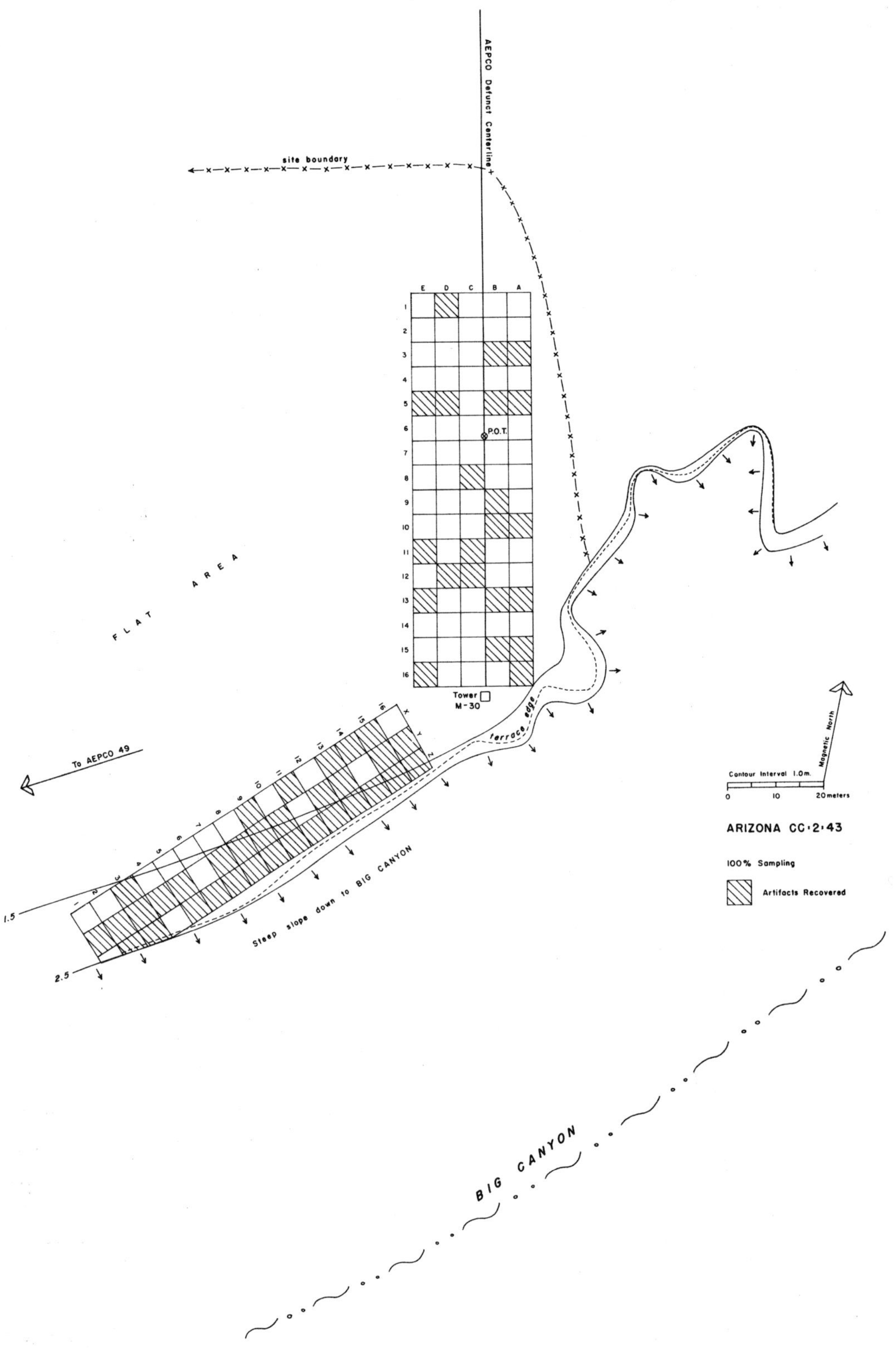

Figure 53. Arizona CC:2:43, overview map.

The site extends far outside the R-O-W and natural boundaries are diffuse, but appear to be defined by the limits of the catchment basin now ringed by creosotebush (Figure 54). Crew members reported a continuous but sparse lithic scatter across the basin; along the R-O-W artifacts noted were at infrequent intervals. Only in the grassland remnant was there an artifact concentration. A 60 m east-west by 135 m north-south column composed of 5 m^2 grids was laid over this concentration, and a 100 percent collection was taken. Thirty-two percent of the squares had artifacts (Figure 55). In addition, a 150 m by 30 m area was gridded in 30 m by 15 m plots and collected (Figure 54).

Water seems to have drained into the basin, silting it in. Artifacts were found directly on this surface; none was even partially buried in the silt. However, to check for subsurface materials, two 1 m^2 test pits were excavated within the artifact concentration. Topsoil consisted of loamy sand and the subsoil was loose and silty with few small stones. At 15 cm below datum a clay substrate was reached. No artifacts were encountered in the test excavations.

No features such as chipping stations, rock piles, or cobble clusters were observed.

Two hundred and twenty-three chipped stone artifacts were collected from this site. These consist of 78 cores, 142 flakes and shatter, and 3 unifaces. Igneous stone was the dominant material represented in the assemblage, with rhyolite comprising 39.4 percent, and basalt 35 percent. Silicates constituted 19.3 percent, with quartzite, obsidian, and unidentified types contributing less than 5 percent each.

Uni-directional cores comprise 79 percent of the cores present while bi-directional cores make up the remaining 21 percent. Platform preparation is evident on 77 percent of all cores. These factors, uni-directionality and platform preparation predominance, indicate standardized techniques prevailed in producing flakes from cores, particularly on basalt and rhyolite, with silicates and quartzite being reduced to a lesser extent. Flakes and shatter dominate the assemblage, constituting 64 percent of all chipped stone. Of the total number, 14.7 percent are primary flakes, 52.8 percent secondary flakes, 23.9 percent tertiary flakes and 8.4 percent shatter. While the high frequency of cores at the site suggests core reduction was a main component of the lithic industry, the comparatively low frequency of primary flakes does not support this assumption. Data are not available to determine the extent of core reduction or to determine the proportion of primary flake removal from cores. However, it may be inferred from the high ratio of secondary and tertiary flakes and shatter that the primary flakes were being reduced to form blanks and tools. Tool resharpening was also a probable activity. Cores may also have been reused as tools, but time did not permit a use study on cores.

Although the tool population is small (17), it is weighted in favor of utilized flakes and cores (77 percent) over formal tools (23 percent). The tool class includes four utilized flakes, six utilized uni-directional

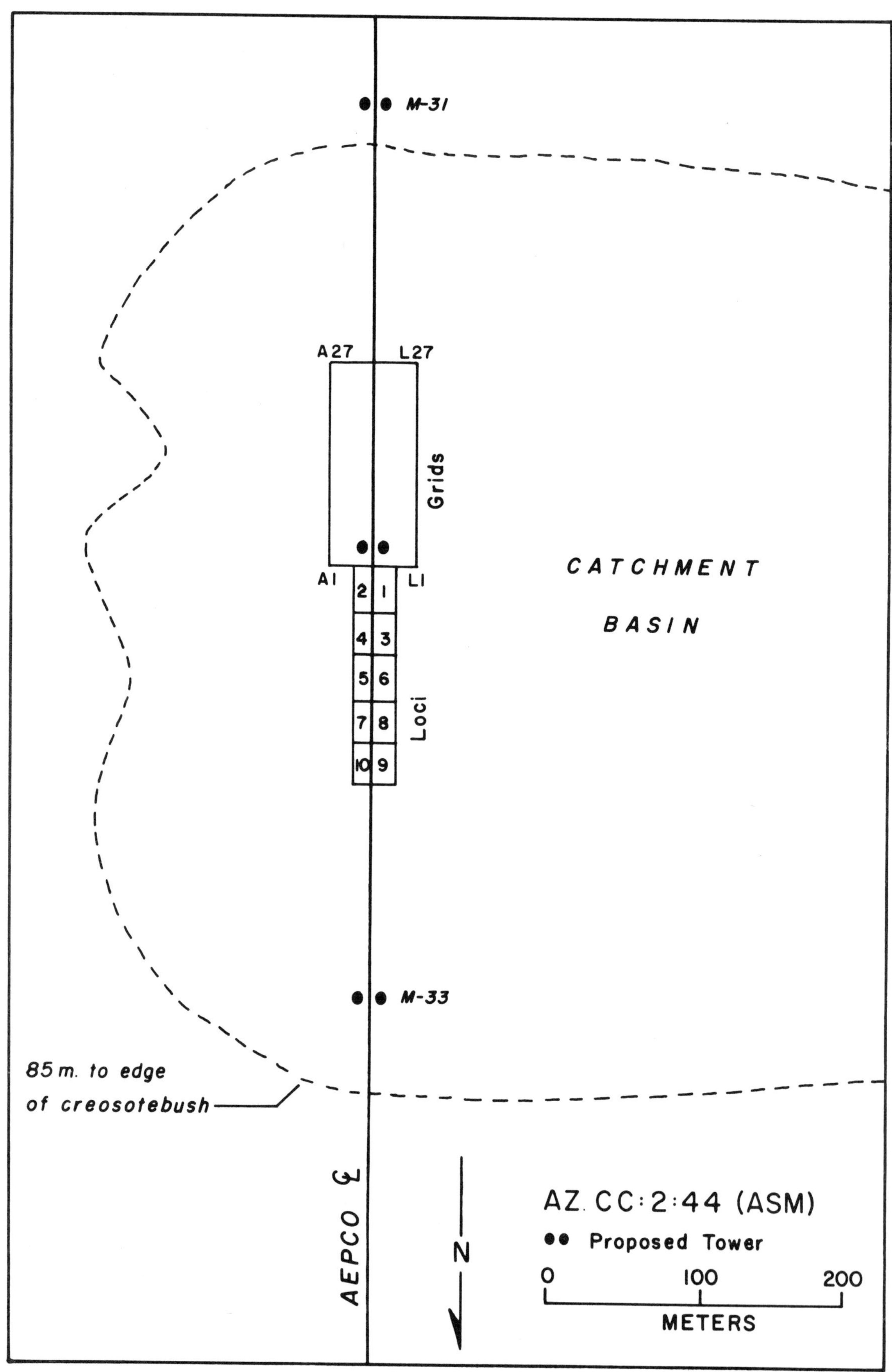

Figure 54. Arizona CC:2:44, overview map

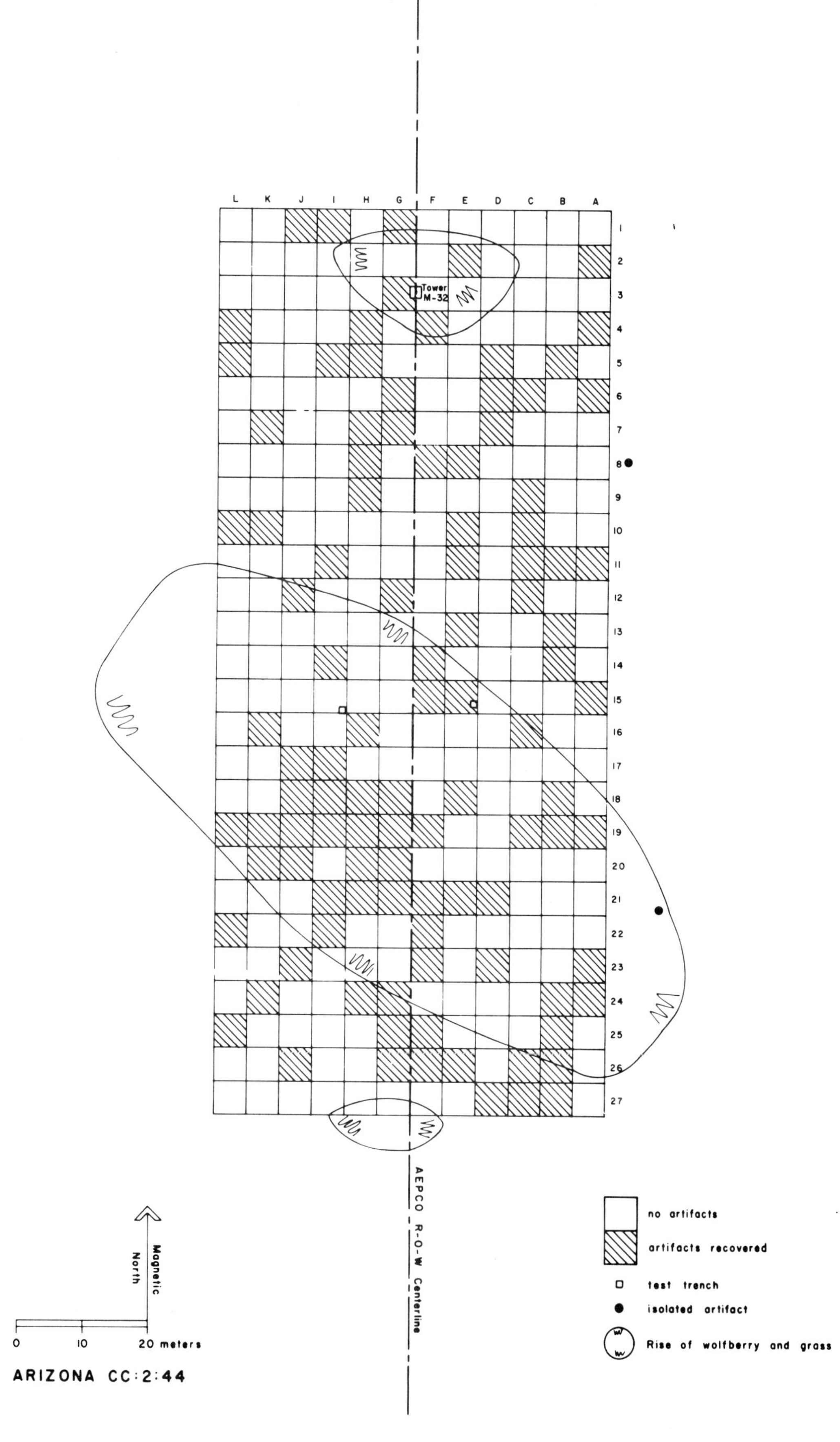

Figure 55. Arizona CC:2:44, site map.

cores, and three unifaces. Interestingly, the utilized flakes and cores are rhyolite and basalt, while of the three unifaces two are silicate and the third is obsidian. This suggests that fine-grained material was preferred for manufacturing formal tools, while unmodified flakes of the coarser textured rhyolite and basalt sufficed for expedient use, or that core manufacture was independent of biface production, or even non-contemporaneous. Two flakes exhibited wear on lateral edges, one on the distal end; two unifaces likewise were used on lateral edges and one on the distal end. Edge angles on utilized pieces rang from 29 to 77 degrees, with a mean of 58.9 degrees. This variability range in steepness may indicate a concomitant range of tasks, possibly involving cutting and scraping.

Arizona CC:2:46

<u>Elevation</u>: 1017-1023 m
<u>Site Size</u>: 1225 m (along the R-O-W) by 60 m (arbitrary boundary)
<u>Field Designation</u>: AEPCO 52

This site is also located in a catchment basin on the lower bajada of the Gila Mountains, 4.8 km north of the Gila River. Big Canyon is 0.72 km east. The basin is ringed by creosotebush but lacks vegetation itself (Figure 49). The south end of the site at the terrace edge has gravelly soil and is dominated by creosotebush; the north end of the site also extends into the creosotebush, but has heavy sheetwash deposition. The basin has Artesia series soils; the rim edge, Tres Hermanos soils.

As cultural materials appeared to be more concentrated at the south end of the site, 5 m^2 grid squares were laid on that rim edge (Figure 56) and a 100 percent collection was made. Feature 4, a remnant of a basalt chipping station, was collected as a unit. The station consisted of eight secondary flakes and two primary flakes. Several rock piles (Figure 48) were present, all of which were very amorphous and haphazardly arranged. All were photographed and one, Feature 1, was tested. A test pit was also excavated near Feature 1 in an artifact concentration. Both 1 m^2 test pits were excavated to a depth of 15 cm; neither pit nor layer outlines nor subsurface cultural material was discerned. Stratigraphy was identical in both; underlying the desert pavement the soil was very gravelly without any stains or evidence of cultural materials or activities. The dimensions for all rock piles in the southern concentration were:

Feature 1: 0.66 m E/W by 0.74 m N/S
Feature 2: 2.00 m E/W by 2.10 m N/S
Feature 3: 1.70 m E/W by 1.40 m N/S
Feature 5: 1.95 m E/W by 0.70 m N/S
Feature 6: 1.40 m E/W by 1.70 m N/S
Feature 7: 1.40 m E/W by 2.00 m N/S
Feature 8: 1.20 m E/W by 1.50 m N/S

Feature 4 is a chipping station near the terrace edge, and could possibly be associated with the rock piles.

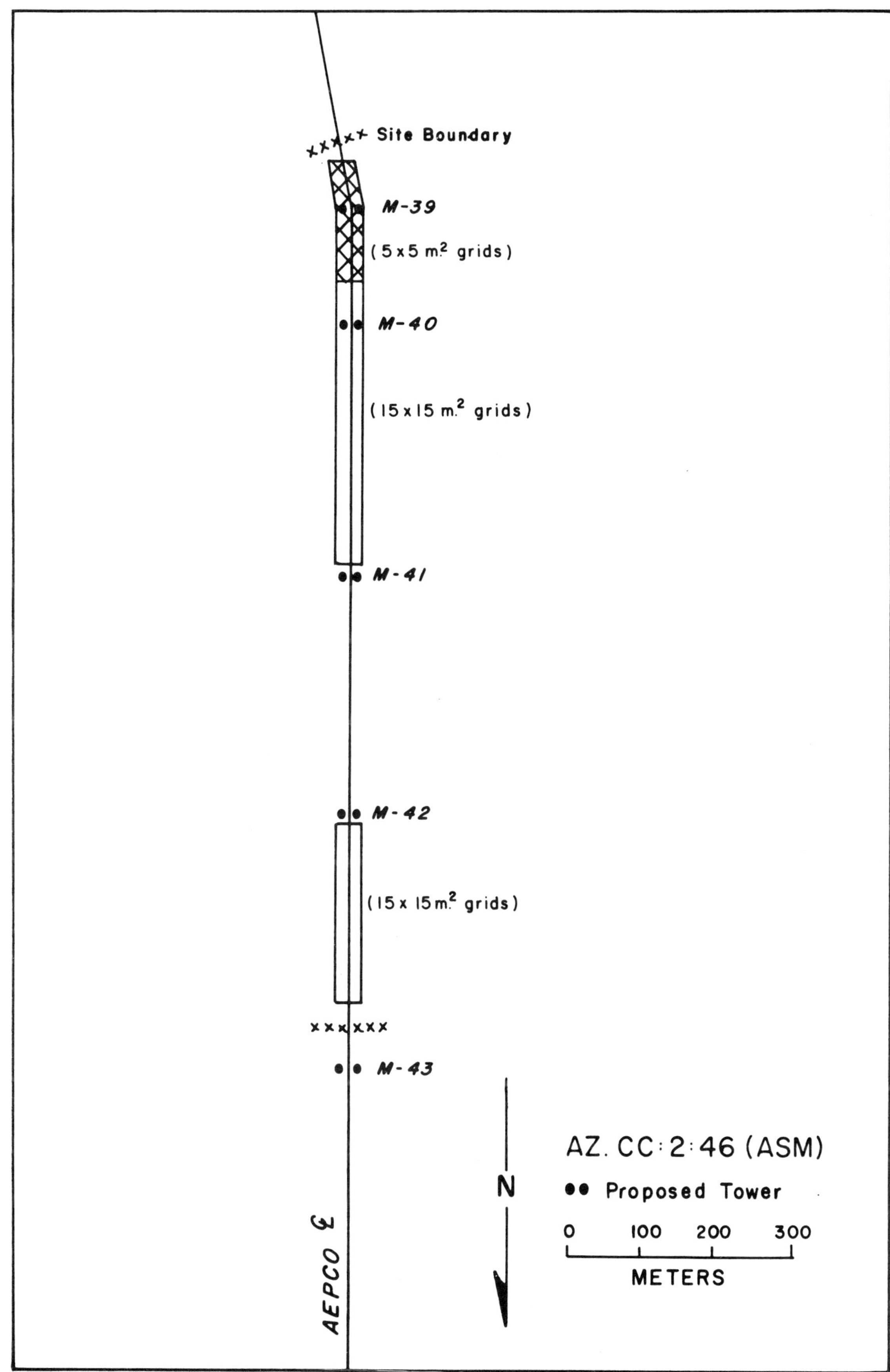

Figure 56. Arizona CC:2:46, site map

For the interior basin 15 m^2 were laid out along the R-O-W (Figure 57). Artifacts were few but clearly visible. Because of the length of the site and evidence of heavy sheet wash erosion in places, pinpoint location of the artifacts was not considered feasible.

Only one feature, Feature 9, was found in the interior basin. It is a rock pile 0.90 m east-west by 1.50 m north-south. The east half of the feature was tested, and no cultural materials were found on or beneath the surface. Fill consisted of aeolian deposition with little gravels. Some stones were buried indicating the pile was not too recent. A caliche hardpan was reached at 30 cm beneath datum level.

In total, 1745 m^2 grid squares and 7615 m^2 grid squares were investigated for a total sampled area of 21,450 m^2. Sixty-nine percent of the site on the R-O-W was investigated. Natural east-west boundaries of the site were not determined.

Collections from this site yielded 30 cores, 214 flakes and shatter, and 12 unifaces, for a combined total of 256 chipped stone artifacts. Analysis of manufacture stage and material type suggests two lithic industries may be present, one focusing on igneous primary core reduction, the other on silicate tool manufacture and use.

Unlike the other two sites in this stratum, silicates predominate in gross material count with 43.8 percent, but are closely followed by basalt (33.6 percent). Rhyolite constitutes only 12.1 percent of the material types, with quartzite and unidentified types contributing 5 percent each.

Following the norm in this stratum, uni-directional cores comprise 73 percent of the core total, with bi-directional cores making up 17 percent and multi-directional cores 10 percent. Platform preparation was evident on 90 percent of the cores, again indicating standardized techniques. Co-occurring with the dominance of uni-directional cores was a dominance of igneous over silicate cores. Basalt and rhyolite combined constitute 84 percent of uni-directional cores and 77 percent of the core total. Silicates make up only 17 percent of the core total. However, silicates lead in the flake category with 45 percent; basalt flakes comprise 34 percent, rhyolite 9 percent, quartzite 5 percent and unidentified types 7 percent. Analysis of debitage yielded a breakdown of 17 percent primary flakes, 36 percent secondary flakes, 30 percent tertiary flakes, and 35 percent shatter.

The tool assemblage, numbering 27 items, is fairly evenly divided between utilized flakes and cores and formal tools. More formal tools were present at this site that at either of the other two sites sampled in this stratum (12 unifaces compared to 5 for Arizona CC:2:43 and 3 for Arizona CC:2:44). The total tool sample consists of 13 utlized flakes, 2 utilized cores, and 12 unifaces. Twelve of the utilized flakes exhibited use on lateral edges, one on the distal end. Nine out of 12 unifaces were used and demonstrated more variation: 4 were utilized on lateral edges, 1 on the perimeter, 3 on the distal end, and 1 on the proximal end. Edge angles on utilized pieces ranged from a minimum of 35 degrees to a maximum of 83 degrees, giving a mean of 49.7 degrees. This wide variance in edge

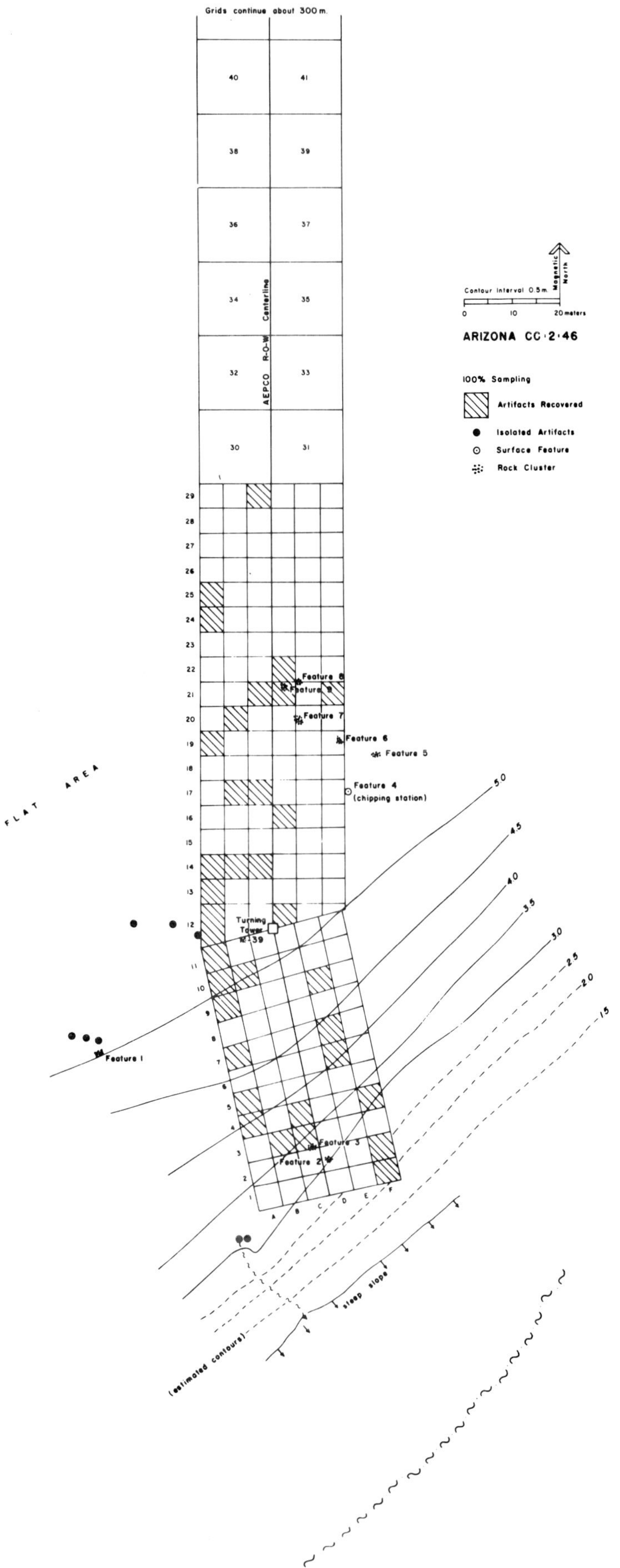

Figure 57. Arizona CC:2:46, overview map.

angle values and more acute mean edge angle sets this site apart from the other two sites in the stratum, and is one of the lowest values for the project area.

Heavy microflaking on utilized pieces occurred in the form of round bifacial scars. While data are lacking on utilization on specific morphological pieces, a general breakdown is as follows. Utilized pieces of chert comprised 75 percent of the total number of utilized items, with quartzite, rhyolite, and basalt contributing 8 percent each. It may be assumed that selection of silicates for tool manufacture (both formalized types and for expedient use) is a prevalent pattern at this site. The range in variation on edge angles may be taken to indicate a concomitant variable range of tool use.

In summary the co-occurrence of small silicate flake selection and acuteness of the mean edge angle suggest fine cutting tools were being manufactured. It may be postulated that butchering and cutting activities prevailed here at one time.

Stratum 4: Upper Bajada of Gila Mountains

This stratum includes the gently rolling uplands of the second oldest geologic terrace of the Gila Valley. The zone has major southwestward flowing washes which break up the otherwise level topography.

The Limpia series clayey loam soils were formed in gravelly, stony, and clayey outwash materials of the sloping fans and terraces of the igneous Gila Mountains. The cobbly soils have few economic uses. There is a moderate cover of grasses such as grama, bluestem, three-awn, and muhley with a few woody plants such as creosotebush, wolfberry, and ocotillo (Figure 59). Paloverde and mesquite grow along the drainages. The stratum's potential for wildlife is fair for rangeland species.

Figure 58. Arizona CC:2:58, overview.

Figure 59. Typical vegetation cover, Stratum 4.

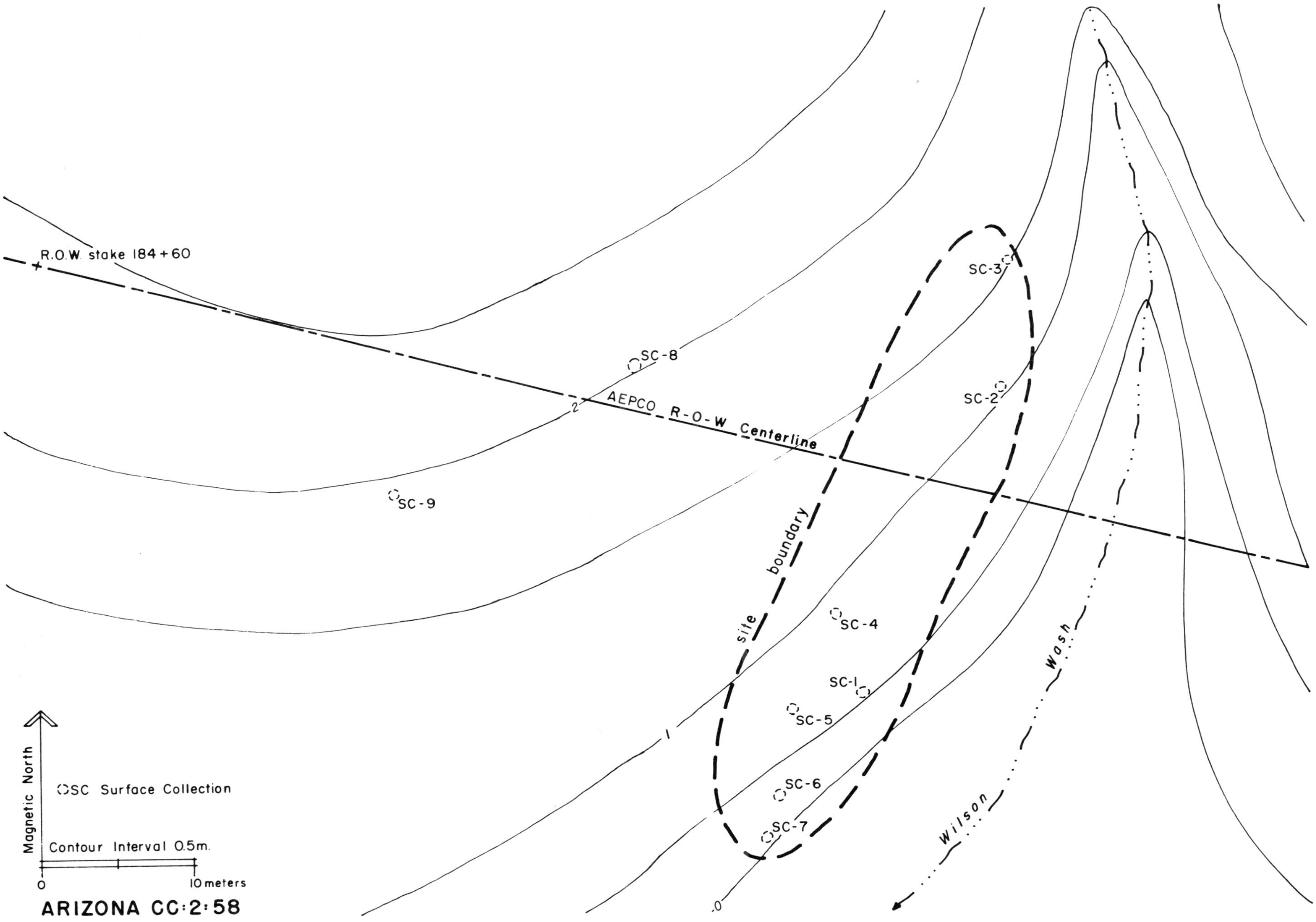

Figure 60. Arizona CC:2:58, site map.

Only two sites were found within the R-O-W corridor transecting this stratum and few isolated artifacts were observed. Both sites were limited activity lithic scatters situated next to a major wash. One site was chosen for mitigation.

Arizona CC:2:58

Elevation: 1082 m
Site Size: 62 m N/S by 15 m E/W
Field Designation: AEPCO 76

The site is a sparse lithic scatter on the west side of a small shallow drainage that flows into the Gila River 6 km to the southwest (Figure 58). Surface topography is a gently southward-sloping bajada, covered with a loose pavement of igneous cobbles, pebbles, and colluvial scree. On-site vegetation includes creosotebush, acacia, *Ephedra*, ocotillo, snakeweed, *Aploppapus*, and, in the drainage, mesquite.

Due to the small size and sparse artifact assemblage, 100 percent data recovery was implemented at this site. A detailed site contour map (Figure 60) was made, and the locations of each artifact pinpointed prior to collection. Twenty-five chipped stone artifacts were collected, all were later identified as debitage; they consisted of two uni-directional unprepared cores and 23 flakes. As was evident from initial survey observations, the majority of material was comprised of rhyolite (56 percent) and basalt (28 percent). Silicates constituted the remaining 16 percent and this material consisted solely of flakes. Because the small size of the artifact collection fell short of the minimum number necessary for statistical analysis, this site was not included in the inter-stratum lithic analysis. However, utilization of available lithic resources (rhyolite and basalt) for tool manufacture is indicated as one activity in this environmental zone.

Stratum 5: Peloncillo Mountain Foothills

These foothills consist of steep, deeply dissected old terrace fronts adjacent to the Gila River Floodplain and of ridges adjacent to the steep basaltic hills and low mountains of the Peloncillo Mountain range (Figures 61-64). Wide, fan-shaped pediments slope gently away from the axial portion of the range. The range is a region of volcanic rock consisting of low hills, generally higher on the west and sloping gently to the east. The eastern surface is characterized by a dendritic drainage pattern and low rounded hills that merge imperceptibly into the pediments. Both mountains and foothills are very dissected, and hundreds of unnamed washes flow southwesterly into the Gila River. The foothills do not have the steep canyons typical of the Peloncillo Mountains (Quaide 1951: 4-5).

The Peloncillo foothills sites have Graham, Tres Hermanos, Pinaleño, Peloncillo, and Limpia soils on ridge tops and Arizo soils in washes; all are poor, shallow, limey soils. These are cobbly or gravelly sandy clay loams which have developed in old alluvium from volcanic sources. Their only present economic use is as rangeland, but they rate no better than fair for livestock, even when in excellent condition. The original plant

Figure 61. Arizona CC:3:26, view of dissected ridges of Peloncillo Mountains.

Figure 62. Typical vegetation cover in Stratum 5.

Figure 63. View of Arizona CC:3:44 from Arizona CC:2:28.

Figure 64. Arizona CC:3:26, overview.

community rapidly deteriorates with overuse. Creosotebush has increased to the detriment of perennial plants palatable to cattle. The vegetation landscape has certainly changed considerably from prehistoric times. In the washes vegetation consists of sparse mesquite stands, whitethorn and catclaw acacia, creosotebush, and annual grasses.

The ridge crests provide little cover for wildlife; adjacent washes are the preferred habitat. Most animal species found are transient between the washes. Present species include snakes, horned toad, rabbit, various rodents, Gambel's quail, and coyote.

Twenty-five sites, all low to moderate density lithic scatters or lithic manufacturing loci, were found in this stratum; ten were investigated. Notable was the number of chipping stations found either within sites or in isolation. Lithics were relatively heterogeneous consisting of cores, cortical flakes, unifaces, a few bifaces and utilized flakes, mostly of basalt, rhyolite, and silicates with some quartzite and obsidian. The ground surface at the sites consisted of desert pavement with workable parent material in abundance. As sites were found on almost every ridge crest in the R-O-W corridor, with many isolated artifacts in between, the entire foothills area appears to have been a lithic use area heavily exploited in the past.

Arizona CC:2:51

Elevation: 944-952 m
Site Size: 140 m N/S by 390 m E/W
Field Designation: AEPCO 58

The site is located on the first major landform above the Gila River floodplain; it is on a Pleistocene terrace situated at the base of a system of east-west trending ridges. At the easternmost edge, the terrace drops down sharply into a large sandy wash that opens out into the Gila River,

0.8 km to the north. The Gila Mountains, across the river, are 3.2 km away. On-site vegetation varies considerably in relation to landform. The easternmost one-third of the site area is a cobblestrewn, disturbed, flat area supporting a sparse cover of creosotebush, acacia, and prickly pear. Westward from this section, the surface slopes down into an alluvial flat, composed of unconsolidated sandy loam intermixed with gravels and supporting a slightly denser vegetation cover of creosotebush, acacia, and grasses. At this point a heavily wooded area begins, which becomes a deep, narrow wash. Vegetation is especially dense along the drainage, and in addition to the above mentioned shrubs, paloverde and mesquite grow along the banks. On either side of the wash within the site area, the surface is relatively flat with sparse creosotebush which increases in density south to the base of the ridge and north toward the edge of the terrace.

Lithic artifacts were concentrated in the eastern portion of the site, becoming increasingly sparse towards the west along the drainage within the R-O-W. The lithic scatter extends southwards up to the base of a high east-west ridge system, and northwards to the edge of the terrace. On-site lithic resources included rhyolite, basalt, and quartzite.

A 30 m wide by 405 m long grid was established along the R-O-W corridor and a surface collection was made from every other 5 m^2 grid square (Figure 65). Two hundred and forty-three squares were investigated of which 81 (33.3 percent) yielded lithic material. One bowl rim sherd of Encinas Red-on-brown was recovered from grid square A41, in the bed of a deep arroyo.

An access road extending outside the transmission line R-O-W to the east was surveyed for 148 meters. All materials located within the 4.5 m wide R-O-W were collected and their location pinpointed on the site map. These materials ceased at the interface of the bench and the terrace above the wash. No materials were found along the access road R-O-W from the interface to a wash approximately 150 m east, where the access road re-enters the transmission line corridor. The materials found in the access road R-O-W could possibly be associated with Feature 1, a cluster of large rocks immediately southwest of the corridor.

Feature 1 (Figure 66) was a roughly oval, collapsed rock pile situated on the lower north slope of a small hill on the east end of the terrace. A surface collection was made of all cultural material occurring within a 10 m area around the center of the feature (Figure 67). This material consisted of two basalt primary flakes, one piece of basalt shatter, one white chert secondary flake, and one white chert utilized flake. A 1 by 3 m north-south trench was placed through the center of the feature (Figure 68). The fill was then trowelled and screened down to the level of the scattered rocks on the outer periphery. One Reserve Red sherd was found on the surface within the feature. Rocks in the center of the feature were discovered to be resting on a level below that of the exterior rocks. Further clearing around these interior rocks revealed a pit outline. The pit was excavated in 5 cm levels until its bottom was reached at a depth of 30 cm below the original ground surface (35 cm below the present ground surface). The fill represented two different deposits. The lower fill

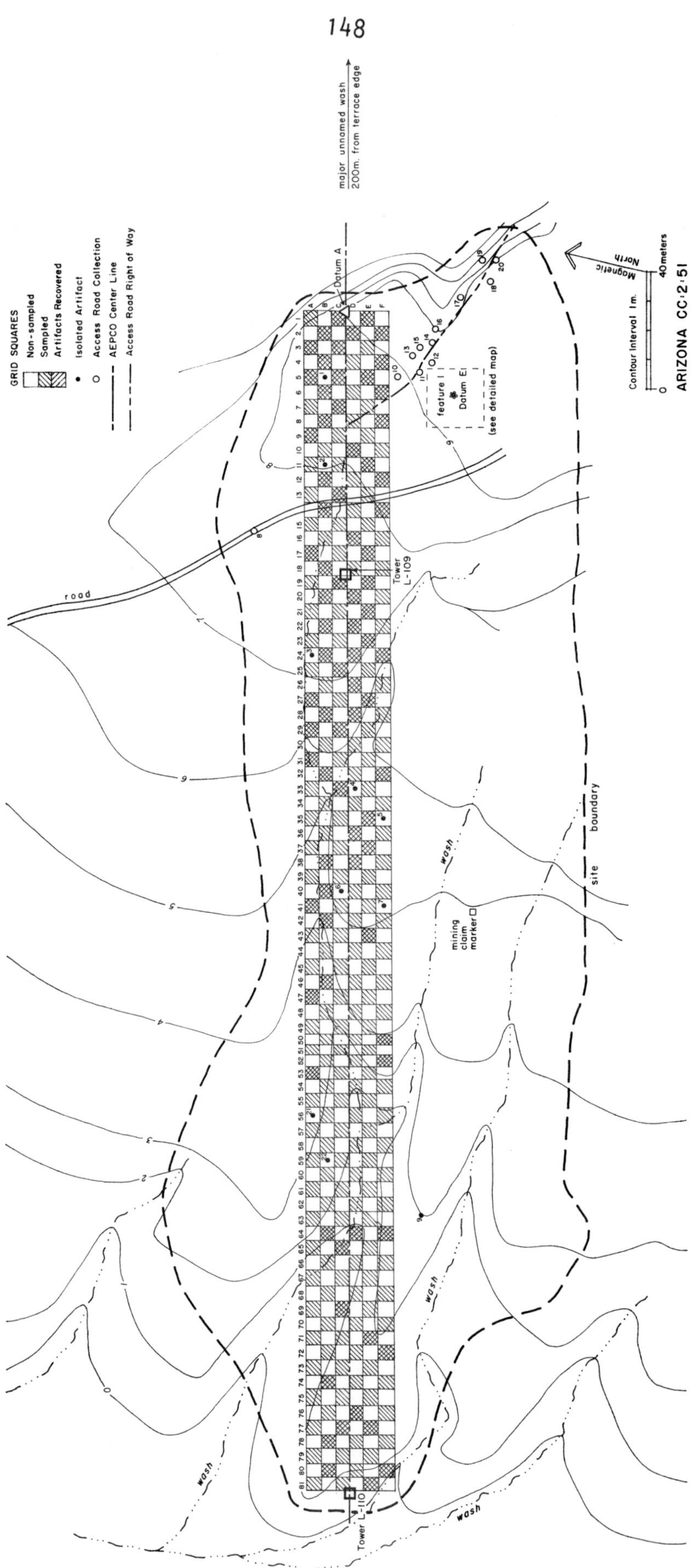

Figure 65. Arizona CC:2:51, site map

consisted of loosely consolidated aeolian-deposited sandy loam with very few gravels, overlain by a natural erosional fill of compacted sandy loam mixed with alluvial gravels. Two bones, were recovered from the pit fill at a depth of 24 below the pit rim. One bone was identified as a right proximal phalanx of a species of Odocoileus, possibly whitetail deer. The second bone is the left radius shaft of a jackrabbit, Lepus sp. Neither of the bones exhibited burning, cutting, or butchering marks. They were probably deposited by rodents.

The original pit excavation had been carried down into the natural substrate, a compact, slightly calichified clay-sand with caliche inclusions. The sides of the pit sloped slightly inwards to a bowl-shaped bottom. The over-all dimensions of the pit were 52 cm north-south, 85 cm east-west, and 30 cm deep. Six small cobbles were set around the rim of the pit; the interior of the pit itself was neither lined nor prepared except for some compaction of the sides. No burned or organic material other than the bones were encountered. Cultural materials were also absent. One pollen sample was taken from the center of the west wall of the pit and one sample from the surface. These samples later were not included in the pollen analysis, since analysis of such specimens was felt to be of limited value.

The function of the large number of rocks around the feature is uncertain, but two amorphous alignments may have at one time served as a foundation for a windbreak. It is possible the pit may have been for storage; at some time rocks were piled up over it, then the rocks were removed and placed rather haphazardly around the pit. The bottom level of these rocks occurs at a level 2-4 cm above that of the stones set around the pit edge, possibly indicating a later deposition.

Figure 66. Arizona CC:2:51, Feature 1.

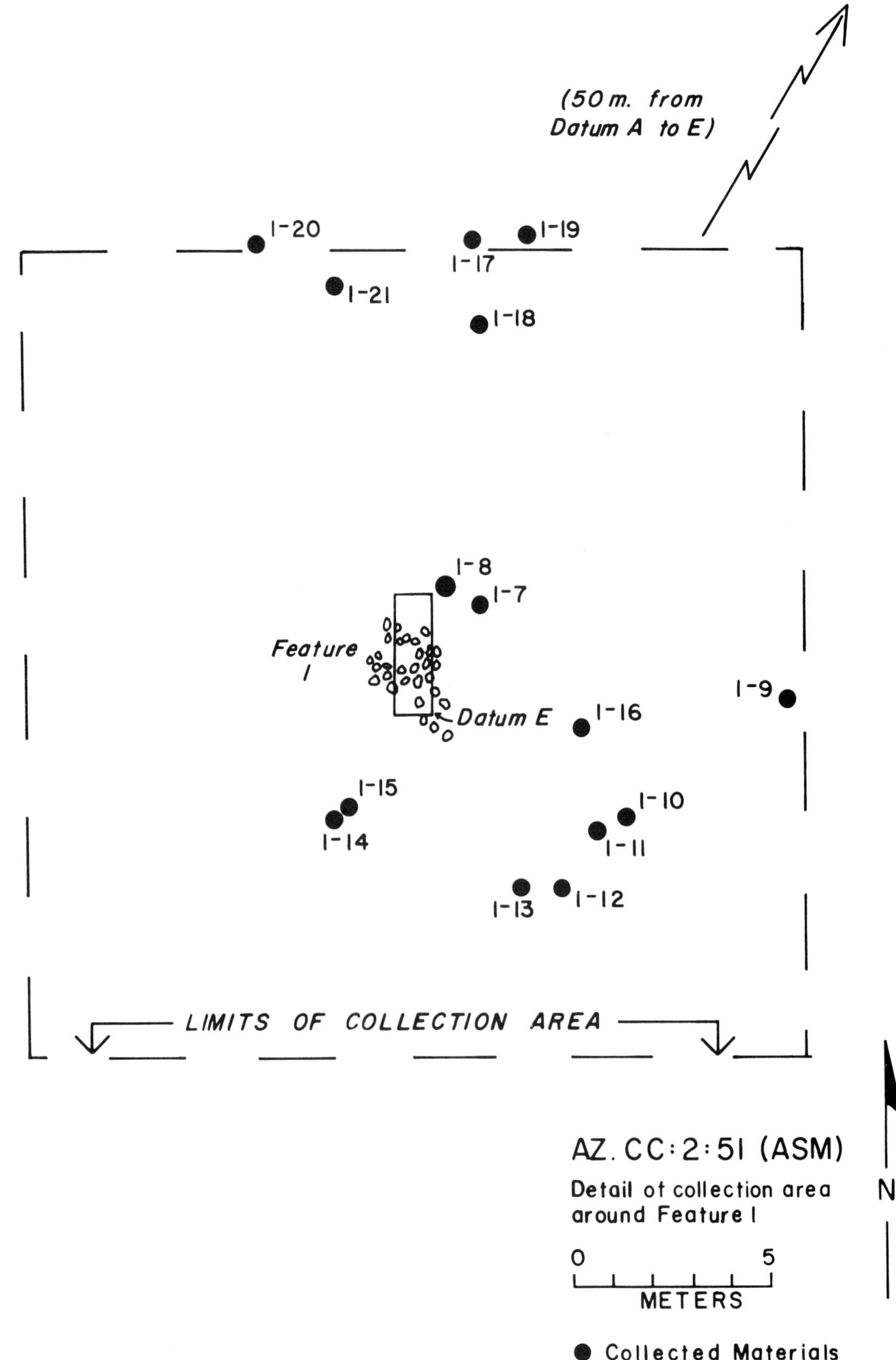

Figure 67. Arizona CC:2:51, detail of collection area around Feature 1

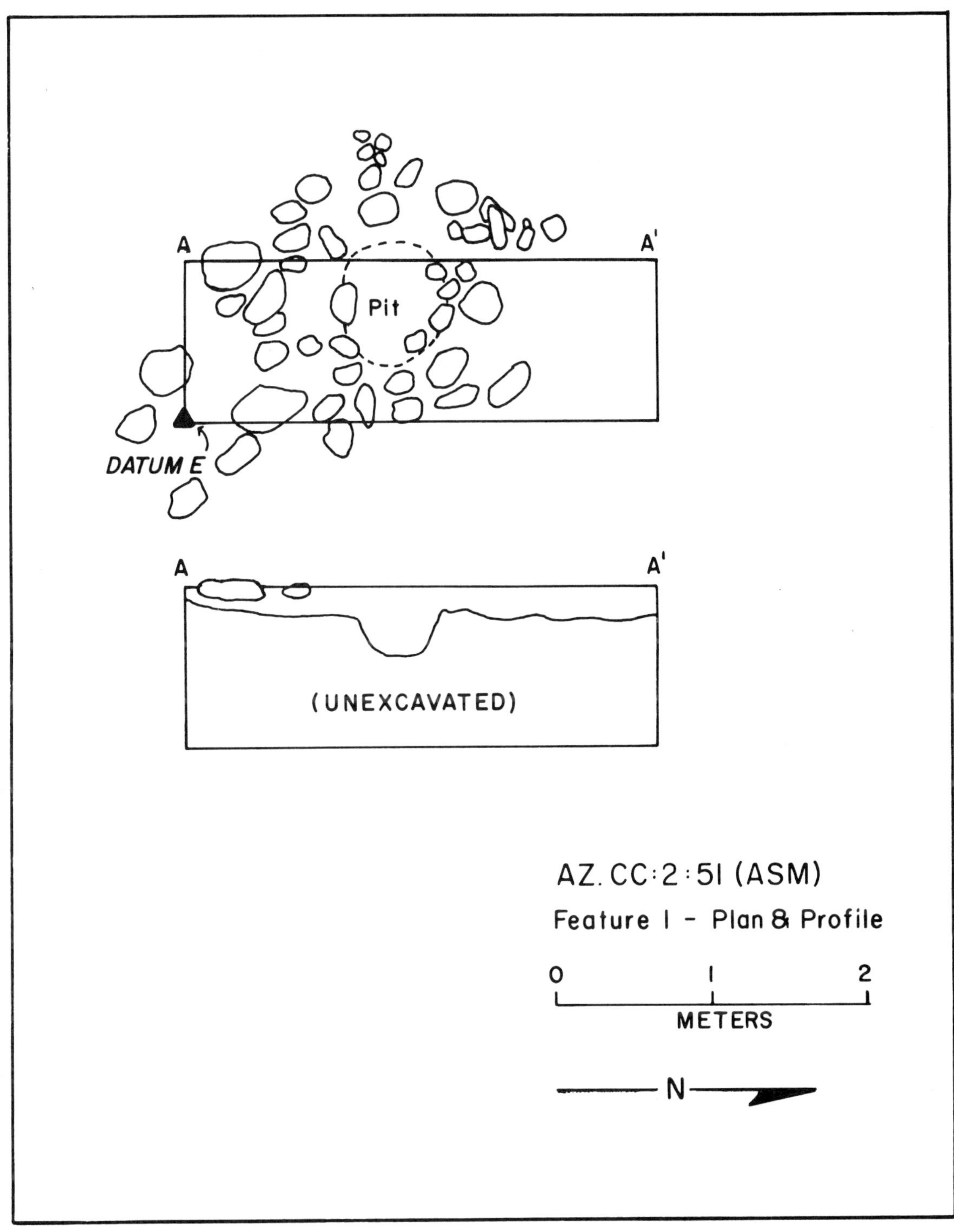

Figure 68. Arizona CC:2:51, Feature 1, plan and profile

A total of 279 chipped stone artifacts was recovered from the transmission line and access road R-O-W corridors. This total comprises 71 cores, 200 flakes and shatter, and eight unifaces. Basalt is the dominant material in the artifact assemblage, constituting 40.9 percent of the total. Rhyolite (26.5 percent) and silicates (25 percent) occur in nearly equal proportion, with obsidian (0.4 percent), quartzite (2.2 percent), and unidentified types (5 percent) occurring in lesser numbers.

Uni-directional cores dominate the core collection at 73 percent; bi-directional cores comprise the remaining 27 percent. Platform preparation was evident on 89 percent of these cores, indicating standardization in core reduction techniques. Basalt and rhyolite primary core reduction was carried out at this site, as is borne out by close ratios of cores to flakes of these respective materials. On the other hand, a very low ratio of silicate cores to flakes (1.11) indicates a low incidence of silicate core reduction. Yet, a high frequency of silicate tools suggests that this material was favored for flake tools. It cannot be ascertained from the data at hand if these attributes reflect technologically distinct lithic industries, or if more esoteric factors are at work. An additional problem is the difficulty in ascertaining use damage on basalt and rhyolite.

Basalt also predominates in the flake collection at 40.5 percent. Silicate flakes occur in greater frequencies (29 percent) than rhyolite (21.5 percent), with unidentified types, quartzite, and obsidian making up the remainder. There are more secondary and tertiary flakes than premary flakes, and shatter represents a respectable 14 percent of the flake and small debitage totals. The relative flake frequencies and percentage of shatter suggest reduction of primary flakes into tool blanks and preforms. The frequency of tertiary flakes (37 percent) indicates tool maintenance and resharpening.

The tools indicate expedient use of flakes and cores over formally produced tools. Sixty-five percent of the tools are made up of ten utilized flakes and five utilized cores; one rhyolite and seven silicate unifaces constitute the remaining 35 percent. Silicate tools along account for 70 percent of the total tool count. The location of edge wear on utilized flakes was quite varied; two exhibited wear on a lateral edge, three on the perimeter, and five on the distal end. One flake showed secondary use. Four unifaces were utilized on a lateral edge and four were used on the perimeter. Microscopic study revealed light-to-medium density microflaking in the form of round bifacial scars. Edge angles ranged from 39 to 86 degrees with a mean of 59.3 degrees. The sum of these attributes suggests that a variable range of tasks were carried out, although intensive use of tools is not indicated.

Arizona CC:2:54

<u>Elevation:</u> 997 - 999 m
<u>Site Size:</u> 160 m N/S by 330 m E/W
<u>Field Designation:</u> AEPCO 61 and 62

This site is situated on two ridge fingers extending northwestward from a high, flat-topped, east-west trending ridge in the Peloncillo

Mountains. Lithics do occur on the upper main ridge well outside the R-O-W corridor, and it is possible Arizona CC:2:54 may be an extension of activities represented on the higher elevations. The Gila River flows 1.04 km to the northwest. Onsite vegetation is sparse, but varied, consisting of creosotebush, ocotillo, whitethorn acacia, _Ephedra_, cane cholla, Santa Rita prickly pear, and barrel cactus. Economic plants in the drainage channels and the wash below the ridge include paloverde and mesquite. Very little soil buildup is present on the ridgetop and upper slopes. Basalt outcrops are numerous and form the bed of a steep drainage through the center of the site. The surface is strewn with basaltic cobbles and gravels, with rhyolite and chalcedony nodules occurring in smaller numbers.

Originally this site had been recorded as two separate sites (AEPCO 61 and 62) because the cultural materials were located on two ridge fingers bisected by a narrow drainage (Figure 69). An analysis of the chipped stone revealed no significant differences between the two loci; and they were therefore combined.

Locus A (AEPCO 62) was gridded along the R-O-W corridor and 50 percent of the grid squares were sampled. Of 81 investigated grid squares, 27 (33.3 percent) yielded artifacts. An intensive survey was conducted to collect materials occurring outside the grid in order to better define the extent of the artifact scatter. Locus B (AEPCO 61) was not gridded due to the sparseness of remains. The site was intensively surveyed and all materials collected. The point provenience of each artifact was plotted on the site map. Most materials were concentrated at the tip of the ridge finger, indicating maximum activity was probably at this locale. Another clustering of material was evident on the southern part of the ridge finger.

A total of 140 chipped stone artifacts was collected from the site; these consisted of 24 cores, 109 flakes and shatter, and 7 unifaces. Material types reflect use of available lithic resources for tool manufacture. Silicates are dominant (41 percent), with basalt contributing 35 percent, and rhyolite 22 percent. Andesite, rarely used at any site in the project area, represented 2 percent of the artifacts.

Uni-directional cores are the dominant core type, constituting 58 percent of the total. Bi-directional and multi-directional cores represent 21 percent each. Platform preparation was evident on 92 percent of the cores. In the total core class, basalt was used for 33 percent, rhyolite for 38 percent, and silicates for 29 percent. These percentages do not differ significantly among themselves to allow postulation of any favored material type. However, the two igneous varieties (rhyolite and basalt) together represent 71 percent, indicating a dominance of coarser textured igneous stone over cryptocrystalline varieties in initial core reduction.

Material types are similarily distributed among the flakes and shatter, with basalt representing 38 percent, rhyolite 20 percent, silicates 39 percent, and andesite 3 percent. Primary flakes consitutes 18.3 percent of the total number of flakes, secondary flakes 40.4 percent, tertiary flakes 24.8 percent, and shatter 16.5 percent. Further distinction

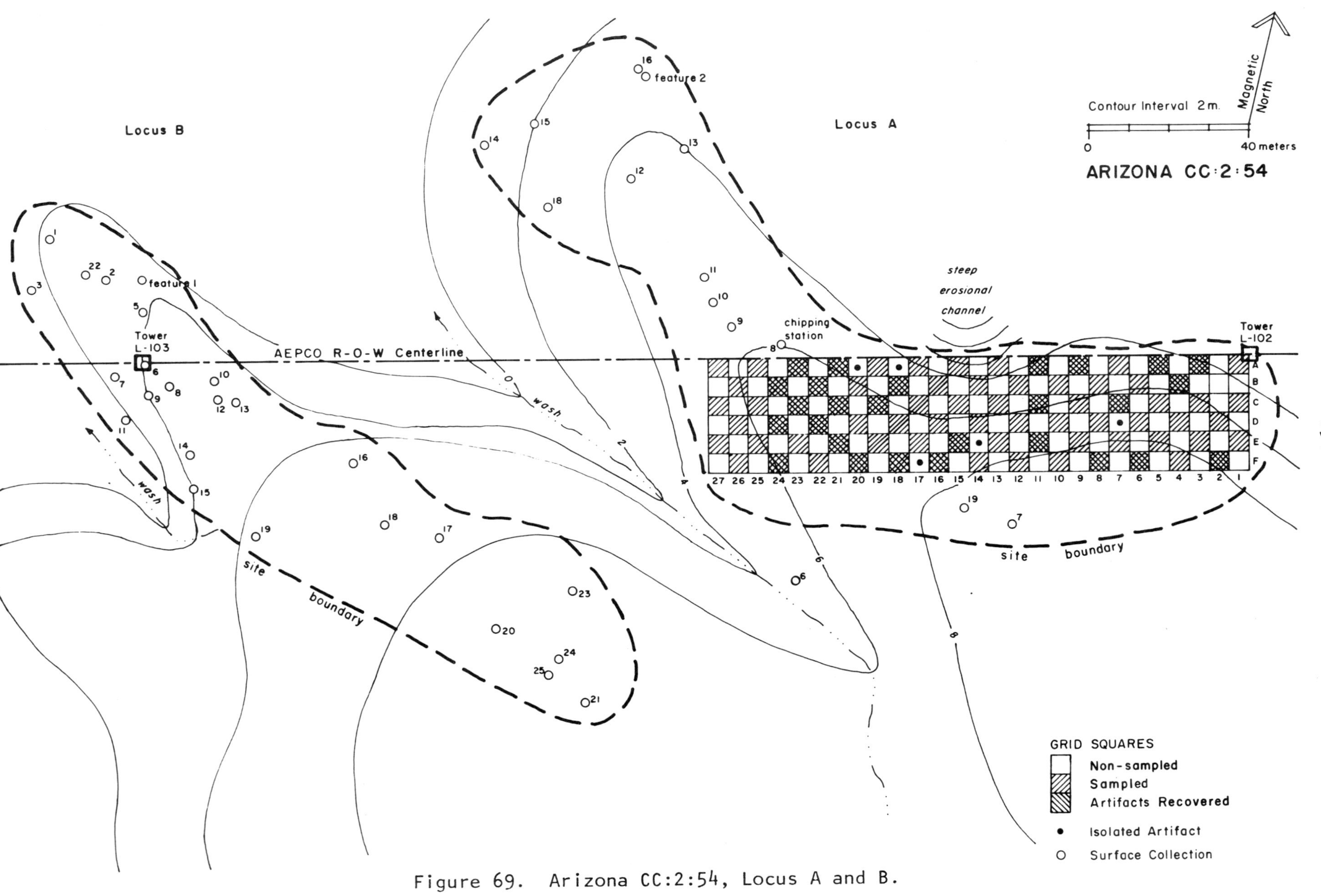

Figure 69. Arizona CC:2:54, Locus A and B.

shows that silicates account for 60 percent of the tertiary flakes. This factor, plus the occurrence of seven silicate unifaces, indicates manufacture and possible resharpening of chert tools as an important activity of the lithic industry at this site.

Four utilized cores and seven silicate unifaces comprise the total tool class. No utilized unmodified flakes were found. Four of the unifaces were utilized, one on a lateral edge, one on the perimenter, and two on the distal end. Edge angles on utilized pieces ranged from 39 to 80 degrees, with a mean of 58.1 degrees. Light intensity microflaking was present as unifacial and bifacial round and trapezoidal scars. The low number of utilized pieces did not allow for valid comparison of activities at this site with those of other sites in the stratum. However, the use of formal tools rather than specially produced flakes for immediate use in an activity is seen as a special aspect of this site.

Arizona CC:2:56

Elevation: 992 - 995 m
Site Size: 175 m N/S by 80 m E/W (along the centerline)
Field Designation: AEPCO 64

This site is situated in a basin-like niche within a system of connected ridge fingers in the Peloncillo foothills. The southern boundary of the site is the base of the high ridges of the Peloncillos, while the northernmost edge is the point where the ridge makes a sheer drop into a wide sandy wash that drains into the Gila River, 1.4 km to the northwest. The northwest portion of the basin area is dominated by a high knoll. Little soil buildup is present on the site, which is strewn with igneous gravels and cobbles. Chert nodules and small Apache tears occur frequently. The vegetation is sparse but varied, consisting of creosotebush, clusters of hedgehog cactus, ocotillo, prickly pear, mesquite (in the drainages), *Ephedra*, pencil cholla, cane cholla, and mammillaria.

The site is a sparse but consistently distributed lithic scatter with a few discrete concentrations. The majority of material is contained within the flat basin portion and along the top of the ridge finger. Artifacts do, however, continue south from the centerline up the slope to the crest of a high ridge. The lithics are made of basalt, rhyolite, chert, chalcedony and obsidian, all of which occur in the vicinity as raw material.

Data recovery at Arizona CC:2:56 was based on a 50 percent sample. A 60 m wide grid column was established perpendicular to the R-O-W centerline for a total length of 170 m (Figure 70). This was done for two reasons: (1) the site's long axis was perpendicular to the centerline and (2) a more stratified sample could be obtained, since the grid covered a high ridge slope, a flat basin-like area, a drainage, a ridge finger, and lower ridge slope. One hundred and ninety-six grid squares were investigated with 70 of these yielding artifacts, a total grid data recovery sample of 35.7 percent. Time was not available in the lithic analysis to test intrasite artifact distribution within the topographical strata.

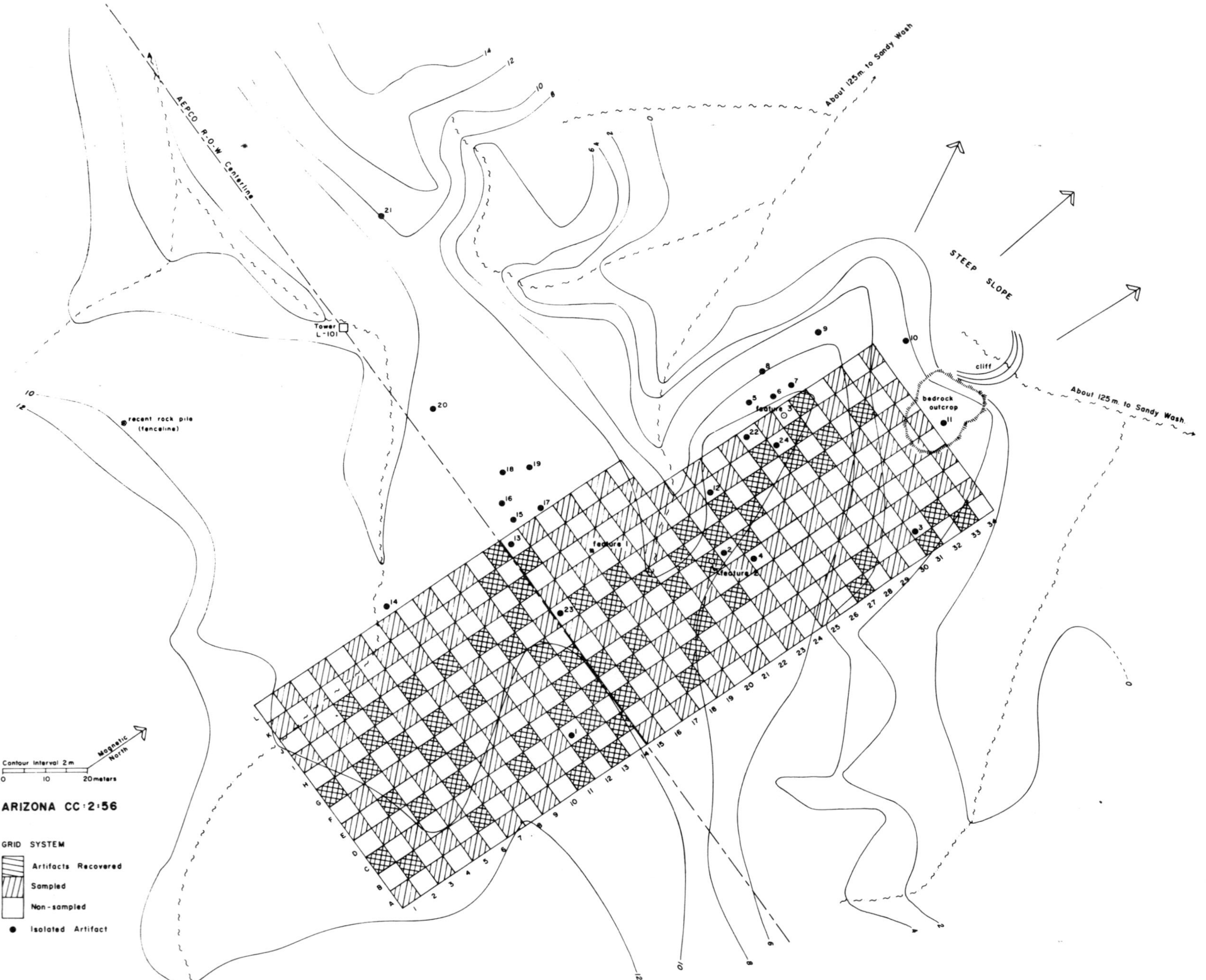

Figure 70. Arizona CC:2:56, site map.

Three features were recorded at the site. Feature 1 was an amorphous cluster of cobbles 1.5 m in diameter with no associated cultural materials. Its function remains unknown. Feature 2 was a grey rhyolite chipping station. The assemblage consisted of a utilized multi-directional core, two primary flakes, nine secondary flakes, and two unifaces. Feature 3, a white chert chipping station, contained one primary flake, three secondary flakes, and one uniface.

Two hundred seventy-six chipped stone artifacts were recovered from the site. A wide variety of material types is present, but silicates are dominant, constituting 48 percent of the total artifacts. Rhyolite makes up 25 percent, basalt 17 percent, with unidentified types, quartzite, and obsidian comprising the remainder.

Thirty-five cores were collected. Platform preparation is present on 83 percent of these, indicating a standardized reduction technique. Uni-directional cores constitute the primary core type at 54 percent; bi-directional cores represent 20 percent, and multi-directional cores 26 percent. Silicate cores comprise 43 percent of the core total, basalt 20 percent, and rhyolite 37 percent. Basalt and rhyolite combined are 37 percent, compared with 43 percent silicate cores. Essentially, core reduction on cryptocrystalline material occurs in nearly equal proportion to reduction of igneous material. It is significant that eight of the nine multi-directional cores, or 89 percent, are silicates. This reflects silicate core reduction on a scale not encountered elsewhere on project sites.

Flakes number 232, or 84 percent of the total artifact collection. Primary flakes represent 16.8 percent, secondary flakes are 39.2 percent, tertiary flakes 27.6 percent, and shatter 16.4 percent of the total flake count. A variety of material is present, dominated by silicates (47 percent). Rhyolite follows with 24 percent and basalt comprises 17 percent. Unidentified types, quartzite, and obsidian occur in lesser numbers. It is notable that the last three material classes are not represented among cores and that most flakes of these materials are secondary and tertiary flakes and shatter. This may indicate that tools of these materials were brought in from elsewhere, and were used and refurbished in connection with activities carried out at this site.

The tool class is divided between utilized debitage (44 percent) and formal tools (56 percent). There are four utilized flakes, three utilized cores, and nine unifaces. Three flakes were used on a lateral edge and one on the distal end. Data are not available on utilized cores. Of the nine unifaces, six showed use wear - five on a lateral edge and one on the perimeter. Both light and heavy microflaking was evident under microscopic viewing, in the form of round unifacial and bifacial scars. Edge angles ranged from 49 to 72 degrees (a mean of 59.5 degrees).

It is noteworthy that all utilized flakes, one core, and all unifaces were made of silicates. The dominance of silicates in the cores, flakes, and tools suggests a complete sequence of lithic procurement, tool manufacture, and tool use. Large pebble-size chert nodules do occur on the site and in the immediate vicinity and evidently were a source of raw material. Manufacturing steps included initial core reduction to obtain flakes, fabrication of tools from flakes, as well as the use of unmodified flakes, and the use of finished tools for specific tasks. At least one lithic workshop is indicated by the data; time did not allow for a more detailed analysis to isolate specific activity areas at the site. Generally, preference of cryptocrystalline material over igneous material for tool manufacture is a characteristic of this site.

Arizona CC:3:26

Elevation: 1130 m
Site Size: 190 m N/S by 110 m E/W
Field Designation: AEPCO 70

This site is situated along the spine of a long, irregularly curved ridge finger, one of many in this area of high dissected ridges in the Peloncillo Mountains (Figures 61 and 64). Several steep erosional channels cut the east and west sides of the ridge and drain into wide sandy washes to the south. The southern extent of the ridge finger curves southwest and slopes down gently into a major southern wash. The ridge-top is covered with colluvium and littered with igneous cobbles. A small saddle divides the ridge crest into two elongated knolls. On-site vegetation is composed of creosotebush, snakeweed, Engelmann and Santa Rita prickly pear, cane cholla, ocotillo, desert Christmas cactus, whitethorn acacia, and *Ephedra*. The lithic scatter included a variety of materials, including chalcedony, chert, rhyolite, and basalt. Small Apache tears occur on the site, but no obsidian artifacts were noted. The R-O-W centerline passes through the narrow saddle portion of the site, at an angle perpendicular to the site's long axis.

Due to the ridgetop's irregular conformation, two separate grid columns were set up, covering the two knolls where artifact distribution was concentrated (Figure 71). Fifty percent of the 5 m^2 grid squares were collected. Of a total of 105 sampled squares, 33 of these (31.4 percent) yielded material.

Two features were recorded during mitigation. Feature 1 was a remnant of a chert chipping station consisting of one primary flake, three secondary flakes, and one piece of shatter. Collected with the lithic flakes was a uni-directional prepared chalcedony core with more than 50 percent cortical material remaining. Feature 2 was a basalt knapping area, consisting of a multi-directional prepared core with more than 50 percent cortical material, one primary flake, and two secondary flakes.

The total collection from this site numbered 149 artifacts. Silicates overwhelmingly dominate the assemblage, comprising 78.4 percent of the total. The remaining material types are basalt (7.4 percent), rhyolite (5.4 percent), quartzite (1.4 percent), and unidentified types (7.4 percent).

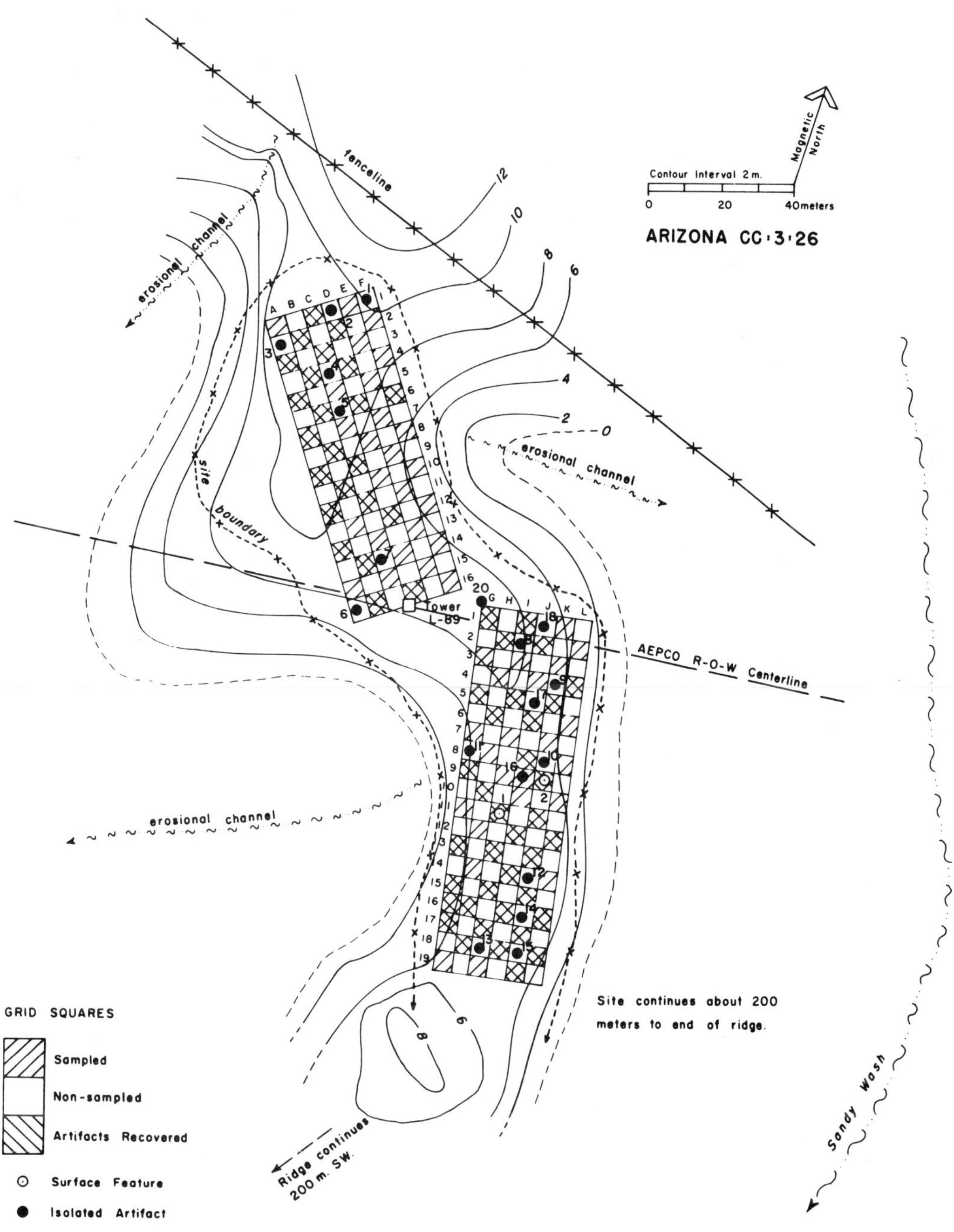

Figure 71. Arizona CC:3:26, site map.

The core total numbered 34, or 23 percent of the total artifact collection. Cores show a bimodal distribution between uni-directional and bi-directional flaking. Noteworthy is that platform preparation is evident on only 59 percent of the cores, primarily on uni-directional cores; lack of this characteristic is most evident on bi-directional silicate cores. This lack of preparedness suggests testing of stones for knapability or a fairly haphazard removal of flakes, or problems with the texture or workability of the material. Seventy-three percent of all cores are silicates, 15 percent are basalt and 12 percent are rhyolite.

A total of 111 flakes and pieces of shatter were collected, representing 74 percent of the artifact total. Primary flakes constitute 18.9 percent, secondary flakes 25.2 percent, tertiary flakes 38.7 percent, and shatter 17.1 percent. As with the cores, silicates dominate the flakes with 79 percent. Basalt contributed 5 percent, rhyolite 4 percent, quartzite 2 percent, and unidentified types 10 percent.

The dominance of silicate cores and flakes indicates preferential selection of these materials for tool manufacture. Basalt and rhyolite are commonly available on the ridge and in the immediate vicinity (as are silicate materials). but were not exploited as thoroughly as the silicates.

Very few tools were found and these consist of three silicate unifaces and three utilized cores. None of the recovered flakes exhibited use. One uniface exhibited usage on the lateral edge, a second on the distal end; the third exhibited no use wear. Edge angle dimensions indicate a range of 29 to 71 degrees. This is not seen as a variety of specific use patterns, but as a result of slight skewing due to the small sample size and by edge angles measured on utilized cores which ordinarily tend to have fairly steep faces.

As at Arizona CC:2:56, the data for Arizona CC:3:26 indicate lithic procurement and silicate tool manufacture with and subsequent tool use as a primary activity at this site. The low number of tools may result from their being transported away from the site or from limited flake damage which produces no visible evidence of use.

Arizona CC:3:28

Elevation: 1100 m
Site Size: 80 m N/S by 300 m E/W
Field Designation: AEPCO 68

This site is located on a ridgetop in an area of highly dissected ridges at the base of the Peloncillo Mountains. The ridges generally run southwest-northeast at this point. There is a deep wash north of the site and smaller wash to the south. These and the surrounding washes drain into the Gila River, 3.4 km to the west-northwest. On-site vegetation includes creosotebush, ocotillo, whitethorn acacia, grasses, pencil cholla, cholla, prickly pear, and barrel cactus.

The group surface is unconsolidated gravel and cobbles predominantly of basalt and quartzite. The soil is classified as a loamy sand.

Because artifacts were widely scattered over the undulating ridgetop, the site was not gridded by standard procedures. Instead, materials were collected and bagged and their locations pinpointed on the contour map (Figure 72). One area did have an artifact concentration which was gridded into six 10 m^2 units and collected separately. Features 3 and 6 occurred within this concentration.

Feature 1 was a rock pile of mostly vesicular basalt 2.70 m north-south by 2.00 m east-west. The largest rock was 35 by 30 cm and the average rock size was 25 by 25 cm. The rock pile was photographed but not tested because it was outside the R-O-W.

Feature 2 was a possible remnant of a chipping station, consisting of four complete secondary flakes.

Feature 3 was a rock circle located on the hill crest in the midst of a lithic concentration (Figure 73). It consisted of four large stones, one of which was recently incised "T.O.L." and "H.A.F." It is 1.00 m north/south by 1.10 m east/west; the largest rock is 35 by 25 cm. The stones were removed from the east half of the feature and the ground surface trowelled to reveal any pit outlines. The east half of the feature was then trenched to 30 cm below the surface. No pit outlines, ash, or subsurface materials were discovered, except for one basalt flake at 1 cm below the surface.

Feature 4 was a rock cluster of unknown function. It was constructed of five vesicular basalt boulders and measures 1 m in diameter (Figure 73).

Feature 5 (Figure 74) was a rock cluster or possible hearth 2.10 m east/west by 1.65 m north/south. Most of the small cobbles are vesicular basalt. One fractured quartzite cobble originally thought to be fire-cracked was also part of the circle. All stones in a 0.75 by 0.50 m trench were removed and the surface trowelled to reveal any possible pit outline; none was found. Sterile substrate was encountered at 15 cm below the surface. No artifacts were present on the surface nor in the trench. As the stones in the circle were not standing on end, no ash or charcoal were present, and the quartzite rock was determined not to be fire-cracked, it seems doubtful that this was a hearth.

Feature 6 was a chipping station consisting of six secondary flakes, seven pieces of variegated chert shatter, and a multi-directional prepared core of the same material. The lack of primary flakes may indicate either that primary flakes were being reduced to form tools, or that they were removed for use elsewhere.

This site had 37 cores, 133 flakes, 18 unifaces, and a tabular knife for a total of 189 artifacts. Silicates comprise 47.3 percent of the artifacts, basalt 25.5 percent, and rhyolite 18.6 percent. Obsidian was used for 1.6 percent, quartz 0.5 percent, and the remaining 6.4 percent was unidentified material.

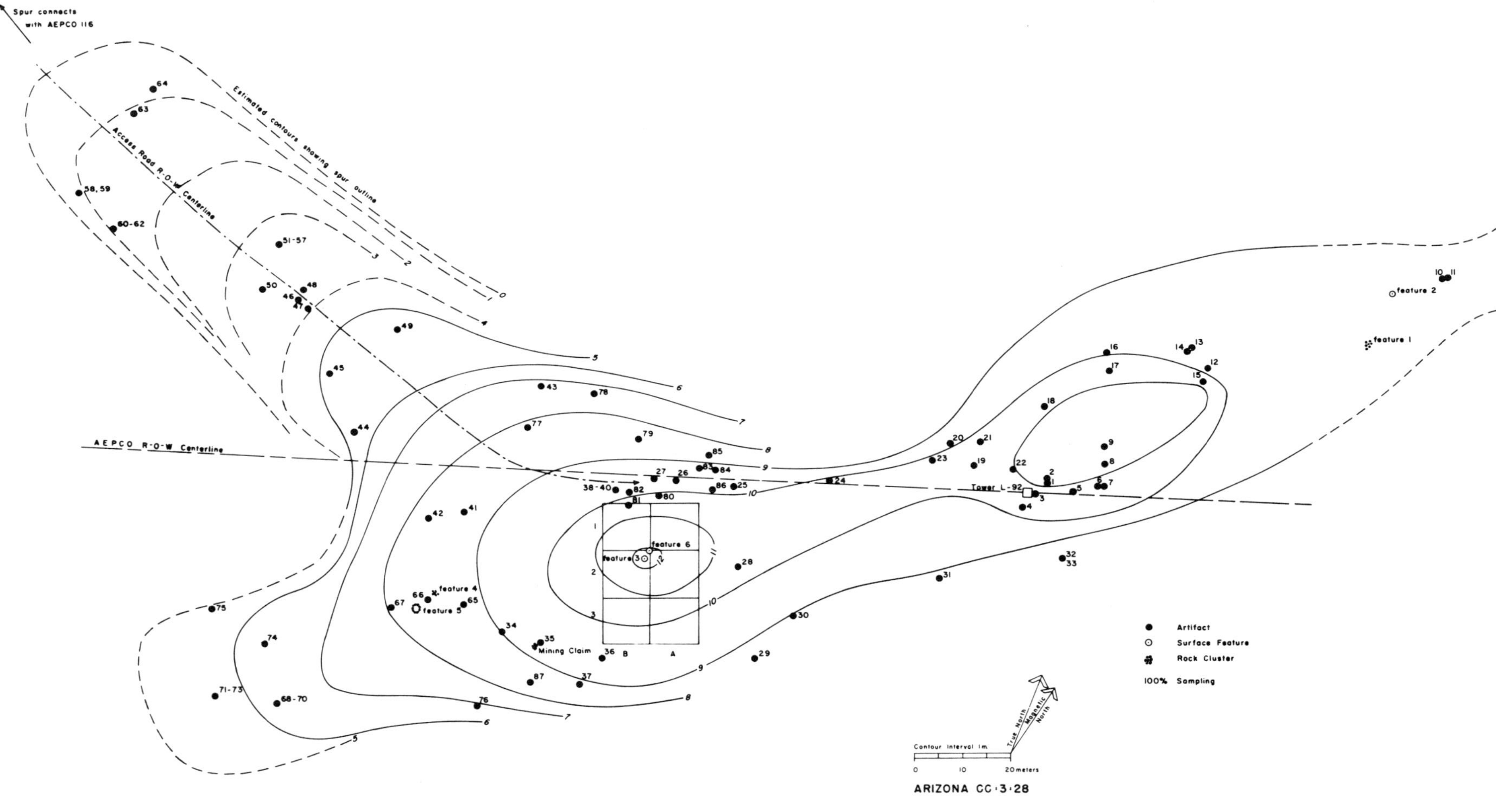

Figure 72. Arizona CC:3:28, site map.

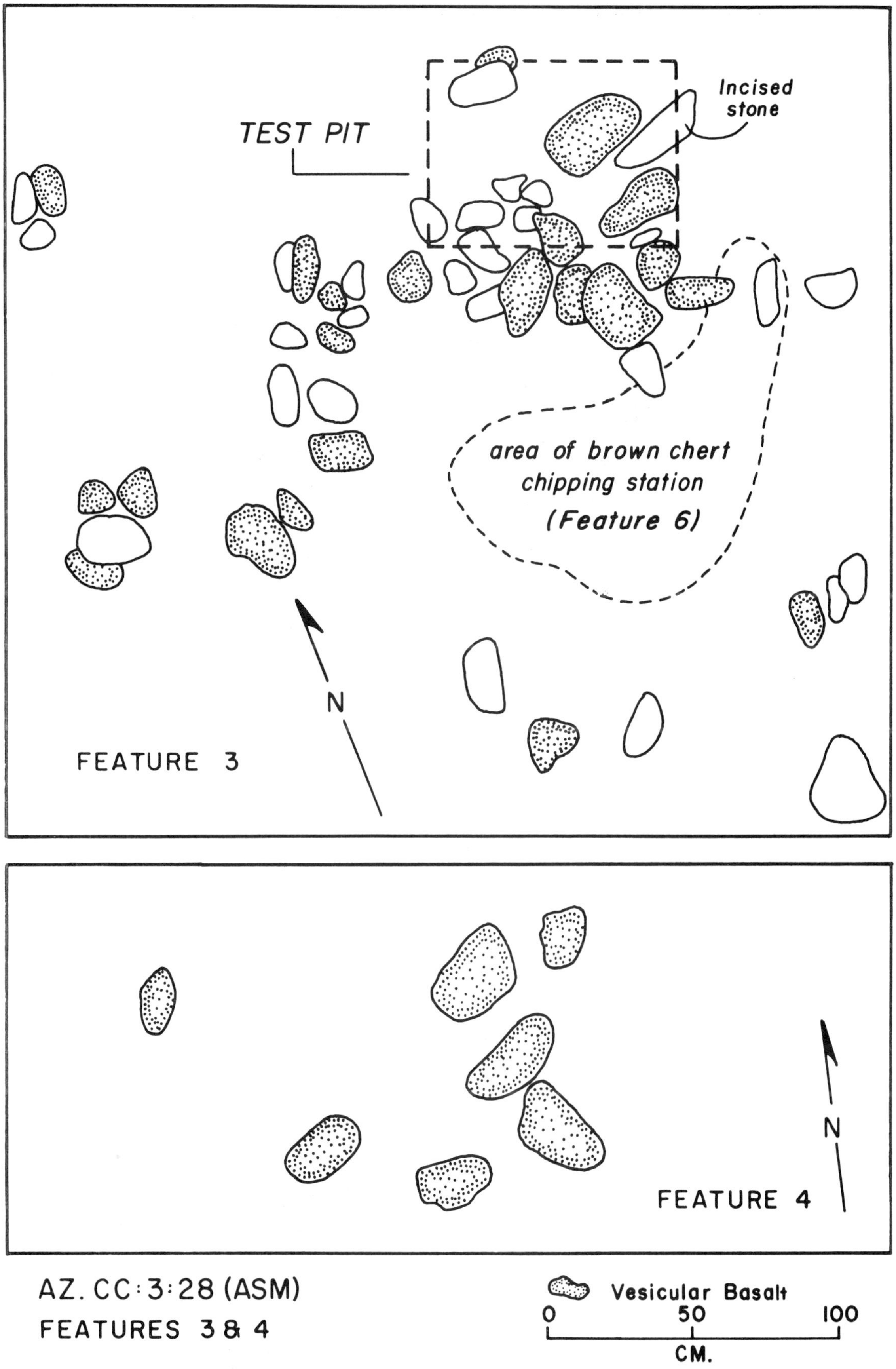

TEST PIT
Incised stone
area of brown chert chipping station
(Feature 6)
N
FEATURE 3
N
FEATURE 4
AZ. CC:3:28 (ASM)
FEATURES 3 & 4
Vesicular Basalt
0
50
100
CM.

Figure 73. Arizona CC:3:28, Features 3 and 4

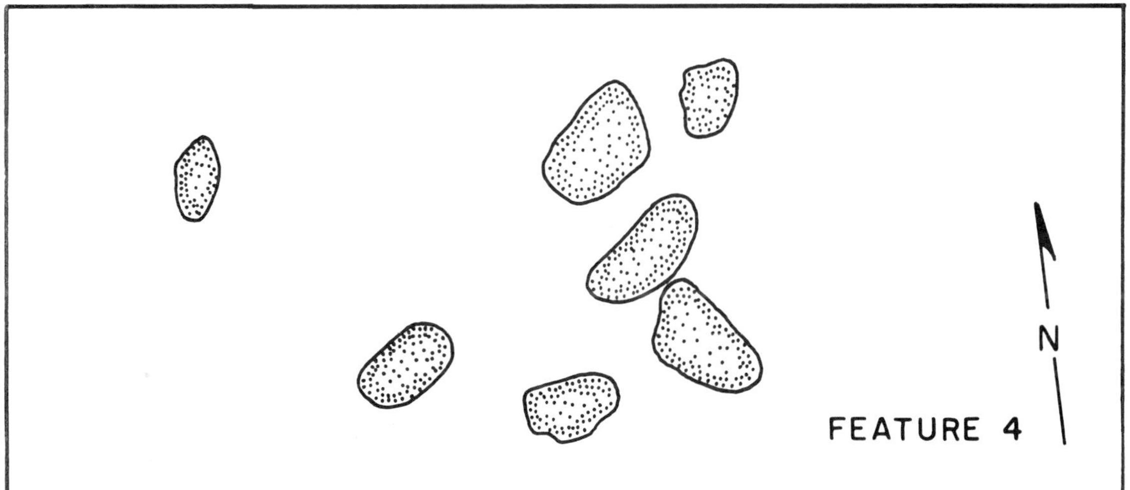

Figure 74. Arizona CC:3:28, Feature 5

Uni-directional cores were the dominant core type making up 65 percent of the core total; bi-directional cores constitute 27 percent, and multi-directional cores the remaining 8 percent. Platform preparation was present on 84 percent of all cores, indicating a standarized flake removal technique. Basalt dominates the core class, particularly the uni-directional and bi-directional cores at 49 percent; rhyolite constitutes 22 percent, silicates a low 16 percent, and unidentified types make up the remaining 14 percent.

Flakes account for 70 percent of the cultural material. Of these 14.3 percent are primary flakes, 42.9 percent are secondary flakes, 26.3 percent tertiary flakes, and 16.5 percent shatter. In contrast to the cores, silicates dominate the flake class with 54 percent, basalt 23 percent and rhyolite 16 percent. Obsidian (2 percent) and unidentified types (5 percent) comprise the remainder. From the foregoing data it may be inferred that basalt and rhyolite core reduction was a primary activity; in addition, tool production or resharpening on silicate flakes represented the primary tool manufacturing aspect.

A total of 18 unifaces, one flake tabular knife (Figure 75) and 8 utilized cores constitute the tool class and represent the highest occurrence of tools at any site in this stratum. However, no utilized flakes were found. Eleven of the unifaces were manufactured from silicates, six were of rhyolite, and one was made of quartz. Use wear on unifaces was predominantly on lateral edges (11 unifaces); 5 were utilized on the perimeter and 1 on the distal end. All types of cores were used as tools and basalt cores were more frequently used than silicate cores. Edge angles on utilized artifacts ranged from 34 to 72 degrees with a mean of 49.7 degrees. This range may indicate a variable range of tasks, but a large standard deviation indicates some skewing in the sample. Light microflaking was evident on utilized edges with round unifacial scars predominating.

In summary, the high frequency of formal tools and absence of utilized flakes suggests that a specialized type of subsistence activity prevailed at this site at one time.

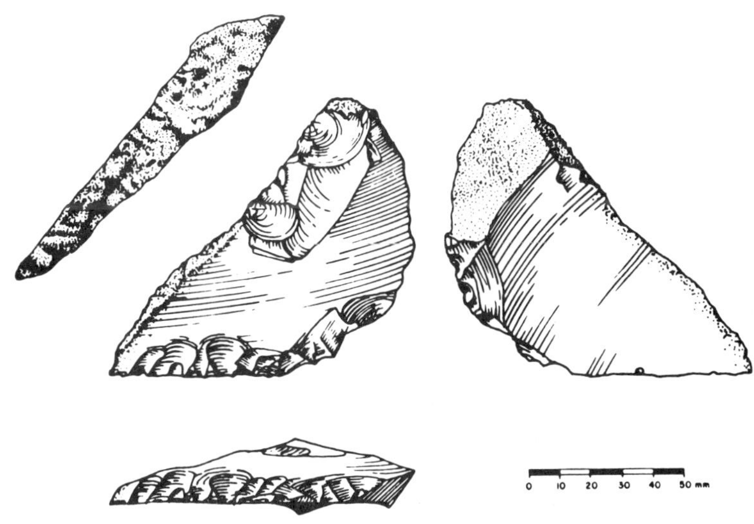

Figure 75. Flake knife from Arizona CC:3:28

Arizona CC:3:44

Elevation: 1073 m
Site Size: 120 m E/W by 40 m N/S
Field Designation: AEPCO 116

This site is located on the flat benches of a ridgetop that extends east to Arizona CC:3:28 (Figure 63). Arizona CC:3:28 and CC:3:44 are separated by a steep saddle but are located on the same ridge system. They were initially suspected to be one site, the absence of cultural material between them related to the steepness of saddle. However, attribute analysis of the artifacts indicated the sites differed significantly, and they were actually two separate sites.

A major wash is to the north/north/west of the site and minor drainages flow south towards Yuma Wash. The Gila River floodplain is visible 3.4 km to the west. Creosotebush is the dominant vegetation.

A small, contained lithic scatter is present over the flat ridge. Because of the low density of cultural materials, 100 percent data recovery was implemented. All artifacts were bagged, their provenience was pinpointed on the site map (Figure 76), and they were collected. The site had two rock piles and two chipping stations.

Feature 1 (Figure 77) was a cobble cluster 1.10 m north/south by 2.00 m east/west and was tested. The stones were removed, the surface scraped for stains or outlines, and a test trench was excavated. At a depth of 40 cm caliche was encountered in one corner of the trench. Three flakes were found in the subsoil; no ash, stratigraphic layering, outlines, or deposition were observed. The flakes consisted of one utilized variegated chert flake and one piece of gray rhyolite shatter; the third flake was later judged not to be man-made.

Feature 2 (Figure 78) was a smaller cobble cluster 2.10 m north/south by 2.15 m east/west. A 1 m east/west by 0.50 m north/south test trench was excavated. There was no pit outline underneath the stones and no second coursing of stones. At 25 cm below the surface caliche substrate was encountered. One pink rhyolite secondary flake was found, but no ash or pit outlines were present.

Feature 3 was a pink rhyolite chipping station consisting of a multi-directional core, two primary flakes, and three secondary flakes.

Feature 4 was a rhyolite chipping station consisting of a cluster of three complete secondary flakes and two pieces of shatter with cortical material on less than half of the dorsal surfaces.

Collections at this site yielded 12 cores, 26 flakes and pieces of shatter, and 4 unifaces. Silicates constituted 47.6 percent of the artifacts, 40.5 percent were made of rhyolite, and 11.9 percent of basalt.

Uni-directional cores comprised 92 percent of the core total. A single multi-directional prepared silicate core represented the remaining 8 percent. Platform preparation was present on only 33 percent of the cores; it was

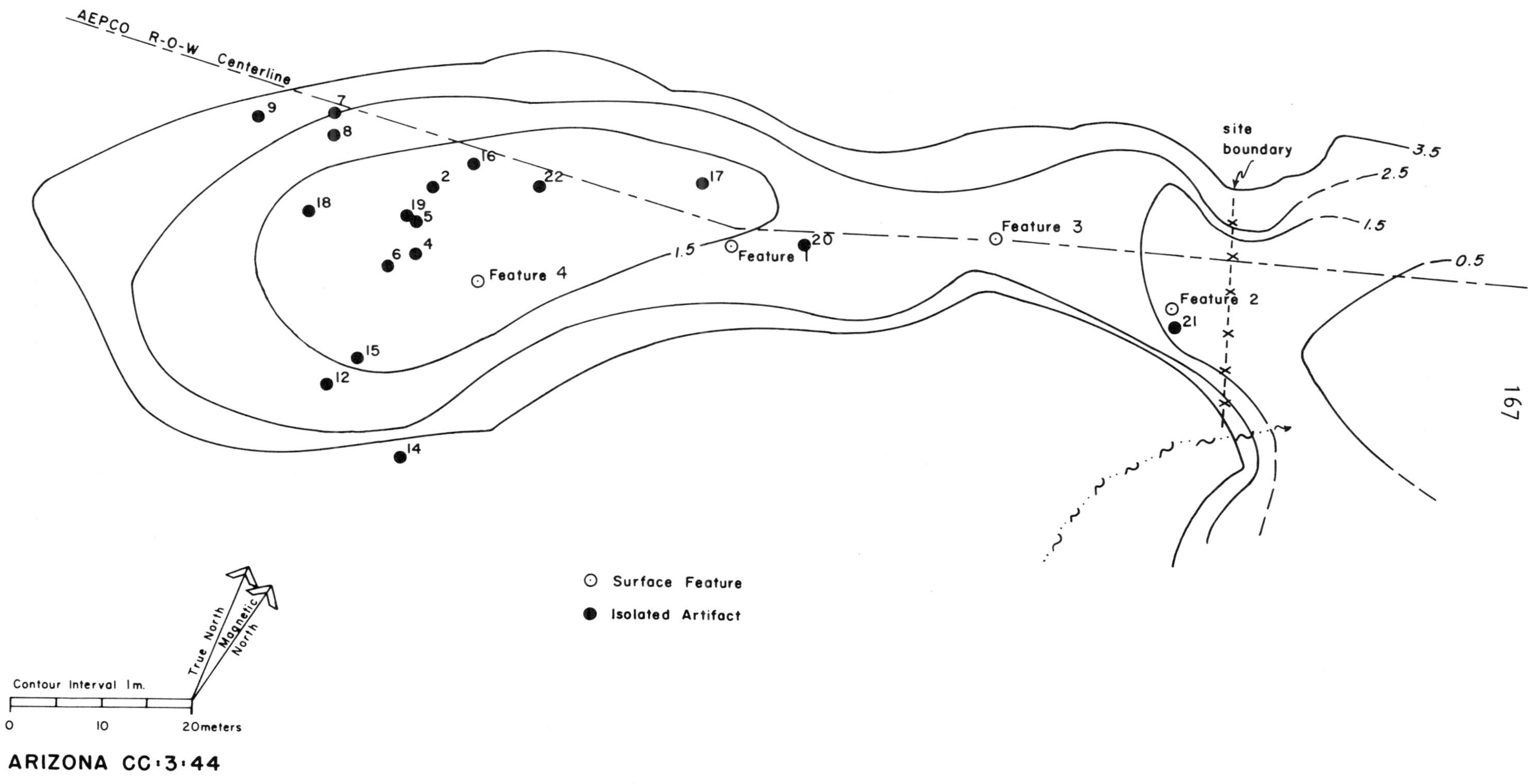

Figure 76. Arizona CC:3:44, site map.

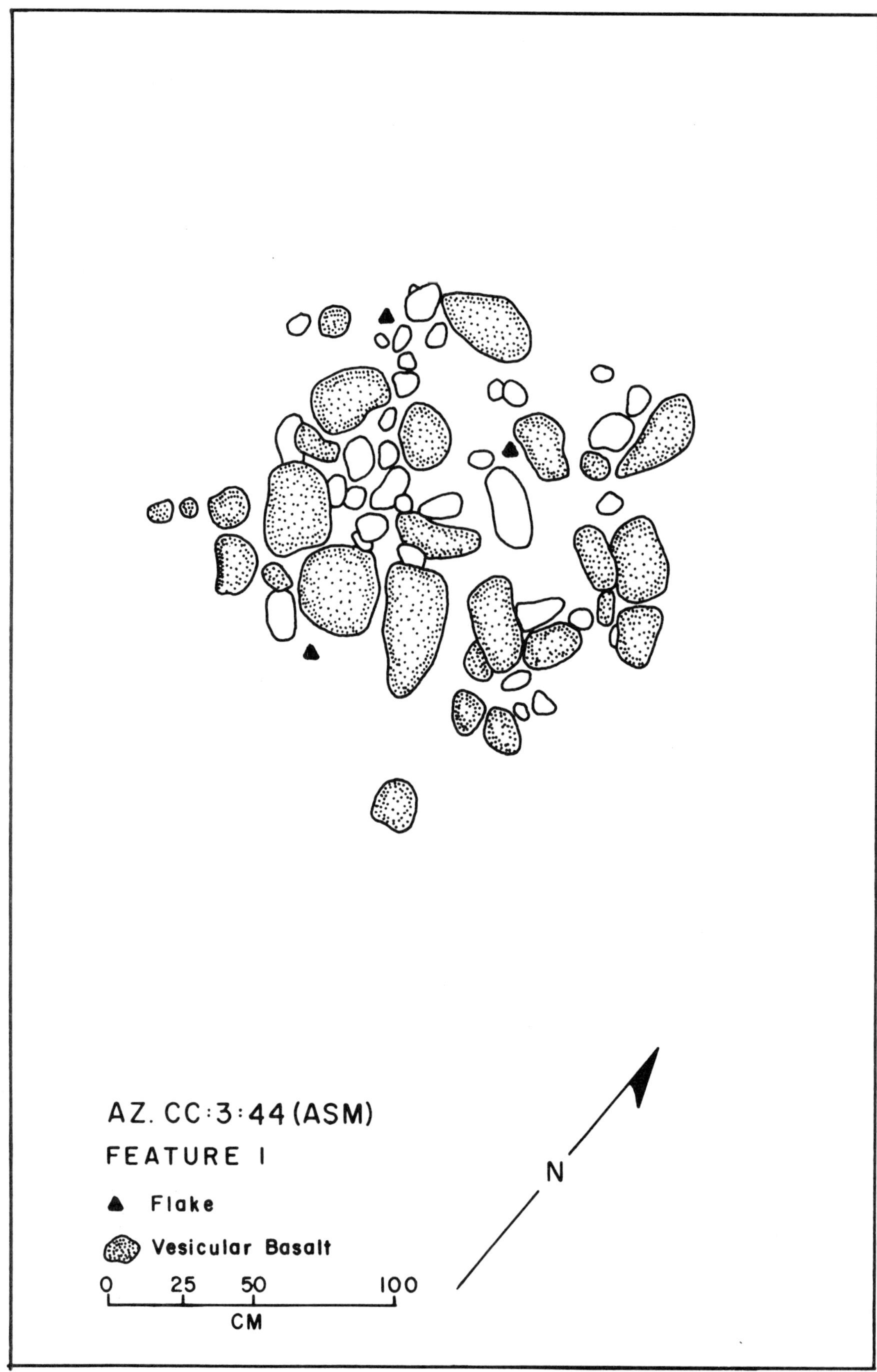

Figure 77. Arizona CC:3:44, Feature 1

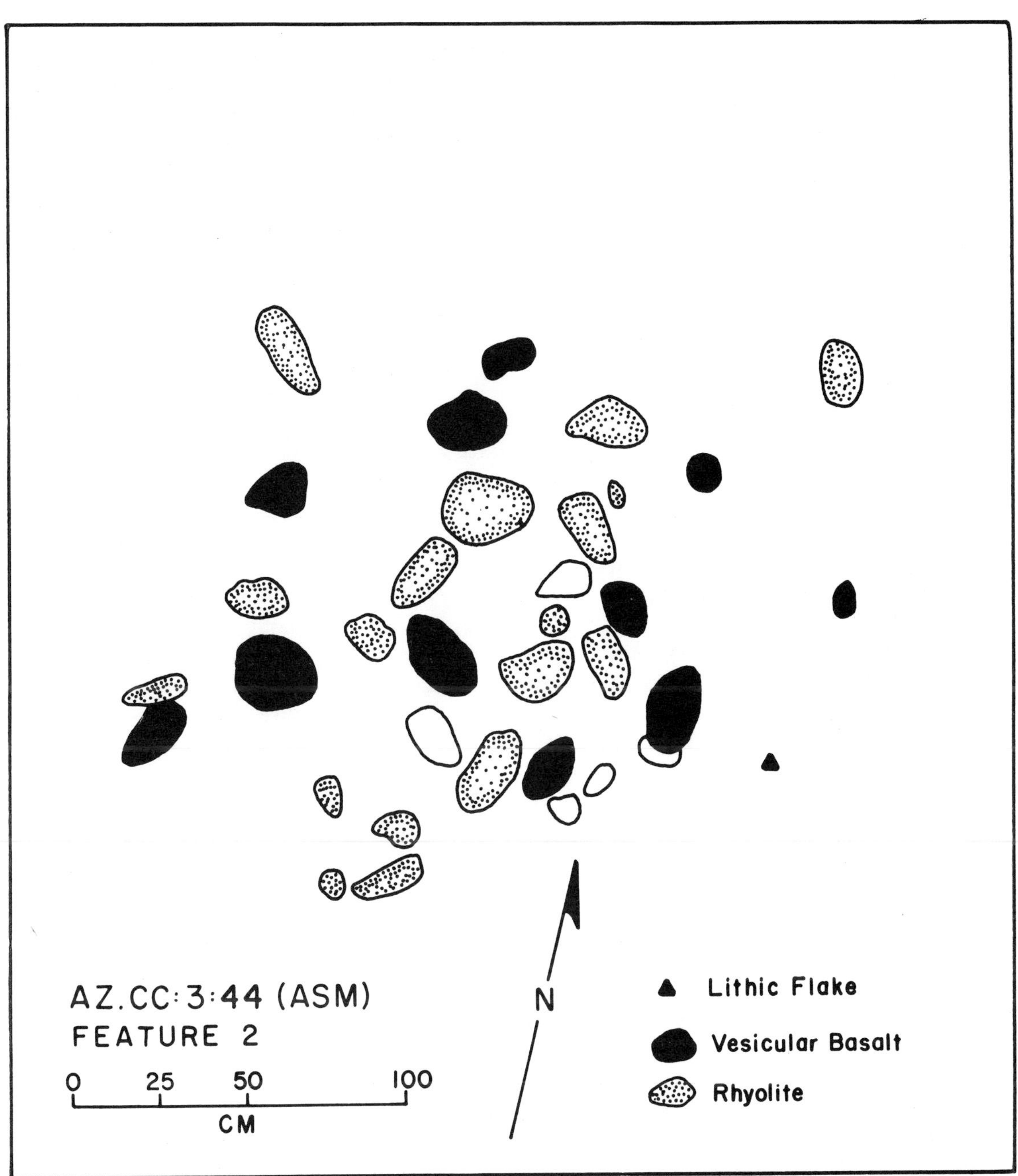

Figure 78. Arizona CC:3:44, Feature 2

lacking on 67 percent of the bi-directionally flaked cores. This is similar to the phenomenon observed at Arizona CC:2:56 and could be the result of testing stones for knapability or haphazard procurement of flakes. Silicates, rhyolite, and basalt were equally represented maong the cores at 33.3 percent each.

Primary flakes constitute only 15.4 percent of the flake total. The majority consists of 50 percent secondary flakes and 34.6 percent tertiary flakes. Silicates and rhyolite dominate the flake assemblage at 50 and 46 percent, respectively. Basalt makes up 4 percent of the flakes.

The tool class is divided between utilized debitage (43 percent) and formal tools (57 percent). Of two utilized flakes one was used on the lateral edge, the second on the perimenter. One uni-directional core exhibited usage. Four unifaces were the only formal tools, all of which were used on a lateral edge. Edge angles on utilized pieces ranged from 37 to 77 degrees with a mean of 59.4 degrees. Although the range of edge angles is fairly wide, the actual number of tools is too low to postulate specific tasks. The salient feature of this site, however, is an apparent preferential selection of silicates to manufacture flakes for expedient use, and manufacturing and sharpening formal tools. No tools of rhyolite were found, but the occurrence of cores and flakes of this material indicates primary and secondary core reduction possibly to obtain flakes for blanks that were taken elsewhere. The single basalt flake, contrasted with four basalt cores suggests large flakes were removed for further reduction or use elsewhere.

Arizona CC:3:24

Elevation: 1154-1169 m
Site Size: 280 m WSW/ENE by 24-53 m NE/SW (Locus 72);
25 m by 20 m (Locus 72S);
50 m E/W by 200 m N/S (Locus 72X);
all arbitrary boundaries
Field Designation: AEPCO 72-72S-72X

This site covers the tops and slopes of two crests and a separating saddle of a northeast/southwest trending ridge at the base of the Peloncillo Mountains. Ridges in the area are dissected by unnamed washes generally flowing towards Yuma Wash. The Gila River is 0.75 miles south/south/east of the site.

Vegetation is dominated by creosotebush, but large stands of prickly pear cactus occur on the northern slopes. The group surface consists of unconsolidated gravels and cobbles. Naturally fractured quartzite, chalcedony, rhyolite, obsidian and, above all, basalt were abundant.

AEPCO 72 was the field designation for the site in the R-O-W corridor. The access road survey revealed that the site was also present on the ridge crest north of the saddle; this area was designated AEPCO 72X. During the data recovery phase it was discovered that there was material in the saddle between the two crests; this was designated AEPCO 72S.

Though initially treated as one continuous lithic scatter, the analysis of the chipped stone industries showed the three areas differed significantly from each other and did not represent a homogeneous scatter. The three field designations have been retained as locus designations. One hundred percent sampling was done at this site.

The grid columns set up on AEPCO 72 (Figure 79) followed the ridge crest. Two hundred and sixty m^2 grid squares were laid out, of which 38 percent had artifacts. Eleven of the 18 irregular grids (at turning points on grid columns) also had artifacts. Forty-five 5 m^2 grids on AEPCO 72X (Figure 80) were laid out over a concentration on the east side of the crest. Sixty percent of these had artifacts. As AEPCO 72S (Figure 81) was an area with small sherds and thinning flakes that were almost impossible to see from a standing position, 56 1.25 m^2 grids were laid out over the concentration and were either screened or trowelled to better reveal any tiny material. Sixty-six percent of the grids yielded material. In addition 10 5 m^2 grids and one irregular grid square were investigated.

Feature 1 of AEPCO 72S (Figure 82) was a cobble cluster of vesicular basalt cobbles and boulders. It was 1.90 m east/west by 0.92 m north/south. Gravel from a large ant hill partially obscured the feature's ground surface. Surface cobbles were removed and the surface trowelled for pit outlines. No second coursing of stones was present. All surface and substrate dirt from the feature was screened, and a 50 cm^2 pit was excavated 20 cm below the surface to the level where caliche was visible. At 10 cm below the surface two naturally fractured obsidian flakes were recovered. No other cultural materials, soil staining, ash, or charcoal were observed in the trench fill. Artifacts were present on the surface in and around the feature.

At AEPCO 72S one bowl body sherd of Mimbres Boldface Black-on-white, one sherd of Mimbres Black-on-white and five jar (?) body sherds of an unidentified corrugated ware were recovered.

Locus 72

Two hundred and sixty-three chipped stone artifacts were collected from Locus 72. These consisted of 44 cores, 213 flakes, and 6 unifaces. Although silicates are most numerous, the percentages of material types do not vary significantly and no material dominates the collection. Silicates compose 32 percent of the artifacts, basalt 24.7 percent, rhyolite 23.2 percent, quartzite 16.3 percent, quartz 2.3 percent and other types 1.5 percent. Notable is the high percentage of quartzite artifacts, which ordinarily occur in low frequencies at project sites.

Uni-directional cores dominate the core class at 59 percent. Bi-directional cores constitute 18 percent and multi-directional cores 23 percent. Platform preparation was evident on 95 percent of the cores, indicating a standardized reduction technique. Numerically, basalt cores are dominant, but the percentage frequencies do not vary significantly among material types to indicate a favored type. Basalt constitutes 41 percent of the cores, rhyolite 32 percent, silicates 23 percent, and quartzite 4 percent. Rhyolite and basalt together constitute 73 percent of the cores.

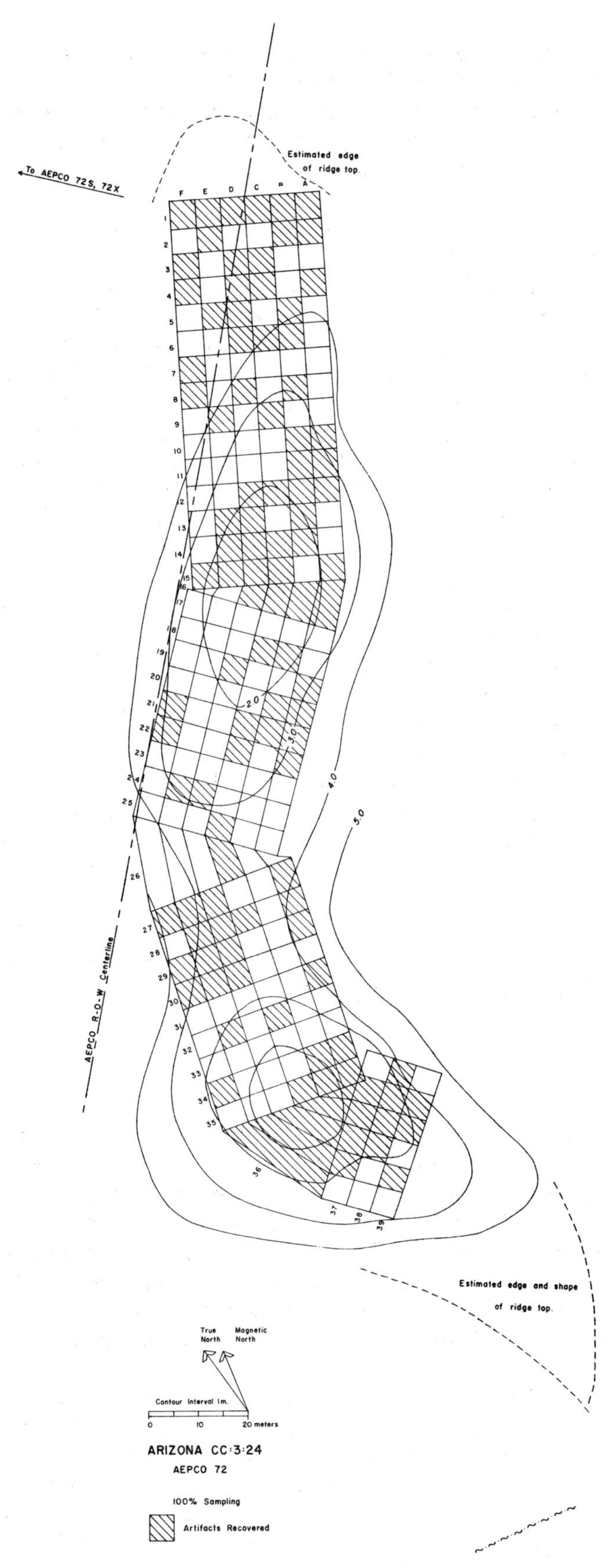

Figure 79. Arizona CC:3:24, Locus 72, site map.

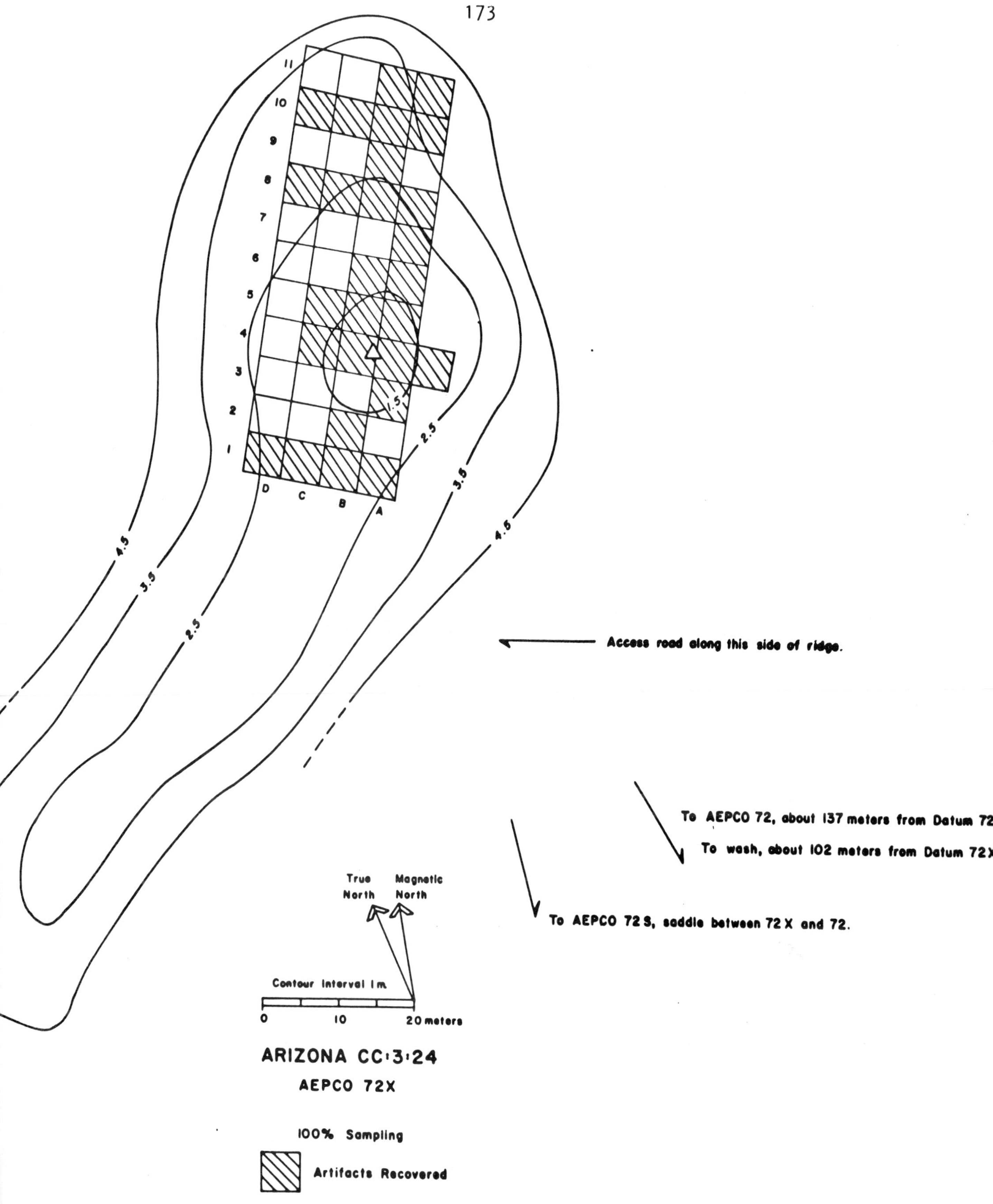

Figure 80. Arizona CC:3:24, Locus 72X, site map

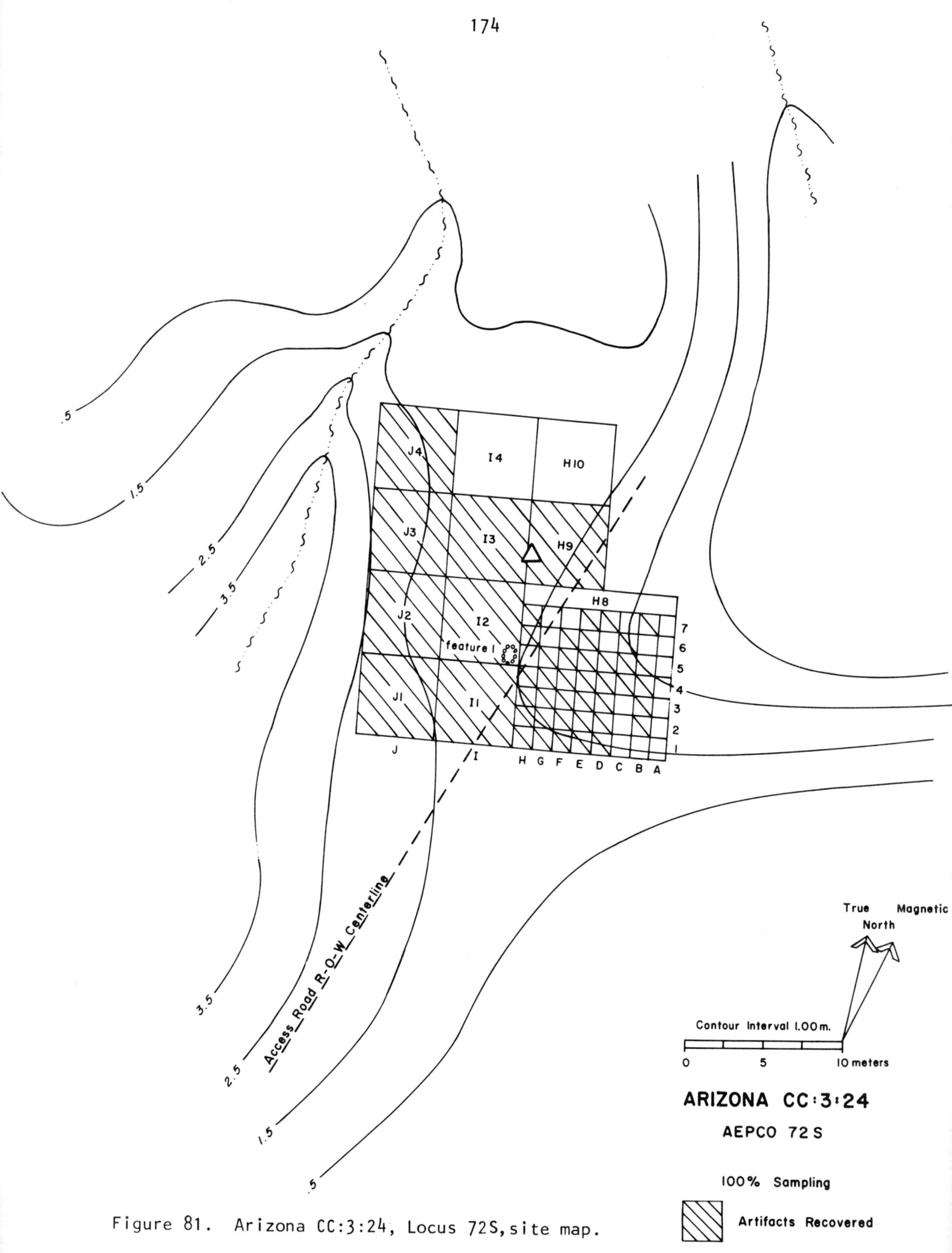

Figure 81. Arizona CC:3:24, Locus 72S, site map.

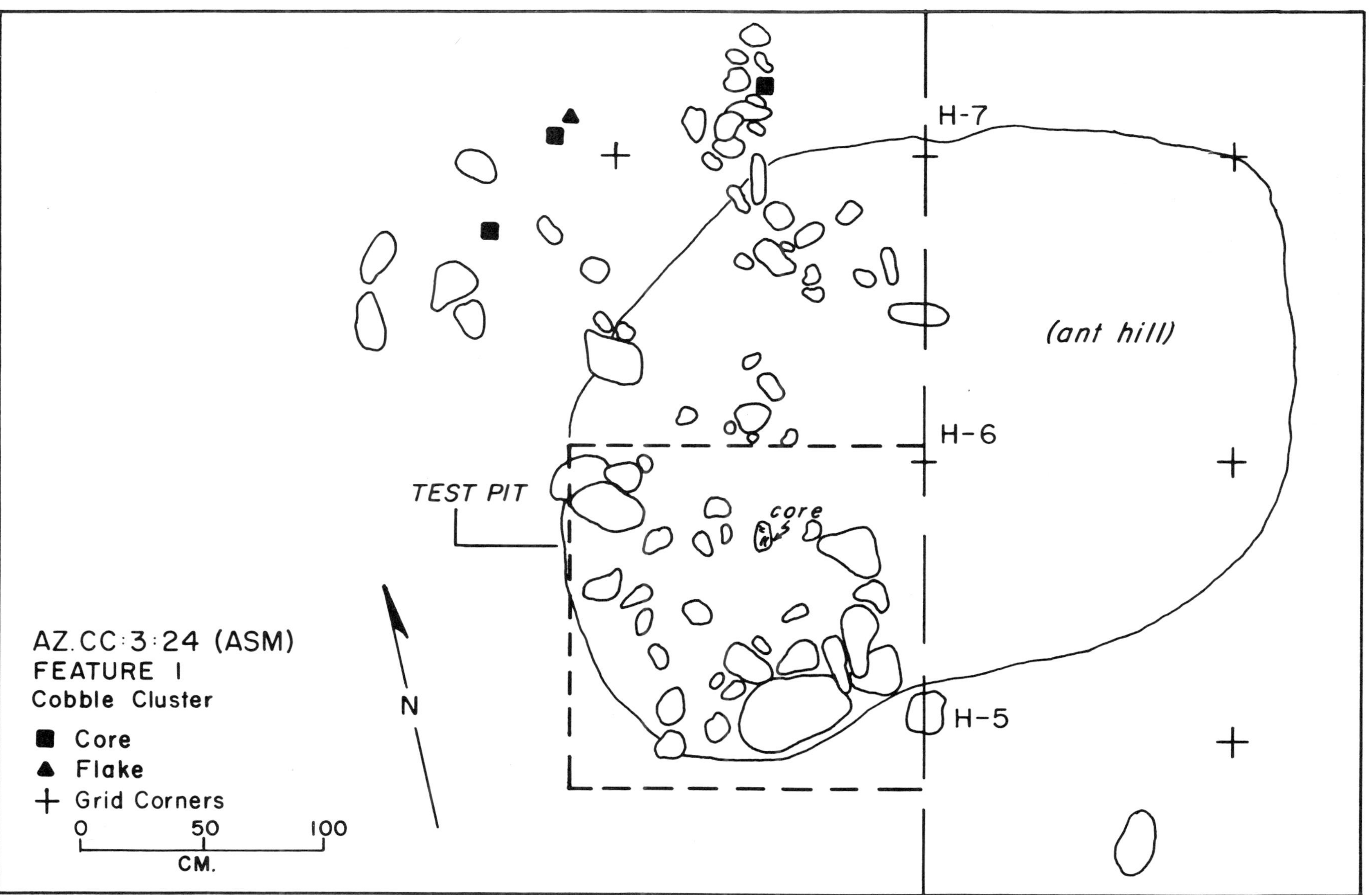

Figure 82. Arizona CC:3:24, Locus 72S, Feature 1

It can be suggested that igneous core reduction predominated over reduction of silicates at this site, a divergence from the observed norm for this stratum.

In the category of flakes and shatter,primary flakes account for 16.4 percent of the total, secondary flakes for 36.6 percent, tertiary flakes for 28.6 percent, and shatter for 18.3 percent. Basalt, rhyolite, silicate, and quartzite flakes occur in close relative frequencies to each other, as was the case for material composition of cores. The available data indicate that primary and secondary core reduction of the above materials was occurring with nearly equal intensity. This is similarily apparent in the tool assemblage.

Tools consists of three utilized flakes, five utilized cores, and six unifaces. No preferential use of material types is indicated for the utilized debitage. Uni-directional and multi-directional cores were both made of rhyolite, basalt, and silicate. Two rhyolite flakes were utilized on the distal end, one silicate flake showed use on a lateral edge. This "mixed bag" of tools reflects a divergence from the norm for sites in this stratum; it appears any handy piece with a usable edge was used; that is, items of a particular material type were not preferentially selected. Selectivity is apparent in the formal tool class, however. Of the six unifaces, five were silicate (the norm) and one was quartzite. Use of these two materials to manufacture tools and for subsequent tool maintenance is reflected in the frequencies of secondary and tertiary flakes of this material (Appendix I, Table 27A). Four unifaces were used on the distal end, one on a lateral edge, and one on the perimeter. Edge angles on utilized pieces ranged from 40 to 83 degrees, with a mean of 60 degrees. Light microflaking occurred in the form of round and elongated unifacial scars on tool exteriors. It appears that unmodified flakes and cores as well as formal tools were used equally to carry out activities at this locus.

Locus 72S

Two hundred and sixty-four chipped stone artifacts were collected from Locus 72S. This number includes 24 cores, 233 flakes and shatter, 6 unifaces, and 1 biface. This locus differs from Locus 72 in that obsidian, absent in the latter, was present and Mimbres branch Mogollon sherds were found in association. Also, a much higher ratio of flakes to cores occurred (10:1 for Locus 72S, compared to 5:1 for Locus 72). The material composition of artifacts is as follows: 40.5 percent silicates, 25.3 percent basalt, 21.6 percent rhyolite, 6.1 percent obsidian, 0.4 percent quartzite, and 6.1 percent unidentified types.

Uni-directional cores constitute 63 percent of the total cores, with bi-directional cores comprising 21 percent and multi-directional cores 16 percent. Platform preparation was evident on 88 percent of all cores. Distribution of material type among cores was fairly consistent among basalt (38 percent), rhyolite (29 percent), and silicates (29 percent). Quartzite comprised the remaining 4 percent.

Of 233 flakes, primary flakes constitute 18.5 percent, secondary flakes are 33.5 percent, tertiary flakes 38.6 percent, and shatter is 9.4 percent. Silicates dominate with 40 percent; basalt follows at 25 percent, rhyolite 21 percent, with obsidian and unidentified types contributing 7 percent each. Based on these data, primary and secondary core reduction on basalt, rhyolite, and silicates is a typical activity. Silicate tool manufacture, use, and refurbishing is also indicated, a typical pattern for this stratum. No cores or tools of obsidian were found; presumably only obsidian tool resharpening was done here.

The tool class is weighed in favor of formal tools over unmodified, utilized debitage. There are five silicate unifaces and one rhyolite uniface, one silicate biface, one utilized rhyolite flake, and two utilized cores. Four of the unifaces are utilized on lateral edges, one on the perimeter and one on the distal end. Light microflaking on utilized edges occurs in the form of round and elongated unifacial scars on tool exteriors. Edge angles range from 43 to 60 degrees with a mean of 53.0 degrees.

The occurrence of sherds with the obsidian thinning flakes may represent the remains of a food gathering kit, assuming obsidian tools were used for obtaining and processing vegetal materials.

Locus 72X

Fifteen cores, 230 flakes, four unifaces, and one biface were collected from this locus, a total of 259 chipped stone artifacts. Again, an even distribution of material types occurs in the artifact assemblage. Silicates constitute 39 percent, basalt 21.6 percent, rhyolite 15 percent, obsidian 17.4 percent, quartzite 6.6 percent, and unidentified types 0.4 percent. Noteworthy is the comparatively high frequency of obsidian, the highest yet recorded for this stratum. Also, this locus has the highest ratio of flakes to cores (16:1) of all sites in this stratum. Two lithic industries may be occurring at this site -- obsidian tool use and refurbishing, and silicate tool manufacture and use.

The low number of cores, coupled with a low frequency of primary flakes, indicate primary core reduction was not a common activity at this site. A consistent variable, however, is that uni-directional cores are the most common (73 percent). Bi-directional cores represent 20 percent and a single multi-directional core contributes the remaining 6 percent. Silicates comprise 40 percent of the cores, rhyolite 27 percent, basalt and quartzite 13 percent each, and one unidentified type 7 percent.

Of the total flake count, primary flakes comprise a low 5 percent, secondary flakes 19.2 percent, tertiary flakes 67.4 percent and shatter 8.4 percent. Silicates account for 39 percent of flakes, basalt 23 percent, obsidian 17 percent, rhyolite 15 percent, and quartzite 6 percent. The high frequency of tertiary flakes suggests flake tool manufacture, use, and resharpening, especially on silicates and obsidian. Other materials were used, but with less emphasis.

The few tools consisted of two utilized silicate flakes, one silicate uniface, three obsidian unifaces, and one obsidian biface. Two unifaces were utilized on lateral edges, one on the perimeter, and one on the distal end. Edge angles on utilized pieces ranged from 44 to 69 degrees with a mean of 57 degrees. Light microflaking occurred in the form of round unifacial scars. The information derived from the debitage and tools at this locus suggests that production and use of formal tools was a primary activity at this site, with utilization of unmodified flakes of secondary importance.

Arizona CC:3:22

Elevation: 1141 m
Site Size: 15 m by 7 m (Locus A; natural boundaries)
75 m (along centerline) by 60 m (arbitrary boundary; Locus B)
Field Designation: AEPCO 74 (now Locus A) and AEPCO 111 (now Locus B)

This site is located on a low, gentle slope trending southwesterly towards a tributary of Yuma Wash. To the northeast is a series of descending southwest-northeast oriented basalt ridges. The area where the site is located is wide and flat with easy access to the surrounding low hills and the Black Hills of the Peloncillo Mountains. These surrounding hills are source areas for basalt and chalcedony. Chert, jasper, quartzite, and obsidian nodules ("Apache tears") are more abundant in the site area than in the higher country to the northeast.

On-site vegetation is predominantly creosotebush; also occurring are ocotillo, paloverde, Mormon tea, prickly pear, pencil cholla, cane cholla, and hedgehog and rainbow cactus. The substrate consists of consolidated igneous outcrops and unconsolidated gravels, cobbles, and boulders eroding from the northwestern basalt ridges. Sandy loam soils are present.

This site was chosen for further exploration because it was one of the many isolated lithic manufacturing loci found in the Peloncillo Mountains foothills, consisting of several chipping stations and a very sparse scatter of lithics.

Locus A is separated from Locus B by a small drainage. Locus A (Figure 83) consisted of a quartzite chipping station (Feature 1 in Figure 83) and a possible basalt chipping station (Feature 2). The basalt assemblage consisted of several cortical flakes and cores that were later determined to be the result of natural fracturing. It was often difficult to distinguish between natural and cultural fracturing of basalt in this basaltic mountain area. All artifacts were bagged, their provenience was pinpointed on the site map, and they collected. Chipping stations were collected as a unit. Only Feature 1, Locus A was drawn in detail (Figure 84). Subsequent lithic analysis revealed specific attributes of each feature.

Feature 1, Locus A (Figure 84) is a lithic concentration consisting of six quartzite flakes, one piece of quartzite shatter, two obsidian

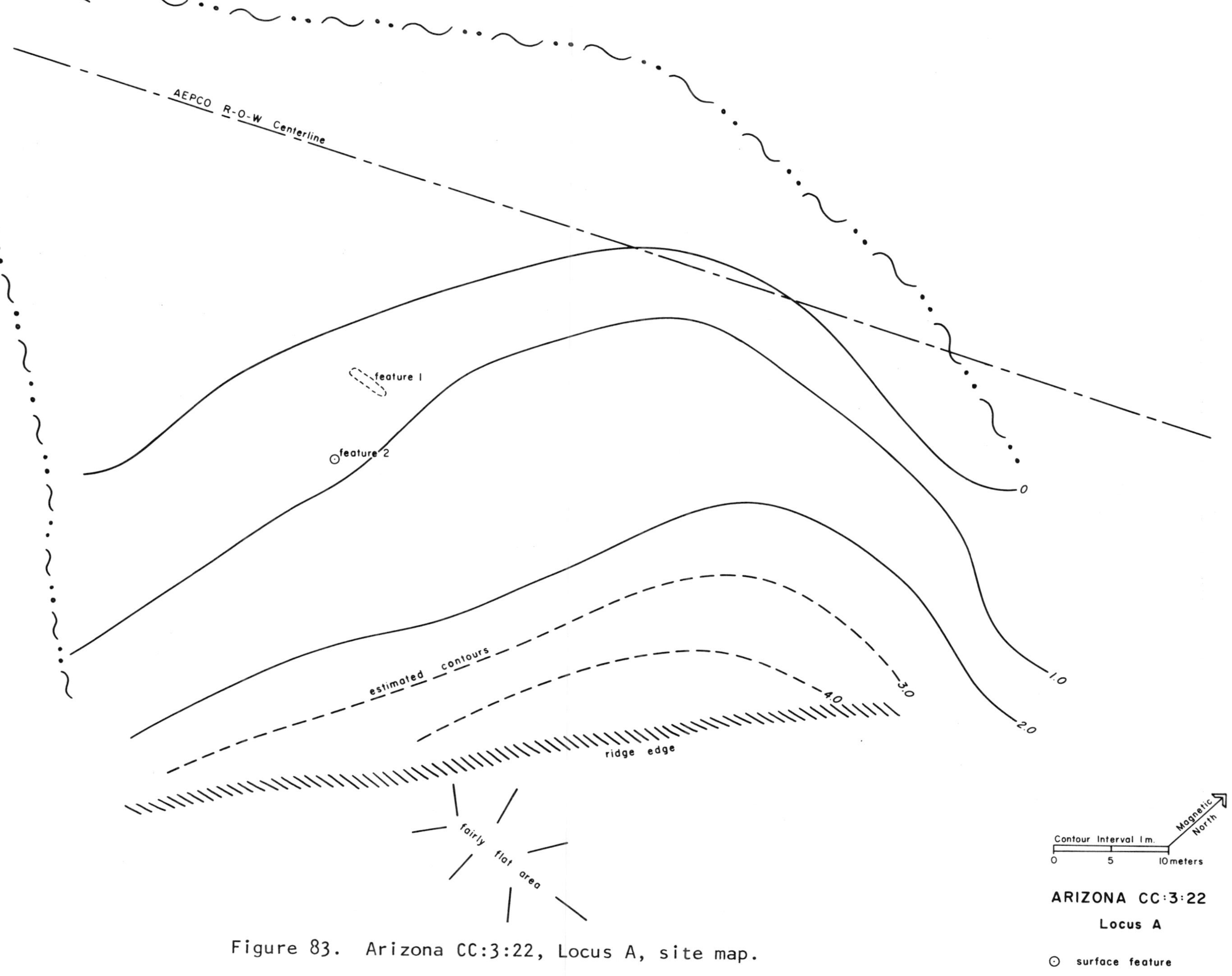

Figure 83. Arizona CC:3:22, Locus A, site map.

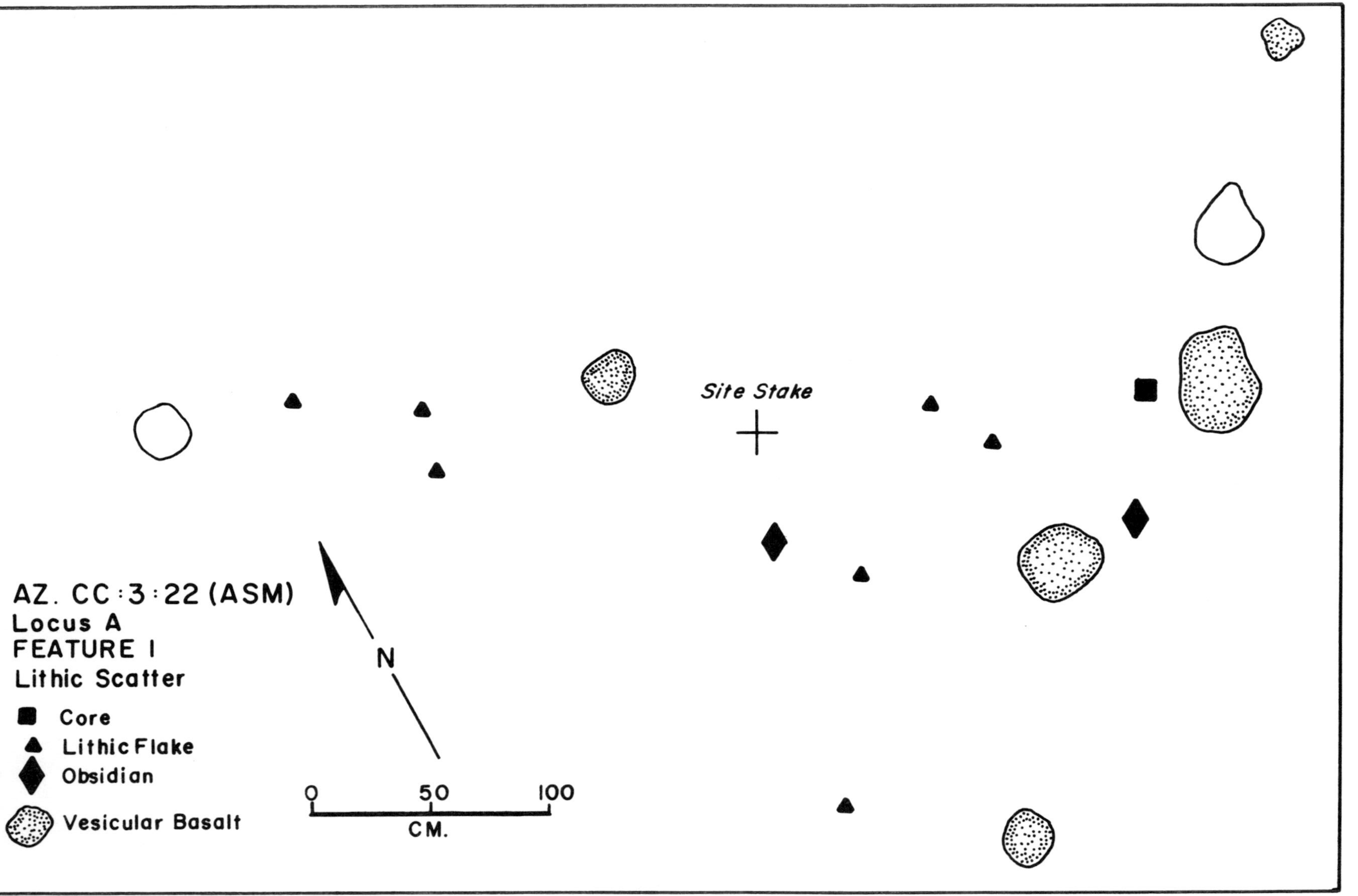

Figure 84. Arizona CC:3:22, Locus A. Feature 1

flakes, and one piece of obsidian shatter. Since no obsidian or quartzite cores occurred on the site, it may be assumed that Feature 1 represents the remains of a flake tool manufacturing or refurbishing station.

Locus B (Figure 85) is an area of at least five chipping stations and a few scattered lithics. As the proposed access road was realigned several times on this site, not all of the site was investigated during the data recovery phase. Only three of the chipping stations located in the impact zone (Features 1, 2, and 3) were collected.

Feature 1, Locus B contained a quartzite uniface, four secondary flakes, and two pieces of shatter. Feature 2, a basalt chipping station contained a uni-directional prepared core, three primary flakes, and four secondary flakes. Feature 3 is another basalt chipping station with one uni-directional prepared core, two primary flakes, and five secondary flakes.

Although they were separated by a drainage, the two loci share a similar pattern of a series of isolated chipping stations and are considered to be loci within a wide lithic "use area." Such a use area naturally has no true boundaries and is discontinuous over a vast area.

Stratum 6: Peloncillo Mountains

All sites in Stratum 6 were avoided by AEPCO and consequently no investigation was carried out.

Stratum 7: Gila River Terraces

This zone includes steep to very steep, deeply dissected old terrace fronts adjacent to the Gila and San Francisco rivers. The Big Lue Mountains are to the north and the Peloncillo Mountains are south of the Gila River. All sites chosen for data recovery occur on the ridges and terrace fronts near small drainages that flow into a major southward drainage of the Gila River.

The surfaces of the sites are strewn with cobbles of rhyolite, basalt, and chert, all of which would provide raw materials for tool production. Small unworked chert nodules were present in great quantities on several sites. All sites are widely dispersed scatters of predominately chert and rhyolite tools and debitage. A few chipping stations occur, but rock piles or possible hearths or sleeping circles are rare.

Included in this unit are areas with soils belonging to the Calciorthids and Torriorthents group. These severely eroded soils occur on rough broken land on low hills. Outcrops of barren and exposed welded tuff and conglomerate also occur. The eroded and deteriorated condition of these areas severely limits vegetative cover. Most wildlife found here are transient between adjacent areas with better cover and food sources.

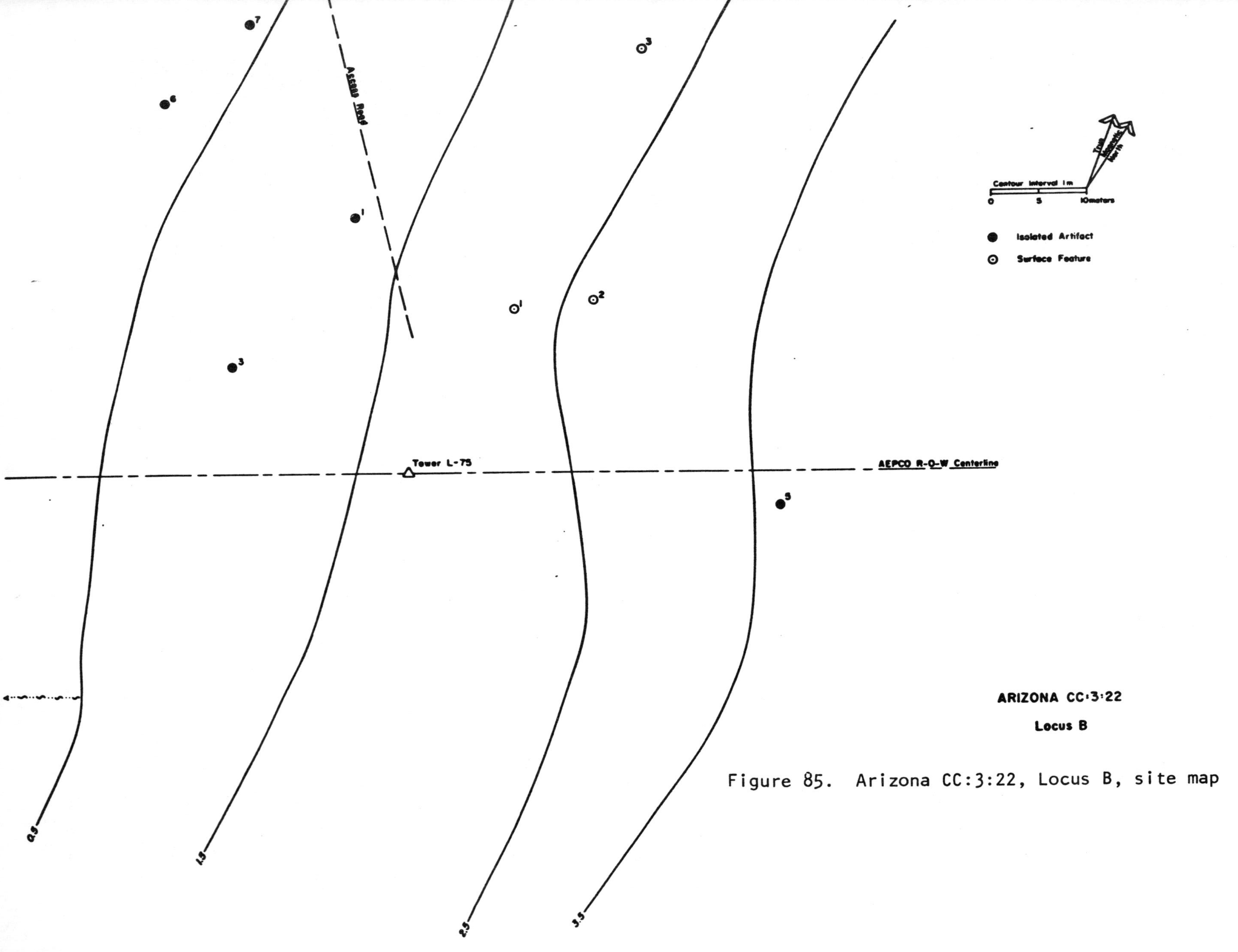

Figure 85. Arizona CC:3:22, Locus B, site map

The majority of soils in this zone belong to the Trés Hermanos soil series. This series, found all along the lower terraces of the Gila Valley, consists of deep, well-drained, calcareous soils that have a gravelly, sandy loam surface layer. The vegetation is mainly creosotebush, cactus and few annual grasses and weeds, but some areas in this stratum, particularly on hill crests, are barren. Acacia, yucca, and mesquite grow in the small drainages.

Arizona CC:3:4

<u>Elevation:</u> 1149-1163 m
<u>Site Size:</u> 105 m N/S by 115 m E/W
<u>Field Designation:</u> AEPCO 25

The site is a lithic scatter situated on the crest and steep eastern slope of a high ridge immediately to the west and above Negro Canyon, the floor of which lies about 200 m below the ridge crest. The ridge (Figure 86) is one of many in an area of high, dissected ridges cut by draingages that flow south to the Gila River, 5.7 km away. In the distance, the Peloncillo Mountains lie 12.5 km to the south. On-site vegetation includes sparsely distributed creosotebush, acacia, <u>Aplopappus</u>, and grasses. Wolfberry grows in several clumps on the ridgetop. The soil is unconsolidated sandy loam intermixed with gravels and small cobbles. The crest of the ridge is littered with cobbles of rhyolite, basalt, and chert. The majority of cultural material was concentrated on the ridge crest, with lithics extending for an undetermined distance north and south, well beyond the R-O-W impact zone. Some material has eroded down the eastern slope. The R-O-W centerline passes through the center of the site's east-west axis, perpendicular to the ridgetop.

Figure 86. Arizona CC:3:4, overview.

Figure 87. Arizona CC:3:19, rock pile.

Figure 88. Arizona CC:3:20, view of Gila River and high terraces.

Figure 89. Arizona CC:3:20, view across north portion on site terrace.

A 30 m wide grid was established over the R-O-W corridor for a total length of 100 m (Figure 90). Fifty percent of the grid squares were sampled and all material from sampled squares was collected. Collections of possible tools were made from five non-sample grid squares. Of the 60 grid squares investigated, 24 yielded material, for a 40 percent data recovery. An intensive survey was conducted in the area outside of the grid to define the true site boundaries on the ridge slope. Along the ridge crest, however, lithics do extend for an undetermined distance north and south, well beyond the R-O-W. In the course of investigation four discrete areas of lithic activity were located; these were designated as features.

Feature 1 was chert concentration consisting of one primary flake, three secondary flakes, one piece of shatter, and one utilized flake.

Feature 2 consisted of one chert uniface and two chert secondary flakes.

Feature 3, a chipping station, consisted of one rhyolite uni-directional prepared core with more than 50 percent cortex remaining, and two rhyolite secondary flakes.

Feature 4 was a lithic cluster containing one utilized uni-directional prepared core of variegated chert without cortex, one chert primary flake, and one chert secondary flake.

Three circular rock features located on the survey were determined to be remnants of an old fenceline. Bits of barbed wire, and boulders wrapped in barbed wire in alignment with the stone circles substantiated this view. In addition, the fenceline corresponds to the section line between Sections 21 and 22 of Zone 12 on the UTM grid.

One isolated historic artifact was collected from the base of the ridge (Surface Collection 2). This is a shattered purple glass telephone or telegraph pole insulator. Embossed around the lower skirt is the following: "...New York/BR...". A reference given in Tibbitts (1967: 11) indicates that this could be an insulator made by the Brookfield Glass Co. of New York City, which produced insulators between the years 1865 and 1920, the latter date being the year when the company ceased production. While several modes of labelling were used on Brookfield insulators (for example, listing of the company address, dates of patents), the "BROOKFIELD, NEW YORK" embossed label was used after 1903. Later insulators read simply "BROOKFIELD."

This site yielded a total collection of 7 cores, 74 flakes, 7 silicate unifaces, and 2 rhyolite bifaces. The lithic assemblage was overwhelmingly dominated by silicates (95.6 percent), with rhyolite constituting the remaining 4.4 percent. This was expected in view of the availability of siliceous material in this stratum. Pebble to fist sized nodules and cobbles of cherts and chalcedonies are frequent on ridgetops in the area, although rhyolites are also common.

It is noteworthy that all of the flakes are composed of silicates. Primary flakes constitute only 9.5 percent of the total flake count, contrasted with 59.5 percent secondary flakes, 25.7 percent tertiary flakes,

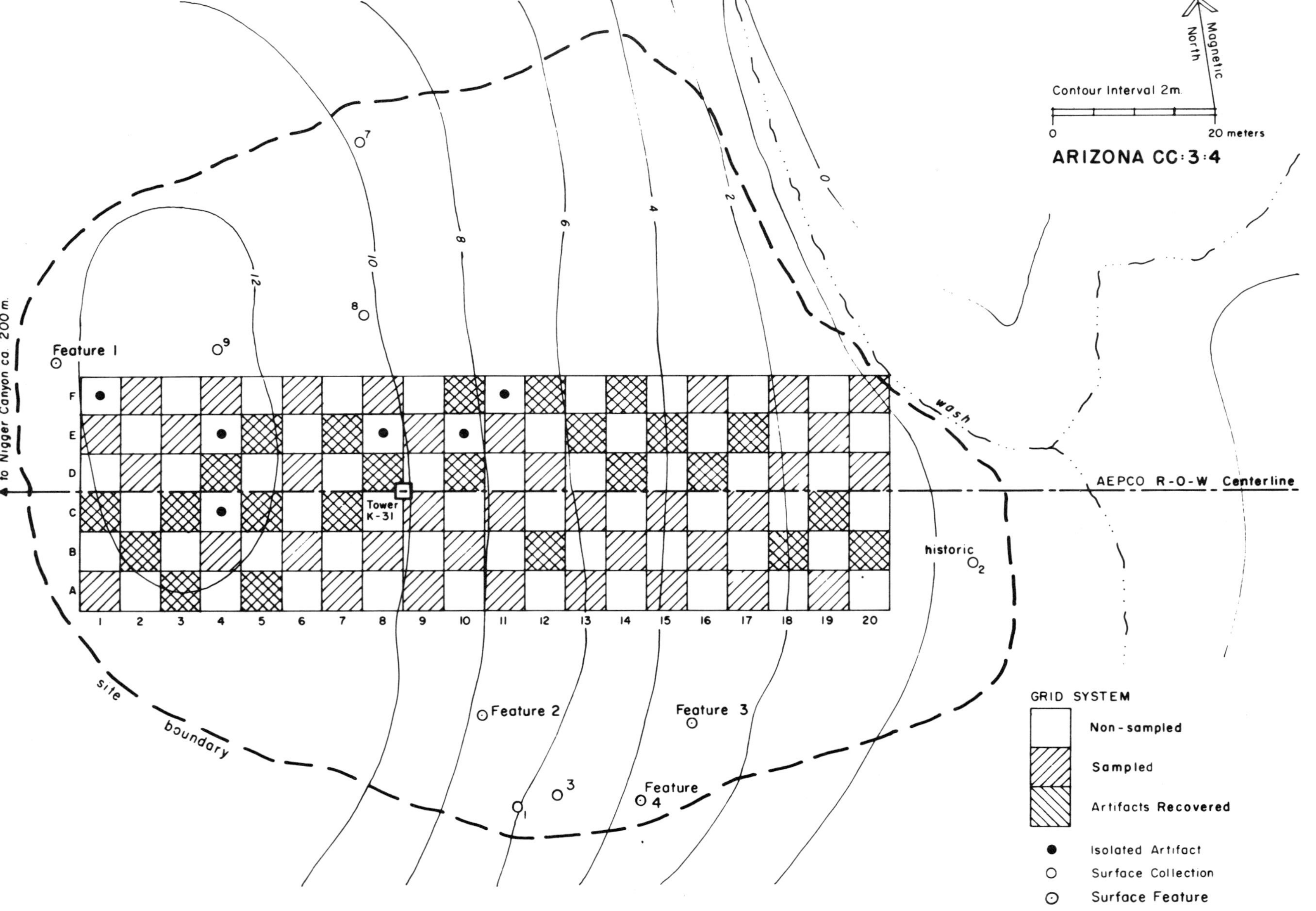

Figure 90. Arizona CC:3:4, site map.

and 5.4 percent shatter. Five of the cores are silicates and two are rhyolite. Uni-directional cores are the dominant form at 86 percent; a single multi-directional silicate core comprises the remaining 14 percent. Platform preparation was present on all but one bi-directional core. The low number of primary flakes and low core count would indicate that core reduction probably was not a primary activity at this site. The high frequency of secondary and tertiary flakes, which together comprise 70 percent of the total lithic assemblage, would seem to indicate that primary flake reduction, tool production, and possibly tool resharpening were occurring at this site. The chipping stations recorded at the site help substantiate this assumption.

The tool assemblage is divided between 57 percent utilized debitage (11 flakes and 1 core) and 43 percent formal tools (7 silicate unifaces and 2 rhyolite bifaces). However, only one uniface and one biface exhibited use. Silicates comprise 96 percent of all tools indicating a possible preferential selection of cherts and chalcedonies for tool manufacture. It is likely that the two rhyolite bifaces were brought in from elsewhere; the data do not support rhyolite tool manufacture at this site.

Edge angles on utilized pieces range from 47 to 70 degrees with a mean of 59.6 degrees. Round bifacial microscars occur on utilized edges. The variable range of acuteness may indicate a variety of cutting and scraping activities at the site. It is not certain if the formal tools and utilized flakes are components of the same tool kit, despite the fact that all are made of silicates. More detailed attribute analysis of tools and intra-site artifact distribution would be necessary to test hypotheses on tool and site functions.

Arizona CC:3:17

Elevation: 1107-113 m
Site Size: 114 m N/S by 72 m E/W
Field Designation: AEPCO 9

The site is located on a south sloping ridge above a small wash draining into tributaries of the Gila River 1.12 km to the south-southwest. The area is between two major rivers, the Gila to the south-southwest and the San Francisco to the northwest. The Peloncillo Mountains lie south of the Gila River. On-site vegetation includes creosotebush, scrub mesquite, *Ephedra*, and *Aplopappus*, all sparsely distributed along the ridgetop. The soil of the ridge and site area is a loamy sand of the Calciorthids and Torriorthents group. A medium-dense cover of gravels and small cobbles covers the surface and becomes increasingly rocky toward the two drainages on the east and west sides of the site. Available lithic resources include cobbles of rhyolite, chert, quartzite, and basalt. The R-O-W centerline passes through the east-central portion of the site.

Data recovery for Arizona CC:3:17 involved a 50 percent non-random sample from within the R-O-W corridor. A grid, 30 m east-west by 115 m north-south was established along the R-O-W centerline and surface collections were made of all materials within every other 5 m^2 grid square.

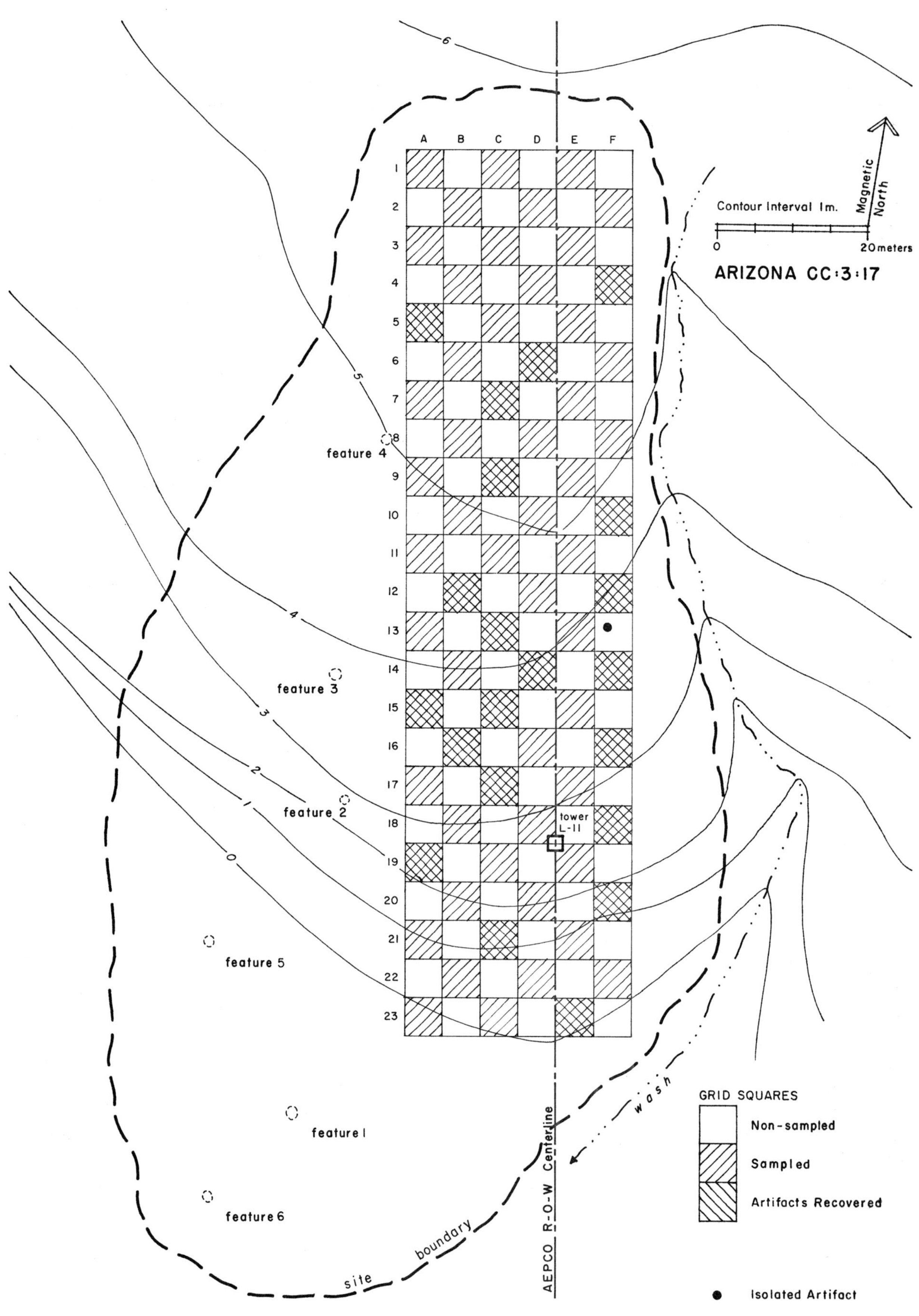

Figure 91. Arizona CC:3:17, site map.

Figure 91 illustrates the grid system and general distribution of material. Of the 69 investigated grids, 21 yielded material, a 30.4 percent data recovery from within the R-O-W corridor. After completion of the grid collection, an intensive survey was made to define the site boundaries and to locate and collect observed chipping stations and possible tools that occurred outside of the R-O-W.

Six lithic concentrations were located adjacent to the R-O-W corridor and were designated as features since they appeared to be discrete localities of knapping activity.

Feature 1 consisted of three white chert secondary flakes and two chert unifaces, and may be a remnant of a chipping station.

Feature 2 consisted of two uni-directional cores, two primary flakes, three secondary flakes, two utilized flakes, and a uniface, all of variegated chert. One of the cores was utilized. The primary utilized flake had an edge angle of 45 degrees with an edge length of 13 mm; the secondary flake had an edge angle of 46 degrees with an edge length of 16 mm. The uniface had an edge angle of 85 degrees with a used edge length of 32 mm. The steep edge angle may indicate a special scraping activity.

Feature 3 consisted of 3 primary flakes, 10 secondary flakes, and 1 utilized uniface, all of white chert. The uniface exhibited traces of cortical material and had an edge angle of 41 degrees with a use edge length of 15 mm. Also collected in association with this feature were a utilized obsidian biface and a utilized secondary flake of variegated chert. The biface had an edge angle of 35 degrees and a use edge length of 20 mm. The flake was utilized on its right lateral edge and had an edge angle of 41 degrees with an edge length of 15 mm.

Feature 4, a lithic concentration, consisted of four complete secondary flakes, one of basalt and three of quartzite, and a complete bi-directional prepared variegated chert core.

Feature 5 consisted of three secondary chert flakes, two pieces of chert shatter, one uni-directional prepared core of unidentified material, and three variegated chert unifaces. The feature may be the remains of a tool manufacturing area.

Feature 6, a chert knapping area, consisted of five secondary flakes, two utilized secondary flakes, one utilized primary flake, and one uniface. The feature probably represents an area where biotic resources were being processed.

A total of 5 cores, 99 flakes, 1 biface and 6 unifaces were recovered from the surface collections at this site. As at Arizona CC:3:4 , silicates dominated the assemblage (84.8 percent), with rhyolite, basalt, quartzite, obsidian, and unidentified types representing less than 5 percent each.

A low ratio of cores to flakes (1:17) is present. The total flake count, broken down into 12.1 percent primary flakes, 44.4 percent secondary flakes, 36.4 percent tertiary flakes, and 7 percent shatter, shows a low frequency of primary flakes contrasted with relatively high frequencies of secondary and tertiary flakes. With secondary and tertiary flakes comprising 80 percent of the flake total, it would appear that primary flake reduction, tool production and tool re-sharpening may have been the primary lithic manufacturing activities. Low core and primary flake frequencies would seem to indicate that core reduction was not an important activity.

Examination of the lithic concentrations (Features 1 through 6) aid in interpreting lithic activity at this site. Features 1, 3, and 6 may represent discrete areas of chert tool production, based on the co-occurrence of flakes and unifaces. Features 2, 3, and 6 additionally contained utilized flakes. This aspect tentatively suggests that tools were being produced for *in situ* exploitation of biotic resources.

The tool assemblage is divided between utilized flakes and formal unifacial and bifacial tools. All of the utilized flakes were composed of silicates and constitute 63 percent of the total tool sample. Five utilized silicate unifaces and one obsidian biface comprise the remaining 37 percent of the tool collection. Of the utilized flakes, 75 percent were used on lateral edges, 16.7 percent on the perimeter, and 8.3 percent on the distal end. Of the utilized unifaces 60 percent were utilized on lateral edges and 40 percent on perimeters. Edge angles of utilized pieces ranged from 35 to 85 degrees with a mean of 50.2 degrees. This variable range, coupled with the frequency of utilization on lateral edges and perimeters of tools may indicate a fairly wide variety of tool functions. Round unifacial microscars occur on tool exteriors. Since no discrimination was made between edge angles on unifaces and those on utilized flakes, it cannot be determined if utilized flakes and formal tools were used for similar or different tasks.

Arizona CC:3:18

Elevation: 1103-111 m
Site Size: 260 m N/S by 125 m E/W
Field Designation: AEPCO 10

The site is located on a broad, flat, high ridgetop west of a tributary of Negro Canyon, which drains into the Gila River 0.96 km to the south-southwest. The ridge is one in an area of dissected ridges between the Gila and San Francisco rivers. The Peloncillo Mountains lie south of the Gila River. Arizona CC:3:17 is located 250 m to the north on a neighboring ridge. On-site vegetation is sparse on the ridgetop and includes creosotebush, snakeweed, yucca, mesquite, whitethorn acacia, teddy bear cholla, cane cholla, Engelmann prickly pear, barrel cactus, Ephedra, and Aploppapus. While sparse on the ridgetop, biotic resources are very dense along and within the drainages to the east and south of the site, consisting of yucca, cane cholla, desert Christmas cactus and barrel cactus. Surface soil of the Tres Hermanos series, is unconsolidated loamy sand with gravels and cobbles forming a medium to dense pavement. The cobbles are of rhyolite, basalt, granite, and chert in a wide range of sizes. The R-O-W centerline passes through the central north-south axis of the site.

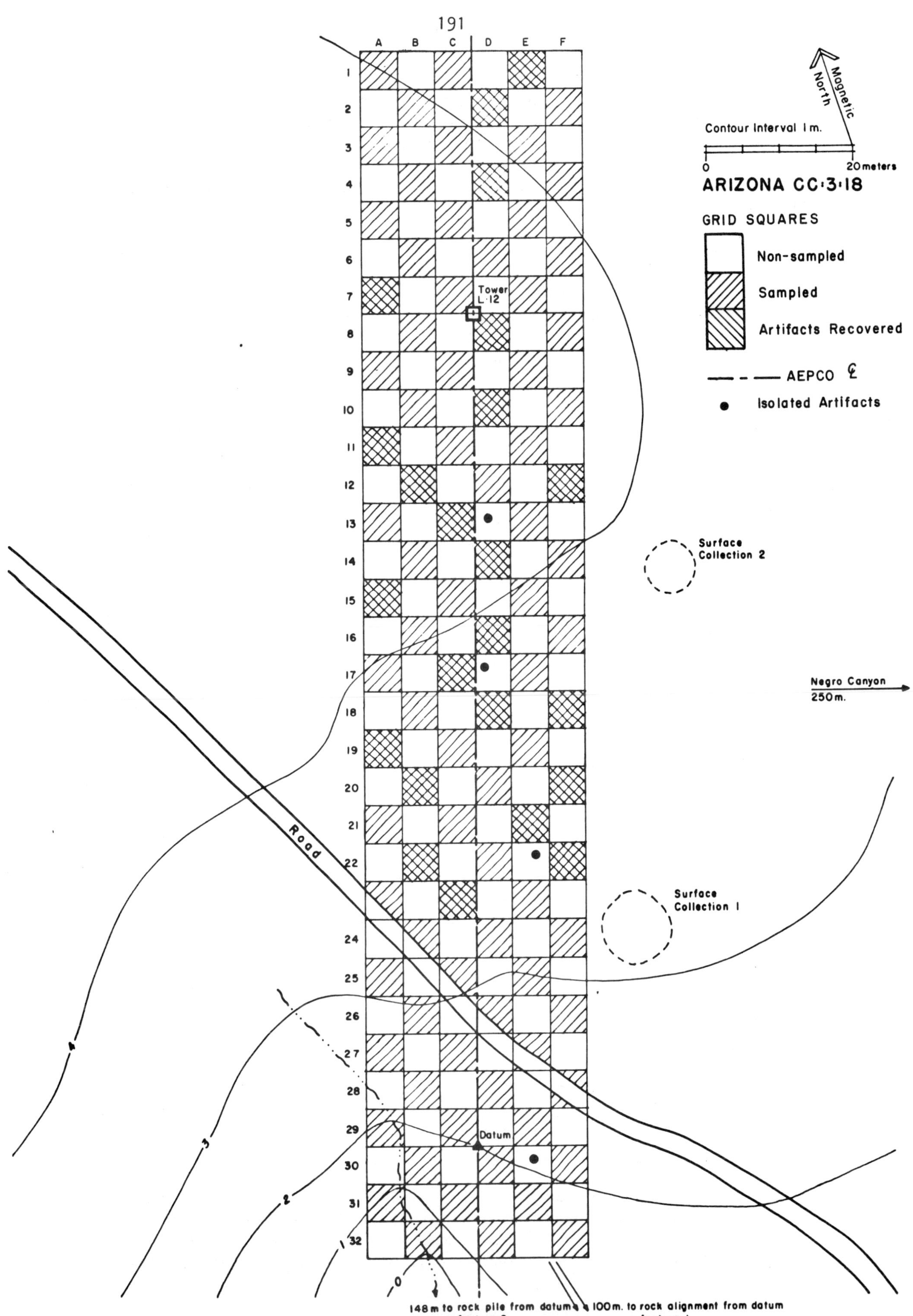

Figure 92. Arizona CC:3:18, site map

A grid was laid out along the R-O-W centerline, 30 m east-west by 160 m north-south and a 50 percent non-random surface collection was made. Figure 92 illustrates the grid and general distribution of lithic materials. Of 96 grid squares investigated, 23 yielded artifactual material, a 24 percent data recovery sample. No ceramics or ground stone were found.

Two rock features, Feature 1 and 2, were recorded south of Arizona CC:3:18 along the crest of a south-trending finger of the main ridge. Feature 1 was an extremely amorphous pile of small decomposing, boulders with no associated cultural materials. It measured 1 m in area and averaged 0.28 m in height. Its function and affiliation are unknown. Feature 2 was a partially collapsed alignment of cobbles, two courses high, lying perpendicular to the dirt road that runs along the ridge crest. It measured 0.50 m wide, 1.0 m long, and averaged 0.37 m in height. No cultural materials were associated with this feature and no interpretation of its function is possible at present.

Seventy-six chipped stone artifacts represent the total sample taken from this site. Silicates constitute the dominant material type (76.3 percent), with rhyolite (14.5 percent) and other types comprising the remainder. The recovered artifact total includes 7 cores, 67 flakes, 1 silicate biface, and 1 silicate uniface.

Flakes constitute the largest artifact category, with 17.9 percent being primary flakes, 43.3 percent secondary flakes, 32.8 percent tertiary flakes, and 6 percent shatter. The core to flake ratio is 1:10 with unifacially reduced cores the primary type represented. Again, primary flake reduction, tool manufacture and possibly tool refurbishing appear to be the main lithic activities at this site.

In contrast to Arizona CC:3:4 and CC:3:17 utilized flakes were few at Arizona CC:3:18; only 7 percent of the total flake collection exhibited microwear. However, in the total tool population, utilized flakes account for 71 percent and formal tools 29 percent, conforming to the general pattern observed for sites in this stratum. Sixty percent of the utilized flakes were used on lateral edges, 20 percent (one flake) on the perimeter and 20 percent (one flake) on the distal end. The single biface was used on the distal end, and the uniface was worn around its perimeter. Edge angles on utilized pieces ranged from 50 to 75 degrees with a mean of 66.2 degrees. This relatively close range of values suggests that tools were discarded when a certain degree of obtuseness was reached.

Arizona CC:3:19

Elevation: 1076-1100 m
Site Size: 380 m N/S (along centerline) by 60 m E/W (arbitrary boundary)
Field Designation: AEPCO 16

This site is located on a flat hill 0.4 km northwest of the Gila River. The hill is surrounded on the east, west, and north by deep washes. The site covers the entire hill and extends down the south and east slopes. Vegetation is predominantly creosotebush, but *Aplopappus*, Mormon tea, whitethorn acacia, yucca, and mesquite are present. Surface soil is a loamy sand

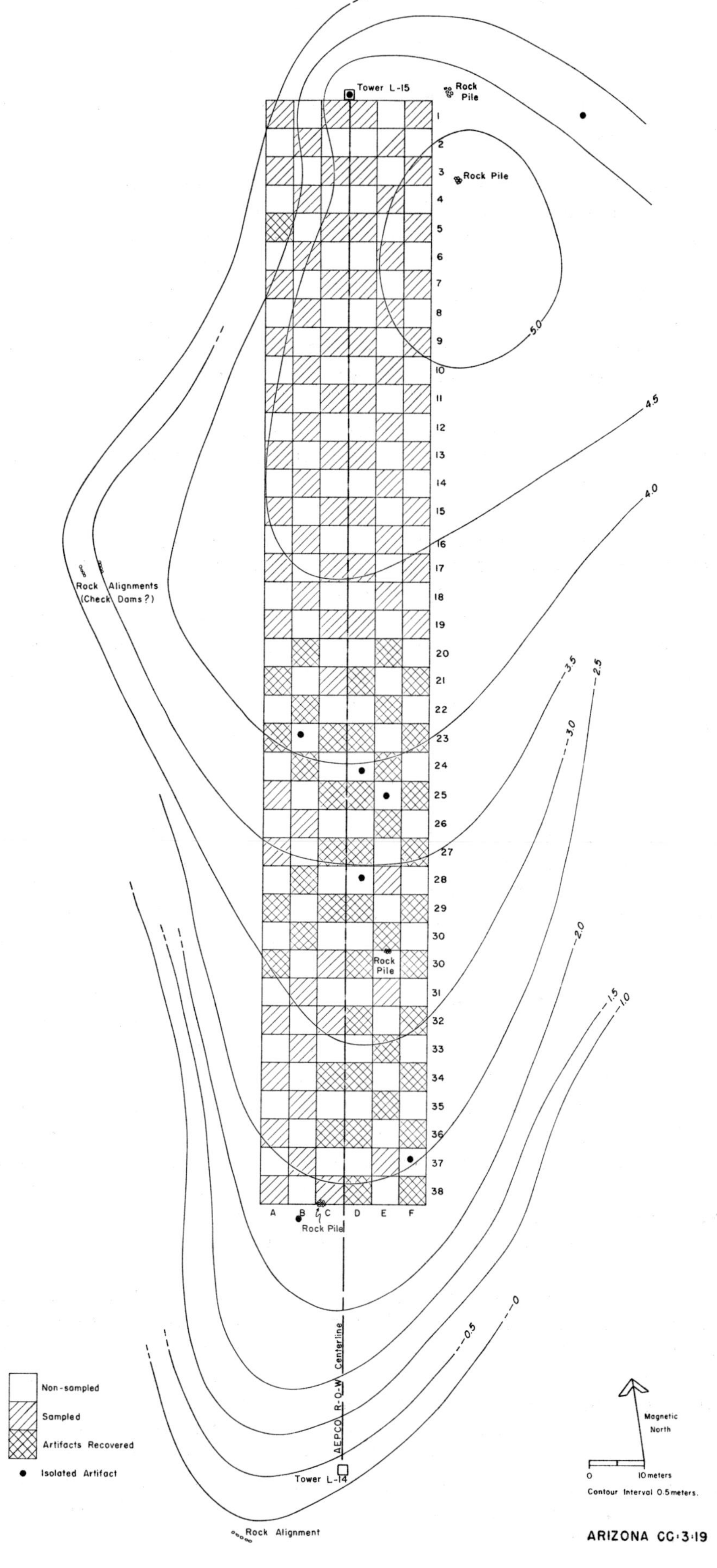

Figure 93. Arizona CC:3:19, site map

of the Tres Hermanos series. The western and southern slopes descend in terrace-like steps.

A grid 30 m east-west and 234 m north-south was laid along the R-O-W and alternate 5 m squares were collected (Figure 93). Thirty-six percent of the squares sampled yielded artifacts which tended to cluster in the south portion of the grid. Eight isolated artifact locations were also mapped, collected, and located by grid square. The site's primary artifact distribution was slightly east of the R-O-W, but since the length of the R-O-W was almost 250 m, it was decided to only sample within the R-O-W and protect the resources outside the R-O-W.

The entire site was strewn with small chert nodules, many of which were collected and examined for use or manufacturing techniques; few showed such evidence.

There are nine rock piles or cobble clusters on the hilltop. All are amorphous in shape, without associated artifacts or an ashy surface. These were mapped and photographed but not tested (Figure 87).

A total of 145 chipped stone artifacts represents the sample taken from this site. Silicates constitute the dominant material type (89 percent), with rhyolite (8.2 percent) and other types comprising the remainder. The recovered artifact total includes 8 cores, 130 flakes and shatter, and 7 unifaces.

The ratio of cores to flakes is again low (1:19). In the total debitage collection, primary flakes constitute 10 percent, secondary flakes 32.3 percent, tertiary flakes 47.7 percent and shatter 10 percent. Silicates comprise 90 percent of the flakes, rhyolite 8.4 percent, and basalt and unidentified types are 0.8 percent each. While the ratio of silicate cores to silicate primary flakes is 1:2, data are lacking to determine if silicate core reduction was occurring; however, the presence of a sparse distribution of large to small-sized silicate pebbles at this site would lend credence to such an assumption. The absence of a larger number of cores and primary flakes does not necessarily mean core reduction was not carried out here; this absence may be a factor of site sampling, since only a fraction of the site was collected. The presence of one obsidian and six silicate unifaces and a high percentage of secondary and tertiary flakes (80 percent of the flake total) may indicate that primary flake reduction and tool manufacture and resharpening (especially on silicates) were important lithic activities.

The tool assemblage constitutes 15 percent of the total artifact collection and consists of 13 utilized flakes, 2 utilized cores, and 7 unifaces. Thus, 68 percent of the tools are easily made and disposable while 32 percent are formally manufactured tools. These frequencies are consistent with those for other sites in this stratum. It is interesting to note that utilized flakes comprise a respectable 10 percent of the total flake count and all show utilization on lateral edges only. Four of the seven unifaces exhibited microwear-- three on lateral edges and one on the distal end. Two uni-directional cores exhibited usage but their function is unknown.

Edge angles on utilized pieces range from 59 to 75 degrees with a mean of 66.6 degrees, the steepest recorded for this stratum. This is unusual, as cryptocrystalline silicates do not generally have steep edge angles, even when retouched. Additionally, microflaking on utilized pieces included trapezoidal scars in addition to round bifacial scars, a characteristic not observed on utilized pieces at other sites in this stratum. It is possible that a specialized activity is indicated for this site.

Arizona CC:3:20 (Component B)

Elevation: 1073 m
Site Size: 220 m N/S by 100 m E/W
Field Designation: AEPCO 104

(Component A is a historic site and is discussed in Chapter 5.)

This site is situated on a high, wide, relatively flat triangular terrace on the north side of the Gila River, which loops around it on the east, south, and west sides. The river flows through a wide, deep gorge in this section, and steep drainages on the east and west sides of the terrace open out into the gorge (Figure 88). To the north are high, dissected hills and ridges supporting a dense creosotebush cover (Figure 89). The terrace supports a relatively sparse vegetation consisting of creosotebush, snakeweed,whitethorn acacia, and yucca. The creosotebush is especially dense along the eastern edge of the terrace where it drops down into a deep arroyo.

The central portion of the terrace is dish-shaped, containing eolian-deposited sandy soil with few gravels and cobbles. The eastern and western edges are littered with cobbles and boulders and the northern extent becomes increasingly rocky as the terrace slopes up into the ridges. At the interface of the ridge base and terrace, an abandoned narrow-gauge railroad grade runs in a west-northwest-east-southeast direction. A dirt road cuts through the western half of the site in a north-south direction; this road eventually will be re-bladed for an access road. Mitigation at this site focused on the access road R-O-W and not the transmission line R-O-W corridor.

The lithic materials at this site are very sparsely distributed over the terrace, with the greatest concentration on the western half, outside the R-O-W corridor but bisected by the dirt road. Two separate 30 m by 100 m grid columns were placed over the road cut and every other 5 m^2 unit was sampled. Figure 94 illustrates the concentrations of recovered cultural material, the majority of which occurred in the south-central portion of the terrace. Of 120 grid squares investigated, 41 (34.2 percent) yielded artifactual material. No prehistoric cultural features were observed within the access road R-O-W.

A 1 m^2 test pit was excavated in the southwest quadrant of grid square I-16 to determine the extent of cultural depth. All fill was sifted through a fine mesh window screen, but no cultural materials were found. Sterile substrate was encountered at 10 cm below the surface, at which level the excavation was closed.

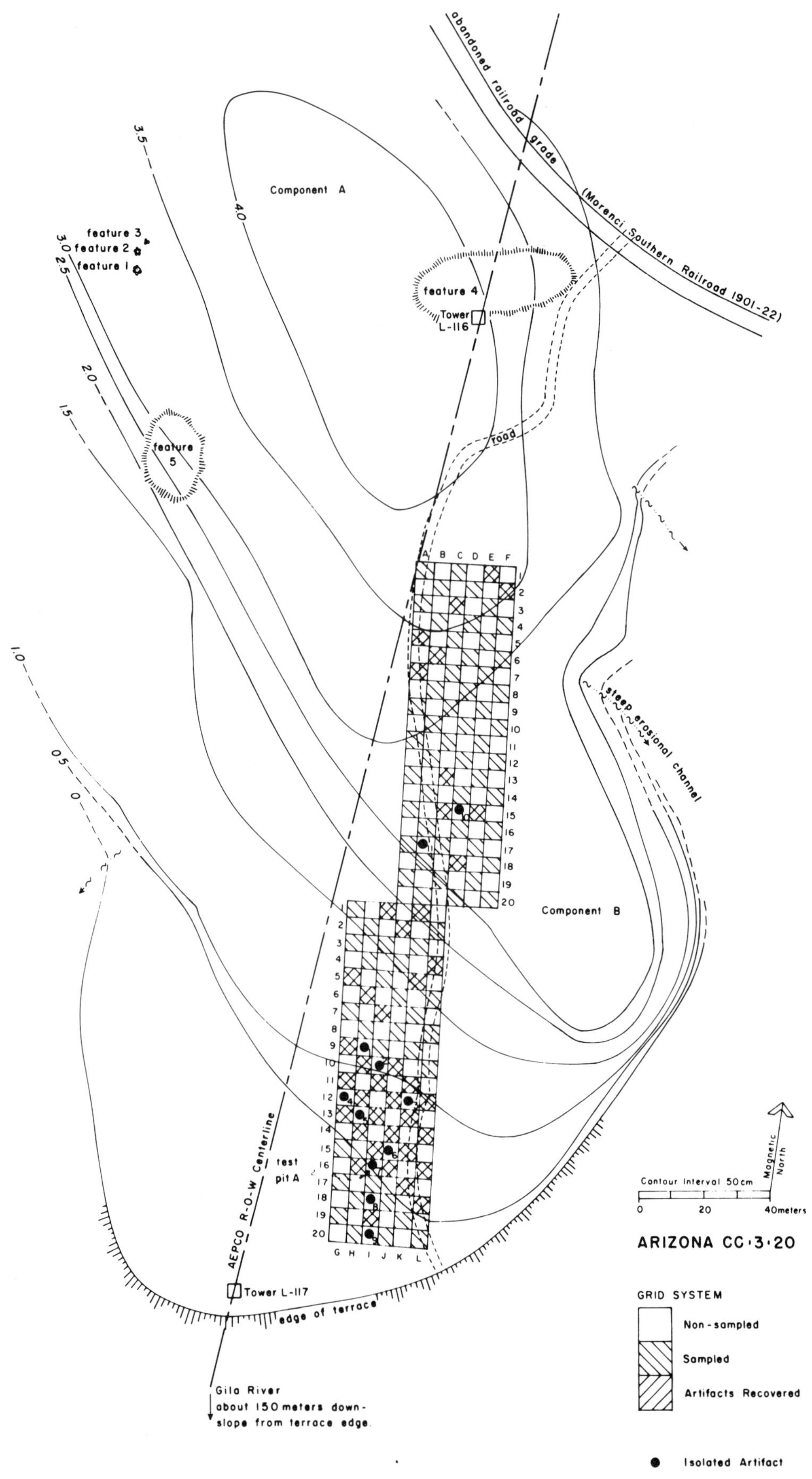

Figure 94. Arizona CC:3:20, Component B, site map.

The collection of material from this site is markedly different from other sites in Stratum 7. Instead of the typical dominance of silicates in the raw material class, artifacts at Arizona CC:3:20 were manufactured from a wider variety of materials. Silicates constitute 31.6 percent and basalt 29.8 percent, with quartzite representing 17.1 percent, rhyolite 11.6 percent, andesite 8.7 percent, obsidian 0.8 percent, and unidentified types 0.4 percent. This variety of exploited raw material is seen as a factor of availability; that is, the site is situated on a broad flat terrace immediately above the Gila River and cobbles could have been acquired from there.

The ratio of cores to flakes (1:38) was much lower at this site; indeed, the lithic assemblage appeared oriented toward finer reduction of material into finished products rather than initial reduction of flake cores to obtain blanks and preforms. Tertiary flakes accounted for 55 percent of the flake total; many of these could be thinning flakes or resharpening flakes. It is notable that 30.5 percent of the tertiary flakes were siliceous material and 30 percent were basalt, indicating that these two materials were probably favored for tools. Of the remaining debitage, primary flakes constituted 2 percent, secondary flakes 18 percent, and shatter 10 percent. Cores accounted for only 3 percent of the total artifact assemblage.

Despite the fact that the debitage indicates tool finishing and refurbishing, only one formal tool, a basalt biface was found. In contrast to other sites in this stratum, utilized debitage was not abundant. The sample yielded six utilized flakes and two utilized cores, equalling only 3 percent of the total collection. However, five of the six utilized flakes were tertiary flakes, indicating a possible preferential selection of a certain flake size for expedient use. This infers that a possible specialized task was carried out with these informal tools.

In summary, the raw data indicate that, although flakes were used for immediate tasks at hand, the high frequency of small flakes suggest that a fair amount of knapping on formal tools took place. It is likely that use of portable formal tools was an important aspect of the complete range of activities at this site.

Stratum 8: San Francisco River Terraces

This zone includes sites bordering the San Francisco River east of its confluence with the Gila River. The San Francisco River flows through a deep, steep-walled chasm which is 34 m deep at its intersection with the transmission line corridor. There is no floodplain development along the channel; only an occasional sandbar rises above the water level. Numerous steep erosional channels and narrow canyons interspersed with high ridges flank the river gorge. Country between the San Francisco and Gila rivers consists of gradually rising terraces of detrital material; the ridges near the San Francisco River are steeper, narrower, and slightly higher in elevation than those along the Gila River.

As in Stratum 7, the soils in Stratum 8 are either of the Calciothids and Torriorthents group or the Tres Hermanos series. Grasses, ocotillo, and sotol were observed to be more common and creosotebush less common than in Stratum 7.

Arizona W:15:15 (Figure 95) is situated south of the San Francisco River. This is a small, contained lithic scatter with rhyolite and chert flakes and cores predominating. Sites north of the San Francisco River (for example, Arizona W:15:17) are larger and more dispersed (Figure 96). The most distinctive feature within this stratum was the high number of rhyolite cores observed on sites, particularly at Arizona W:15:15. Worked and unworked hematite, rare in any stratum, was present at two sites. One rock shelter, Arizona W:15:18, was found during the data recovery phase (Figure 97).

Arizona W:15:15

<u>Elevation:</u> 1107 m
<u>Site Size:</u> 39 m N/S by 64 m E/W
<u>Field Designation:</u> AEPCO 33

The site is located on the top of a high ridge overlooking the San Francisco River. The ridge is in an area of high, deeply channelled ridges bordering the River (Figure 95). The ridgetop supports a sparse cover of creosotebush, acacia, and snakeweed. Ocotillo, prickly pear, cane cholla, barrel cactus, and sotol grow on the upper and lower slopes. The vegetation is especially dense in the erosional channels that flank the ridge. Soils in the vicinity of the site belong to the Calciothids and Torriorthents group. There is very little soil buildup and the surface is strewn with rhyolite cobbles and boulders; several decomposing rhyolite outcrops occur near the edges of the ridge crest. Basalt, andesite, and jasper occur in smaller numbers.

Tower N-20, an angle tower, is situated in the area of greatest lithic density. A dirt road cuts through the southern part of the site.

Due to the small size and well-defined artifact assemblage obvious on the surface, complete (100 percent) data recovery was initiated. All materials were bagged, their provenience was pinpointed on the site map, and they were collected (Figure 99). A peculiar phenomenon at Arizona W:15:15 not encountered at any other site was the high percentage of rhyolite cores, indicating the site to be a possible small quarry area. The majority of artifacts were clustered on the flat portion of the ridgetop and the north-facing upper slope.

Four cobble features were recorded for this site during survey. Feature 1 was an area of three amorphous rock piles which were difficult to isolate from the general surface scree of naturally occurring cobbles. Its tentative location was mapped in.

Feature 2 was tentatively identified as a remnant of a rhyolite chipping station. It consisted of one primary flake and three secondary flakes. All flakes were complete but showed no evidence of a platform or utilization.

Figure 95. Arizona W:15:15, general overview.

Figure 96. Arizona W:15:17, general overview.

Figure 97. Arizona W:15:18, rock-shelter.

Figure 98. Arizona W:15:17, Feature 5, Petroglyph Boulder 1.

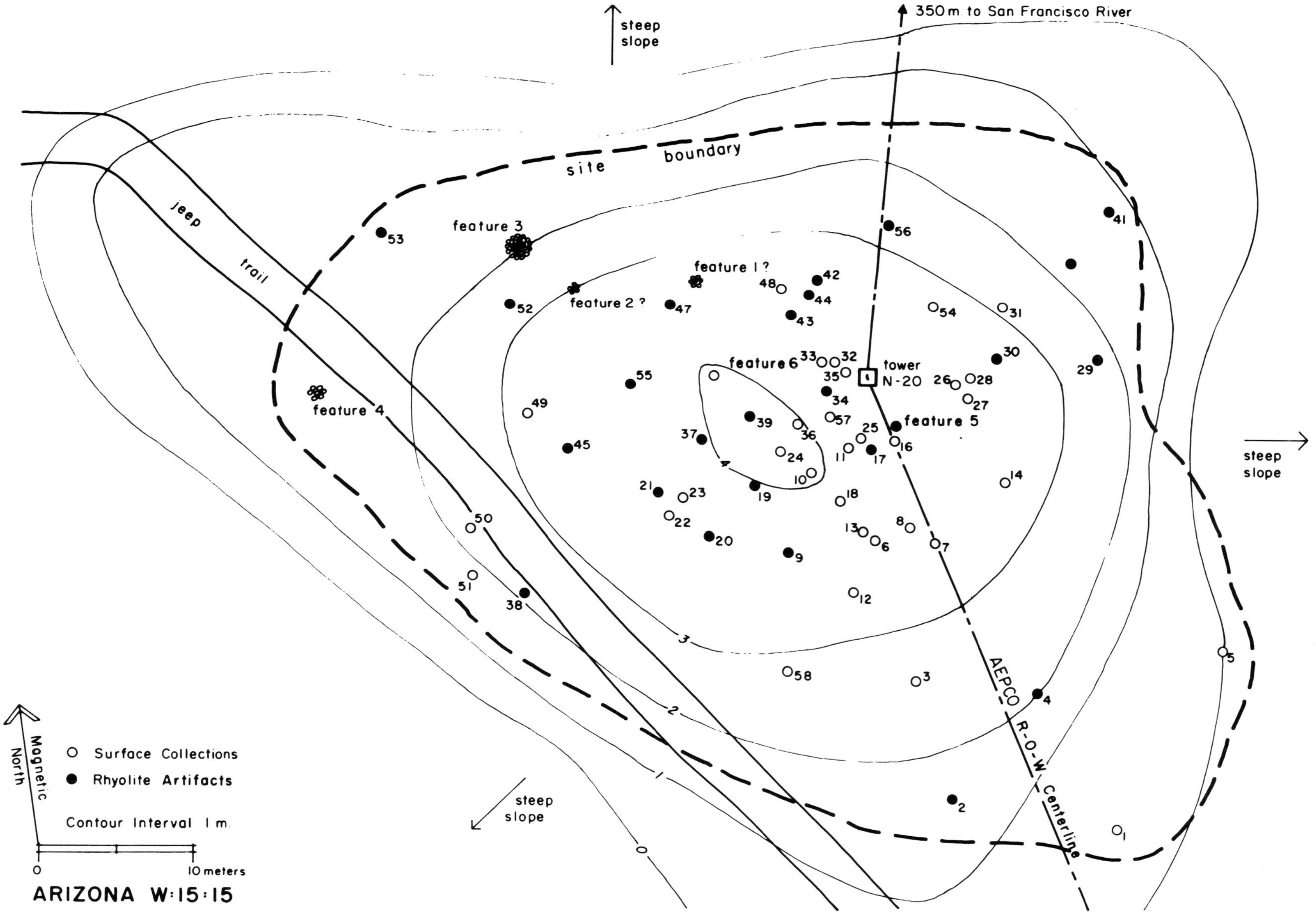

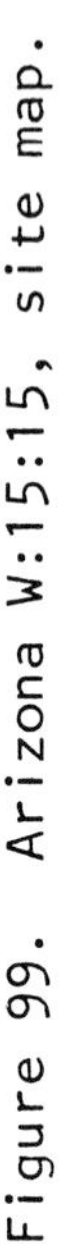

Figure 99. Arizona W:15:15, site map.

Feature 3 was a large oval rock pile measuring 1.65 m north-south by 1.55 m east-west and 0.35 m in heights. In the center were 12 hematite cobbles forming a nucleus, around and upon which were piled large cobbles of basalt, rhyolite, vesicular basalt, and several irregular chunks of conglomerate. The rock pile was composed of three rough tiers. Surface rocks were removed from the eastern half and modern glass was discovered on the ground surface beneath the first layer of rocks. The ground was troweled to check for a pit outline and then dug to a depth of 10 cm. A red clayey soil was encountered 4 cm below the ground surface. No cultural materials were present. It was concluded that this was a recent rock pile, although the reasons for its construction are unknown.

Feature 4 was a circular arrangement of five large irregular boulders, laid on the present ground surface. No deposition was present and the large size of the boulders did not indicate this to be a pot rest or feature of similar function. It may have functioned as a marker; a jeep trail lies less than 1 m to the north.

Feature 5 was a rhyolite chipping station, containing one uni-directional prepared core, a bi-directional core, two primary flakes, three secondary flakes, and one piece of shatter.

Feature 6, a lithic cluster that may represent a remnant of a rhyolite chipping station, contained one uni-directional prepared core, one primary flake, one tertiary flake, one piece of shatter, and a uniface.

The artifact assemblage recovered from this site numbered 59 cores, 68 flakes, and 3 unifaces, totalling 130 items. The assemblage indicates that this site may have been a primary core reduction area, using the natural abundance of rhyolite cobbles on the ridgetop. Rhyolite accounts for 83.1 percent of the raw material, with silicates representing 7.7 percent, basalt 4.6 percent, quartzite 0.8 percent, and unidentified types 3.8 percent.

The core to flake ratio is nearly equal (59 cores to 68 flakes), with rhyolite cores comprising 86 percent of the cores and rhyolite flakes accounting for 79 percent of the total flake count. The dominance of uni-directional prepared cores (69 percent) indicates there is a standardized core reduction technique. Bi-directional prepared cores (17 percent) and multi-directional prepared cores (12 percent), while occurring in smaller frequencies, also reflect possible standardized methods. Essentially, careful preparation of platform prior to flake detachment is indicated as an important factor in the lithic industry.

The flake total is broken down into 23.5 percent primary flakes, 54.4 percent secondary flakes, and 22 percent tertiary flakes. The close ratio of cores to primary flakes (1:2) indicates initial core reduction as one activity. The combined frequencies of secondary and tertiary flakes (76.4 percent of the flakes) indicates primary flake reduction, possibly into preforms. That some tool finishing was also carried out is indicated by three rhyolite bifaces. Evidence for utilization of lithic tools is rare; one flake, two unifaces, and five cores show use, but no microflaking is present. In view of the abundant biotic resources in the immediate vicinity, one would expect more utilized pieces at this site; however this lack may be a factor of inability to identify use evidence on rhyolite, cursory use of tools such that an observable wear pattern did not develop, or skewing as a result of the artifically-drawn boundaries of the R-O-W corridor. Sites exhibiting food procurement and processing tasks may well occur in areas outside the R-O-W. The best that can be said for this site is that it represents a small source of lithic raw material that was exploited for manufacturing tools apparently for use elsewhere.

Arizona W:15:17

Elevation: 1073-1083 m
Site Size: 190 m N/S by 68 m E/W
Field Designation: AEPCO 35

Arizona W:15:17 is situated on the top of a high, very steep ridge on the north side of the San Francisco River (Figure 96). The ridge drops eastward into a deeply cut un-named side canyon of the San Francisco River gorge. Directly across the canyon from the site is an abandoned gravel operation. The surface of the ridgetop is extremely rocky and the northern half of the site has been disturbed by heavy equipment. The southern portion of the ridgetop flattens out somewhat, is partially cleared of cabbles, then drops down sharply to the San Francisco River. Most of the cultural materials were clustered in this lower, southern portion (Figure 100).

Soils belong to the Tres Hermanos series and the vegetation, although sparse, is quite varied, consisting of creosotebush, Englemann prickly pear, ocotillo, catclaw acacia, sotol, cane cholla, pencil cholla, barrell cactus, and various grasses. At the interface of the ridge base and canyon floor is a dense mesquite bosque. Lithic resources include rhyolite, basalt, chalcedony, jasper, and hematite.

The cultural materials present at Arizona W:15:17 were generally very sparsely and irregularly distributed over the ridgetop, with a concentration located at the flat, southern tip of the ridge. All cultural material was collected and all artifact provenience locations were pinpointed on the site map. Four features were also mapped and recorded. Features 1, 2, and 3 are rock rings, constructed of large irregular boulders. Feature 2 exhibited some deposition and was selected for testing. Surface soil was cleared away by troweling down to the base of the rocks. No cultural materials were recovered from this level. Natural substrate was reached at a depth 0.7 cm below the surface. No pit or occupation surface was present.

The alignment of Features 1, 2, and 3 and the presence of broken glass and metal objects suggests that these features may in some way be associated with a utility line, now abandoned. Whether it was associated with the abandoned gravel operation on the opposite side of the canyon cannot be positively determined, although this seems likely. It could also be associated with an abandoned railroad grade which is 0.4 km southeast.

Feature 4 was a parallel alignment of boulders, each row averaging 4.5 m long, 1.0 m apart from each other, oriented north-south. The boulders had been set into the machinery-disturbed fill and, therefore, are quite recent.

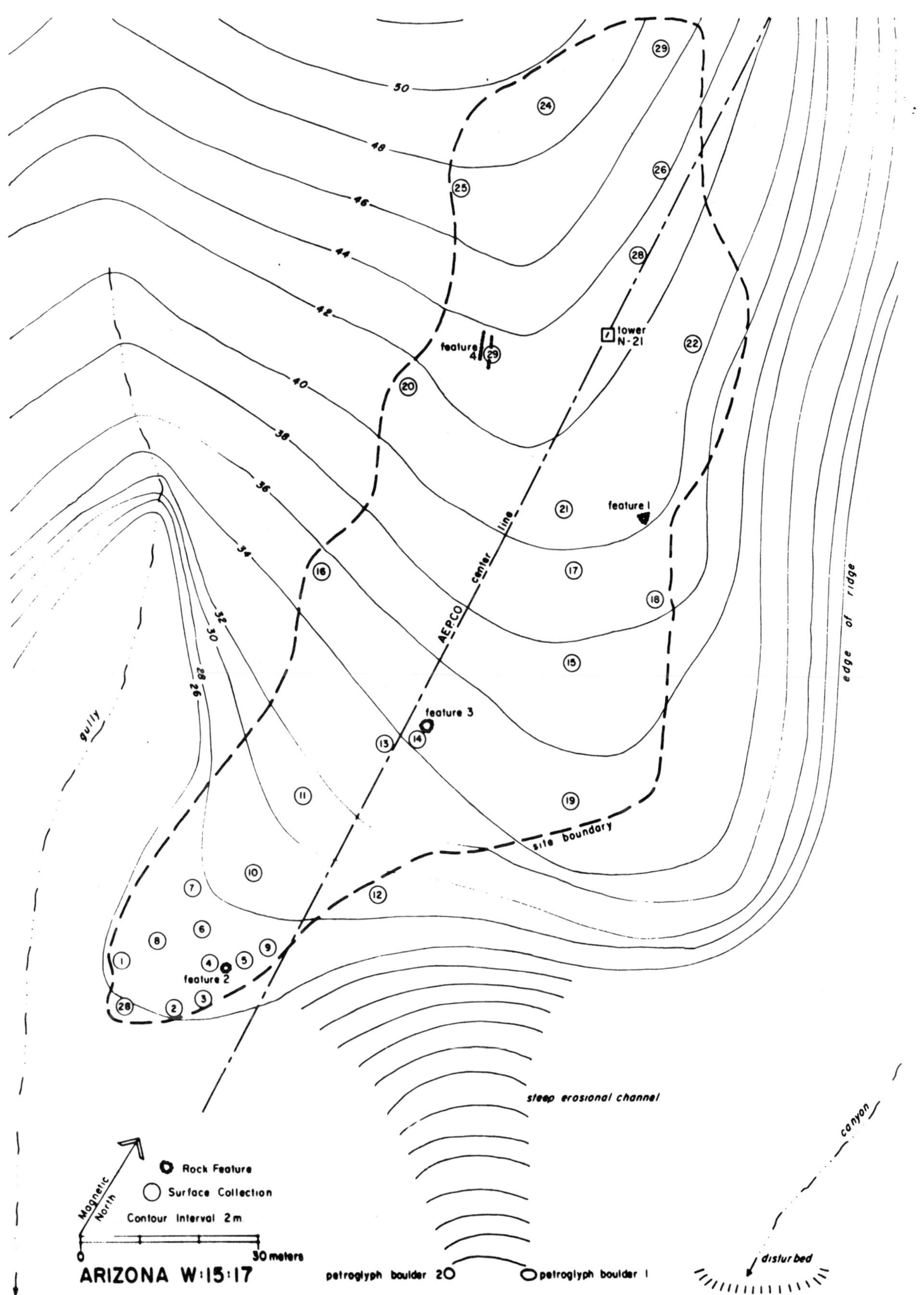

Figure 100. Arizona W:15:17, site map

Feature 5, a petroglyph locale, was discovered upon climbing the ridge slope to the site. It is not certain if it is associated with Arizona W:15:17, but was included with this site for recording purposes and for protection against possible disturbance by line construction. Additionally, the two boulders comprising this feature are situated on a very steep slope, subject to natural erosional processes and possible future dislocation.

Boulder 1 of Feature 5, is a pinkish-tan, oval sandstone boulder situated approximately 25 m above the floor of an unnamed canyon. The boulder measures 67 cm long, 42 cm wide, and is 19 cm high. It is intact, although somewhat eroded. The glyphs (Figures 98 and 101) are formed by dense, but shallow pecking, and no paint is evident. At least five glyphs are present, but this is only an estimate, since the elements tend to run into each other. However, three dominant motifs are evident: a bull's-eye, a vertical line with short horizontal bars, and a bull's-eye with wavy lines radiating out from it.

Boulder 2 is of reddish-tan sandstone, is situated 12.4 m upslope (west) from Boulder 1, and rests on a bedrock outcrop. It measured 40 cm long, 36 cm wide, and 19 cm high. It is also intact, but badly eroded; motifs are difficult to define and are nearly completely obscured in the central part of the panel. The glyphs were formed by dense, but shallow pecking. Both geometric and curvilinear elements similar to those on Boulder 1 are apparent (Figure 102).

Photographs and tracings of the two petroglyphs were sent to Polly Schaafsma of Arroyo Hondo, New Mexico, for consultation regarding their cultural affinities. It was originally thought that the glyphs might be Apache; however, Schaafsma (1977, personal communication) indicates they are neither Apache nor Hohokam, although the Hohokam did make abstract curvilinear patterns. According to Schaafsma, the petroglyphs resemble Archaic work. She states that glyphs such as these are pre-Hohokam and have been found over an area extending westward from Texas through New Mexico and into Arizona, a region occupied by the southwestern archaic culture.

This site, situated directly across the San Francisco River from Arizona W:15:15, reflects a very different lithic assemblage from that of W:15:15. While rhyolite occurs in abundance naturally, silicate artifacts outnumber rhyolite artifacts 35 to 39 percent. Basalt constitutes 16.5 percent of the raw material, with unidentified types, quartzite and obsidian following in number. The total collection of 79 artifacts consists of 21 cores, 55 flakes, 2 unifaces, and 1 biface.

Among the cores, rhyolite is the dominant material type (67 percent). As at Arizona W:15:15, platform preparation is a strong attribute. In contrast to the high frequency of rhyolite cores, only 23 percent of the flakes are rhyolite, with silicates and other fine-grained materials comprising 77 percent of the flakes. The total flake count consists of 16.4 percent primary flakes, 45.5 percent secondary flakes, 12.7 percent tertiary flakes, and 25.5 percent shatter. Viewing the collection as a whole, it would appear that two different lithic industries occurred at this site, one focusing

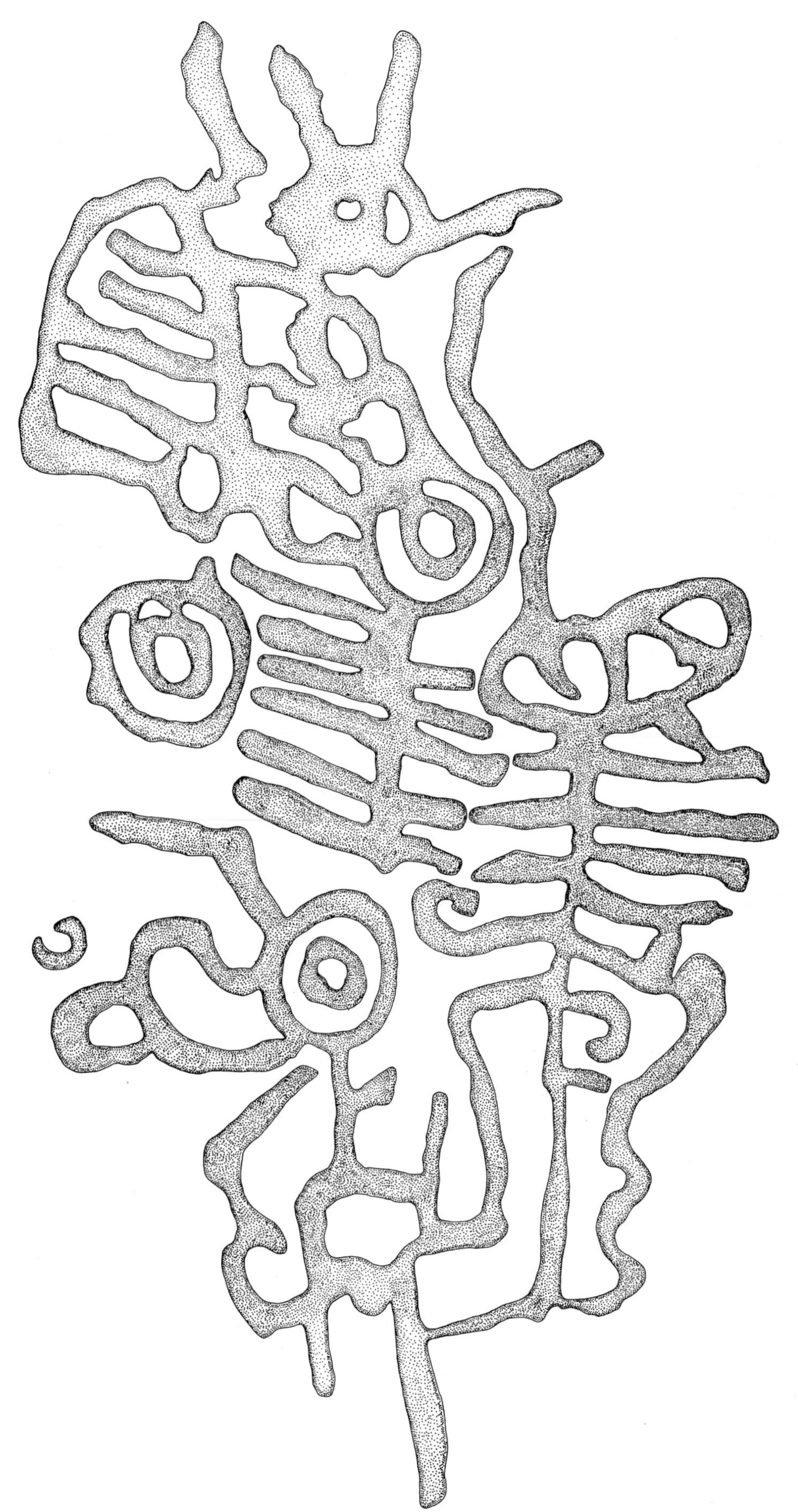

Figure 101. Arizona W:15:17, Feature 5, Petroglyph 1

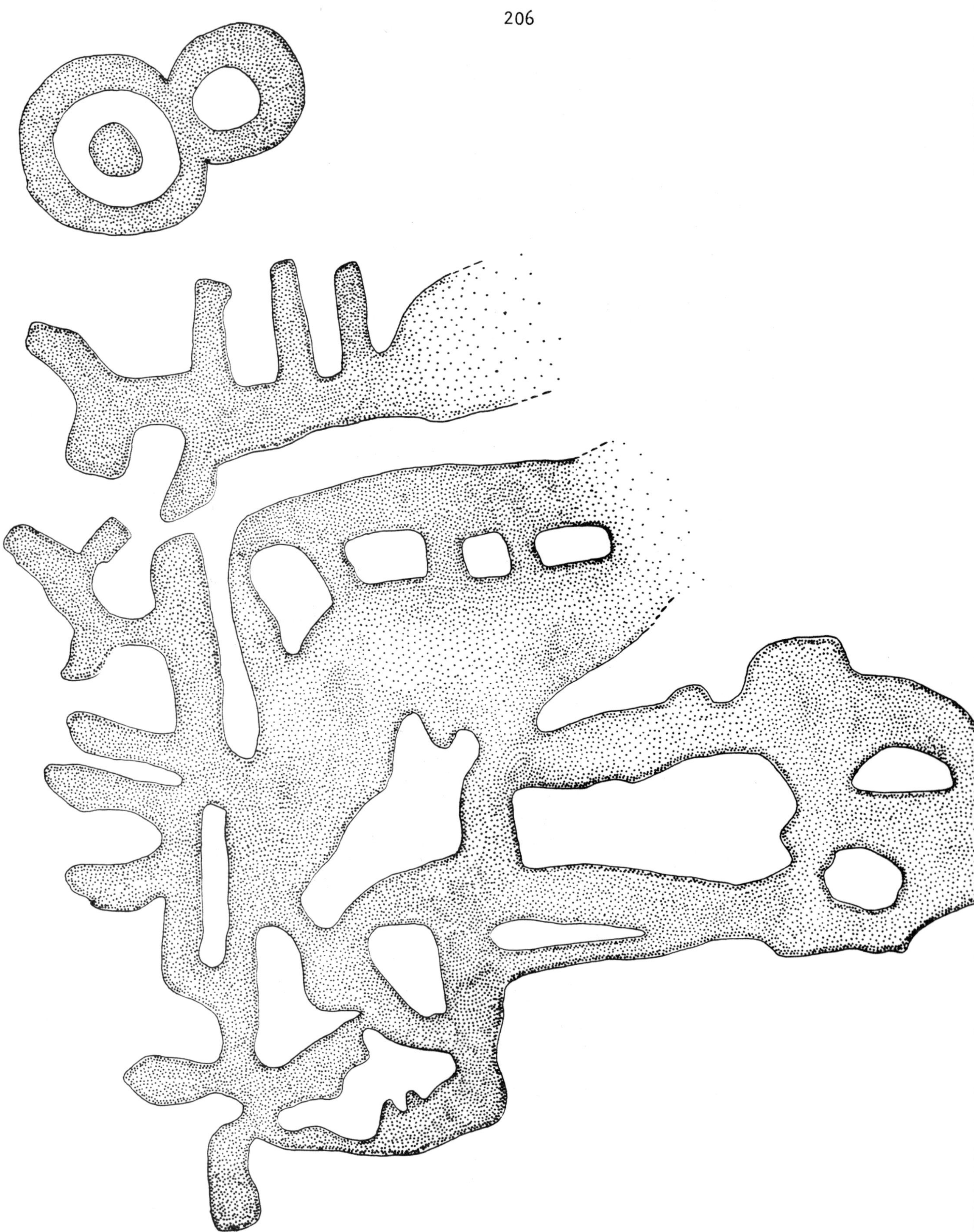

Figure 102. Arizona W:15:17, Feature 5, Petroglyph 2

on rhyolite core reduction with the resulting flakes taken elsewhere, the other focusing on finishing and resharpening tools of other materials (silicates and basalt).

Only 8 percent of the artifacts could be classified as tools; these consisted of two unifaces, one biface, one utilized core, and two utilized flakes. On the formal tools utilization was apparent on only the two unifaces; microflaking was present in the form of round unifacial scars on lateral edges. The sample of utilized pieces is too small to draw valid conclusions regarding site function. At best, one can suggest possible hunting and gathering activities, in addition to lithic procurement tasks.

In addition to mitigation activities at Arizona W:15:17 a brief survey was conducted up the side canyon to determine if other features or sites were present that might aid in understanding the cultural context of Arizona W:15:17. Approximately 100 m north up the canyon a small rockshelter (Arizona W:15:18) was located in the west wall, 10 m above the canyon floor. The rockshelter is a naturally formed concavity eroded out of the cemented alluvial strata forming the canyon sides. A small ledge juts out from the base of the shelter allowing for shallow soil buildup, supporting a small, sparse community of prickly pear, acacia, and a few perennial shrubs (Figure 97).

The shelter measures approximately 15 m long (north-south), 7 m high, and 5 m deep. The ceiling is heavily sooted and light spalling is evident. The floor of the shelter is covered with dry, powdery, grayish soil, approximately 25-30 cm deep. The surface is strewn with bunches of dry grass, but it is not known if these were brought in by humans or animals. A burned area occurs at the north end of the rock shelter but no definable hearth is evident. A sparse artifact scatter consisting of sherds and obsidian and rhyolite lithics is distributed across the surface; a few of these items were collected.

Identification of the ceramic collection revealed three Mogollon sherds of Reserve Plain Corrugated and one unidentified smudged plainware sherd. Analysis of the lithics revealed one utilized siliceous flake and one utilized obsidian flake. The remaining seven lithic items consist of debitage. Only future research can determine if the rock shelter has any relationship to Arizona W:15:17.

Stratum 9/10: Big Lue-Gila River Canyonlands

This zone includes steep to very steep, deeply dissected old terrace fronts adjacent to the upper Gila River floodplains and bottomlands, south of the Big Lue Mountains, and east of the confluence of the Gila and San Francisco rivers. The land is dissected by a few large canyons, instead of many washes as in adjacent Stratum 7, resulting in fairly smooth topography (Figure 105).

Continental soils formed in alluvial material from mixed igneous rocks are present; they have a gravelly or cobbly sandy loan surface layer. Today these soils are not irrigated or farmed, but are used for rangeland. The relationship between plants, soil, and water is good, and under favorable (climax) conditions annual herbage production is high. These soils provide a habitat for moderate to large numbers of wildlife. Rabbits, quail, doves, and deer prefer these habitats especially in areas near the mountains (Gelderman 1970: 13, 31-32).

Present day vegetation consists of a sparse cover of snakeweed, Aplopappus and other grasses, yucca and hedgehog cacti. Creosotebush is present but not dominant. Acacia and mesquite are present in drainages. Juniper is present in Cold Creek Canyon. The broad terraces between canyons are almost devoid of vegetation.

Ground surface is gravelly and occasional outcrops appear, but cobbles of workable material are not as plentiful as in other strata.

Though few sites occur in this stratum, they are distinctive in that obsidian artifacts occur in relatively high frequencies and many formal tools are present. Arizona CC:4:5, 6, and 9 are extensive lithic scatters without apparent natural boundaries. Features such as rock piles, amorphous rock alignments, and chipping stations are present. The other sites in the stratum, Arizona CC:4:4, 7 and 8 are small concentrations of tools or flakes. Two obsidian projectile points, as well as occasional rhyolite flakes, were found in isolation along the line.

Arizona CC:4:5

Elevation: 1217-1218 m
Site Size: 40 m (along centerline) by 60 m (arbitrary boundary)
Field Designation: AEPCO 17

Arizona CC:4:5 is located along a small intermittent drainage between Willow and Cold creeks on Wire Corral Mesa. The mesa forms a low, broad, gently sloping transitional zone between the Big Lue Mountains and the dissected ridges to the northeast and the Gila River, 5.6 to 6.4 km to the southwest. The site has been disturbed on the extreme southern end by a paved road, on the eastern section by a Civilian Conservation Corps terrace, and by cattle grazing and rodent burrowing. The ground surface is extremely stoney. Yucca, mesquite, and acacia are present along the stream channel, and creosotebush occurs on the plain.

The site consists of a sparse lithic scatter extending at least 1.6 km along its east-west boundaries. To the north and south, outside the impact zone natural boundaries could not be determined (Figure 106). A grid 30 m wide by 120 m long sectioned into 5 m^2 squares was laid out along the R-O-W corridor. Every other grid square was collected for a total of 71 collected grid squares (1750 m^2). Of these, 22 squares, or 40 percent of the area sampled, contained artifacts. Isolated artifacts were also collected from one non-sample grid square and one square outside the grid.

Features 1 and 2 were lithic concentrations that may be the remains of chipping stations. Feature 1 consisted of a cluster of six rhyolite secondary flakes, and Feature 2 contained one primary, and three secondary rhyolite flakes.

Although no cores were found in direct association with the flake clusters, rhyolite cores do occur elsewhere on the site.

Five rock piles were recorded; two, Features 3 and 4, were located within the R-O-W and were tested. Both were constructed of randomly stacked stones (Figure 104). Feature 3 (Figure 107) was 2.25 m north/ south by 4.15 east/west and stood 0.40 m high. Feature 4 was 0.80 m east/ west by 0.70 m north/south. Surface cobbles were removed from half of each feature and a cross-section test pit was excavated. The soil was very rocky with many large cobbles. A sterile clay substrate was encountered approximately 10 cm below the surface. No artifacts were found underneath the rock piles nor in the shallow topsoil. The possible function of the rock piles, all of which lie along the arroyo edge, will be discussed in the site summary.

This site yielded a small but definitive assemblage of 73 chipped stone artifacts, consisting of 9 cores, 50 flakes, 6 unifaces, 7 bifaces, and 1 projectile point. The assemblage was dominated by rhyolite (68.5 percent), with obsidian comprising 17.8 percent, basalt 11 percent, and silicates the remaining 2.7 percent.

Although cores are few they exhibit characteristics that indicate very selective processes. Seven are uni-directional prepared cores, all of rhyolite. The remaining two are made of silicates, one a uni-directional unprepared core, the other a bi-directional prepared core. The significance of rhyolite reduction at this site will be discussed below.

Flakes also show significant patterns in material type distribution. As with the cores, rhyolite dominates the flakes, constituting 74 percent of all flakes, while basalt represents 16 percent, and obsidian the remaining 10 percent. A breakdown of stage of manufacture shows a dominance of secondary and tertiary flakes (Appendix I, Table 38A). The flake total is comprised of 8 percent primary flakes, 70 percent secondary flakes, 20 percent tertiary flakes, and 2 percent shatter.

Debitage frequencies correlate well with the two chipping stations (Features 1 and 2) to indicate primary and secondary core reduction on rhyolite as a dominant lithic industry. Additionally, all of the six unifaces found at the site are made of rhyolite, and apparently represent the end products of a complete lithic manufacturing sequence. It is likely, therefore, that the rhyolite assemblage represents a discrete lithic workshop.

Tools represent 26 percent of the total chipped stone collection. In addition to the above-mentioned rhyolite unifaces, there are seven obsidian bifaces and a Chiricahua stage Cochise hydrated obsidian point. Since no obsidian cores and only four flakes were found, obsidian tool production was probably not occurring on the site, but tools may have been brought in from elsewhere. It is possible that some of these bifaces may be point preforms, while others may have been manufactured for butchering game. Use of the bifaces for butchering is only a tentative assumption; extremely few obsidian resharpening flakes were found and none of the recovered bifaces showed use.

Figure 103. Arizona CC:4:6, general overview.

Figure 104. Arizona CC:4:5, rock pile.

Figure 105. General topographic overview of southeastern slope of Democrat Mesa.

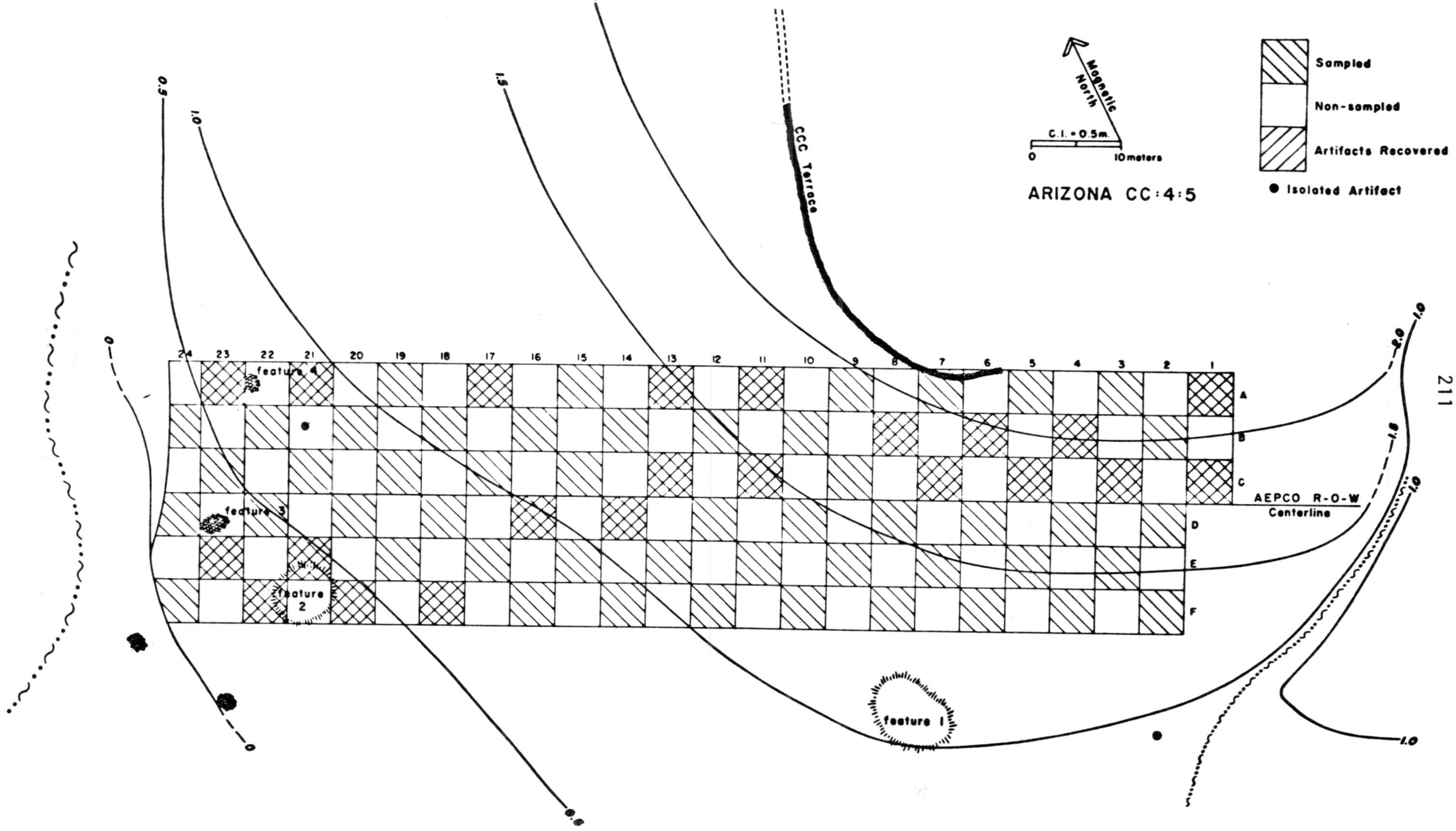

Figure 106. Arizona CC:4:5, site map

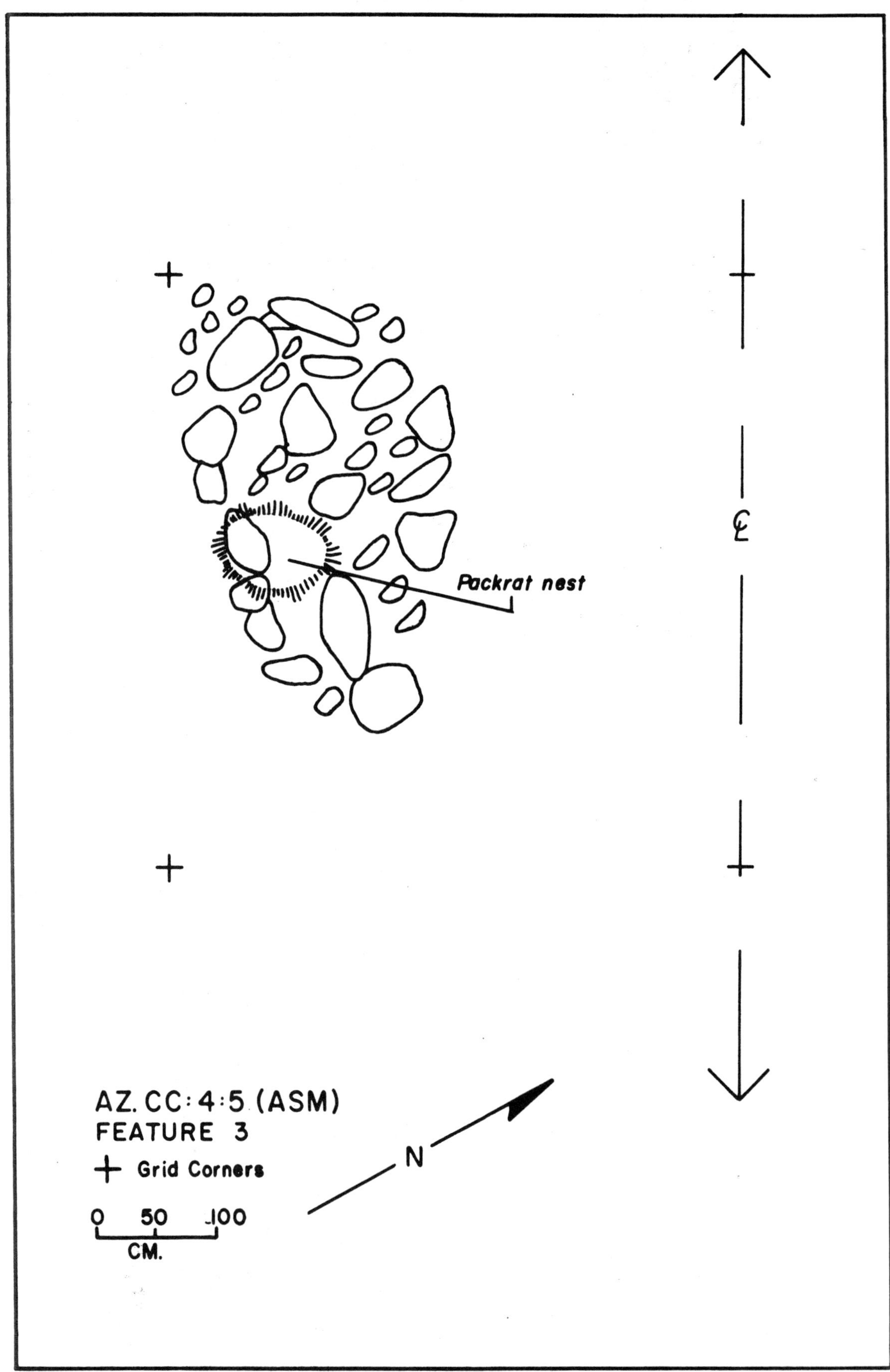

Figure 107. Arizona CC:4:5, Feature 3

Utilized debitage comprises the remaining tools. These are one rhyolite core, two rhyolite flakes, one obsidian, and one basalt flake. All the flakes were utilized on lateral edges with light microflaking present in the form of round unifacial scars. Edge angles ranged from 65 to 78 degrees, with a mean of 71.7 degrees, the steepest recorded for the entire project area. This narrow range indicates that a fairly steep edge angle was a constant factor of tools and suggests a specialized use technique.

In summary, it may be postulated that the chipped stone population at Arizona CC:4:5 represents portions of a hunting tool kit. It is likely that the co-occurrence of finished obsidian tools and a complete rhyolite unifacial tool production sequence represent tasks relating to procuring and processing game. That few of the tools exhibit use may be tentatively explained in part by arguing from negative evidence--useful tools may have been saved, or tools were not used intensively enough to develop an observable wear pattern.

The occurrence of a single Chiricahua stage Cochise projectile point is an interesting aspect of this site, but it does not assure that all the lithic objects at the site were produced by Cochise culture people. The area is recognized as one that was exploited periodically by transhumant groups over a long period of time; therefore one must be cautious about assigning cultural identification to this site on the basis of a single projectile point. Also, surface contexts mean association is poor. However, the close association of the discrete lithic assemblages at one locus would argue in favor of Arizona CC:4:5 being an archaic site.

Prior to data recovery it was noted that the majority of lithics tended to cluster about the rock piles along the arroyo bank. While only the two rock piles occurring within the R-O-W corridor were investigated, the co-occurrence of lithics with rock piles and the significant size of Feature 3 merit special consideration. It is possible that some of the rock piles are hunting blinds and their associated lithics are the remains of hunting tool kit production and maintenance (Debowski and others 1976: 92). Although data are lacking on specialized isolated hunting sites in the vicinity of the project area, data from archaeological resources elsewhere and ethnographic data may aid in supporting the contention that Arizona CC:4:5 represents a specialized example of subsistence activity.

Investigations in the proposed Buttes Reservoir district (Debowski and others 1976: 92-93) west of the AEPCO project area identified several sites as "hunting stations." Such sites conformed to a set of criteria cited below:

(1) Located on present or pre-historic game trails.

(2) Small size, reflecting occupation by a few individuals.

(3) Presence of hunting and animal processing tools and features, that is, projectile points, knives, hunting blinds.

(4) Absence or scarcity of implements not directly related to hunting activities.

Use of blinds for hunting deer has been demonstrated ethnographically for the Walapai (Kroeber 1935: 61-63):

> ...the deer had the most general distribution over the territory. They were hunted in a variety of ways. One method was to construct a low wall or "hide"...about three or four feet high, of rock near a deer runway. One or more hunters would lie in wait there with bows and arrows while others chased the game past.

The features and artifact assemblage at Arizona CC:4:5 satisfy the criteria listed above, save for the first; game trails were not noted on the survey. However, salient environmental and topographic features of the site allow some inferences to be drawn. One is that the site is situated within a transitional zone between the riverine and montane environmental zones, a habitat congenial to deer since it offers water, browse, and cover within an approximately 10 km^2 area. Although data are lacking on deer population behavior in this specific area, mule deer are known to occur in the area (Gelderman 1970: 13, 13-32). Drainage systems are natural passages between the mountainous higher elevations and the Gila River, and support herbage communities of varying densities.

Given, then, the possibility that the arroyo may be a game passage, the location and size of the rock piles, and the lithic assemblage, it is likely that Arizona CC:4:5 represents a specialized game killing and butchering site although no cultural or chronological affiliation can be positively determined at the present time.

Arizona CC:4:6

<u>Elevation:</u> 1206-1208 m
<u>Site Size:</u> 130 m E/W (along centerline) by 60 m N/S (arbitrary boundary)
<u>Field Designation:</u> AEPCO 18

Arizona CC:4:6 (Figure 103) is located on the rim of Cold Creek Canyon west of Wire Corral Mesa. The mesa is a long, gently sloping area extending from dissected ridges and the Big Lue Mountains to the north-northwest. The site is 6.44 km north/northwest of the Gila River. About 1 km north of the mesa the slope increases to form low dissected ridges. The sparse vegetation is dominated by snakeweed, <u>Aplopappus</u>, unidentified grasses, and yucca. Juniper is present along the canyon edge. Cresotebush is not on the site but is found nearby. Ground surface consists of a sandy loam strewn with cobbles and boulders.

As the AEPCO centerline crosses the northeastern periphery of the main artifact concentration an additional grid column was laid down adjacent to the R-O-W grid column in order to sample the main concentration (Figure 108). A total of 90 5 m^2 grids (2250 m^2) were collected; 73 percent of the squares sampled had artifacts.

Feature 1, an amorphous stone circle outside the main concentration, was photographed but not tested. Feature 2 (Figure 109), a stone circle within the main artifact concentration, was tested. Surface stones were drawn and photographed. The north half of the circle was excavated to a depth of 10 cm. No pit outlines, ash, or cultural material were encountered. The surface was quite cobbly, with many outcrops, making it difficult to differentiate between natural and cultural stone alignments.

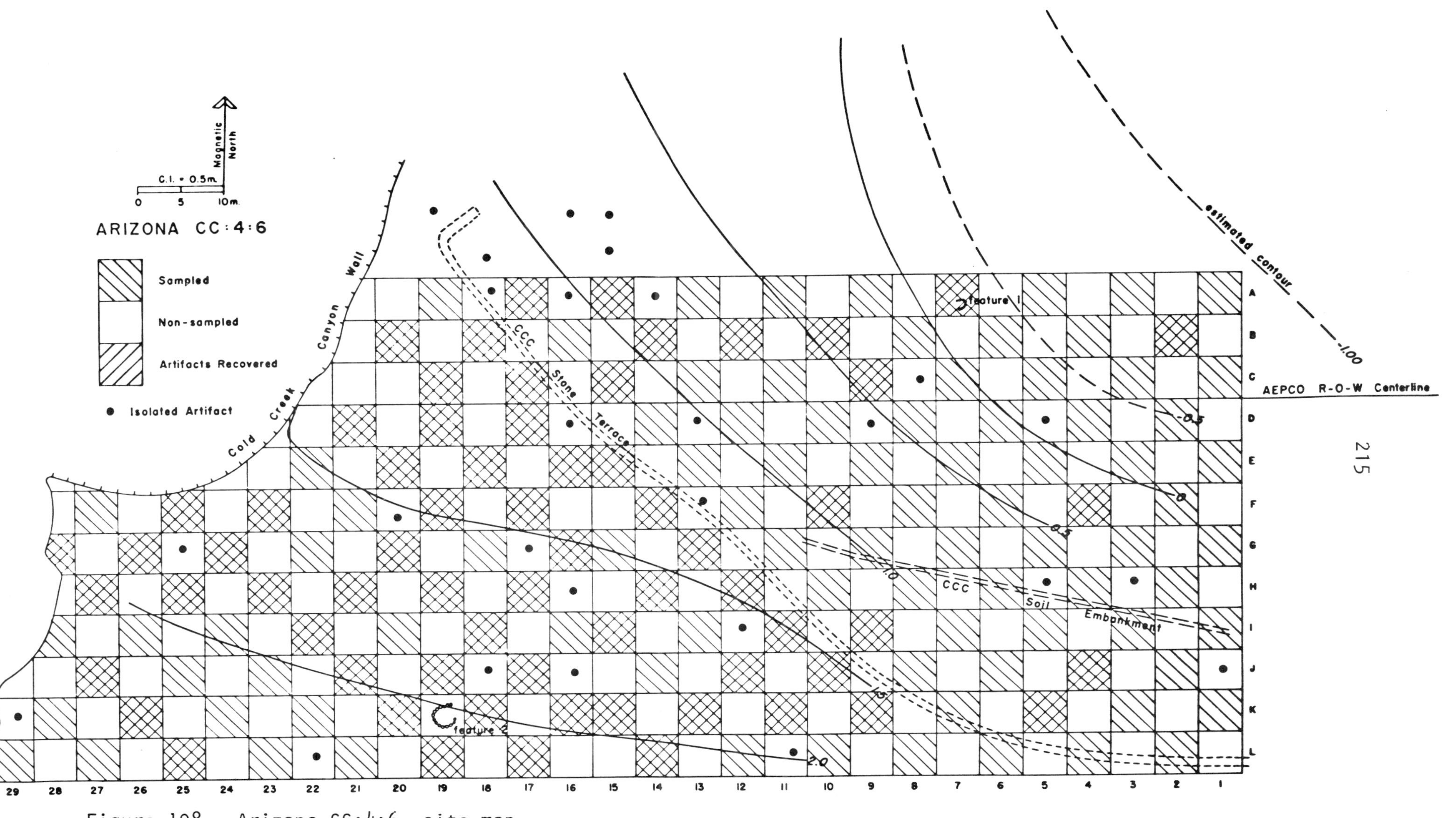

Figure 108. Arizona CC:4:6, site map

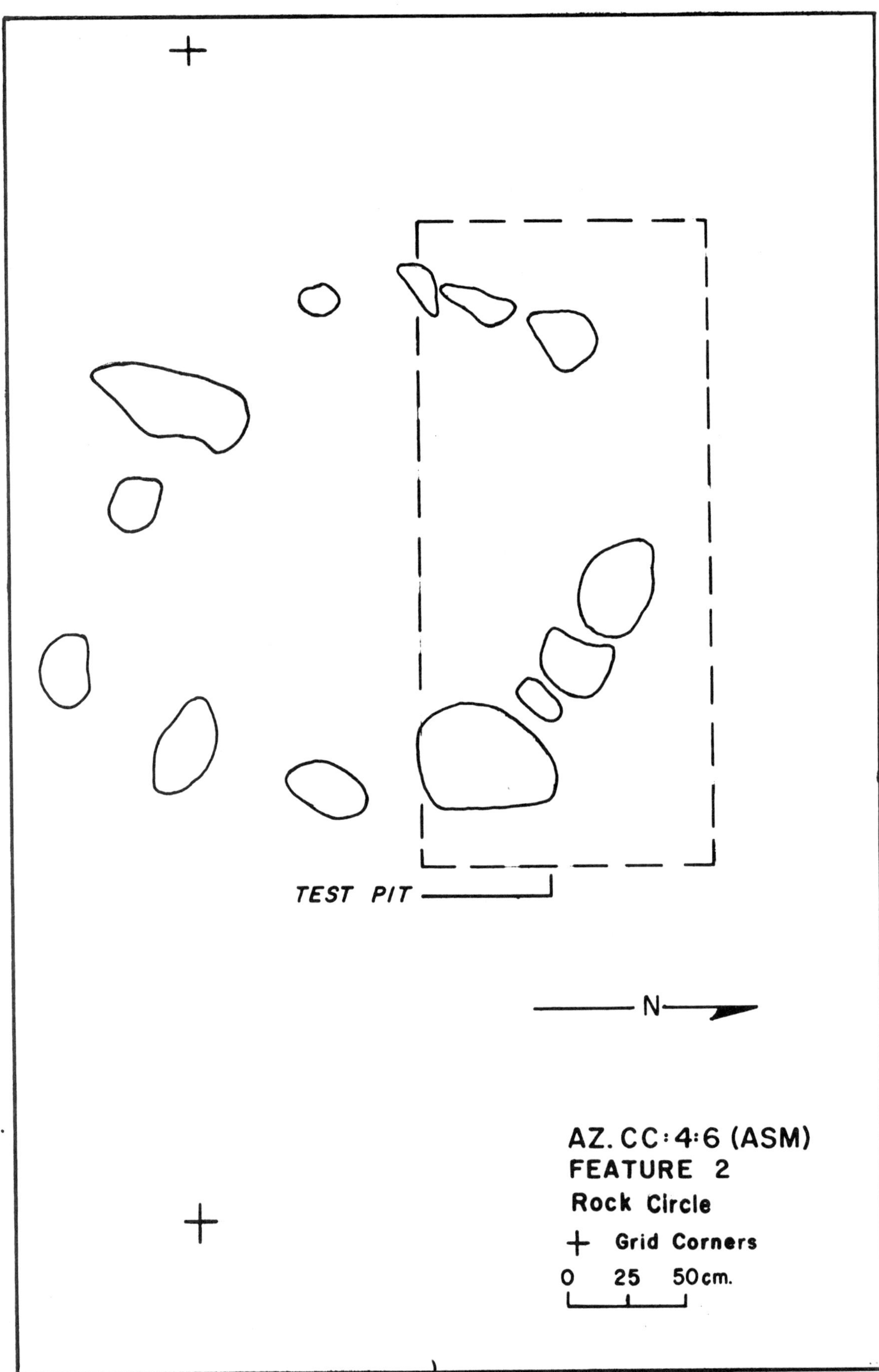

Figure 109. Arizona CC:4:6, Feature 2

The chipped stone collection from this site consists of 4 cores, 194 flakes, 46 unifaces, 8 bifaces, and 1 projectile point for a total of 253 artifacts. The total tool sample, including both formal tools and utilized debitage, comprises a hefty 31 percent of the total assemblage, the highest frequency of any site in the R-O-W corridor. This site differs from Arizona CC:4:5 in having a different material type distribution among artifacts and exhibiting only minimal core reduction tasks.

Silicates dominate the collection at 57.8 percent; rhyolite comprises only 14.6 percent, basalt 5.1 percent, quartzite 0.8 percent, and unidentified types 3.6 percent. Obsidian contributes 18.2 percent, which is nearly the same as for Arizona CC:4:5. However, obsidian was used for both bifaces and unifaces, whereas at Arizona CC:4:5 it was used almost exclusively for bifacial tools.

Three stages of manufacture are represented by the cores. One is a silicate uni-directional core, two are silicate bi-directional cores and a fourth is a basalt multi-directional core. Platform preparation is present on all examples. This very low frequency of cores is significant because it supports the assumption that this site is a specialized tool finishing and tool use area, and was not exploited as a lithic procurement site. This is further borne out by the occurrence of a lone primary cortical flake of unidentified material. Secondary flakes account for 32 percent of all flakes, tertiary flakes 55 percent, and shatter 13 percent. Fifty-six percent of the flakes are silicates; rhyolite constitutes 18 percent, and obsidian 16 percent. Quartzite, basalt, and other types each contribute 5 percent or less.

Formal tools outnumber utilized debitage two to one, yet this site had higher frequencies of utilized flakes than any other site in the project corridor. Formal tools include unifaces, bifaces, and one non-diagnostic projectile point. Significant patterns are evident in the distribution of material types among the formal tools. In gross counts silicates comprise 65 percent of the total, obsidian 26 percent, rhyolite 5.5 percent, and basalt 4 percent. Salient differences are evident when bifaces are separated from unifaces; 62.5 percent of the bifaces are made of obsidian and the remaining 37.5 percent are silicates. This suggests a relationship with Arizona CC:4:5 with its obsidian biface assemblage. Conversely, silicates comprise 69.6 percent of the unifaces and 85 percent of the utilized flakes, whereas the unifaces at Arizona CC:4:5 were all made of rhyolite.

The extraordinarily high uniface frequency is unique to CC:4:6 and is not encountered elsewhere in the project area. It is noteworthy that the majority were formed on secondary and tertiary silicate flakes and are relatively small in size. Given the probability that this site, like Arizona CC:4:5, may reflect hunting activities, the unifaces could well be tools made for processing game. Detailed information that would allow the postulation of specific tasks performed with unifaces is lacking, however, and until more discriminant attributes can be studied on the unifacial tools, this suggestion must be considered tentative.

Twenty-three, or 12 percent, of the collected flakes exhibited utilization. Twenty of these were used on lateral edges, one on the perimeter, and two on the distal end. None of the bifaces exhibited use wear. Usage was apparent on 35 percent of the unifaces; six were utilized on lateral edges, three on the perimeter, and one on the distal end. In summation, 79 percent of the utilized pieces were used on lateral edges, 9 percent on the distal end, and 12 percent on the perimeter. Marginal retouch, found on tools only at this site, was evident on three flakes, three unifaces, and three bifaces. Edge angles on utilized pieces ranged from 39 to 72 degrees with a mean of 57.5 degrees. This fairly variable range may indicate a similarily variable range of tool function, but is a hypothesis that needs further testing.

Summarizing the above data, it is evident that Arizona CC:4:6 is a specialized limited activity site. Lack of time prevented a more detailed intra-site analysis of the functions and relationships among the three discrete lithic assembalges-obsidian bifaces, silicate unifaces, and utilized silicate flakes. Not only are there problems in attempting to understand stylistic and functional attributes, but chronological differences may also be present that are not immediately apparent. Nevertheless, the close association of all the various tools in a singular localized context argues for an integrated set of tasks associated with procuring and processing of game.

Summary of the AEPCO Lithic Industry and Inter-stratum Relationships

Introduction

Three categories were defined for recovered chipped stone materials: (1) cores, the cobbles and nodular pieces from which flakes were removed, (2) debitage (flakes and shatter), the by-products of core reduction and/or tool manufacture and (3) tools, bifaces, unifaces, and projectile points with or without utilization or marginal retouch, and unmodified cores and flakes that are marginally retouched or exhibit use wear. Lithic analyses identified 651 cores, 2839 flakes, 385 pieces of shatter, and 387 tools.

Initially artifacts were sorted into the core, debitage, or tool category. Later, each specimen's attributes were described and the total artifact inventory mathematically analyzed (Appendix I). Distributional data on these attributes were derived by using the Statistical Package for Social Sciences (SPSS) and relevant subprograms. DISCRIMINANT, CONDESCRIPTIVE, FREQUENCY, and CROSSTAB (Nie and others 1972; Klecka and others 1975). Interpretation of computer output aided in answering research questions about aboriginal activities and local cultural traditions.

One problem in the AEPCO lithic analysis involved identifying core tools. Microscopic inspection suggested that many cores were initially prepared for flake production and later re-used as tools. A second problem was identifying the stage of tool manufacture; for example, a uniface could have been first utilized as a flake and later percussion-reduced into a formal tool.

Research Objectives

The research design for the lithic analysis was oriented toward two research goals. First, to identify aboriginal activities at project sites and relate these to prehistoric land use patterns and, secondly, to clarify problems of regional culture history. A thorough descriptive analysis aided by computerized statistical data manipulation best suited the goals of the lithic study. Thus, objectives were to obtain information on (1) reduction and manufacture methods, (2) tool types, and (3) tool uses.

Aboriginal Activities

The first research objective was obtained by generating hypotheses about aboriginal activities in distinct environmental strata within the project area. Tool attributes like edge angles, presence/absence of microwear, stage of manufacture, metric dimensions, ratio of different stages of manufacture, and material type were studied to diagnose land use patterns and site activities.

Ten environmental strata, each with different topographic features and biotic communities, were transected by the transmission line right-of-way. It was assumed that the lithics reflected some of the varied activities occurring in each strata. The implicit assumption was that isolation of variability within and among strata was possible. Because the right-of-way transected only a narrow portion of each stratum it cannot be assumed that the lithic assemblages reflect <u>all</u> activities. Also, some site types (for example, habitation sites) were avoided by AEPCO. However, it was felt that a representative, comparable sample was nevertheless obtained from the field investigations. The environmental strata were established as sampling strata with the intention of observing variation among artifact assemblages within and among strata. Different frequencies of attributes occurring within artifact assemblages could be indicative of (1) differing resource procurement, (2) non-contemporaneity of sites, (3) different cultures or, (4) different natural or cultural formation processes. Stratum and site differentiation would be documented by comparing divergent raw material quantities and tool use intensity and by identifying an artifact's stage of manufacture.

The activity hypotheses discussed below are confined to sites occurring <u>within</u> the R-O-W in each of the seven environmental strata. Postulated activities were hunting and butchering of game, plant collecting and processing, quarrying, core reduction, tool manufacture and, tool resharpening activities. Hunting could be documented by the presence of projectile points and utilized flakes. Butchering could be indicated by the presence of utilized flakes, cores, unifaces, and bifaces (Bayham 1976). Plant collecting tool kits consist primarily of perishable items, but large and small cutting and scraping tools might be expected (Goodyear 1975b). Plant processing could be indicated by pounding, cutting, and grinding implements as well as storage facilities. Quarrying could be identified by the presence of tested cobbles and split nodules, while reduction would be indicated by a predominance of cortical flakes and tools. Tool resharpening would be indicated by small flakes with or without edge damage

(Teague 1975). Based on the above assumptions and present environmental data, hypothesized activities are presented for each stratum.

Stratum 1: Gila River Terraces. As this area has floodplain and desert riparian growth, tool assemblages reflecting farming, plant collecting and processing, hunting and fishing activities are expected. Tools indicating wood cutting may also be expected.

Stratum 2: San Simon River Valley. This stratum is similar to Stratum 1 and should also reflect agricultural potential. Butchering tools, plant collecting instruments, and ground stone processing equipment were anticipated. It is interesting to note that one site in the stratum, Arizona CC:2:40 is associated with gridded gardens.

Stratum 3: Pleistocene terraces and lower bajada of the Gila River. Deeply dissected terraces in a tobosa grassland environment characterize this stratum. Gravels abound on the terraces. It was hypothesized that cobble quarrying and reduction activities would be present. Flakes and core tools used for plant processing activities and flakes used for butchering game could also be expected.

Stratum 4: Upper bajada of the Gila Mountains. Varied plant cover and terrace gravels indicate the possibility of various subsistence activities. It was expected that tools and re-sharpening flakes from plant collecting and butchering activities and debris from cobble quarrying and reduction would be present.

Stratum 5: Peloncillo Mountains foothills. The creosotebush and cactus vegetation, cobble ground cover and basalt outcrops differentiate this stratum from the others. Hunting and gathering as well as rhyolite and basalt reduction were hypothesized activities.

Stratum 7: Gila River terraces. This deeply dissected terrace system has a creosotebush cover. Cactus is present and gravels are available for artifact production. Flake tools for hunting and gathering were expected as well as the use of local cherts in tool manufacture.

Stratum 8: San Francisco River terraces. Similar to Stratum 7, this stratum has denser vegetal cover and rockier slopes. Rhyolite outcrops are common. It was anticipated that sites would reflect rhyolite reduction activities. Temporary collecting stations, indicated by tools, were expected.

Stratum 9/10: Big Lue Mountains-Gila River Canyonlands and Democrat Mesa. Chert reduction and tool manufacture were postulated activities. It was anticipated that hunting and plant processing would be indicated by the tool assemblage.

Cultural Background

Southeastern Arizona contains a confusing interplay of several cultural traditions. Thus it is imperative to carefully describe techniques of manufacture that might be culturally or chronologically specific.

Attributes useful in the recognition of technological traditions overlap with those helpful in the recognition of aboriginal activities. Multiple technological traditions are considered present if differences between or within assemblages can be established where these differences are not dependent upon material types or their availability (Sackett 1977). Another indicator of possible cultural affiliation is the presence of diagnostic artifact types on sites. For example, Mogollon ceramics were present on the Gila floodplain villages and the gridded garden complex, and suggest that the lithic scatter sites might be associated with these.

It was assumed that Cochise, Mogollon, Hohokam, Salado, and Apache tool manufacturing systems would each have different clusters of technological traits. Homogeneity within traditions and heterogeneity among traditions was assumed. However, other factors can create distinct traditions of toolmaking besides separate cultural affiliations. These include chronological continuity, different social groups within the same culture, and different tool kits for exploitation of varying resources. Rather than attempt to assign the chipped stone to a specific culture, the focus was to isolate discrete methods of manufacture, and interpret them. Laboratory analysis of core reduction and tool manufacturing techniques would assist in identifying styles of tool fabrication indicative of cultural traditions (Sackett 1977).

Description of SPSS Subprogram Results

As noted previously, the AEPCO project utilized the SPSS computer program (Nie and others 1972; Klecka and others 1975) to expedite interpretation of the lithic collection. Distributional data on artifact attributes were used to ascertain if samples showed significant departures from expectations for variables occurring at sites or within strata.

The SPSS subprogram FREQUENCY (Klecka and others 1975) computes and presents one-way frequency distribution tables, for example, the frequency of unifaces in a given stratum. The subprogram DISCRIMINANT provides a way to tabulate data and set up classifications. Specifically it tabulates the number of cases for each value of a variable. Thus, a variable would be material type and values thereof would be chert, rhyolite, basalt, and so forth. The subprogram CONDESCRIPTIVE (continuous descriptive statistics) computes summary measures of central tendency. Statistical outputs of this subprogram delineate the minimum, maximum, and range of a given variable, for example, tool edge angles. Mean values and standard deviation are also derived from this subprogram and are useful for comparing tool dimensions within and among strata.

The AEPCO sample had three anomalous features. First, despite the presence of numerous cores, hammerstones were absent. Second, although chert flakes predominated, cores were primarily of rhyolite. Third, formal tools evidenced little use.

The sample total is 651 cores, 3278 flakes and shatter (debitage), and 387 tools. Seven strata produced this collection. Table 4 illustrates the artifact types and their respective material composition. When

	Cores	Flakes	Shatter	Unifaces	Bifaces	Projectile Pts	Utilized Cores	Utilized Flakes	Utilized Unifaces	Utilized Bifaces	Utilized Pts		Percent of Total Assemblage
Rhyolite	262 / 27.3	582 / 60.8	50 / 5.2	10 / 1.0	5 / .5		24 / 2.5	11 / 1.2	11 / 1.2	3 / 0.3		958	22.2
Silicates	140 / 7.7	1251 / 68.8	175 / 9.6	26 / 1.4	4 / 0.2		21 / 1.2	109 / 6.0	90 / 5.0	2 / 0.1		1818	42.1
Quartz		1 / 100										1	0.02
Quartzite	24 / 12.4	139 / 71.7	15 / 7.7	4 / 2.1			1 / 0.5	3 / 1.5	7 / 3.6	1 / 0.5		194	4.5
Obsidian		129 / 71.3	23 / 12.7	9 / 5.0	13 / 7.2		3 / 1.6		2 / 1.1		2 / 1.1	181	4.2
Basalt	213 / 21.9	659 / 67.6	77 / 7.9	3 / 0.3	1 / 0.1		17 / 1.7	5 / 0.5				975	22.6
Andesite	4 / 8.7	38 / 82.6	4 / 8.7									46	1.1
Other	8 / 5.6	94 / 65.7	41 / 20.7									143	3.3
Total	651	2893	385	52	23		63	131	110	6	2	4316	
% of assemblage	15.0	67.0	9.0	1.2	0.5		1.5	3.0	2.6	0.14	0.05		100

Table 4. Chipped Stone Crosstabulation: Material Type by Stage of Manufacture.

	Rhyolite	Silicates	Quartz	Quartzite	Obsidian	Basalt	Andesite	Other	Totals	Percent of Assemblage
Stratum 2	72 / 22.3	56 / 17.3		25 / 7.7	8 / 2.5	132 / 40.9	10 / 3.1	20 / 6.2	323	7.7
Stratum 3	181 / 26.1	210 / 30.3		33 / 4.8	4 / .6	236 / 34		29 / 4.2	693	16.6
Stratum 4	14 / 56	4 / 16				7 / 28			25	.6
Stratum 5	393 / 20.7	781 / 41	1 / .05	55 / 2.9	124 / 6.5	468 / 24.6		82 / 4.3	1904	45.6
Stratum 7	64 / 9.2	455 / 65.2		55 / 7.9	6 / .9	86 / 12.3	24 / 3.4	8 / 1.1	698	16.7
Stratum 8	136 / 65.1	41 / 19.6		3 / 1.4	1 / .5	19 / 9.1	9 / 4.3		209	5
Stratum 9	87 / 26.7	148 / 45.4		2 / .6	59 / 18.1	21 / 6.4		9 / 2.8	326	7.8
Total	947	1695	1	173	202	969	43	148	4178	
% of assemblage	22.7	40.6	.02	4.2	4.8	23.2	1.0	3.5		100

Table 5. Chipped Stone Crosstabulation: Material Type by Strata

analyzing the varying frequencies of strata totals it must be emphasized that site artifact totals within each stratum may vary. For example, Stratum 5 included 10 sites while Stratum 9/10 had only two. The material from Stratum 4 was not included in the comparative inter-stratum analysis because the small artifact sample (less than 30 specimens) required separate statistical tests.

Of the total 4316 artifacts three material types are dominant (Table 5): silicates (42.1 percent), primarily chert, basalt (26.7 percent), and rhyolite (22.2 percent). Significant patterns of occurrence of material types are apparent within particular strata. Strata 2 and 3 showed primarily basalt use, Strata 4 and 8 primarily rhyolite use, and silicates were most frequent in Strata 5, 7, and 9. Obsidian, rarely encountered on project sites, showed high percentages in Strata 5 and 9. Notable is the use of several local materials in each stratum following a dominant material type. In Stratum 2 basalt and rhyolite were worked, in Stratum 3 basalt and silicates, in Stratum 5 silicates and basalt, and in Stratum 9 silicates and rhyolite. Strata 7 and 8 do not conform to this pattern. Differential procurement of a variety of available local material is reflected in these changing frequencies from stratum to stratum.

Table 6 illustrates the frequency of artifact types within each stratum. Three general classes of artifacts will be discussed: cores, debitage, and tools.

Table 7 illustrates the occurrence of discrete core types within each stratum (see Appendix I for an explanation of core classes). Cores were classified by attributes based on direction of flake removal and platform preparation. Implicit in the discussion of core classes is the assumption that these classes reflect differing stages of reduction. The data indicate that different material types were subject to certain patterns of reduction. For example, Class 1 cores (uni-directional prepared) were primarily manufactured from rhyolite and basalt, whereas Class 5 cores (multi-directional prepared) were found to be mostly of chert. One explanation for this polarity is that raw silicates were occurring in small nodules whereas rhyolite and basalt much more often occurred in large outcrops. The smaller chert nodules could only produce a small number of flakes from a given platform and would require the use of multiple platforms, thus becoming multi-directional cores.

Strata 5, 3, 2, and 8 produced the most cores, respectively. Uni-directional prepared cores (Class 1) were the dominant type and were most frequently made of rhyolite and basalt. Uni-directional prepared and unprepared cores were generally larger than the other core classes and were probably a factor of raw material size (angular fragments of basalt and rhyolite). Silicates predominated in core Classes 3 through 6 (bi-directional and multi-directional cores). Prepared cores were more common although techniques of preparation were unsophisticated (Appendix I). One anomalous feature in the total core sample is that Stratum 8 produced the most Class 5 cores (multi-directional prepared) even though the collection from this stratum was dominated by rhyolite. Generally, as noted previously, Class 5 cores were found to be made primarily from silicates. Important in discerning

	Cores	Flakes	Shatter	Unifaces	Bifaces	Points	Utilized Cores	Utilized Flakes	Utilized Unifaces	Utilized Bifaces	Utilized Pts	Total	Percent
Stratum 2	115/35	181/55	11/3.3		5/1.6		6/1.8	6/1.8	4/1.2	1/.3		329	7.6
Stratum 3	124/17.5	458/64.4	80/11.3	3/.4			13/1.8	18/2.5	15/2.1			711	16.5
Stratum 4	2/8	23/92	-									25	.6
Stratum 5	269/14	1321/68.7	211/11	7/.3	2/.1		31/1.6	23/1.2	59/3.1			1923	44.5
Stratum 7	30/4	583/78.3	54/7.2	7/.9	3/.4		5/.7	47/6.3	14/1.9	2/.3		745	17.3
Stratum 8	99/41.6	109/45.9	14/5.9	1/.4	1/.4		7/2.9	7/2.9				238	5.5
Stratum 9	12/3.5	218/63.2	15/4.3	34/9.8	12/3.5		1/.3	30/8.7	18/5.2	3/.9	2/.6	345	8
Total Cores	651	2893	385	52	23		63	131	110	6	2	4316	100
Precentage	15	67	8.9	1.2	.5		1.5	3.3	2.5	.1	.04		

Table 6. Chipped Stone Crosstabulation: Frequency of manufacture stages and tool classes by strata.

	Uni-directional prepared	Uni-directional unprepared	Bi-directional prepared	Bi-directional unprepared	Multi-directional prepared	Multi-directional unprepared	Total	Percentage of all cores
CLASS	1	2	3	4	5	6		
Stratum 2	72/59.5	17/14.0	22/18.2	2/1.7	8/6.6		121	16.9
Stratum 3	73/53.3	29/21.2	25/18.2	2/1.5	8/5.8		137	19.2
Stratum 4		2/100					2	0.3
Stratum 5	156/52	36/12	60/20	15/5	33/11		300	42
Stratum 7	20/57.2	6/17.1	1/2.9	2/5.7	6/17.1		35	5.0
Stratum 8	51/48.1	1/1	17/16		37/34.9		106	14.8
Stratum 9	8/61.5	1/7.7	3/23.1			1/7.7	13	1.8
Total Cores	380	92	128	21	92	1	714	
Percentage	53.2	12.9	18.0	2.9	13.9	0.1		100

Table 7. Chipped Stone Crosstabulation: Core Classes by Strata.

patterns of reduction within strata is an inspection of the ratios of cores to flakes for each of the dominant material types (Table 4). These ratios are silicates 1:8, basalt 1:3, and rhyolite 1:2. The ratios for basalt and rhyolite are low in comparison to the silicates, which suggests that primary reduction of basalt and rhyolite may not have been occurring at project sites and that perhaps silicate flakes were preferred over other materials.

Flakes dominated the lithic assemblages in Strata 5, 7, and 9, and Stratum 5 had the highest percentage of debitage. Flakes were classified according to the percentage of cortex present. In some ways this manner of classification is arbitrary, since observations concering raw material size which are critical in a determination of manufacture stage were not taken (for example, small cortical flakes may be final finishing flakes). Thus, gross categories of amount of cortex may mask potentially varying frequencies.

Tertiary and secondary flakes predominated in the total flake assemblage (Table 8). Reduction techniques within strata may be discussed by examining the percentages of flake types in the assemblage. Three strata, 5, 7, and 9 show tertiary, secondary and primary flakes in

	Primary Flake	Secondary Flake	Tertiary Flake	Shatter	Total	Percent of all debitage
Stratum 2	55 / 28.6	71 / 37	55 / 28.6	11 / 5.7	192	5.9
Stratum 3	77 / 14.3	205 / 38.1	176 / 32.7	80 / 14.9	538	16.4
Stratum 4	4 / 17.4	13 / 56.5	6 / 26.1		23	.7
Stratum 5	236 / 15.4	514 / 33.6	571 / 37.2	211 / 13.8	1532	46.7
Stratum 7	50 / 7.8	207 / 32.5	326 / 51.2	54 / 8.5	637	19.4
Stratum 8	25 / 20.3	62 / 50.4	22 / 17.9	14 / 11.4	123	3.8
Stratum 9	5 / 2.1	97 / 41.6	116 / 49.9	15 / 6.4	233	7.1
Total	452	1169	1272	385	3278	
Percentage	13.7	35.7	38.9	11.7		100

Table 8. Chipped Stone Crosstabulation: Frequencies of debitage by strata.

decreasing percentages. Two strata, 2 and 8, have more secondary than primary or tertiary flakes, and Strata 3 and 4 show secondary, tertiary and then primary flakes in decreasing amounts. An examination of flake percentages confirms the impression that primary reduction was occurring in all strata. In Strata 2 and 8, however, it appears that secondary flakes are more frequent than elsewhere, indicating secondary reduction of flakes into tools.

Tools were defined in two ways: (1) as formal tools like unifaces, bifaces and projectile points, with or without utilization and (2) as pieces that displayed utilization or marginal retouch. The combined strata produced 387 tools, 312 of which were utilized (the remainder being unfinished unifaces and bifaces). Few pieces showed retouch (Table 9). In the combined total, primary and secondary flakes were

	UNSHAPED UTILIZED ARTIFACTS				SHAPED TOOLS-UTILIZED			SHAPED TOOLS-NON-UTILIZED				
	Cores	Primary Flakes	Secondary Flakes	Tertiary Flakes	Unifaces	Bifaces	Projectile Pts	Unifaces	Bifaces	Projectile Pts	Total	Percent
Stratum 2	6 / 27.3	3 / 13.6	2 / 9.1	1 / 4.5	4 / 18.2	1 / 4.5			5 / 22.8		22	5.7
Stratum 3	13 / 26.5	2 / 4.1	11 / 23.4	5 / 10.2	15 / 30.7			3 / 6.1			49	12.7
Stratum 4	-	-	-	-	-	-	-	-	-	-	-	-
Stratum 5	31 / 25.4	5 / 4.1	13 / 10.7	5 / 4.1	59 / 48.4			7 / 5.7	2 / 1.6		122	31.5
Stratum 7	5 / 6.4	4 / 5.1	31 / 39.7	12 / 15.4	14 / 18	2 / 2.6		7 / 9	3 / 3.8		78	20.2
Stratum 8	7 / 43.7	2 / 12.5	1 / 6.2	4 / 25				1 / 6.3	1 / 6.3		16	4.1
Stratum 9	1 / 1		17 / 17	13 / 13	18 / 18	3 / 3	2 / 2	34 / 34	12 / 12		100	25.8
Total	63	16	75	40	110	6	2	52	23	-	387	
Percentage	16.3	4.1	19.4	10.3	28.4	1.6	.5	13.4	6	-		100

Table 9. Chipped Stone Crosstabulation: Frequencies of tool types by strata.

most commonly utilized followed in frequency by unifaces and cores. Unifaces were the most common formal tool type especially in Strata 9 and 5. Utilized flakes predominated over other utilized pieces in all strata except Stratum 5, where utilized unifaces were most frequent. Stratum 5 produced 36.7 percent of all tools with Strata 9 and 7 following in frequency.

Analysis of the utilized cores reveals that Class 1 (uni-directional prepared cores) were most often utilized, especially in Stratum 5 (Table 10). Utilized cores also accounted for a good portion of the utilized material. About 80 percent of all formal tools were utilized.

	Class 1	Class 2	Class 3	Class 4	Class 5	Class 6	Total	Percentage
Stratum 2	3 / 50				3 / 50		6	9.5
Stratum 3	8 / 61.5	4 / 30.8			1 / 7.7		13	20.6
Stratum 4	-	-	-	-	-	-	-	-
Stratum 5	12 / 38.7	2 / 6.4	10 / 32.3		7 / 22.6		31	49.2
Stratum 7	3 / 60	1 / 20			1 / 20		5	8
Stratum 8	3 / 42.9		1 / 14.2		3 / 42.9		7	11.1
Stratum 9	1 / 100						1	1.6
Total	30	7	11		15		63	
Percentage	47.6	11.1	17.5		23.8			100

Table 10. Chipped Stone Crosstabulation: Frequencies of utilized cores by strata.

Stratum 5 produced the most utilized material of all the combined strata with 36.2 percent (Table 11). However, Stratum 9 showed the greatest proportion of utilized material within its own assemblage, perhaps indicating a greater intensity of tool use than in other strata. The distribution of use damage revealed that right lateral and left lateral edges on flakes most often exhibited wear (Table 12). This clustering of location of use wear may indicate a particular type of function for utilizing flakes. Generally only light evidence of microflaking was apparent on tools (only tools from Arizona CC:4:6 exhibited heavy wear damage). This suggests that tools were only slightly used before being discarded, which may relate to the availability of raw material for tool replacement.

The dimensions of utilized pieces indicate that size variation occurs among strata except in edge length and edge angle values (Table 13). In terms

	Artifact Total	Number of Utilized Artifacts	Percentages of Assemblage Utilized	Percentage of all Utilized Artifacts
Stratum 2	329	17	5.1	5.4
Stratum 3	711	46	6.4	14.7
Stratum 4	25	0	0	0
Stratum 5	1923	113	5.8	36.2
Stratum 7	745	68	9.1	21.7
Stratum 8	238	14	5.8	4.4
Stratum 9/10	345	54	15.6	17.3
Total	4316	312		

Table 11. Chipped Stone Crosstabulation: Percentage of utilized artifacts by strata.

	Proximal end	Distal end	Lateral right edge	Lateral left edge	Perimeter	Notch	Other (retouch and cores)	Total
Stratum 2		1	4	4	2		6	17
Stratum 3	1	8	10	13	1		13	46
Stratum 4								
Stratum 5		20	22	21	19		31	113
Stratum 7		6	25	24	8		5	68
Stratum 8		4	3				7	14
Stratum 9		3	17	15	4		15	54
Total	1	42	81	77	34		77	312

Table 12: Chipped Stone Crosstabulation: Location of use wear and occurrence of marginal retouch on tools by strata.

	Mean Length	Mean Width	Mean Thickness	Mean Edge Angle	Mean Edge Length
Stratum 2	66.8	51.7	34.2	63.5°	36.7
Stratum 3	51.3	41.7	20.5	51.5	40
Stratum 4					
Stratum 5	42.6	38.3	19.6	56	37
Stratum 7	31.5	23.1	9.0	59.4	25.8
Stratum 8	56.2	55.5	27.2	65.3	35.9
Stratum 9	37.8	27.7	11	64.6	28.9
Total	47.7	39.6	20.2	60.0°	34.0

Table 13. Chipped Stone Crosstabulation: Mean metric values by strata.

of edge length Strata 2, 5, and 8 cluster as do Strata 7 and 9. Strata 2, 8 and 9 have similar edge angle means as do Strata 3, 5, and 7. Stratum 3 appears not to cluster with either group. To more fully elucidate edge angle values, histograms were compiled for the utilized pieces (Figures 110-114).

The greatest percentage of all utilized pieces cluster between 61 and 70 degrees (Figure 110). It was expected that cores would have wider angles than bifaces, since difference in edge angle is related to the striking angle necessary to successfully remove flakes from the artifact. The core and biface histograms (Figures 111 and 112) indicate that edge angle values conform to these expectations. However, the histograms for utilized flakes and unifaces (Figures 113 and 114) indicate that edge angle values for these tools cluster around similar degrees of acuteness. This is a departure from expectations because one would expect utilized flake edges to be more acute than those on unifaces. Marginal retouch produced during surface flaking of unifaces creates a steep angle before utilization occurs. Possible explanations for the closely related edge angle values for utilized flakes and unifaces are: (1) selection of flakes with steep spine plane angles; (2) utilization of flakes that were later retouched to form unifaces; (3) discarding flakes at a specific edge angle regardless of the original edge angle; (4) variation in standard deviation between minimum and maximum edge angle values that may cloud possible differences.

Perusal of the initial output of the SPSS subprograms FREQUENCY, DISCRIMINANT, and CONDESCRIPTIVE revealed several obvious patternings in artifact attribute distribution. Overall the primary stone for manufacture was rhyolite, yet few tools were made from this material. Conversely, silicate cores occurred in low frequencies although the majority of tools were made from chert. Basalt was consistently found in all stages of manufacture.

Morphological variables were compared using the SPSS subprogram CROSSTABS (Klecka and others 1975: 70), which is designed to investigate the relationship between two or more variables. For example, the high incidence of rhyolite cores was interrelating with platform preparation and the consistent removal of flakes. Rhyolite cores most often had prepared platforms and uni-directional or bi-directional flaking. On the other hand, chert and other silicate cores had limited platform preparation and the consistent, but unpatterned, removal of flakes. Studies of co-occurrence of manufacturing attributes supported the rhyolite core/chert flake dichotomy. Platform preparation was often observable on the rhyolite cores and seldom on the chert flakes, a correspondence with the high incidence of chert flakes from unprepared multidirectional cores. Cortical surfaces were often still present on the chert primary flakes.

Among utilized materials, large utilized primary percussion flakes and primary cores were over-represented when their frequency of occurrence was compared to the industry as a whole. Exhausted cores and smaller flakes with little cortex rarely were utilized.

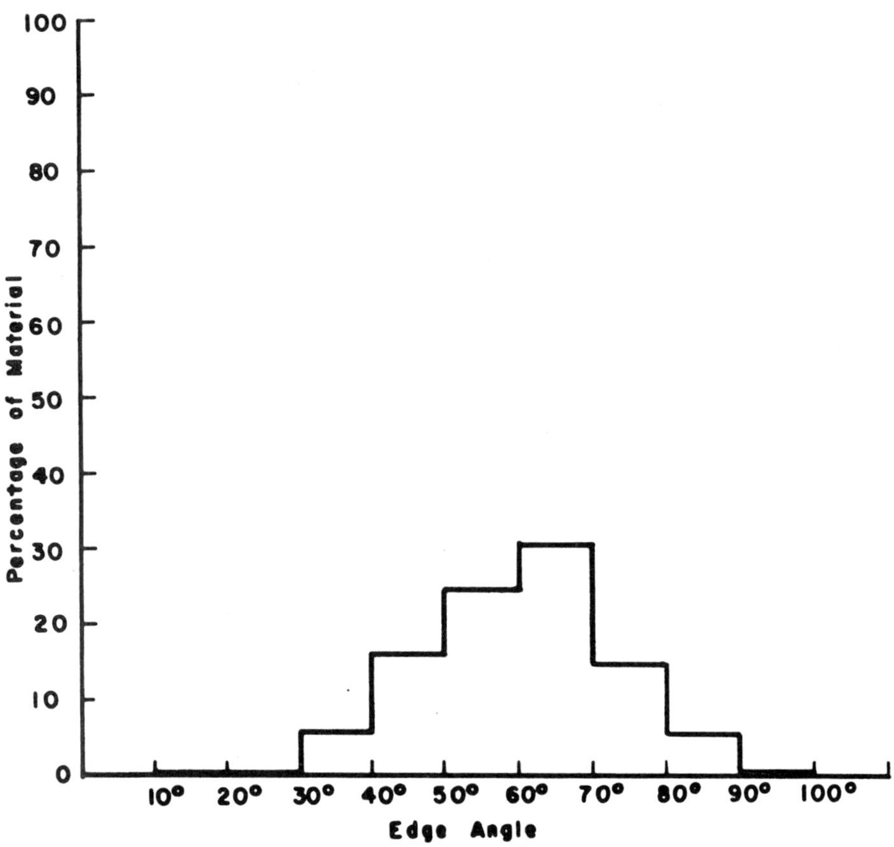

Figure 110. Edge angle values of all utilized material

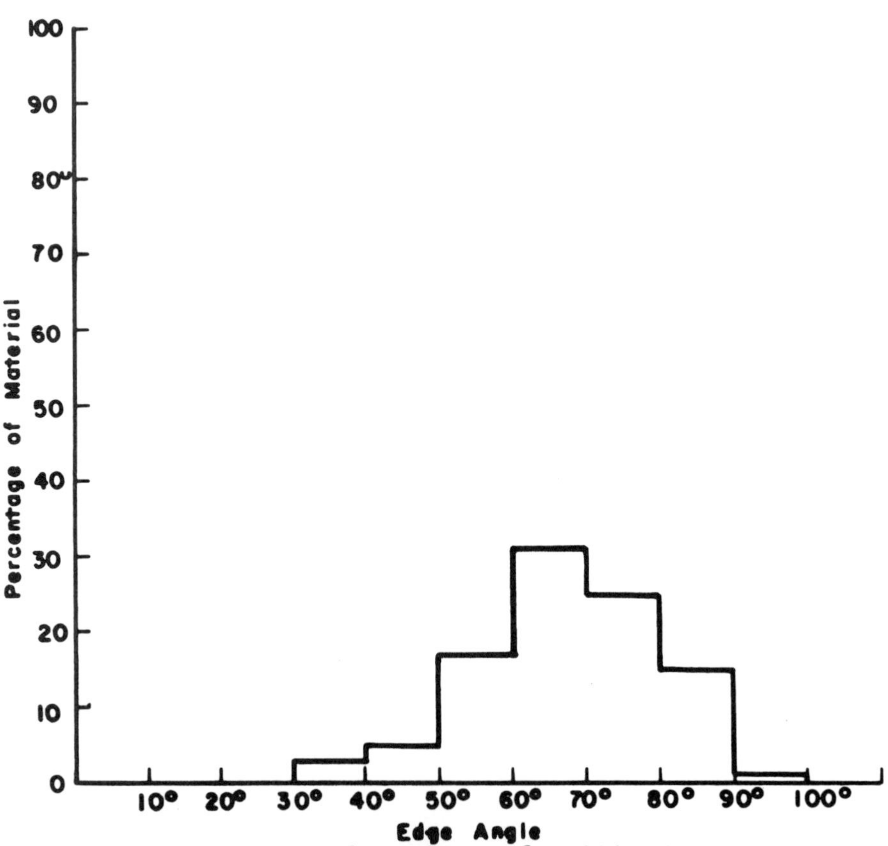

Figure 111. Edge Angle values of utilized cores

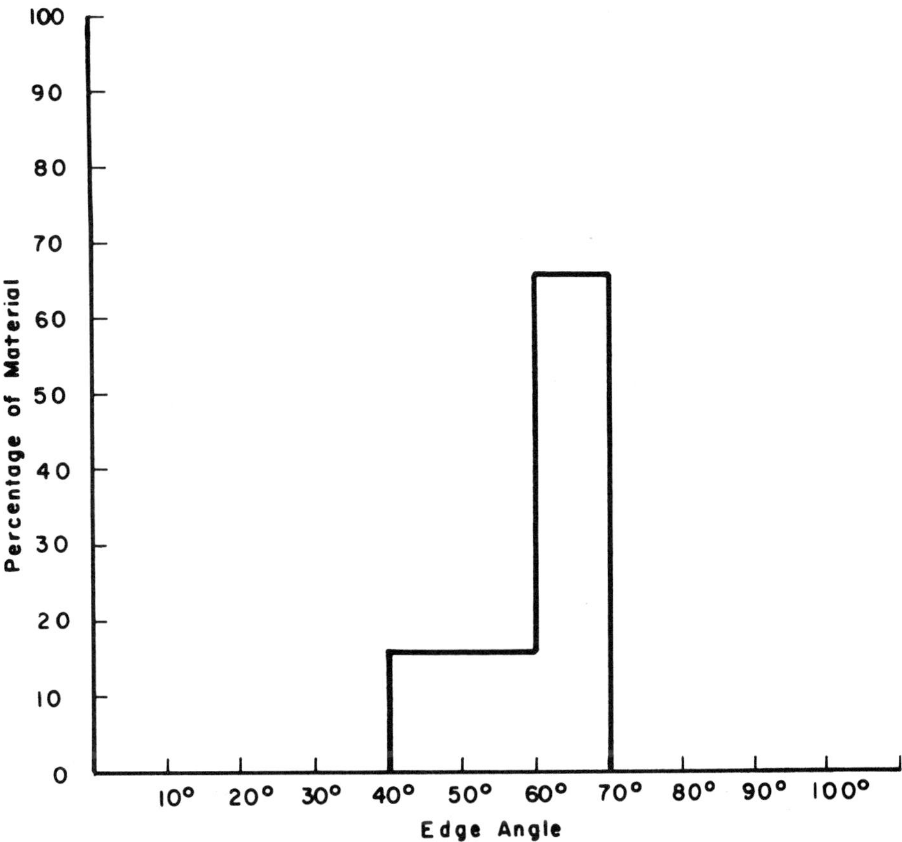

Figure 112. Edge angle values of utilized bifaces

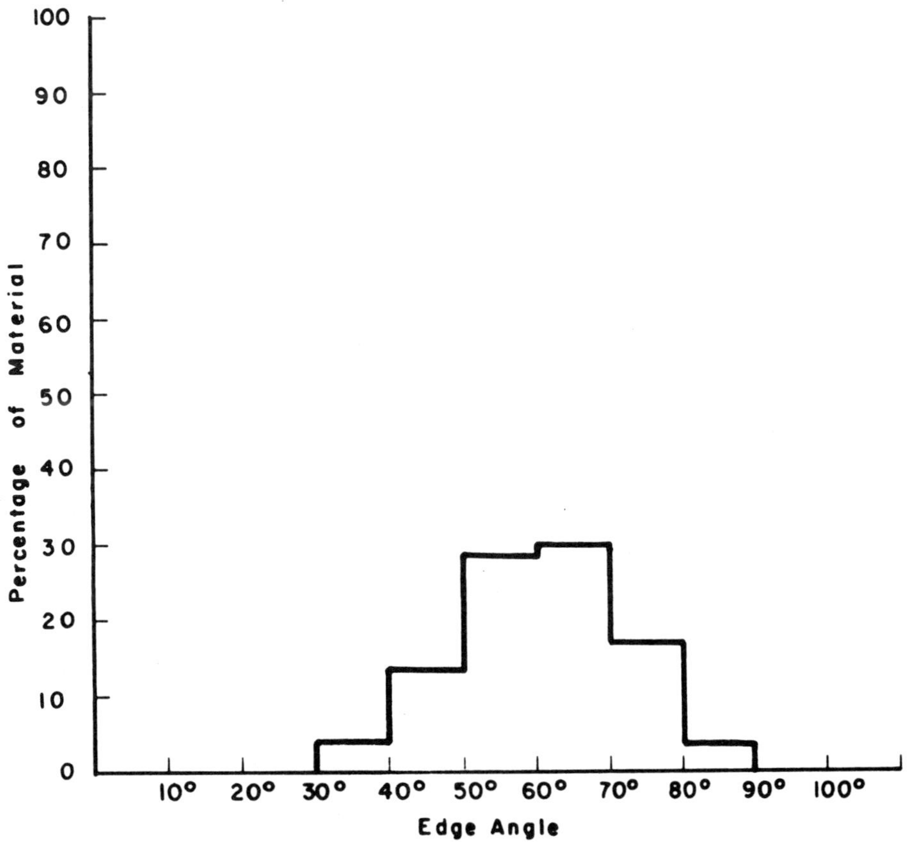

Figure 113. Edge angle values of utilized flakes

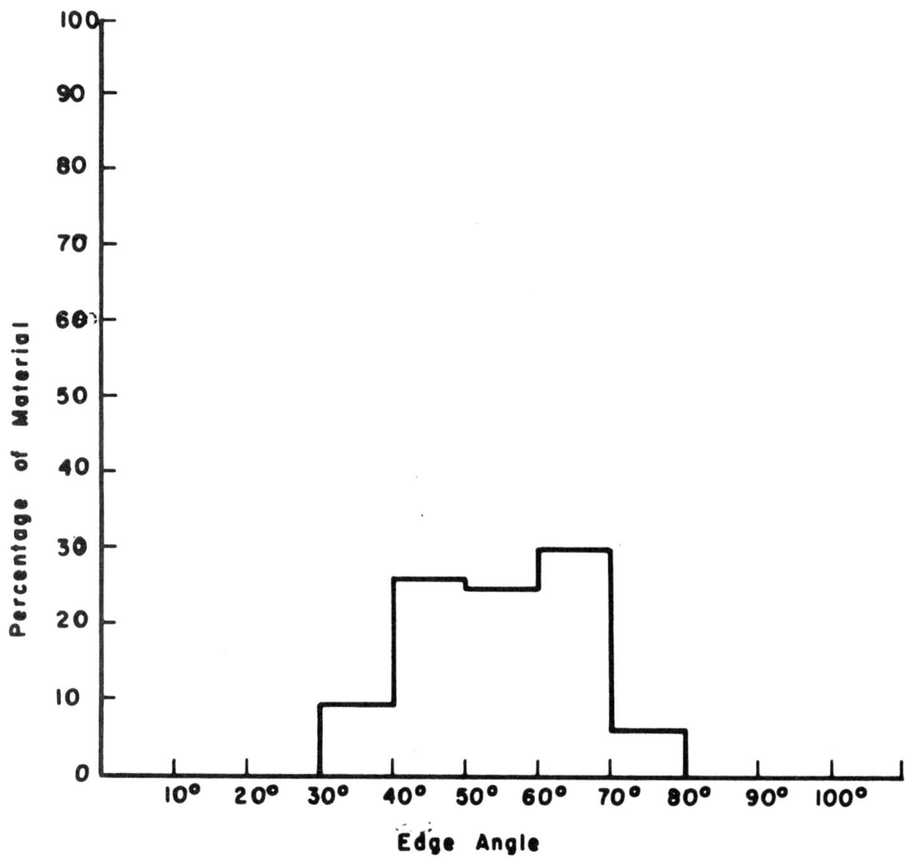

Figure 114. Edge angle values of utilized unifaces

Within strata some co-occurrences were noteworthy and were useful in supporting hypotheses on strata differentiation. In Strata 2 and 3 rhyolite cores were over-represented, whereas in Strata 5 and 7 chert flakes predominated. Stratum 9/10 with its chert and obisidian unifaces and bifaces was again completely distinct from other sampled units. The distribution of material and manufacture stage values in Stratum 8 may indicate that sites within this sample were more dissimilar than previously expected (a heterogeneity of sample).

In all strata the highest incidence of utilized material was chert and basalt although these were infrequently worked into finished tools. Rhyolite tools also evidenced little use. In Stratum 9/10, 50 percent of all chert tools were utilized, perhaps indicating a quite specific tool-kit.

Frequency of individual variables and their co-occurrence indicate that stage of reduction, materials employed, and incidence of utilized artifacts may differentiate one stratum from another.

Discussion

To facilitate discussion cultural material was grouped by manufacturing stage: debitage (flakes and shatter), cores, and tools.

Debitage. The flake debitage from the Greenlee-Dos Condado sites reflected the reduction of chert, rhyolite, and basalt. All stages of manufacture were apparent in the debitage, from initial cortical flakes to small trimming flakes; however, partially cortical flakes predominated. The higher frequency of cortical flakes with unprepared platforms may be interpreted in two ways. Either little flake and core reduction for tool manufacture was occurring at the sites so that few non-cortical flakes were found; or non-cortical flakes were removed from the sites for use elsewhere. The absence of numerous trimming flakes partially confirms the first explanation. The second hypothesis is not readily testable as the argument rests on negative evidence.

Flake breakage was uncommon, perhaps because most materials involved were sturdy and did not shatter easily. Breakage can occur when material is redeposited. The low incidence of fragmentation along with the absence of tumbling appear to indicate that most material was *in situ*.

Cores. Three core reduction systems appear to be present. First, cobble and nodular cores were found that have unprepared cortical platforms and uni-directional flake scars (Class 2 cores). Some of these were "tested" cores, that is, only the quality of material was ascertained before the piece was abandoned. A second type of core used a flake scar as a platform and flakes were removed from this area (Class 1 cores). A third core form had numerous prepared and unprepared platforms and flake removal occurred from all platforms (Classes 5 and 6 cores).

Class 1 and 2 cores (Figure 115) appear to have resulted from the hard-hammer percussion removal of flakes from a central platform. In this case, an oblong cobble was selected by the knapper and diagonally split. Flake scars were deep and long, indicating that this type of core was used to produce thick, large flakes. The Class 3 and 4 cores (Figures 116 and 117) represent a continuation of flake-making. The flake scars from the initial reduction process were substituted for a cortical platform and additional flakes were removed. Flake removal was either uni-directional or bi-directional. Class 5 and 6 cores departed from the other styles. Not only was chert the common stone used, but limited platform preparation and the removal of small flakes was characteristic of this type. Multi-directionality may be a product of the material employed. Replication experiments with local cherts from the project area revealed that inclusions in material create unpredictable fracture patterns. In order to obtain usable flakes these imperfections had to be avoided, resulting in a multi-directional core.

On cores, platform preparation was simple. Platform edges were neither rounded nor did they have numerous small stepped flakes. These features are associated with the use of an abrader to prepare a platform. No abraders were recovered during fieldwork. Aside from cortex removal no other attempts at platform preparation were common; however, two chert cores in the sample apparently were ground and roughened slightly prior to flake removal.

Core reduction was probably exclusively by freehand percussion using a leg rest. An absence of abrasion opposite core platforms suggested that anvil use was not employed.

Tools. Tools were produced on flakes, cores, and occasionally on cobbles of quartzite, rhyolite, or basalt. At many sites only primary flakes of silicates and occasionally rhyolite became tools. Retouching and notching were rare enough to be insignificant. Two sites had unique tool assemblages. Arizona CC:4:6 in Stratum 9/10 had a high incidence of unifaces; again these were manufactured on primary flakes. The second site, Arizona CC:2:44 in Stratum 2, had a number of unifacially reduced cobbles and nodules that had step fracturing on concave edge portions. This cannot be attributed to platform preparation (which should occur on the convex section) and indicates use as a tool. Therefore, this site had utilized cores and large uni-facially and bi-facially reduced cobbles as well as flake tools.

Unshaped flake tools were classified into three types and were sorted by edge preparation and edge angle. These were utilized flakes having evidence of use damage (microflaking); uni-facially retouched flakes with serial flaking on one face; and notched and retouched flakes with pressure notching and bi-facial retouching.

Other tool types found included utilized cores and large, uni-facially reduced cobbles. The latter created a problem in the analysis since although morphologically they resembled tools, such as choppers,

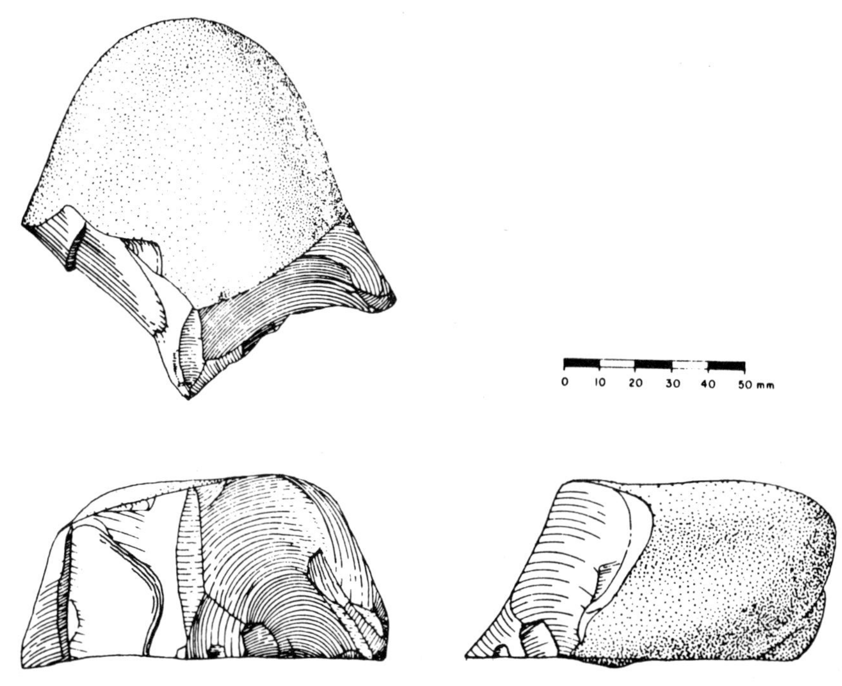

Figure 115. Unifacially reduced cobble

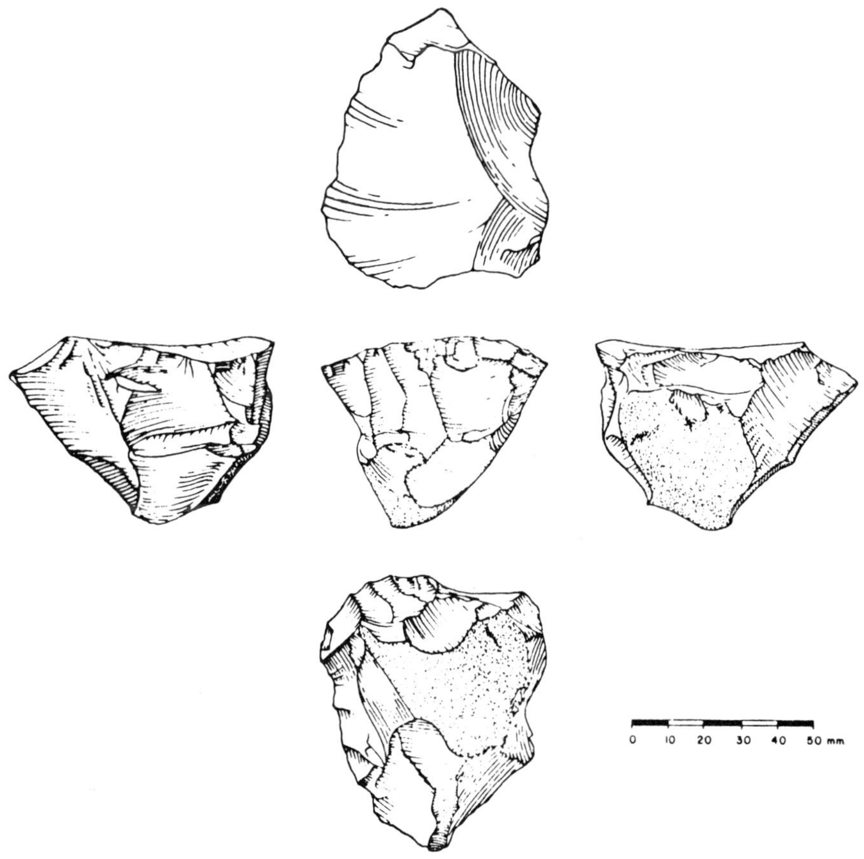

Figure 116. Bi-directional prepared core

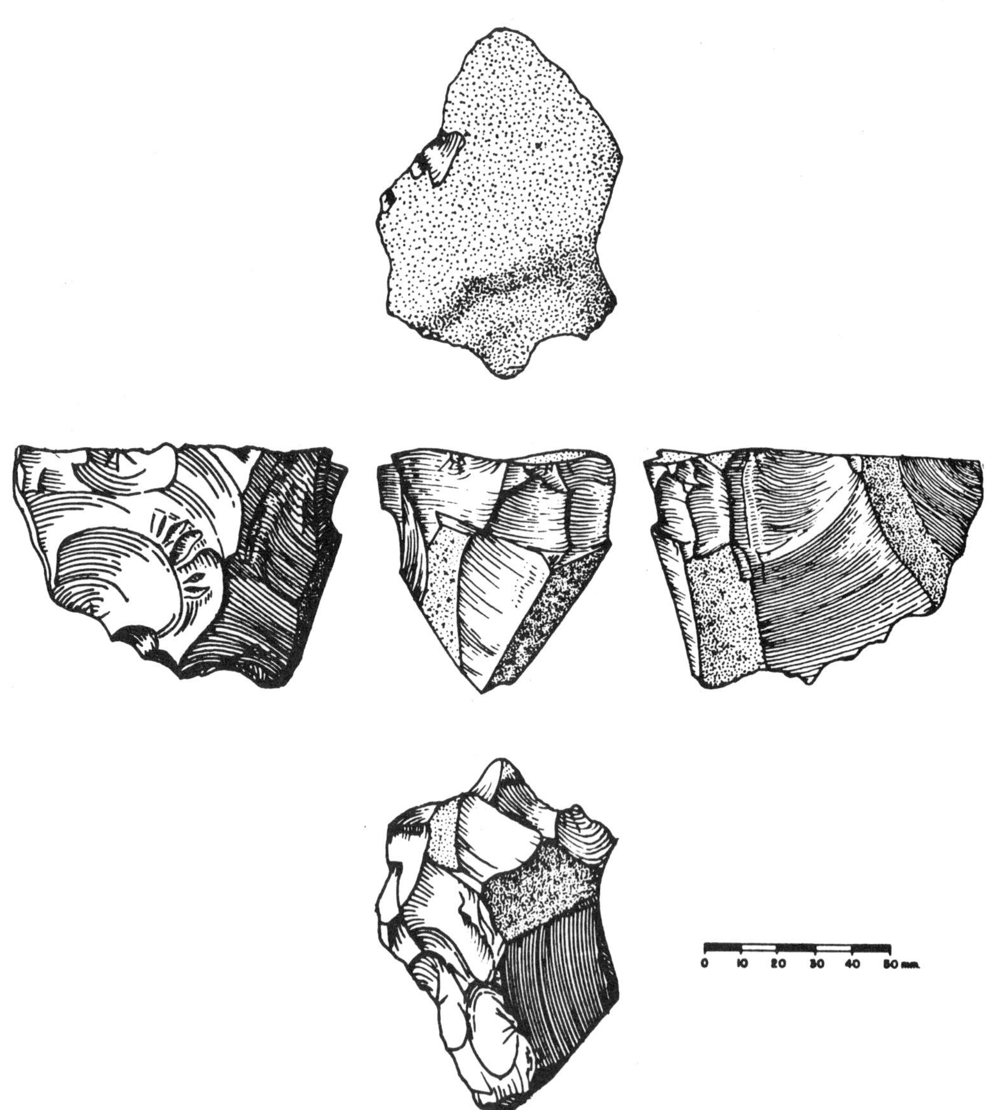

Figure 117. Bi-directional unprepared core

they exhibited no utilization. On these cobbles scar lengths were seldom more than 1 cm long and the edge was occasionally denticulated by hard-hammer notching (Figure 118). These attributes were interpreted as tool manufacture and sharpening rather than flake production.

Shaped tools consisted of unifaces (Figure 119), bifaces, and projectile points. Bifaces and unifaces are a reduction category of shaped pieces where utilization is absent. Some bifaces functioned as projectile points or perhaps knives but many appeared to have been discarded before final shaping. One broken biface in the sample may have been a drill. Bifaces average less than 3 cm in length with the exception of one hydrated obsidian specimen. Only one point, from Arizona CC:4:6, had known chronologic affiliations. Several examples of flake tools are illustrated in Figures 120 and 121.

Flake tools were inspected with a 30-power binocular microscope to identify patterns of edge damage. Round, elongated, and trapezoidal microflake shapes were present. Scraping and shaving activities produce rounded scars. Trapezoid or "stepped" scars develop when hard materials (like bone or antler) are worked (Tringham and others 1974: 188-89). The AEPCO lithic material did not show distinct wear patterns and extensive (heavy) damage was only observed on tools from Arizona CC:4:6. The distribution of scars on these tools was uneven, which may indicate cutting activities (Tringham and others 1974: 188).

Testing Research Objectives

Aboriginal Land Use Patterns. To test our hypotheses that different types of land use were occurring in different topographic zones, tool and debitage frequencies in site sampling strata were compared. Strata 2 and 3 appear quite similar as both reflect reduction of rhyolite cores and the occasional use of the products of this activity. Strata 5 and 7 have higher site densities and greater artifact variety. High frequencies of chert primary flakes and cores occur with additional basalt and rhyolite flakes. A slight differentiation between the two strata results from a decrease in the use of igneous rock in Stratum 7. Stratum 8, a small sample, was similar to Stratum 2 but lacked significant amounts of basalt. Finally Stratum 9/10 with its projectile points and high ratio of tools to debitage appears quite distinct. How these distinctions support our test implications is discussed below.

Stratum 2

For this stratum it was hypothesized that small tools and food processing equipment would be found. Little ground stone was recovered from this stratum, so evidence of food processing was minimal. Fewer small tools were recovered than expected and more cores were found. The original hypothesis was not supported but an alternative suggestion is that chert and rhyolite tool production was a primary activity here. At the very least, wild food procurement is suggested by the limited tool assemblage.

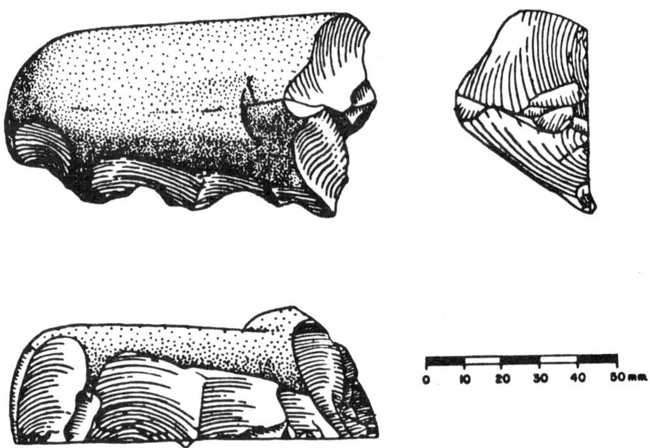

Figure 118. Core tool

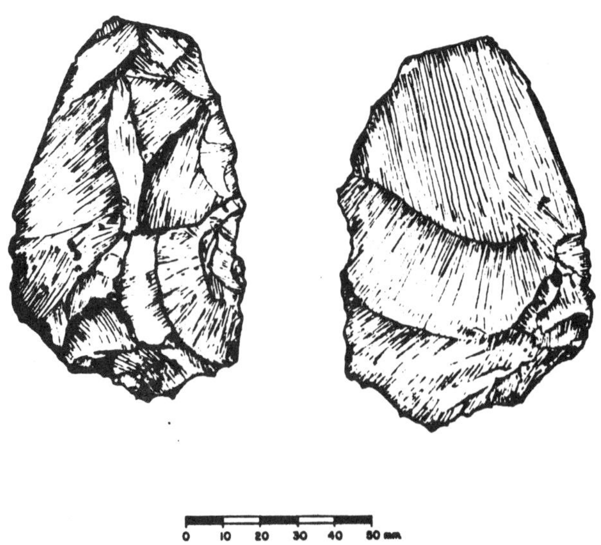

Figure 119. Uniface

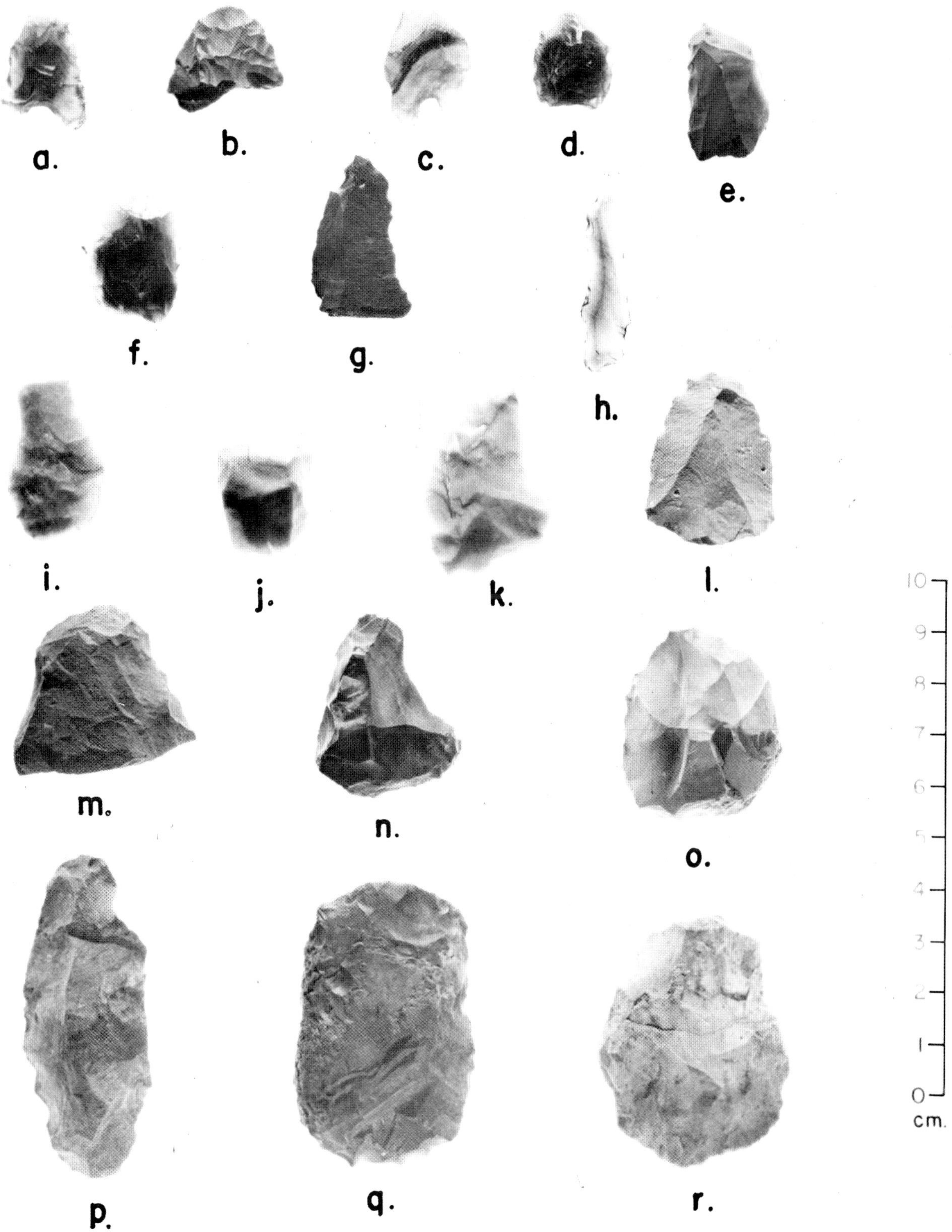

Figure 120. Tools from AEPCO Project sites: a) obsidian point; b) biface tip of hydrated obsidian; c) notched obsidian tool; d) bifacially pressure flaked obsidian piece; e) retouched flake; f) obsidian biface; g) basalt flake; h) retouched obsidian bladelet; i) chert drill; j) retouched chert uniface; k) chert uniface; l) rhyolite uniface; m) retouched basalt flake; n) jasper utilized flake; o) utilized chert uniface; p) rhyolite biface; q) utilized rhyolite uniface; r) chert biface.

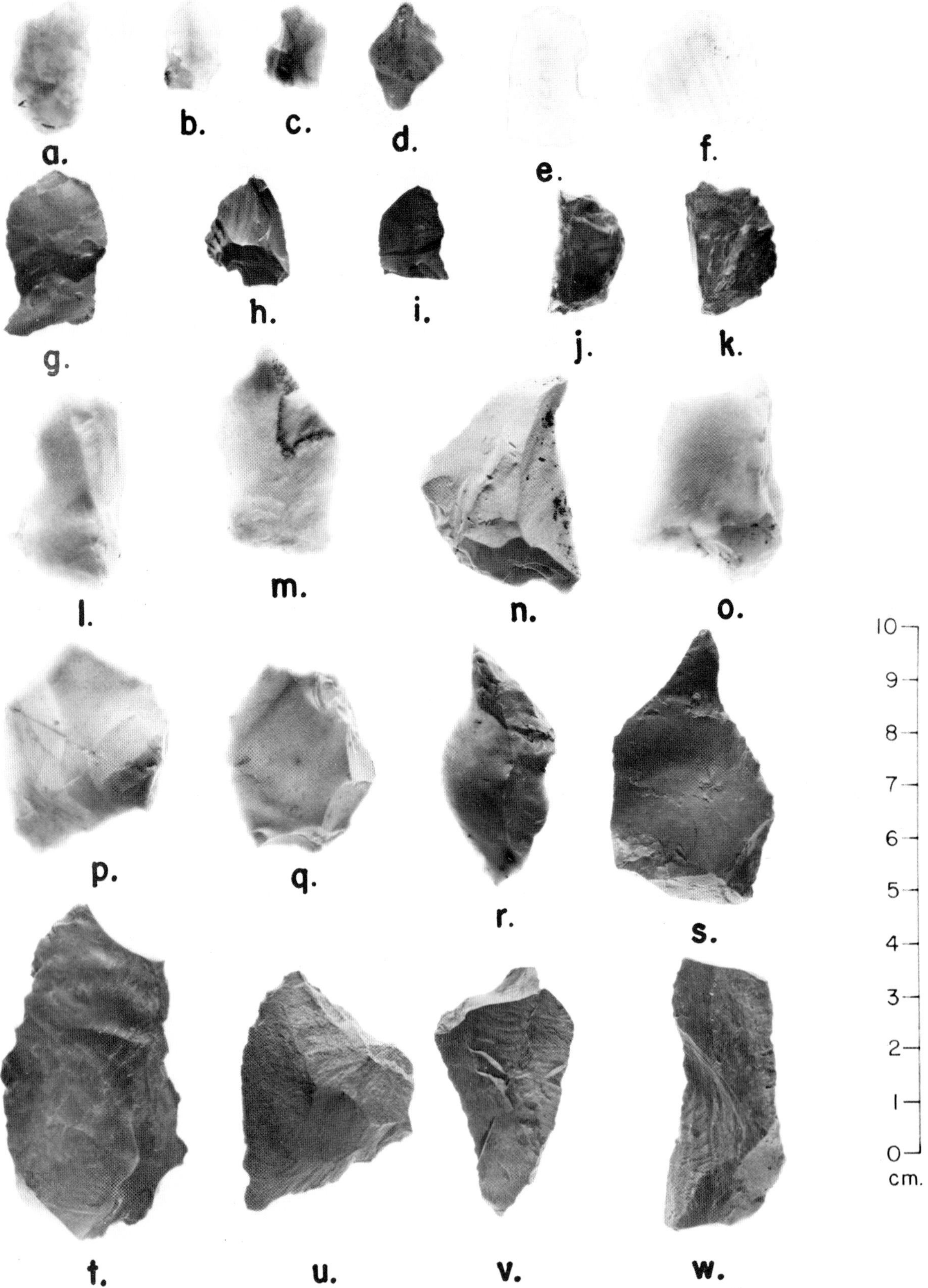

Figure 121. Tools from AEPCO Project sites: a-f) utilized chert and chalcedony flakes; g,h) utilized rhyolite flakes; i,j) utilized jasper flakes; k) utilized chert flake; l-q) utilized chert flakes; r,s) utilized jasper flakes; t,u) retouched rhyolite flakes; v) serially retouched basalt flake; w) retouched rhyolite flake.

Stratum 3

Stratum 3 conformed more to original expectations. Numerous tested cores were identified, which supports the hypothesis that tool manufacture was carried out. Seventy-three utilized cores which could have been used in plant processing were found. However, small flakes, that would be evidence of butchering, were lacking.

Stratum 4

Internal site diversity indicating varied activities within the stratum was anticipated. Since the only site sampled in this stratum had fewer than 30 artifacts, our ideas on land-use could not be tested.

Stratum 5

It was thought that Stratum 5 would be a basalt and rhyolite quarrying area because of the occurrence of local outcrops. Along with evidence for working these materials, chert flakes were also extensively used. The paucity of chert cores may indicate "curation" of these for other activities and only local use of flakes. Although not anticipated, the processing of obsidian was also occurring. Small utilized flakes suggest scraping and cutting of hard materials, perhaps wood or bone.

Stratum 6

No material was recovered and hypotheses remain untested.

Stratum 7

Local terraces provided diverse cobbles (chert, rhyolite, basalt) for tool making, but few cores were recovered. Instead, chert debitage and tools were found. The occurrence of 14 unifaces suggests tool finishing activities and possibly the use of bifaces (5 were found) for activities associated with hunting. These data support the initial hypothesis.

Stratum 8

In this area local rhyolite use was projected. The occurrence of cores manufactured from a distinctive pink rhyolite found in the stratum substantiated the hypothesis. Equipment for plant processing and identified tools for butchering were few. Only seven utilized cores and seven utilized flakes were collected; no unifaces nor bifaces were found.

Stratum 9/10

Stratum 9/10 was different from expectations. It was thought chert reduction and tool manufacture would be major activities in the canyonlands. Few cores were encountered and debitage was minimal. Instead chert and obsidian unifaces and bifaces, evidence for hunting and tool finishing, were found. Numerous bifaces were collected and many appeared to have been in the initial stages of point production.

Stratum Activities

Four types of activities can be identified in the AEPCO industry: rhyolite, chert, and obsidian tool manufacture; use of small-flake cutting or scraping tools, manufacture of projectile points; and use of cores and large cobble tools. The activities appear to occur in certain separate strata. Rhyolite reduction was documented in Strata 2 and 3; obsidian reduction in Stratum 5 (Arizona CC:3:24), and chert reduction in Stratum 5. The presence of cores and debitage among these strata suggest tool production of local material.

Use of small tools was observed at many sites but the collection from Stratum 9/10 more specifically indicates that scraping and cutting tools may have been the object of flake manufacture. Also in this stratum, Arizona CC:4:6 reveals local manufacture and use of projectile points.

Arizona CC:2:44, in Stratum 3, had both unifacially reduced cobble tools and large flake tools. These robust tools are suggestive of specialized collecting or processing needs in the tobosa grassland section where the sites were located. The artifacts also exhibited post-fabrication oxidation which may indicate a greater antiquity for this site than for the other project loci.

Testing Problems of Regional Culture History. It was hypothesized that if differing traditions of tool manufacture were present then different cultures were represented. As noted previously, the authors are aware that other variables, such as chronological continuity and functionally different tool kits, contribute to observable differences in artifact assemblages. Nevertheless, an attempt was made to determine possible cultural attributes in order that the AEPCO sites might in some way be related to a known cultural group. However, the sample was limited to fewer than 4500 pieces so identifying distinct systems of tool-making was difficult. A lack of hammerstones and flint-knapping abraders complicates the reconstruction of probable techniques. However, two materials predominate, and their methods of manufacture appear distinct.

Chert from stream and terrace cobbles was being selected and reduced to make flake tools which averaged 4.5 cm in length and 3.5 cm in width. These primary flakes were the object of core reduction techniques. Any core face capable of producing a moderate size flake was struck; hence multi-directional cores developed. In contrast, rhyolite reduction produced uni-directional and bi-directional core and cobble artifacts. The cobbles and cores both developed sinuous edges and both were used as tools. Thus rhyolite manufacturing objectives included not only flake tools, but also large core and cobble tool production as well as reuse of cores.

The difference between chert and rhyolite core use and manufacture would not be noteworthy except that they occur at separate sites, cores and tools seldom occur together, and rhyolite cores and cobbles are often in an advanced state of weathering. These separate manufacturing goals and accompanying material selection may be interpreted as separate traditions of tool manufacture. This implication should be tested in future studies.

These techniques of flake and core tool production and their accompanying core types are unlike techniques described by Levine-Lischka (1975) from Salado sites along Miami Wash, Pinal County, Arizona. Similarly, they are different from Hohokam technology as described by Crabtree (1973). It is suspected that silicate tool manufacturing techniques are contemporaneous with what appears to be a local Mogollon tradition. The rhyolite manufacture debris and tool complex at Arizona CC:2:44 may be earlier than Mogollon, and may perhaps be Cochise. Cochise tool production systems have yet to be described so suspicions cannot now be confirmed.

Speculations on culture history have been based upon a sample of 29 sites. This sample reflects activities occurring within and adjacent to the R-O-W. Due to time and cost factors comparisons were only made on an inter-stratum basis and with all strata combined. Although the percentage of area surface collected varied from stratum to stratum our samples appear to be relatively comparable. It may be assumed that the sample was regionally representative.

It is felt that the material reflects a complicated history of cultural interplay in an area which served as a focus of activity for various branches of the Mogollon tradition. The variety of tools and techniques is not great. The tool kit is uniformly simple, unsophisticated, and shows expedient tool use (many more utilized flakes occured than shaped tools). A statistical test for homogeneity within and among strata indicated that internal variation was as great as external, with the exception of Arizona CC:4:6 in Stratum 9/10. Although it is felt that differing traditions of lithic technology are represented by the cultural material, this idea cannot as yet be fully supported by the data.

Conclusions

AEPCO data recovery yielded lithic samples from 29 sites in seven distinct physiographic zones. The collections represented only those activities occurring in or adjacent to the right-of-way and can be considered regionally representative and a predominant pattern for non-habitation sites in the study area.

Twenty-eight sites produced 30 or more specimens and could be statistically analyzed. Frequency of attribute occurrence suggests that two sites are distinct, Arizona CC:4:6 and CC:2:44. The remaining have common activities of core reduction, tool manufacture, and small tool use.

From this limited analysis it was concluded that most of the investigated strata were the sites of temporary hunting or collecting stations, and not permanent or long-term settlements. Extensive use of regional stone resources was documented and from the manufacture debris two primary methods of core reduction are indicated.

It was impossible to substantiate the cultural affiliation of the inventory. Further research and comparison of this material with that of the Gila floodplain villages may confirm a Mogollon origin suggested by the presence of isolated sherds at some of the sites. It is hoped that such research would clarify relationships between habitation sites and lithic scatters by focusing on inter-regional site distribution problems. The AEPCO lithic analysis revealed differences between chert and rhyolite manufacturing techniques and tool types and this is suggestive of the presence of two cultural traditions in the area. Also, these differences in manufacturing techniques occur in different strata.

It is hoped that further research on intra-stratum and intra-site distributions may someday be undertaken with the AEPCO material. Due to time and contract considerations such analyses could not be done at present.

In summary, the inventory consists of the products of unsophisticated manufacture and expedient, disposable tool use. Few formal tools are present and hammerstones and abraders are totally absent. Two manufacturing techniques appear to be present although cultural affiliations are questionable. Ceramics and ground stone and storage facilities are virtually absent, suggesting grinding and storage activities were not important at the sites.

Further study, particularly of the core and core-tool complex, and study of flake selection and use may yield important data on regional technological traditions which are unclear at present. Interpretation of regional land use will remain a problem if sites remain undifferentiated and if tools fail to reveal distinct stylistic modes of manufacture and diagnostic use wear patterns.

REFERENCES

Arizona Highway Department
1965a Atlas of Graham County. Phoenix.

1965b Atlas of Greenlee County. Phoenix.

Arizona State Museum
1976 Arizona State Museum Site Survey Form Instruction Manual. MS. Arizona State Museum, University of Arizona, Tucson.

Avery, Ben
1942 Morenci's copper bolsters America. Phoenix Republic, Feb. 22, 1942.

Bandelier, Adolf A.
1892 Final report of investigations among the Indians of the southwestern United States, carried on mainly in the years from 1880 to 1885, pt. 2. Papers of the Archaeological Institute of America. American Series, Vol. 4.

Barber, Edwin A.
1970 Marks of American potters (reprint of 1904 edition). Cracker Barrel.

Bartholomew, Ed
1970 1000 Bitters Bottles. Bartholomew House, Publishers, Ft. Davis, Texas.

Basso, Keith H.
1971 Western Apache raiding and warfare. University of Arizona Press, Tucson.

Bayham, Frank E.
1976 Appendix II: Lithics in "Desert Resources and Hohokam Subsistence: The CONOCO Florence Project," by William Harper Doelle. Arizona State Museum, Cultural Resource Management Section, Archaeological Series 103.

Bell, William A.
1869 New Tracks in North America Vols. I and II. Chapman and Hall, London.

Benninghoff, W. S.
1962 Calculation of Pollen and Spores Density in Sediments by Addition of Exotic Pollen in Known Quantities. Pollen et Spores 6(2): 332-33. Paris.

Bitting, A. W.
1937 Appertizing or the art of canning: Its history and development. The Trade Pressroom. San Francisco.

Bohrer, Vorsila L.
1972 Paleoecology of the Hay Hollow Site, Arizona. Fieldiana: Anthropology 63(1): 1-30.

Breternitz, David A.
1959 Excavations at Nantack Village, Point of Pines, Arizona. Anthropological Papers of the University of Arizona 1.

1966 An appraisal of tree-ring dated pottery in the Southwest. Anthropological Papers of the University of Arizona 10.

Brown, Jeffrey L.
1973 The origin and nature of Salado: Evidence from the Safford Valley, Arizona. Doctoral dissertation, Department of Anthropology, University of Arizona, Tucson. University Microfilms, Ann Arbor.

1974 Pueblo Viejo Salado Sites and their relationship to Western Pueblo culture. The Artifact 12(2).

Bullard, W. R. Jr.
1962 The Cerro Colorado Site and pithouse architecture in the southwestern United States prior to A.D. 900. Peabody Museum of American Archaeology and Ethnology, Harvard University Papers 44(2).

Burkham, D. E.
1972 Channel changes of the Gila River in Safford Valley, Arizona 1846-1970. USGS Professional Paper 665-G.

Burns and McDonnel Engineering Company
1974 Report on the environmental analysis for Apache Electric Station Units No. 2 and No. 3 and related transmission for Arizona Electric Power Cooperative. Kansas City, Missouri.

Butler, P.
1959 Palynological Studies of Barstable Marsh, Cape Cod, Massachusetts. Ecology 40: 735-37.

Cameron, Cathy
1976 Chipped stone assemblages from the Baca Float Sites, in "Excavations in the Middle Santa Cruz River Valley, Southeastern Arizona," by David E. Doyel. Arizona State Museum, Contributions to Highway Salvage Archaeology in Arizona 44: 139-55.

Canouts, Veletta, Assembler
1975 Archaeological resources of the Orme Reservoir. Arizona State Museum, Cultural Resource Management Section, Archaeological Series 92.

Canouts, Veletta, Edward Germeshausen, and Robert Larkin
1972 Archaeological survey of the Santa Rosa Wash. Arizona State Museum, Cultural Resource Management Section, Archaeological Series 18.

Carlson, Roy L.
1970 White Mountain Redware: A pottery tradition of east-central Arizona and western New Mexico. Anthropological Papers of the University of Arizona 19.

Chapman, Richard
1973 Lithic analysis techniques. Human Systems Research Technical Manual, pp. 305-25.

Cleland, Robert G.
1952 A history of Phelps Dodge: 1834-1950. Alfred A. Knopf, New York.

Cosgrove, H. S. and C. B. Cosgrove
1932 The Swarts Ruin: A typical Mimbres site in southwestern New Mexico. Papers of the Peabody Museum of American Archaeology and Ethnology, Harvard 15(1).

Cowgill, George L.
1975 A selection of samplers: Comments on archaeostatistics. In Sampling in Archaeology, edited by J. W. Mueller, pp. 258-76. University of Arizona Press, Tucson.

Cox, Dellon N.
1973 Soil survey of Hidalgo County New Mexico. USDA Soil Conservation Service.

Crabtree, Donald E.
1972 An introduction to flintworking. Occasional Papers of the Idaho State University Museum 28.

1973 Experiments in replicating Hohokam points. Tebiwa 16(1): 10-45.

Cruess, William V.
1948 Commercial fruit and vegetable products, 3rd edition. McGraw-Hill, New York.

Danson, Edward B.
1957 An archaeological survey of west central New Mexico and east central Arizona. Papers of the Peabody Museum of American Archaeology and Ethnology, 44(1).

Davis, Alex
1967 Package and print: The development of container and label design. Clarkson N. Potter, Inc., New York.

Davis, M. B.
1959 Three Pollen Diagrams from central Massachusetts. American Journal of Science 256: 540-70.

Davis, R. B.
1967 Pollen Studies of near-surface sediments in Maine Lakes. In Quaternary Paleoecology, edited by E. J. Cushing and H. E. Wright Jr., pp. 143-73.

Debowski, Sharon, Anique George, Richard Goddard, and Deborah Mullon.
1976 An archaeological survey of the Buttes Reservoir. Arizona State Museum, Cultural Resource Management Section, Archaeological Series 93(1)

Devner, Kay
1968 Patent medicine picture. The Tombstone Epitaph. Tombstone.

Dick, Herbert
1965 Bat Cave. Monographs of at the School of American Research 27. Santa Fe.

DiPeso, Charles C.
1956 The upper Pima of San Cayetano del Tumacacori. The Amerind Foundation 7.

1974 Casas Grandes, a fallen trading center of the Gran Chichimeca, Vols. 1-3. Northland Press, Flagstaff.

1976 Gila Polychrome in the Casas Grandes region. The Kiva 42(1): 57-63.

Doyel, David E.
1972 An archaeological survey of the San Juan-Vail 345 kV power transmission line, Clifton-Vail section. Arizona State Museum Cultural Resource Management Section, Archaeological Series 15.

Ellis, Florence Hawley
1970 Irrigation and waters in the Rio Grande. MS. Report for water control symposium, 1970 Pecos conference. University of Arizona Arizona State Museum, Tucson.

Elmore, F. W.
1944 Ethnobotany of the Navajo. University of New Mexico Press, Albuquerque.

Emory, Lieut. Col. William H.
1848 Notes of a military reconnaissance from Fort leavenworth in Missouri to San Diego in California. U.S. Congress Senate, Executive Document 41, 30th Congress, 1st Session.

Evenari, Michael, Leslie Shanan, and Naphtali Tadmor
1971 The Negev: Challenge of a desert. Harvard University Press, Cambridge.

Faulk, Odie B.
1973 Destiny road: The Gila trail and the opening of the Southwest. Oxford University Press, New York.

Fewkes, Jesse Walter
1904 Two summers work in Pueblo Ruins. Twenty-second Annual Report of the Bureau of American Ethnology, Part I, pp. 168-96.

Fitting, J. E.
1977 *Mitigation of adverse effects to archaeological resources on the Foote Wash conservation and development project.* Commonwealth Associates Inc., Jackson, Michigan.

Fontana, Bernard and J. Cameron Greenleaf
1962 Johnny Ward's ranch. *Kiva* 28(1-2):1-115.

Gelderman, Frederick W.
1970 *Soil survey of the Safford area, Arizona.* USDA Soil Conservation Service.

Gifford, J. C.
1957 Archaeological explorations in caves of Point of Pines region. MS. Master's thesis, University of Arizona, Department of Anthropology, Tucson.

Gilman, Patricia L. and Peter Sherman
1975 An archaeological survey of the Graham-Curtis Project: Phase II. Arizona State Museum, Cultural Resource Management Section, *Archaeological Series* 65.

Gladwin, Harold S.
1957 *A history of the ancient Southwest*. The Bond Wheelwright Co., Portland.

Gladwin, Harold S., Emil W. Haury, E. B. Sayles, and Nora Gladwin
1937 Excavations at Snaketown, material culture. Medallion Papers 25. (Reprinted 1965, University of Arizona Press, Tucson.)

Gladwin, Winifred and H. S. Gladwin
1930 Some southwestern pottery types. Series II. *Medallion Papers* 70.

1935 The eastern range of the Red-on-buff culture. *Medallion Papers* 16.

Goodyear, Albert C., III
1975a A general research design for highway archaeology in South Carolina. *The Institute of Archaeology and Anthropology notebook* 7(1) .

1975b Hecla II and III: An interpretative study of archaeological remains from the Lakeshore Project, Papago Reservation, south central Arizona. *Arizona State University, Anthropological Research Paper* 9.

Granger, Byrd H.
1960 *Will C.Barnes' Arizona place names,* University of Arizona Press, Tucson.

Hack, John T.
1942 The changing physical environment of the Hopi Indians of Arizona. *Peabody Museum Papers* 35(1).

Hastings, James Rodney
1958-59 Vegetation Change and Arroyo Cutting in Southeastern Arizona during the past century: An historical review. *Arid Lands Colloquia*, University of Arizona.

Haury, Emil W.

1936 Some Southwestern pottery types: Series IV. Medallion Papers 140.

1950 The stratigraphy and archaeology of Ventana Cave. University of Arizona Press, Albuquerque and Tucson.

1958 Evidence at Point of Pines for a prehistoric migration from northern Arizona. In "Migrations in New World Culture History," edited by Raymond H. Thompson, pp. 1-16. University of Arizona Bulletin 29(2), Social Science Bulletin 27.

1976 The Hohokam: Desert farmers and craftsmen. University of Arizona Press, Tucson.

Hayden, Julian D.

1957 Excavations, 1940 at University Indian Ruin, Tucson, Arizona. Southwestern Monuments Association Technical Series, Vol. 5.

1965 Fragile-pattern areas. American Antiquity 31(2): 272-76.

Heindle, L. A. and McCullough R. A.

1961 Geology and the availability of water in the lower Bonita Creek area, Graham County, Arizona. USGS Water-Supply Paper 1589

Herskovitz, Robert M.

1975 Identification and analysis of material from Fort Bowie National Historic Site, Arizona. MS. Arizona State Museum, University of Arizona, Tucson.

Hevly, R. H., P. J. Mehringer, Jr. and H. G. Yocum

1963 Modern pollen rain in the Sonoran Desert. Journal of the Arizona Academy of Science 3(3): 123-35.

Hole, Frank and Robert F. Heizer

1965 An introduction to prehistoric archaeology. Holt, Rinehart, and Winston. New York.

Hough, Walter

1907 Antiquities of the Upper Gila and Salt River valleys in Arizona and New Mexico. Bureau of American Ethnology Bulletin 35.

Hunt, Charles B.

1959 Dating of mining camps with tin cans and bottles. Geotimes 3(8): 8-10, 34.

Hyde, A. H.

1959 Atmospheric pollen in relation to land use. Nature 1(183): 1694-95.

Irwin-Williams, Cynthia

1967 Picosa: The elementary southwestern culture. American Antiquity 32(4): 441-45.

Iverson, J.

1941 Landnam i Denmarks Stendlder. Danm. Geol. Unders. 2(RK 66): 1-68.

Jelinek, Arthur J.
1976 "Form, Function and Style in Lithic Analysis." In cultural change and Continuity: Essays in Honor of James Bennett Griffin, edited by Charles E. Cleland.

Jewitt, Llewellyn
1970 Ceramic art of Great Britain (Reprint of 1883 edition). Wardlock Reprints.

Johnson, Alfred E.
1965 The development of western pueblo culture. Doctoral dissertation, Department of Antrhopology, University of Arizona, Tucson. Univerwity of Microfilms, Ann Arbor.

Johnson, Alfred E. and William Wasley
1966 Archaeological excavation near Bylas, Arizona. Kiva 31(4): 205-53.

Jones, May
1968 The bottle trail. Southwest Offset Inc., Hereford, Texas.

Kearney, T. H. and R. H. Peebles
1951 Arizona flora. University of California Press, Berkeley.

Kinkade, Gay M.
1975 Foote Wash--No Name Wash project. Arizona State Museum, Cultural Resource Management Section, Archaeological Series 67.

1976 Cultural resource management program: BLM Safford District. Arizona State Museum, Cultural Resource Management Section, Archaeological Series 100.

Klecka, William R., Norman H. Nie, and C. Hadlai Hull
1975 SPSS Primer: Statistical package for the social sciences primer. McGraw-Hill Book Company, NY

Knechtel, M. N.
1938 Geology and ground water resources of the valley of Gila River and San Simon Creek, Graham County, Arizona. USGS Water Supply Paper 796: 181-222.

Krebs, Roland
1953 Making friends is our business: 100 years of Anheuser-Busch.

Kroeber, Alfred
1935 Walapai Ethnography. American Anthropological Association Memoir 42.

Lapham, M. H. and Neill, N. P.
1904 Soil survey of the Solomonsville area, Arizona. USDA, Field Oper. Bur. Soils.

LeBlanc, Steven and Ben Nelson
1976 The Salado in southwestern New Mexico. Kiva 42(1): 71-80.

Levine-Lischka, Leslie
1975 Lithic analysis and cultural inferences from the Miami Wash Project. Doctoral dissertation, Department of Anthropology, University of Arizona, Tucson. University Microfilms, Ann Arbor.

Lindgren, W.
1905a The copper deposits of the Clifton-Morenci district, Arizona. USGS Professional Paper 43.

1905b Description of the Clifton quadrangle. USGS Geological Atlas Folio 129.

Lindsay, Alexander J., Jr. and Calven H. Jennings (ed.)

1968 Salado Red Ware conference, ninth southwestern ceramic seminar. Museum of Northern Arizona, Ceramic Series 4.

Lowe, Charles H.
1964 Arizona's natural environment. University of Arizona Press, Tucson.

McGregor, John
1965 Southwestern Archaeology, 2nd edition. University of Illinois Press, Urbana.

Maher, Louis J., Jr.
1964 Ephedra Pollen in Sediments of the Great Lakes Region. Ecology: 45(2): 391-95.

Martin, Paul S.
1963 The last 10,000 years. University of Arizona Press, Tucson.

Martin, Paul S. and Fred Plog
1973 The archaeology of Arizona. Doubleday Natural History Press, New York.

Martin, Paul S. and John B. Rinaldo
1950 Sites of the Reserve phase, Pine Lawn Valley, western New Mexico. Fieldiana: Anthropology 38(1).

Martin, Paul S., John B. Rinaldo, Elain Bluhm, Hugh C. Culter and Roger Grange, Jr.
1952 Mogollon cultural continuity and change. The stratigraphic analysis of Tularosa and Cordova caves. Fieldiana: Anthropology 40.

Masse, Bruce
in preparation Agricultural systems. In "The Peppersauce Wash project: Excavations at three multi-component sites in the San Pedro Valley, Arizona." MS. Arizona State Museum, Universtiy of Arizona, Tucson.

1974 Prehistoric southwestern agricultural and water control features: terminology and description. MS. Arizona State Museum Library, University of Arizona, Tucson.

McClellan, Carole
1976 Archaeological survey of Vail-Bicknell transmission line. Arizona State Museum, Cultural Resource Management Section, Archaeological Series 97.

McGregor, John
1965 *Southwestern Archaeology*, 2nd edition, University of Illinois Press, Urbana

McKearin, George S. and Helen McKearin
1941 *American Glass.* Crown Publishers, New York.

Mehringer, P. J., Jr.
1967 Pollen Analysis of the Tule Springs Area, Nevada. In "Pleistocene studies in southern Nevada," edited by H. M. Wormington and D. Ellis. *Nevada State Museum Anthropological Papers* 13, part 3: 120-200.

Mitchell, G. F.
1956 Post-Boreal Pollen Diagrams from Irish raised bogs. *Proceedings of the Royal Irish Academy of Science* Section B 57: 185-251.

Moolick, R. T. and J. J. Durek
1966 The Morenci district. In *Geology of the porphyry copper deposits southwestern North America*, edited by S. R. Titley and C. L. Hicks, pp. 221-32. University of Arizona Press, Tucson.

Moratto, Michael J.
1975 On the concept of archaeological significance. Paper prepared for the annual meeting of the Society of California Archaeology, Fresno State University.

Morris, Earl H.
1932 Private correspondence to A. E. Douglas. University of Arizona, Tucson .

Munsey, Cecil
1970 *The illustrated guide to collecting bottles.* Hawthorn Books, Inc. New York.

Myrick, David F.
1966 The strange story of the El Paso and Southwestern Trains. *Trains* Feb., pp. 44-49.

1968 *Pioneer Arizona railroads.* Colorado Railroad Museum, Golden, Colorado.

1975 *Railroads of Arizona* Vol 1, *The Southern Roads.* Howell-North Books, Berkeley.

Nichol, A. A.
1952 The natural vegetation of Arizona (revised by W. S. Phillips). *University of Arizona, Agricultural Experiment Station,Technical Bulletin* 127.

Nie, H. Norman, C. Hadlai Hull, Jean G. Jenkins, Karin Steinbrenner, and Dale H. Bent
1975 *Statistical package for the social sciences,* 2nd edition. McGraw Hill Company, New York.

Noyes, Edward
1962 The glass bottle industry of Milwaukee, a sketch. *Historical Messenger* 18(3): 2-7. Milwaukee County Historical Society.

Olmstead, F. H.
1919 Gila River flood control: A report on flood control of the Gila River in Graham County, Arizona. U. S. Congress, Senate Document 436, 65th Congress, 3rd session.

Olson, A. P.
1959 An evaluation of the phase concept in Southwestern Archaeology. MS. Doctoral dissertation, University of Arizona, Tucson.

O'Neill, Ralph E.
1973 A resumé of Clifton's heritage: 1873-1973. Clifton centennial special newspaper publication, October 26, 27, 28.

Pattie, James O.
1930 The personal narrative of James O. Pattie of Kentucky. Lakeside Press, Chicago.

Potter, Loren D. and Joanne Rowley
1960 Pollen rain and vegetation, San Agustin Plains, New Mexico. The Botanical Gazette 122(1): 1-25.

Poulson, E. N. and F. O. Youngs
1938 Soil survey of the upper Gila Valley area, Arizona. USDA Bureau of Chemistry and Soils Series 1933(15).

Quaide, W. L.
1951 Geology of central Peloncillo Mountains Hidalgo County, New Mexico. MS. Master's htesis, University of California, Berkeley.

Quinn, Kathleen and John Roney
1973 The archaeological resources of the San Simon and Vulture units of the Bureau of Land Management. Arizona State Museum, Cultural Resource Management Section, Archaeological Series 34.

Raab, L. Mark
1973 Research design for investigation of archaeological resources in Santa Rosa Wash: Phase I. Arizona State Museum, Cultural Resource Management Section, Archaeological Series 26.

Raynor, G. S., E. C. Ogden and J. V. Hayes
1973 Dispersal of pollens from low-level, crosswind line sources. Agricultural Meterology 9: 177-95.

Redman, Charles
1975 Productive sampling strategies for archaeological sites. In Sampling in Archaeology, edited by J. W. Mueller, pp. 147-54, University of Arizona Press, Tucson.

Redman, Charles L. and Patty Jo Watson
1970 Systematic, intensive surface collection. American Antiquity 35(3) 279-91.

Rinaldo, John B. and Elaine A. Bluhm
1956 Late Mogollon pottery types of the Reserve area. Fieldiana: Anthropology 38: 7.

Robbins, W. W., J. P. Harrington and B. Freire-Marreco
1916 Ethnobotany of the Tewa Indians. Bureau of American Ethnology Bulletin 55.

Robinson, R. F. and A. Cook
1966 The Safford copper deposit, Lone Star Mining district, Graham County, Arizona. In Geology of the porphyry copper deposits, southwestern North America, edited by S. R. Titley and C.L. Hicks, pp. 251-66, University of Arizona Press, Tucson.

Rosenthal, E. Jane
in preparation The Quijotoa Valley project. Western Archeological Center, National Park Service. U.S. Government Printing Office, Washington.

Sackett, James R.
1977 The meaning of style in Archaeology: A general model. American Antiquity 43(3) 369-80.

Saur, Carl and Donald Brand
1930 Pueblo sites in southeastern Arizona. University of California Publications in Geography 3(7) 415-58.

Sayles, E. B.
1936 Some Southwestern pottery types, Series V. Medallion Papers 21.

1945 The San Simon Branch, excavations at Cave Creek and in the San Simon Valley. I: Material culture. Medallion Papers 34

Sayles, E. B. and Ernst Antevs
1941 The Cochise culture. Medallion Papers 29.

Schaafsma, Curtis F.
1977 Archaeological excavations and lithic analysis in the Abiquiu Reservoir district, New Mexico: Phase IV. School of American Research, Santa Fe.

Schwennesen, A. T.
1917 Ground water in San Simon Valley, Arizona and New Mexico. USGS Water-Supply Paper 425.

Scovill, Douglas H., Garland J. Gordon, and Keith M. Anderson
1972 Guidelines for the preparation of statements of environmental impact on archaeological resources. MS. Western Archeological Center, National Park Service, Tucson.

Sellers, William D. and R. H. Hill
1974 Arizona climate 1931-1972. Rev., 2nd edition, University of Arizona Press, Tucson.

Shreve, F. and I. L. Wiggins
1964 Vegetation and flora of the Sonoran Desert Vol. 1. Stanford University Press, Palo Alto.

Solomon, Allen M.
n.d. Pollen evidence of past land-use at Tesuque, Nambe, and Pojoaque Pueblos. MS. University of Arizona Library, Tucson.

Solomon, Allen M. and D. F. Kroener
1971 The effects of urban development on airborn pollen: Pollen deposited in reservoir muds. Bulletin of the New Jersey Academy of Science, 15(1-2): 30-44.

Spaulding, Albert C.
1973 The concept of artifact types in archaeology. Plateau 45: 149-64.

Spicer, Edward H.
1962 Cycles of conquest. University of Arizona Press, Tucson.

Stevenson, Matilda Coxe
1915 Ethnobotany of the Zuni Indians. 30th Annual Report of the Bureau of American Ethnology, 1908-09, pp. 35-102.

Stewart, Guy R.
1940 Conservation in Pueblo agriculture I, Primitive practices. The Scientific Monthly 51(3): 201-20.

Stockton, C. W. and Fritts, H. C.
1968 Conditional probability of occurrence for variations in climate based on widths of annual tree rings in Arizona. Laboratory of tree-ring research annual report. University of Arizona, Tucson.

Stout, Wilbur
1923 History of the clay industry in Ohio. Geological survey of Ohio. 4th series, Bulletin 26, pp. 7-102. n.p., Columbus, Ohio.

Teague, George A.
1975 Foote Wash-No Name Wash F.R.S. Archaeological studies research design. MS. Arizona State Museum, University of Arizona, Tucson.

Teague, Lynn S.
1974 The archaeological resources of the Winkleman and Black Hills unit of the Bureau of Land Management. Arizona State Museum, Cultural Resource Management Section, Archaeological Series 47.

Tibbitts, John C.
1967 A guide for insulator collectors. The Little Glass Shack, Sacramento.

Toulouse, Julian
1971 Bottle makers and their marks. T. Nelson, New York.

Travis, Russel B.
1955 Classification of rocks. Quarterly of the Colorado School of Mines 50(1). Golden, Colorado.

Tringham, Ruth, Glen Cooper, George Odell, Barbara Voytek, and Anne Whitman
1974 Experimentation in the formation of edge damage: A new approach to lithic analysis. Journal of Field Archaeology 1: 171-96.

Tuck, Frank J.
1963 History of mining in Arizona, 2nd edition. Dept. of Mineral Resources, State of Arizona, Phoenix.

Tuohy, Donald R.
1960 Archaeological survey and excavation in the Gila River channel between Earven Dam Site and Buttes Reservoir Site, Arizona. MS. Arizona State Museum, University of Arizona, Tucson.

Tuthill, Carr
1950 Notes on the Dragoon complex. In For the Dean, pp. 51-59. Hohokam Museum Association and Southwestern Monuments Assoc., Tucson and Santa Fe.

U. S. Bureau of the Census
1924 Biennial census of manufacturers, 1921. GPO, Washington.

U. S. Department of the Interior, Bureau of Land Management
1971 Safford District visitor map.

U. S. Soil Conservation Service
1973a General soil map Graham County, Arizona. USDA-SCS Portland.

U. S. Soil Conservation Service
1973b General Soil Map Greenlee County, Arizona. USDA-SCS Portland.

Vivian, R. Gwinn
1974 Conservation and diversion: Water control systems in the Anasazi Southwest. In "Irrigation's impact on society," edited by T. Downing and M. Gibson, pp. 95-112. Anthropological Papers of the University of Arizona 25. University of Arizona, Tucson.

Vivian, R. Gwinn and Raymond H. Thompson
1973 A proposal for an archaeological program to mitigate the effects of the Santa Rosa Wash Project Phase I. MS. Arizona State Museum, University of Arizona, Tucson.

Wagoner, Jay J.
1975 Early Arizona: Prehistory to Civil War. University of Arizona Press, Tucson.

Wasley, William W.
1962 A ceremonial cave on Bonita Creek, Arizona. American Antiquity 27(3) 380-94.

Weaver, Donald E.
1976 Salado influences in the lower Salt River Valley. Kiva 42(1): 17-26.

Wendorf, Fred
1950 A report on the excavation of a small ruin near Point of Pines, east-central Arizona. University of Arizona Bulletin 21(3), Social Science Bulletin 19, Tucson.

Whalen, Norman M.
1971 Cochise culture sites in the San Pedro drainage, Arizona. PhD Dissertation. University of Arizona, Tucson.

1973 Agriculture and the Cochise. Kiva 39(1): 89-96.

1975 Cochise site distribution in the San Pedro Valley. Kiva 40(3): 203-22.

Wheat, Joe Ben
1955 Mogollon culture prior to A.D. 1000. Memoirs of the Society for American Archaeology 10.

Whiting, A. F.
1939 Ethnobotany of the Hopi. Museum of Northern Arizona Bulletin 15.

Wilcox, David R.
1973 The entry of Athabascans to the Southwest: The problem today. MS. Arizona State Museum Library, University of Arizona. Tucson.

Williams, O. A.
1937 Settlement and growth of the Gila Valley as a Mormon colony 1879-1900. Master's thesis, University of Arizona, Tucson.

Wilmsen, Edwin
1970 Lithic analysis and cultural inference: A Paleo-Indian case. University of Arizona Anthropological Papers 16.

Wilson, Bill and Betty
1969 Western bitters. NW Printing Company, Santa Rosa, California.

1971 19th century medicine in glass. 19th Century Hobby and Publishing Co.

Wilson, Eldred D.
1962 A resume of the geology of Arizona. Arizona Bureau of Mines Bulletin 171.

1965 Guidebook 1-Highways of Arizona U.S. Highway 666. Arizona Bureau of Mines Bulletin 174.

Windmiller, Ric
1973 The late Cochise culture in the Sulphur Spring Valley, southeastern Arizona: Archaeology of the Fairchild Site. Kiva 39(2): 131-70

Woodbury, Richard B.
1961 Prehistoric agriculture at Point of Pines, Arizona. Society for American Archaeology Memoir 17.

Wothke, C. A. and W. H. Yarbough
1953 Economic study of Graham County. Arizona State College, Tempe.

APPENDIX I

LITHIC ANALYSIS METHODOLOGY AND SITE MATERIAL CULTURE

by

Jeanette L. Dickerson

Introduction

Along the Greenlee-Dos Condado transmission line, 29 sites produced a chipped stone inventory of 4185 artifacts. The quantity of material recovered and the project's time limitations necessitated computerized statistical data analysis. Prerequisites for such analysis included consistent methods of data recovery and a minimal sample size (Rosenthal in preparation).

The research goals for the lithic analysis were first, the identification of activities occurring at project sites and their relation to aboriginal land use, and second, possible clarification of regional chronologic problems. Objectives were to obtain information on artifact categories, uses, and methods of manufacture.

Because previous archaological data recovery in the project area was very minimal, it was decided that the lithic study should be oriented descriptively rather than typologically. A computerized statistical program designed along these lines would be most efficient; however, little published information was available concerning computerized lithic analysis programs. Schaafsma's (1977) lithic code developed for the Abiquiu Reservoir materials was chosen as a model for the AEPCO Project analysis.

Lithic analysis was carried out by Dickerson. Rosenthal assisted in the formulation of the core classification and identification of microflaking. Analysis and interpretation of the statistical output was carried out by Rosenthal and Dickerson.

The Code

The lithic code was designed to systematically observe attributes related to material, procurement, manufacture, and use. Stage of manufacture, direction of flaking, and presence or absence of cortex were all recorded to determine what manufacturing activities occurred at a site. Platform preparation was recorded to indicate the method of reduction occurring in tool manufacture. Location of utilization and determination of microflaking and dimensions helped in defining possible technological traditions. Alterations to artifacts by design or through use provided data for tool utilization experiments.

The purpose of defining the variables was to make consistent observations and to remove as much subjectivity as possible from the study. However, some variables remained impressionistic because values were non-quantitatively ranked.

Procedures

Following Spaulding (1973), observations nad measurements of discrete and continuous attributes and variables were made. Attributes were considered discrete properties observable on particular artifacts; for example, a discrete variable would be a flake. A continuous attribute would be the measure of a flake's length. Sets of mutually exclusive attributes were then organized into dimensions. Thus, dimensions were seen as a formally defined aspect of a groups of objects, such as "materials," which included specific types such as rhyolite and chert. Following Schaafsma (1977), the dimensions chosen for observation were: material, stage of manufacture, cortex, fragmentation, metrics, utilized portion, and marginal retouch.

Because lithic analysis accompanied fieldwork, analysis record forms were developed prior to data recovery. This created problems during analysis because Schaafsma's model code was oriented toward careful description of flake attributes. As analysis proceeded, it became evident that this system had limited applicability for some of the AEPCO site collections which were dominated by cores. The original code was augmented to provide new observations on flaking and platform preparation. These observations formed the basis of the core classification which was later established but was not part of the original code. Further additions were made to facilitate the recording of atrributes for the microflaking analysis.

The morphologic, stylistic, and metric attributes observed on the lithics were recorded on IBM Fortran coding sheets. These attributes became numerical variables with ordinal scale values. Each attribute was termed a "field" (a series of numerical blocks ranging from one to four columns (Figure 123). After recording lithic dimensions, the information was transferred to computer cards and statistically processed.

Figure 122. Analysis Code

Field	Content	Code	Definition	Column
1	Analysis Type	1	Lithics	1-2
		2	Ceramics	
		3	Ground Stone	
2	Site Number	1-999	taken from artifact bag	3-5
3	Grid Number	1-9999	taken from artifact bag	6-9
4	Provenience	1-9999	taken from artifact bag	10-13
5	Artifact Number	1-99	given only to tools	14-15
6	Material type	1	Rhyolite	16-17
		2	Gray Rhyolite	
		3	Pink Rhyolite	

Figure 122 (continued)

Field	Content	Code	Definition	Column
6	Material type	3	Pink Rhyolite	
		4	Chert	
		5	White Chert	
		6	Variegated Chert	
		7	Gray Chert	
		8	Chalcedony	
		9	Jasper	
		10	Red Jasper	
		11	Yellow Jasper	
		12	Obsidian	
		13	Quartz	
		14	Quartzite	
		15	Andesite	
		16	Basalt	
		17	Granite	
		18	Sandstone	
		19	Flint	
		20	Shale	
		21	Gneiss	
		22	Hematite	
		23	Unknown	
7	Stage of Manufacture	1	Primary Core	18-19
		2	Secondary Core	
		3	Exhausted Core	
		4	Primary Flake	
		5	Secondary Flake	
		6	Tertiary Flake	
		7	Shatter	
		8	Uniface	
		9	Biface	
		10	Projectile Point	
8	Platform	1	None	20
		2	Prepared	
		3	Unprepared	
9	Surface Flaking	1	Unidirectional	21
		2	Bidirectional	
		3	Multidirectional	
10	Fragmentation	1	Complete	22
		2	Incomplete	
11	Cortex	1	None	23
		2	Greater than 50%	
		3	Less than 50%	
12	Length	1-999	measured to nearest mm.	24-26
13	Width	1-999	measured to nearest mm.	27-29
14	Thickness	1-999	measured to nearest mm.	30-32
15	Primary Edge Angle	1-999	measured to nearest mm.	33-35
16	Secondary Edge Angle	1-999	measured to nearest mm.	36-38
17	Primary Edge Length	1-999	measured to nearest mm.	39-41
18	Secondary Edge Length	1-999	measured to nearest mm.	42-44

Figure 122 continued

Field	Content	Code	Definition	Column
19	Primary Utilized Portion	1	None	45-46
		2	Proximal end	
		3	Distal end	
		4	Lateral edge left	
		5	Lateral edge right	
		6	Perimeter	
		7	Notch	
20	Secondary Utilized Portion	1	None	47-48
		2	Proximal end	
		3	Distal end	
		4	Lateral edge left	
		5	Lateral edge right	
		6	Perimeter	
		7	Notch	
1	Marginal Retouch Primary Edge	1	None	49
		2	Unifacial	
		3	Bifacial	
22	Marginal Retouch Secondary Edge	1	None	50
		2	Unifacial	
		3	Bifacial	
23	Microflaking Shape	1	Trapezoid	51
		2	Round	
		3	Elongated	
		4	Trapezoid, Round	
		5	Round, Trapezoid	
		6	Round, Trapezoid	
		7	Round, Elongated	
		8	Elongated, Round	
		9	Round, Elongated	
		10	Trapezoid, Elongated, Round	
		11	Elongated, Round, Trapezoid	
		12	Round, Elongated, Trapezoid	
		13	Trapezoid, Elongated	
	Location	1	Exterior	52
		2	Interior	
		3	Both	
	Faces	1	Unifacial	53
		2	Bifacial	
	Intensity	1	Light	54
		2	Medium	
		3	Heavy	

Analysis of frequency of occurrence, co-occurrence, and condescriptive statistical tests were performed using the programs based on the Statistical Package for the Social Sciences (SPSS) (Nie and others 1970). The sub-programs FREQUENCIES, CROSSTABS, CONDESCRIPTIVE, and DISCRIMINANT were employed for these purposes, results were studied and inferences drawn.

Terminology

Two operational definitions are important in understanding the code and lithic analysis in general. Artifacts were classed as debitage if they represented residual lithic material from reduction sequences (Crabtree 1972: 58). Non-utilized cores, flakes, and shatter were considered debitage. Cores were later removed from the category and analyzed in terms of morphological classes. Any artifact showing evidence of use or retouch was considered a tool. The tool category further included bifaces, unifaces, and projectile points even if utilization and retouch were not evident.

Operational Definitions for the Code

Material

Rock types were classified using the conventions of Travis (1955). Identification was assisted by Paul Dunlevy (Safford BLM regional geologist) and Robert O'Haire (Arizona Bureau of Mines). Schaafsma's (1977) original material dimension included rock type, color, transparency and, identification of inclusions. The AEPCO analysis combined color with material, and later eliminated variations of transparency because a single specimen often had clear and opaque areas. Further code reductions occurred when it was recognized that some rock types were not present in the project area.

Stage of Manufacture

Schaafsma's (1977) dimension for stage of manufacture included morphological categories rather than sequential steps in tool manufacture. His attribute descriptions were expanded by incorporating ideas presented by Crabtree (1972), Chapman (1973), Cameron (1976), and Rosenthal (in preparation). Ten attributes were defined:

1. Primary core. A piece of parent material, often nodular in form, which has been reduced and shows multiple flake scars.

2. Secondary core. A large flake with numerous flakes removed and therefore displaying multiple negative scars.

3. Exhausted core. A stone piece with multiple negative flake scars less than 3 cm in length and having multiple unrecoverable platforms.

4. Primary flake. A complete stone piece detached from a core which displays various "hertzian" features (Crabtree 1972). These include a bulb of percussion, platform, lip, fissures, striations, and radii. Primary flakes contain more than 50 percent cortex. "Complete" signifies that lateral and distal edge as well as ventral and dorsal surfaces are identifiable.

5. Secondary flake. A complete stone piece detached from a core which displays "hertzian" features and has less than 50 percent cortex.

6. Tertiary flake. A complete stone piece detached from a core which displays "hertzian" features and retains no cortex.

7. Shatter. Irregular pieces of material displaying some "hertzian" features and retaining no coretex.

8. Uniface. A flake tool that displays pressure or direct percussion retouch on one surface but does not necessarily display utilization, resharpening, or edge modification (marginal retouch).

9. Biface. A flake tool that displays pressure or direct percussion retouch on both surfaces but does not necessarily display utilization or resharpening or edge modification (marginal retouch).

10. Projectile Point. A flake tool that displays bifacial retouch on both surfaces, as well as marginal retouch, usually triangular in plan view. A discrete type that is self-explanatory. A projectile point was classified as a tool.

11. Platform. On cores this is the table or surface receiving the force necessary to detach a flake or blade (Crabtree 1972: 84). Three attributes were included in this dimension: absent, prepared, and unprepared. Platform preparation was identified by multiple small flake scars on the platform. On prepared cores, platforms were singly or multiply scarred, with uni-directional negative scars running perpendicular to the platform. Other forms of platform preparation, such as abrasion, were absent on the AEPCO material.

Surface Flaking

Surface flaking is a core attribute that refers to the planar direction of flake removal, as oriented from the striking platform. Surface flaking attributes are uni-directional, bi-directional, and multi-directional.

Fragmentation

This dimension refers to whether a specimen is complete or broken.

Cortex

The cortex is defined as a natural surface or rind on an artifact. The percentage of coretex on the face and platform was evaluated.

Length, Width, Thickness

Measurements of greatest length, width, and thickness were made perpendicular to or parallel to the striking platform on tools. It was hoped these measurements would indicate possible selectivity of debitage for specific tools.

Edge Angle

The inclination of utilized edges was measured with a goniometer to the nearest degree. Edge angles were measured on the actual utilized bit rather than the "spine-plane angle" (Wilmsen 1970). It was hoped that this measurement, in conjunction with observations on microflaking, would indicate specific tasks undertaken at project sites.

Edge Length

The length of the utilized edges were measured in mm with a sliding caliper.

Utilized Portion

Utilized pieces exhibiting wear patterns were recorded according to their location in relation to the striking platform following Chapman (1973: 312-13). These locations were recorded for both primary and, where applicable, secondary utilized edges. The edge exhibiting the greatest utilization was called the primary utilized portion.

Microflaking

Microscar shape was observed under 30 power microscope following Tringham and others (1974). Microscar shapes were defined as trapezoid, round, and elongated. On the code sheet various combinations of the above shapes are present. The dominant scar shape in the combination is underlined.

Location

The location of the microflaking was identified as being on either the ventral (interior) or dorsal (exterior) surface or both.

Faces

The identification of microflaking was identified as being either unifacial or bifacial.

Intensity

Intensity ranked the extent of damage. Light microflaking was classed as the presence of a single visible scar; medium microflaking as an almost continuous series of scars; and heavy microflaking as the presence of overlapping scars.

The Core Typology

Initial perusal of the statistical output led to the establishment of a core classification. Based on the co-occurrence of direction of flaking and platform preparation, six core classes were set up. Cores were divided into classes rather than types. This was done because establishing types pre-supposed some cultural regularity. Because of the paucity of research in the area, it is uncertain whether the different classes reflect a continuum in core reduction or whether the specific classes reflect specific cultural types. Each core class then is a recognizable group of artifacts in a collection that share a specified set of attributes. The core classes are:

1. Uni-directional Prepared
2. Uni-directional Unprepared
3. Bi-directional Prepared
4. Bi-directional Unprepared
5. Multi-directional Prepared
6. Multi-directional Unprepared

The tables that follow summarize A) frequencies of raw material types and stage of manufacture, and B) use-wear location on utilized artifacts. Table 40, at the end of this appendix, compares the mean metric attributes and edge angles of tools from specific AEPCO sites, organized by strata.

The AEPCO Chipped Stone Industry

Stratum 2: San Simon River Valley

Arizona CC:2:33. This site produced 71 chipped stone artifacts. Rhyolite, silicates, and basalt were respectively the most common materials for artifact manufacture. Flakes, followed by cores, were the common artifact types (Table 14A). The formal tool types consisted of four bifaces. Only 5.6 percent of all artifacts were utilized including one uni-directional prepared core, one multi-directional prepared core, and two primary cortical flakes (Table 14B).

Use analysis indicated light microflaking in the form of round and trapezoidal unifacial scars on tool interiors.

Ground stone consisted of two pieces of a possible basalt pestle. The total dimensions are 106 mm in length, 56 mm in width. One end is absent. No grinding striations or battering were evident but the surface was polished. It is possible that grinding marks were present on the missing end.

Arizona CC:2:34. This site provided 45 chipped stone artifacts for analysis, of which basalt was the commonest material represented. Cores and flakes respectively were the most common artifact types (Table 15A). No formal tools were present in the sample. Of 45 artifacts, only two (4.4 percent),

TABLE 14A. Arizona CC:2:33

STAGE \ MATERIAL TYPE	RHYOLITE	SILICATES	QUARTZ	QUARTZITE	OBSIDIAN	BASALT	ANDESITE	OTHER	TOTALS	PERCENTAGE OF ASSEMBLAGE
Uni-directional Prepared Core	7/38.9	5/27.8				4/22.2		2/11.1	18	25.4
Uni-directional Unprep'd Core	2/50					2/50			4	5.6
Bi-directional Prepared Core	1/20	2/40		1/20		1/20			5	7.0
Bi-directional Unprep'd Core										
Multi-directional Prepared Core						1/100			1	1.4
Multi-directional Unprep'd Core										
Primary Cortical Flake	7/46.7	5/33.3				2/13.3		1/6.7	15	21.1
Secondary Cortical Flake	4/18.3	4/18.2		3/13.6		7/31.8		4/18.2	22	31.0
Tertiary Flakes	1/50	1/50							2	2.8
Shatter										
Uniface										
Biface	4/100								4	5.6
Projectile Point										
TOTALS	26	17		4		17		7	71	
PERCENTAGE OF ASSEMBLAGE	36.6	23.9		5.6		23.9		9.8		99.9

NOTE: Number to left of slash indicates quantity; number to right of slash indicates percentage of the quantity for that particular stage.

TABLE 14B. Arizona CC:2:33

STAGE \ WEAR LOCATION	PROXIMAL END	DISTAL END	LATERAL EDGE RIGHT	LATERAL EDGE LEFT	PERIMETER	NOTCH	OTHER	TOTALS	PERCENTAGE OF TOTAL ASSEMBLAGE
Uni-directional Prepared Core							1/100	1	1.4
Uni-directional Unprep'd Core									
Bi-directional Prepared Core									
Bi-directional Unprep'd Core									
Multi-directional Prepared Core							1/100	1	1.4
Primary Cortical Flake		1/50	1/50					2	2.8
Secondary Cortical Flake									
Tertiary Flake									
Shatter									
Uniface									
Biface									
Projectile Point									
TOTAL		1	1				2	4	5.6

NOTE: Number to left of slash indicates quantity; number to right of slash indicates percentage of the quantity for that particular stage.

TABLE 15A. Arizona CC:2:34

STAGE \ MATERIAL TYPE	RHYOLITE	SILICATES	QUARTZ	QUARTZITE	OBSIDIAN	BASALT	ANDESITE	OTHER	TOTALS	PERCENTAGE OF ASSEMBLAGE
Uni-directional Prepared Core	1/9.1					8/72.7		2/18.2	11	24.4
Uni-directional Unprep'd Core				1/20		4/80			5	11.1
Bi-directional Prepared Core				1/25		3/75			4	8.9
Bi-directional Unprep'd Core	1/50					1/50			2	4.4
Multi-directional Prepared Core						1/100			1	2.2
Multi-directional Unprep'd Core										
Primary Cortical Flake	1/14.3					4/57.1		2/28.6	7	15.6
Secondary Cortical Flake						3/60		2/40	5	11.1
Tertiary Flakes	1/14.2					3/42.9		3/42.9	7	15.6
Shatter					2/66.7			1/33.3	3	6.7
Uniface										
Biface										
Projectile Point										
TOTALS	4			2	2	27		10	45	
PERCENTAGE OF ASSEMBLAGE	9.0			4.4	4.4	60.0		22.2		100

NOTE: Number to left of slash indicates quantity; number to right of slash indicates percentage of the quantity for that particular stage.

TABLE 15B. Arizona CC:2:34

STAGE \ WEAR LOCATION	PROXIMAL END	DISTAL END	LATERAL EDGE RIGHT	LATERAL EDGE LEFT	PERIMETER	NOTCH	OTHER	TOTALS	PERCENTAGE OF TOTAL ASSEMBLAGE
Uni-directional Prepared Core							1/100	1	2.2
Uni-directional Unprep'd Core									
Bi-directional Prepared Core									
Bi-directional Unprep'd Core									
Multi-directional Prepared Core							1/100	1	2.2
Primary Cortical Flake									
Secondary Cortical Flake									
Tertiary Flake									
Shatter									
Uniface									
Biface									
Projectile Point									
TOTAL							2	2	4.4

NOTE: Number to left of slash indicates quantity; number to right of slash indicates percentage of the quantity for that particular stage.

a uni-directional prepared core and a multi-directional prepared core, displayed utilization (Table 15B).

Ground stone from Arizona CC:2:34 consisted of a rectangular sandstone grinding slab and a fragment of an andesite grinding slab. The former was 20 mm long, slightly concave in profile and showed little evidence of modification. A rotary grinding motion was suggested by the wear pattern. The andesite fragment was also slightly concave with clear striations and a light polish on the grinding facet.

Arizona CC:2:40. This site yielded 207 chipped stone artifacts. Basalt was the most representative lithic material and flakes, followed by cores, were the most common artifact types. The high frequency of uni-directional prepared cores is significant, perhaps indicating that the production of these cores and their possible reduction were central in the activities of thss site (Table 16A).

Unifaces, bifaces, and a tabular knife represented formal tool types. The four unifaces exhibited utilization as did the single tabular knife. Only 5.3 percent of the entire assemblage is utilized including two cores and four flakes (Table 16B). Use analysis indicated light microflaking in the form of round and trapezoidal unifacial scars on tool interiors.

Stratum 3: Gila River Pleistocene Terraces and Lower Bajada of the Gila Mountains

Arizona CC:2:43. This site had an assemblage of 214 chipped stone artifacts. Basalt, and to a lesser degree rhyolite, were the most common materials to be exploited. Flakes were the most common artifact type (Table 17A).

Three unifaces were the only formal tools present, and all were utilized. Four and one-tenth percent of the assemblage displayed utilization; however, cores comprised a little over one-half of all utilized material (Table 17B). Use analysis indicated light microflaking in the form of round and trapezoidal unifacial scars on tool interiors and exteriors.

Arizona CC:2:44. The sample from Arizona CC:2:44 consisted of 223 chipped stone artifacts with rhyolite, followed closely by basalt, the most frequent artifact materials. Flakes and then cores were the most common artifact types. The high percentage of uni-directional prepared cores suggests that preparation of these cores and their reduction to obtain flake blanks was central to activities carried out at this site (Table 18A).

Unifaces were the only formal tool type and all exhibited utilization. Two unifaces were also marginally retouched. Of the entire assemblage, 5.8 percent was utilized (Table 18 B). Evidence of retouch was also found on one flake. Use analysis revealed light to medium microflaking in the form of round and elongated unifacial scars on tool exteriors.

TABLE 16A. Arizona CC:2:40

STAGE \ MATERIAL TYPE	RHYOLITE	SILICATES	QUARTZ	QUARTZITE	OBSIDIAN	BASALT	ANDESITE	OTHER	TOTALS	PERCENTAGE OF ASSEMBLAGE
Uni-directional Prepared Core	14/32.5	2/4.7		1/2.3		26/60.5			43	20.8
Uni-directional Unprep'd Core	4/50.0			1/12.5		3/37.5			8	3.9
Bi-directional Prepared Core	3/23.1	1/7.7		8/61.5		1/7.7			13	6.3
Bi-directional Unprep'd Core										
Multi-directional Prepared Core		1/16.7				5/83.3			6	2.9
Multi-directional Unprep'd Core										
Primary Cortical Flake	5/15.2	5/15.2			5/15.2	16/48.4		2/6.0	33	15.9
Secondary Cortical Flake	4/9.0	9/20.5		6/13.6		16/36.4		9/20.5	44	21.2
Tertiary Flakes	11/24.0	14/30.4		2/4.3		17/37.0		2/4.3	46	22.2
Shatter	1/12.5	2/25.0		1/12.5		4/50.0			8	3.9
Uniface		4/100							4	1.9
Biface		1/50.0			1/50.0				2	1.0
Projectile Point										
TOTALS	42	39		19	6	88		13	207	
PERCENTAGE OF ASSEMBLAGE	20.3	18.8		9.2	2.9	42.5		6.3		100

NOTE: Number to left of slash indicates quantity; number to right of slash indicates percentage of the quantity for that particular stage.

TABLE 16B. Arizona CC:2:40

STAGE \ WEAR LOCATION	PROXIMAL END	DISTAL END	LATERAL EDGE RIGHT	LATERAL EDGE LEFT	PERIMETER	NOTCH	OTHER	TOTALS	PERCENTAGE OF TOTAL ASSEMBLAGE
Uni-directional Prepared Core							1/100	1	0.4
Uni-directional Unprep'd Core									
Bi-directional Prepared Core									
Bi-directional Unprep'd Core									
Multi-directional Prepared Core							1/100	1	0.9
Primary Cortical Flake					1/100			1	0.4
Secondary Cortical Flake				2/100				2	0.9
Tertiary Flake			1/100					1	0.4
Shatter									
Uniface			1/25	2/50	1/25			4	1.9
Biface			1/100 (knife)					1	0.4
Projectile Point									
TOTAL			3	4	2		2	11	5.3

NOTE: Number to left of slash indicates quantity; number to right of slash indicates percentage of the quantity for that particular stage.

TABLE 17A. Arizona CC:2:43

MATERIAL TYPE / STAGE	RHYOLITE	SILICATES	QUARTZ	QUARTZITE	OBSIDIAN	BASALT	ANDESITE	OTHER	TOTALS	PERCENTAGE OF ASSEMBLAGE
Uni-directional Prepared Core	1/12.5	3/37.5		2/25		2/25			8	3.7
Uni-directional Unprep'd Core	4/40			1/10		5/50			10	4.7
Bi-directional Prepared Core	3/50					3/50			6	2.8
Bi-directional Unprep'd Core										
Multi-directional Prepared Core	2/40	3/60							5	2.3
Multi-directional Unprep'd Core										
Primary Cortical Flake	9/47.4	2/10.5				8/42.1			19	8.9
Secondary Cortical Flake	20/37.7	14/26.4		2/3.8		11/20.8		6/11.3	53	24.8
Tertiary Flakes	19/24.7	20/26		3/3.9	1/1.3	34/44.1			77	36.0
Shatter	4/12.1	11/33.3		2/6.1		9/27.3		7/21.2	33	15.4
Uniface		2/66.7			1/33.3				3	1.4
Biface										
Projectile Point										
TOTALS	62	55		10	2	72		13	214	
PERCENTAGE OF ASSEMBLAGE	29	25.7		4.7	0.9	33.7		6.0		

NOTE: Number to left of slash indicates quantity; number to right of slash indicates percentage of the quantity for that particular stage.

TABLE 17B. Arizona CC:2:43

STAGE \ WEAR LOCATION	PROXIMAL END	DISTAL END	LATERAL EDGE RIGHT	LATERAL EDGE LEFT	PERIMETER	NOTCH	OTHER	TOTALS	PERCENTAGE OF TOTAL ASSEMBLAGE
Uni-directional Prepared Core							3/100	3	1.4
Uni-directional Unprep'd Core							2/100	2	0.9
Bi-directional Prepared Core									
Bi-directional Unprep'd Core									
Multi-directional Prepared Core									
Primary Cortical Flake									
Secondary Cortical Flake			1/100					1	0.4
Tertiary Flake									
Shatter									
Uniface		1/33.3	1/33.3	1/33.3				3	1.4
Biface									
Projectile Point									
TOTAL		1	2	1			5	9	4.1

NOTE: Number to left of slash indicates quantity; number to right of slash indicates percentage of the quantity for that particular stage.

TABLE 18A. Arizona CC:2:44

STAGE \ MATERIAL TYPE	RHYOLITE	SILICATES	QUARTZ	QUARTZITE	OBSIDIAN	BASALT	ANDESITE	OTHER	TOTALS	PERCENTAGE OF ASSEMBLAGE
Uni-directional Prepared Core	22/47.8	2/4.3		1/2.2		21/45.7			46	20.6
Uni-directional Unprep'd Core	4/25	3/18.7		1/6.3		8/50			16	7.2
Bi-directional Prepared Core	4/28.6	1/7.1		2/14.3		7/50			14	6.3
Bi-directional Unprep'd Core						2/100			2	0.9
Multi-directional Prepared Core										
Multi-directional Unprep'd Core										
Primary Cortical Flake	8/38.1	4/19				9/42.9			21	9.4
Secondary Cortical Flake	36/48	11/14.7		6/8		22/29.3			75	33.6
Tertiary Flakes	10/29.4	17/50			1/3	6/17.6			34	15.2
Shatter	4/33.3	3/25				3/25	2/16.7		12	5.4
Uniface		2/66.7			1/33.3				3	1.4
Biface										
Projectile Point										
TOTALS	88	43		10	2	78	2		223	
PERCENTAGE OF ASSEMBLAGE	39.4	19.3		4.5	0.9	35	0.9			100

NOTE: Number to left of slash indicates quantity; number to right of slash indicates percentage of the quantity for that particular stage.

TABLE 18B. Arizona CC:2:44

STAGE \ WEAR LOCATION	PROXIMAL END	DISTAL END	LATERAL EDGE RIGHT	LATERAL EDGE LEFT	PERIMETER	NOTCH	OTHER	TOTALS	PERCENTAGE OF TOTAL ASSEMBLAGE
Uni-directional Prepared Core							4/100	4	1.8
Uni-directional Unprep'd Core							2/100	2	0.9
Bi-directional Prepared Core									
Bi-directional Unprep'd Core									
Multi-directional Prepared Core									
Primary Cortical Flake									
Secondary Cortical Flake		2/66.7	1/33.3					3	1.3
Tertiary Flake				1/100				1	0.5
Shatter									
Uniface		1/33.3	1/33.3	1/33.3				3	1.3
Biface									
Projectile Point									
TOTAL		3	2	2			6	13	5.8

NOTE: Number to left of slash indicates quantity; number to right of slash indicates percentage of the quantity for that particular stage.

Arizona CC:2:46. This site yielded a collection of 256 chipped stone artifacts. Silicates, followed by basalt were the most common materials; flakes were the most common artifact type. As at Arizona CC:2:44, uni-directional prepared cores are the dominant core type (Table 19A).

The only formal tool type was represented by 12 unifaces of which nine exhibited marginal retouch. Nine and four-tenths percent of the assemblage was utilized and flakes were the most common artifact displaying edge wear (Table 19B). Use analysis indicated heavy microflaking in the form of round unifacial scars on tool interiors.

Stratum 4. Upper Bajada of the Gila Mountains

Arizona CC:2:58. This site provided 25 chipped stone artifacts for analysis. Rhyolite was the most common material exploited and flakes the most common artifact type (Table 20).

No formal tools were presented nor were any of the artifacts utilized. Out of 279 artifact, only 8.2 percent showed utilization including 5 cores, and 10 flakes (Table 21B). Use analysis indicated light to medium microflaking in the form of round unifacial scars along tool exteriors.

Stratum 5. Peloncillo Mountain Foothills

Arizona CC:2:51. This site was represented by 279 chipped stone artifacts, among which basalt was the commonest artifact material. Flakes and cores respectively were the dominant artifact types and of the cores, uni-directionally prepared cores predominated (Table 21A).

Unifaces represented the only formal tools, all of which were utilized. Out of 279 artifacts, only 8.2 percent showed utilization including 5 cores, and 10 flakes (Table 21B). Use analysis indicated light medium microflaking in the form of round unifacial scars along tool exteriors.

Arizona CC:2:54. This site provided 140 chipped stone artifacts for analysis. Silicates, followed by basalt, were the most common materials, while flakes were the most common artifact type (Table 22A).

The only formal tools were seven unifaces of which four were utilized. Only 6 percent of the 140 artifacts exhibited utilization, and 50 percent of the utilized pieces were cores (Table 22B). Use analysis indicated light microflaking in the form of round and trapezoidal unifacial scars on tool interiors.

Arizona CC:2:56. Two hundred-seventy-six chipped stone artifacts represent the sample from this site. Silicates were the most common materials with flakes the most common artifact type (Table 23A).

TABLE 19A. Arizona CC:2:46

STAGE \ MATERIAL TYPE	RHYOLITE	SILICATES	QUARTZ	QUARTZITE	OBSIDIAN	BASALT	ANDESITE	OTHER	TOTALS	PERCENTAGE OF ASSEMBLAGE
Uni-directional Prepared Core	8/42.1	3/15.8				8/42.1			19	7.4
Uni-directional Unprep'd Core						3/100			3	1.2
Bi-directional Prepared Core				2/40.0		3/60.0			5	2.0
Bi-directional Unprep'd Core										
Multi-directional Prepared Core	1/33.3	2/66.7							3	1.2
Multi-directional Unprep'd Core										
Primary Cortical Flake	3/8.1	16/43.3		2/5.4		14/37.8		2/5.4	37	14.4
Secondary Cortical Flake	4/5.1	35/45.5		1/1.3		31/40.3		6/7.8	77	30.0
Tertiary Flakes	10/15.4	26/40.0		7/10.8		17/26.2		5/7.6	65	25.4
Shatter	2/5.7	21/60.0		1/2.9		10/28.5		1/2.9	35	13.7
Uniface	3/25	9/75.0							12	4.7
Biface										
Projectile Point										
TOTALS	31	112		13		86		14	256	
PERCENTAGE OF ASSEMBLAGE	12.1	43.8		5.0		33.6		5.5		100

NOTE: Number to left of slash indicates quantity; number to right of slash indicates percentage of the quantity for that particular stage.

TABLE 19B. Arizona CC:2:46

STAGE \ WEAR LOCATION	PROXIMAL END	DISTAL END	LATERAL EDGE RIGHT	LATERAL EDGE LEFT	PERIMETER	NOTCH	OTHER	TOTALS	PERCENTAGE OF TOTAL ASSEMBLAGE
Uni-directional Prepared Core							1/100	1	0.4
Uni-directional Unprep'd Core									
Bi-directional Prepared Core									
Bi-directional Unprep'd Core									
Multi-directional Prepared Core							1/100	1	0.4
Primary Cortical Flake			1/50	1/50				2	0.8
Secondary Cortical Flake		1/14.2	3/42.9	3/42.9				7	2.7
Tertiary Flake			2/50	2/50				4	1.6
Shatter									
Uniface	1/11.1	3/33.3		4/44.4	1/11.1			9	3.5
Biface									
Projectile Point									
TOTAL	1	4	6	10	1		2	24	9.4

NOTE: Number to left of slash indicates quantity; number to right of slash indicates percentage of the quantity for that particular stage.

TABLE 20. Arizona CC:2:58

STAGE \ MATERIAL TYPE	RHYOLITE	SILICATES	QUARTZ	QUARTZITE	OBSIDIAN	BASALT	ANDESITE	OTHER	TOTALS	PERCENTAGE OF ASSEMBLAGE
Uni-directional Prepared Core										
Uni-directional Unprep'd Core	1/50					1/50			2	8
Bi-directional Prepared Core										
Bi-directional Unprep'd Core										
Multi-directional Prepared Core										
Multi-directional Unprep'd Core										
Primary Cortical Flake	3/75	1/25							4	16
Secondary Cortical Flake	8/61.5	3/23.1				2/15.4			13	52
Tertiary Flakes	2/33.3					4/66.7			6	24
Shatter										
Uniface										
Biface										
Projectile Point										
TOTALS	14	4				7			25	
PERCENTAGE OF ASSEMBLAGE	56	16				28				100

NOTE: Number to left of slash indicates quantity; number to right of slash indicates percentage of the quantity for that particular stage.

TABLE 21A. Arizona CC:2:51

STAGE \ MATERIAL TYPE	RHYOLITE	SILICATES	QUARTZ	QUARTZITE	OBSIDIAN	BASALT	ANDESITE	OTHER	TOTALS	PERCENTAGE OF ASSEMBLAGE
Uni-directional Prepared Core	21/46.7	4/8.9		1/2.2		19/42.2			45	16.1
Uni-directional Unprep'd Core	1/14.3					6/85.7			7	2.5
Bi-directional Prepared Core	8/44.4	1/5.6		1/5.6		8/44.4			18	6.5
Bi-directional Unprep'd Core								1/100	1	0.4
Multi-directional Prepared Core										
Multi-directional Unprep'd Core										
Primary Cortical Flake	6/19.4	7/22.6		1/3.2	1/3.2	13/41.9		3/9.7	31	11.1
Secondary Cortical Flake	15/22	16/23.5		2/3		30/44.1		5/7.4	68	24.4
Tertiary Flakes	14/19.2	30/41.1				27/37		2/2.7	73	26.2
Shatter	8/28.6	5/17.8		1/3.6		11/39.3		3/10.7	28	10
Uniface	1/12.5	7/87.5							8	2.8
Biface										
Projectile Point										
TOTALS	74	70		6	1	114		14	279	
PERCENTAGE OF ASSEMBLAGE	26.5	25.0		2.2	0.4	40.9		5.0		100

NOTE: Number to left of slash indicates quantity; number to right of slash indicates percentage of the quantity for that particular stage.

TABLE 21B. Arizona CC:2:51

STAGE \ WEAR LOCATION	PROXIMAL END	DISTAL END	LATERAL EDGE RIGHT	LATERAL EDGE LEFT	PERIMETER	NOTCH	OTHER	TOTALS	PERCENTAGE OF TOTAL ASSEMBLAGE
Uni-directional Prepared Core							3/100	3	13.0
Uni-directional Unprep'd Core							2/100	2	8.7
Bi-directional Prepared Core									
Bi-directional Unprep'd Core									
Multi-directional Prepared Core									
Primary Cortical Flake	3/75				1/25			4	17.4
Secondary Cortical Flake				2/66.7	1/33.3			3	13.0
Tertiary Flake	2/66.7				1/33.3			3	13.0
Shatter									
Uniface	1/12.5			3/37.5	4/50			8	34.8
Biface									
Projectile Point									
TOTAL	6			5	7		5	23	99.9

NOTE: Number to left of slash indicates quantity; number to right of slash indicates percentage of the quantity for that particular stage.

TABLE 22A. Arizona CC:2:54

STAGE \ MATERIAL TYPE	RHYOLITE	SILICATES	QUARTZ	QUARTZITE	OBSIDIAN	BASALT	ANDESITE	OTHER	TOTALS	PERCENTAGE OF ASSEMBLAGE
Uni-directional Prepared Core	7/58.3	2/16.7				3/25			12	8.6
Uni-directional Unprep'd Core						2/100			2	1.4
Bi-directional Prepared Core	1/20	2/40				2/40			5	3.6
Bi-directional Unprep'd Core										
Multi-directional Prepared Core	1/20	3/60				1/20			5	3.6
Multi-directional Unprep'd Core										
Primary Cortical Flake	4/20	7/35				9/45			20	14.3
Secondary Cortical Flake	8/18.2	14/31.8				22/50			44	31.4
Tertiary Flakes	8/29.6	16/59.3				3/11.1			27	19.3
Shatter	2/11.1	6/33.3				7/38.9	3/16.7		18	12.8
Uniface		7/100							7	5.0
Biface										
Projectile Point										
TOTALS	31	57				49	3		140	
PERCENTAGE OF ASSEMBLAGE	22	41				35	2			100

NOTE: Number to left of slash indicates quantity; number to right of slash indicates percentage of the quantity for that particular stage.

TABLE 22B. Arizona CC:2:54

STAGE \ WEAR LOCATION	PROXIMAL END	DISTAL END	LATERAL EDGE RIGHT	LATERAL EDGE LEFT	PERIMETER	NOTCH	OTHER	TOTALS	PERCENTAGE OF TOTAL ASSEMBLAGE
Uni-directional Prepared Core							3/100	3	37.5
Uni-directional Unprep'd Core									
Bi-directional Prepared Core									
Bi-directional Unprep'd Core									
Multi-directional Prepared Core							1/100	1	12.5
Primary Cortical Flake									
Secondary Cortical Flake									
Tertiary Flake									
Shatter									
Uniface			2/50	1/25	1/25			4	50.0
Biface									
Projectile Point									
TOTAL			2	1	1		4	8	100

NOTE: Number to left of slash indicates quantity; number to right of slash indicates percentage of the quantity for that particular stage.

TABLE 23A. Arizona CC:2:56

STAGE \ MATERIAL TYPE	RHYOLITE	SILICATES	QUARTZ	QUARTZITE	OBSIDIAN	BASALT	ANDESITE	OTHER	TOTALS	PERCENTAGE OF ASSEMBLAGE
Uni-directional Prepared Core	9/69	1/8				3/23			13	4.7
Uni-directional Unprep'd Core		5/83.3				1/16.7			6	2.1
Bi-directional Prepared Core	3/43	1/14				3/43			7	2.5
Bi-directional Unprep'd Core										
Multi-directional Prepared Core	1/11.1	8/88.9							9	3.3
Multi-directional Unprep'd Core										
Primary Cortical Flake	8/20.5	24/61.5		1/2.6		6/15.4			39	14.1
Secondary Cortical Flake	21/23	47/51.6		4/4.4		19/21			91	33.0
Tertiary Flakes	20/31.3	26/40.6		3/4.7	2/3.1	11/17.2		2/3.1	64	23.2
Shatter	7/18.4	11/29.0		4/10.5		4/10.5		12/31.6	38	13.8
Uniface		9/100							9	3.3
Biface										
Projectile Point										
TOTALS	69	132		12	2	47		14	276	
PERCENTAGE OF ASSEMBLAGE	25	48		4.3	.7	17		5		100

NOTE: Number to left of slash indicates quantity; number to right of slash indicates percentage of the quantity for that particular stage.

TABLE 23B. Arizona CC:2:56

STAGE \ WEAR LOCATION	PROXIMAL END	DISTAL END	LATERAL EDGE RIGHT	LATERAL EDGE LEFT	PERIMETER	NOTCH	OTHER	TOTALS	PERCENTAGE OF TOTAL ASSEMBLAGE
Uni-directional Prepared Core							2/100	2	15.4
Uni-directional Unprep'd Core									
Bi-directional Prepared Core									
Bi-directional Unprep'd Core									
Multi-directional Prepared Core							1/100	1	7.7
Primary Cortical Flake									
Secondary Cortical Flake		1/25	2/50	1/25				4	30.7
Tertiary Flake									
Shatter									
Uniface			1/16.1	4/66.6	1/16.7			6	46.2
Biface									
Projectile Point									
TOTAL		1	3	5	1		3	13	

NOTE: Number to left of slash indicates quantity; number to right of slash indicates percentage of the quantity for that particular stage.

Unifaces were the only formal tools of which 67 percent were utilized. Only 4.7 percent of the 276 artifacts showed utilization and 76.9 percent of the tools were utilized flakes with left lateral edge wear predominating (Table 23B).

Use analysis showed light and heavy microflaking in the form of round unifacial scars on exteriors of tools.

Arizona CC:3:26. This site yielded 149 chipped stone artifacts for analysis. Silicates were the most common materials represented, with flakes and cores respectively the most common artifact types (Table 24A).

Only 2.8 percent of the 149 artifacts were utilized; these were two bi-directional prepared cores, and two unifaces (Table 24B). Use analysis revealed no evidence of microflaking.

Arizona CC:3:28. This site provided 188 chipped stone artifacts. Silicates were the most commonly exploited materials with flakes the most common artifact type (Table 25A).

Unifaces, and one rhyolite flake knife were the only formal tools persent and all showed utilization. Of 188 artifacts, 13.8 percent were utilized, with 69.2 percent of these being unifaces and 30.8 percent cores. Class 3 cores were most commonly utilized (Table 25B). Use analysis revealed light microflaking in the form of round bifacial scars on exteriors and interiors of tools.

Arizona CC:3:44. The site yielded 42 chipped stone artifacts of which silicates were predominant, followed closely by rhyolite. Flakes and cores respectively were the most common artifact types (Table 26A).

Unifaces were the formal tool type and all were utilized. Of the total assemblage, 14.3 percent exhibited utilization including one core and two flakes (Table 26B). Use analysis indicated light microflaking in the form of round bifacial scars on tool interiors and exteriors.

Arizona CC:3:24 (Locus 72). This locus had an assemblage of 263 chipped stone artifacts. Silicates were the primary artifact material and flakes the most common artifact type (Table 27A).

Unifaces represented the formal tool type and all showed some utilization. Of the entire assemblage, only 5.3 percent was utilized (Table 27B). Use analysis revealed light microflaking in the form of round and elongated unifacial scars in tool exteriors.

Arizona CC:3:24 (Locus 72S). This locus was represented by 264 chipped stone artifacts. Silicate materials predominated and flakes were the most common artifact type (Table 28A).

TABLE 24A. Arizona CC:3:26

STAGE \ MATERIAL TYPE	RHYOLITE	SILICATES	QUARTZ	QUARTZITE	OBSIDIAN	BASALT	ANDESITE	OTHER	TOTALS	PERCENTAGE OF ASSEMBLAGE
Uni-directional Prepared Core	1/7.1	10/71.4				3/21.4			14	9.5
Uni-directional Unprep'd Core		3/100							3	2.0
Bi-directional Prepared Core		4/66.7				2/33.3			6	4.1
Bi-directional Unprep'd Core	3/27.3	8/72.7							11	7.4
Multi-directional Prepared Core										
Multi-directional Unprep'd Core										
Primary Cortical Flake	2/9.5	16/76.2		1/4.8		2/9.5			21	14.2
Secondary Cortical Flake	1/3.6	17/60.7		1/3.6		3/10.7		6/21.4	28	19.0
Tertiary Flakes		38/88.4				1/2.3		4/9.3	43	29.0
Shatter	1/5.3	17/89.4						1/5.3	19	12.8
Uniface		3/100							3	2.0
Biface										
Projectile Point										
TOTALS	8	116		2		11		11	148	
PERCENTAGE OF ASSEMBLAGE	5.4	78.4		1.4		7.4		7.4		100

NOTE: Number to left of slash indicates quantity; number to right of slash indicates percentage of the quantity for that particular stage.

TABLE 24B. Arizona CC:3:26

STAGE \ WEAR LOCATION	PROXIMAL END	DISTAL END	LATERAL EDGE RIGHT	LATERAL EDGE LEFT	PERIMETER	NOTCH	OTHER	TOTALS	PERCENTAGE OF TOTAL ASSEMBLAGE
Uni-directional Prepared Core									
Uni-directional Unprep'd Core									
Bi-directional Prepared Core							2/100	2	1.4
Bi-directional Unprep'd Core									
Multi-directional Prepared Core									
Primary Cortical Flake									
Secondary Cortical Flake									
Tertiary Flake									
Shatter									
Uniface	1/50	1/50						2	1.4
Biface									
Projectile Point									
TOTAL	1	1					2	4	2.8

NOTE: Number to left of slash indicates quantity; number to right of slash indicates percentage of the quantity for that particular stage.

TABLE 25A. Arizona CC:3:28

STAGE \ MATERIAL TYPE	RHYOLITE	SILICATES	QUARTZ	QUARTZITE	OBSIDIAN	BASALT	ANDESITE	OTHER	TOTALS	PERCENTAGE OF ASSEMBLAGE
Uni-directional Prepared Core	5/27.8	2/11.1				7/38.9		4/22.2	18	9.6
Uni-directional Unprep'd Core	1/16.7					5/83.3			6	3.2
Bi-directional Prepared Core	2/20	2/20				5/50		1/10	10	5.3
Bi-directional Unprep'd Core										
Multi-directional Prepared Core		2/66.7				1/33.3			3	1.6
Multi-directional Unprep'd Core										
Primary Cortical Flake	4/21.1	8/42.1			1/5.2	6/31.6			19	10.1
Secondary Cortical Flake	6/10.5	30/52.6			1/1.8	13/22.8		7/12.3	57	30.3
Tertiary Flakes	8/22.9	18/51.4				9/25.7			35	18.6
Shatter	3/13.6	16/72.7			1/4.6	2/9.1			22	11.7
Uniface	6/33.3	11/61.1	1/5.6						18	9.5
Biface										
Projectile Point										
TOTALS	35	89	1		3	48		12	188	
PERCENTAGE OF ASSEMBLAGE	18.6	47.3	0.5		1.6	25.5		6.4		99.9

NOTE: Number to left of slash indicates quantity; number to right of slash indicates percentage of the quantity for that particular stage.

TABLE 25B. Arizona CC:3:28

STAGE \ WEAR LOCATION	PROXIMAL END	DISTAL END	LATERAL EDGE RIGHT	LATERAL EDGE LEFT	PERIMETER	NOTCH	OTHER	TOTALS	PERCENTAGE OF TOTAL ASSEMBLAGE
Uni-directional Prepared Core							1/100	1	0.5
Uni-directional Unprep'd Core							1/100	1	0.5
Bi-directional Prepared Core							5/100	5	2.7
Bi-directional Unprep'd Core									
Multi-directional Prepared Core							1/100	1	0.5
Primary Cortical Flake									
Secondary Cortical Flake									
Tertiary Flake									
Shatter									
Uniface		1/5.6	7/38.9	4/22.2	5/27.7			17	9.6
Biface							1/100 (knife)	1	0.5
Projectile Point									
TOTAL		1	7	4	5		9	26	13.3

NOTE: Number to left of slash indicates quantity; number to right of slash indicates percentage of the quantity for that particular stage.

TABLE 26A Arizona CC:3:44

STAGE \ MATERIAL TYPE	RHYOLITE	SILICATES	QUARTZ	QUARTZITE	OBSIDIAN	BASALT	ANDESITE	OTHER	TOTALS	PERCENTAGE OF ASSEMBLAGE
Uni-directional Prepared Core	2/66.7	1/33.3							3	7.1
Uni-directional Unprep'd Core	2/25	2/25				4/50			8	19.1
Bi-directional Prepared Core										
Bi-directional Unprep'd Core										
Multi-directional Prepared Core		1/100							1	2.4
Multi-directional Unprep'd Core										
Primary Cortical Flake	2/50	2/50							4	9.5
Secondary Cortical Flake	8/61.5	5/38.5							13	31.0
Tertiary Flakes	3/33.3	5/55.6				1/11.1			9	21.4
Shatter										
Uniface		4/100							4	9.5
Biface										
Projectile Point										
TOTALS	17	20				5			42	
PERCENTAGE OF ASSEMBLAGE	40.5	47.6				11.9				100

NOTE: Number to left of slash indicates quantity; number to right of slash indicates percentage of the quantity for that particular stage.

TABLE 26B.Arizona CC:3:44

STAGE \ WEAR LOCATION	PROXIMAL END	DISTAL END	LATERAL EDGE RIGHT	LATERAL EDGE LEFT	PERIMETER	NOTCH	OTHER	TOTALS	PERCENTAGE OF TOTAL ASSEMBLAGE
Uni-directional Prepared Core							1/100	1	2.4
Uni-directional Unprep'd Core									
Bi-directional Prepared Core									
Bi-directional Unprep'd Core									
Multi-directional Prepared Core									
Primary Cortical Flake					1/100			1	2.4
Secondary Cortical Flake			1/100					1	2.4
Tertiary Flake									
Shatter									
Uniface			2/50	2/50				4	9.5
Biface									
Projectile Point									
TOTAL			3	2	1		1	7	14.3

NOTE: Number to left of slash indicates quantity; number to right of slash indicates percentage of the quantity for that particular stage.

TABLE 27A. Arizona CC:3:24, Locus 72

STAGE \ MATERIAL TYPE	RHYOLITE	SILICATES	QUARTZ	QUARTZITE	OBSIDIAN	BASALT	ANDESITE	OTHER	TOTALS	PERCENTAGE OF ASSEMBLAGE
Uni-directional Prepared Core	9/37.5	3/12.5				12/50.0			24	9.1
Uni-directional Unprep'd Core				2/100					2	0.8
Bi-directional Prepared Core	3/37.5	4/50.0				1/12.5			8	3.0
Bi-directional Unprep'd Core										
Multi-directional Prepared Core	2/20.0	3/30.0				5/50.0			10	3.8
Multi-directional Unprep'd Core										
Primary Cortical Flake	6/17.1	8/22.9			19/54.3	2/5.7			35	13.3
Secondary Cortical Flake	35/44.9	18/23.1			3/3.8	22/28.2			78	29.7
Tertiary Flakes	4/6.6	37/60.7		2/3.3	6/9.8	12/19.6			61	23.2
Shatter	2/5.1	6/15.4		1/2.6	15/38.5	11/28.2		4/10.2	39	14.8
Uniface		5/83.3		1/16.7					6	2.3
Biface										
Projectile Point										
TOTALS	61	84		6	43	65		4	263	
PERCENTAGE OF ASSEMBLAGE	23.2	32.0		2.3	16.3	24.7		1.5		100

NOTE: Number to left of slash indicates quantity; number to right of slash indicates percentage of the quantity for that particular stage.

TABLE 27B. Arizona CC:3:24, Locus 72

STAGE \ WEAR LOCATION	PROXIMAL END	DISTAL END	LATERAL EDGE RIGHT	LATERAL EDGE LEFT	PERIMETER	NOTCH	OTHER	TOTALS	PERCENTAGE OF TOTAL ASSEMBLAGE
Uni-directional Prepared Core							2/100	2	0.8
Uni-directional Unprep'd Core									
Bi-directional Prepared Core									
Bi-directional Unprep'd Core									
Multi-directional Prepared Core							3/100	3	1.1
Primary Cortical Flake									
Secondary Cortical Flake		2/66.7	1/33.3					3	1.1
Tertiary Flake									
Shatter									
Uniface		4/66.6	1/16.7	1/16.7				6	2.3
Biface									
Projectile Point									
TOTAL		6	2	1			5	14	5.3

NOTE: Number to left of slash indicates quantity; number to right of slash indicates percentage of the quantity for that particular stage.

TABLE 28A. Arizona CC:3:24, Locus 72S

STAGE \ MATERIAL TYPE	RHYOLITE	SILICATES	QUARTZ	QUARTZITE	OBSIDIAN	BASALT	ANDESITE	OTHER	TOTALS	PERCENTAGE OF ASSEMBLAGE
Uni-directional Prepared Core	2/16.7	2/16.7		1/8.3		7/58.3			12	4.6
Uni-directional Unprep'd Core	2/66.7	1/33.3							3	1.1
Bi-directional Prepared Core	2/40	1/20				2/40			5	1.9
Bi-directional Unprep'd Core										
Multi-directional Prepared Core	1/25	3/75							4	1.5
Multi-directional Unprep'd Core										
Primary Cortical Flake	5/11.6	12/27.9			12/27.9	7/16.3		7/16.3	43	16.3
Secondary Cortical Flake	26/33.3	28/35.9			3/3.8	21/27.0			78	29.5
Tertiary Flakes	10/11.1	52/57.8			1/1.1	24/26.7		3/3.3	90	34.1
Shatter	8/36.4	2/9.0				6/27.3		6/27.3	22	8.3
Uniface	1/16.7	5/83.3							6	2.3
Biface		1/100							1	0.4
Projectile Point										
TOTALS	57	107		1	16	67		16	264	
PERCENTAGE OF ASSEMBLAGE	21.6	40.5		0.4	6.1	25.3		6.1		100

NOTE: Number to left of slash indicates quantity; number to right of slash indicates percentage of the quantity for that particular stage.

TABLE 28B. Arizona CC:3:24, Locus 72S

STAGE \ WEAR LOCATION	PROXIMAL END	DISTAL END	LATERAL EDGE RIGHT	LATERAL EDGE LEFT	PERIMETER	NOTCH	OTHER	TOTALS	PERCENTAGE OF TOTAL ASSEMBLAGE
Uni-directional Prepared Core									
Uni-directional Unprep'd Core									
Bi-directional Prepared Core							1/100	1	0.4
Bi-directional Unprep'd Core									
Multi-directional Prepared Core							1/100	1	0.4
Primary Cortical Flake									
Secondary Cortical Flake	1/100							1	0.4
Tertiary Flake									
Shatter									
Uniface	1/16.6	3/50	1/16.6	1/16.6				6	2.3
Biface									
Projectile Point									
TOTAL	2	3	1	1			2	9	3.5

NOTE: Number to left of slash indicates quantity; number to right of slash indicates percentage of the quantity for that particular stage.

Six unifaces and one biface, represented the formal tool types and all unifaces were utilized. Three and one-half percent of the assemblage exhibited some utilization; this included two cores and one flake (Table 28B). Use analysis indicated light microflaking in the form of round unifacial scars on the exterior of tools.

Arizona CC:3:24 (Locus 72X). This locus yielded 259 chipped stone artifacts. Silicates were the most commonly exploited material (39 percent), but obsidian, rare in other sites in this stratum, comprised 17.4 percent of available material. Flakes were the most common artifact type (Table 29A).

Only 2.7 percent of the assemblage displayed utilization; of these four unifaces, one secondary flake, and two tertiary flakes were utilized (Table 29B). Use analysis revealed light microflaking in the form of round unifacial scars on tool interiors.

Arizona CC:3:22. This site produced 44 chipped stone artifacts. Basalt was the most common material exploited and flakes the most common artifact type (Table 30A).

A simple utilized uniface represented the only formal tool at the site. Only 4.6 percent of the 44 artifacts was utilized including one uni-directional unprepared core (Table 30B). Use analysis indicated no evidence of microflaking.

Stratum 7. Gila River Terraces

Arizona CC:3:4. This site had a sample of 90 chipped stone artifacts. Silicates were the primary materials exploited at this site, and flakes were the most common artifact type. Table 31A summarizes the stage of manufacture and material type of the assemblage.

Unifaces, followed by bifaces, were the most common formal tool types present at Arizona CC:3:4. Of these, two of the seven unifaces and one of the two bifaces were utilized. Only 18.8 percent of the entire assemblage was utilized. Table 31B summarizes the stage of manufacture and location of edge wear on the utilized material.

Use analysis revealed light microflaking was present in the form of round bifacial scars on tool interiors and exteriors.

Arizona CC:3:17. The site produced 112 chipped stone artifacts. Silicates were the most exploited material with flakes the most common artifact type (Table 32A).

Six unifaces and one biface represented formal tools. Of these five (83 percent) of the unifaces and the single biface were utilized. The biface also showed evidence of marginal retouch. Of the 112 artifacts, 16.1 percent were utilized. Besides the formal tools, some flakes were also utilized (Table 32B). Use analysis showed evidence of light microflaking in the form of round unifacial scars on exteriors of tools.

TABLE 29A. Arizona CC:3:24, Locus 72X

STAGE \ MATERIAL TYPE	RHYOLITE	SILICATES	QUARTZ	QUARTZITE	OBSIDIAN	BASALT	ANDESITE	OTHER	TOTALS	PERCENTAGE OF ASSEMBLAGE
Uni-directional Prepared Core	4/40	3/30		1/10		1/10		1/10	10	3.9
Uni-directional Unprep'd Core		1/100							1	0.4
Bi-directional Prepared Core										
Bi-directional Unprep'd Core		2/66.7				1/33.3			3	1.1
Multi-directional Prepared Core				1/100					1	0.4
Multi-directional Unprep'd Core										
Primary Cortical Flake	4/33.3	1/8.3		1/8.3	4/33.3	2/16.8			12	4.6
Secondary Cortical Flake	11/23.9	14/30.4		3/6.5	4/8.6	14/30.4			46	17.8
Tertiary Flakes	19/11.8	70/43.4		11/6.8	26/16	35/21.7			161	62.2
Shatter	1/5	9/45			7/35	3/15			20	7.7
Uniface		1/25			3/75				4	1.5
Biface					1/100				1	0.4
Projectile Point										
TOTALS	39	101		17	45	56		1	259	
PERCENTAGE OF ASSEMBLAGE	15.0	39.0		6.6	17.4	21.6		0.4		100

NOTE: Number to left of slash indicates quantity; number to right of slash indicates percentage of the quantity for that particular stage.

TABLE 29B. Arizona CC:3:24, Locus 72X

STAGE \ WEAR LOCATION	PROXIMAL END	DISTAL END	LATERAL EDGE RIGHT	LATERAL EDGE LEFT	PERIMETER	NOTCH	OTHER	TOTALS	PERCENTAGE OF TOTAL ASSEMBLAGE
Uni-directional Prepared Core									
Uni-directional Unprep'd Core									
Bi-directional Prepared Core									
Bi-directional Unprep'd Core									
Multi-directional Prepared Core									
Primary Cortical Flake									
Secondary Cortical Flake			1/100					1	0.4
Tertiary Flake			2/100					2	0.8
Shatter									
Uniface		1/25	1/25	1/25	1/25			4	1.5
Biface									
Projectile Point									
TOTAL		1	4	1	1			7	2.7

NOTE: Number to left of slash indicates quantity; number to right of slash indicates percentage of the quantity for that particular stage.

TABLE 30A. Arizona CC:3:22

STAGE \ MATERIAL TYPE	RHYOLITE	SILICATES	QUARTZ	QUARTZITE	OBSIDIAN	BASALT	ANDESITE	OTHER	TOTALS	PERCENTAGE OF ASSEMBLAGE
Uni-directional Prepared Core	1/20	2/40				2/40			5	11.4
Uni-directional Unprep'd Core		1/100							1	2.3
Bi-directional Prepared Core	1/100								1	2.3
Bi-directional Unprep'd Core										
Multi-directional Prepared Core										
Multi-directional Unprep'd Core										
Primary Cortical Flake				4/33.3	1/8.3	6/50		1/8.3	12	27.2
Secondary Cortical Flake				1/9.1	1/9.1	8/72.7		1/9.1	11	25.0
Tertiary Flakes		1/12.5		1/12.5		3/37.5		3/37.5	8	18.1
Shatter		1/20		1/20	1/20			2/40	5	11.4
Uniface				1/100					1	2.3
Biface										
Projectile Point										
TOTALS	2	5		8	3	19		7	44	
PERCENTAGE OF ASSEMBLAGE	4.5	11.4		18.1	6.8	43.2		16.0		100

NOTE: Number to left of slash indicates quantity; number to right of slash indicates percentage of the quantity for that particular stage.

TABLE 30B. Arizona CC:3:22

STAGE \ WEAR LOCATION	PROXIMAL END	DISTAL END	LATERAL EDGE RIGHT	LATERAL EDGE LEFT	PERIMETER	NOTCH	OTHER	TOTALS	PERCENTAGE OF TOTAL ASSEMBLAGE
Uni-directional Prepared Core									
Uni-directional Unprep'd Core							1/100	1	2.3
Bi-directional Prepared Core									
Bi-directional Unprep'd Core									
Multi-directional Prepared Core									
Primary Cortical Flake									
Secondary Cortical Flake									
Tertiary Flake									
Shatter									
Uniface					1/100			1	2.3
Biface									
Projectile Point									
TOTAL					1		1	2	4.6

NOTE: Number to left of slash indicates quantity; number to right of slash indicates percentage of the quantity for that particular stage.

TABLE 31A Arizona CC:3:4

STAGE \ MATERIAL TYPE	RHYOLITE	SILICATES	QUARTZ	QUARTZITE	OBSIDIAN	BASALT	ANDESITE	OTHER	TOTALS	PERCENTAGE OF ASSEMBLAGE
Uni-directional Prepared Core	2/40	3/60							5	5.6
Uni-directional Unprep'd Core		1/100							1	1.1
Bi-directional Prepared Core										
Bi-directional Unprep'd Core										
Multi-directional Prepared Core		1/100							1	1.1
Multi-directional Unprep'd Core										
Primary Cortical Flake		7/100							7	7.8
Secondary Cortical Flake		44/100							44	48.9
Tertiary Flakes		19/100							19	21.1
Shatter		4/100							4	4.4
Uniface		7/100							7	7.8
Biface	2/100								2	2.2
Projectile Point										
TOTALS	4	86							90	
PERCENTAGE OF ASSEMBLAGE	4.4	95.6								100

NOTE: Number to left of slash indicates quantity; number to right of slash indicates percentage of the quantity for that particular stage.

TABLE 31B. Arizona CC:3:4

STAGE \ WEAR LOCATION	PROXIMAL END	DISTAL END	LATERAL EDGE RIGHT	LATERAL EDGE LEFT	PERIMETER	NOTCH	OTHER	TOTALS	PERCENTAGE OF TOTAL ASSEMBLAGE
Uni-directional Prepared Core							1/100	1	1.1
Uni-directional Unprep'd Core									
Bi-directional Prepared Core									
Bi-directional Unprep'd Core									
Multi-directional Prepared Core									
Primary Cortical Flake			1/100					1	1.1
Secondary Cortical Flake			1/33.3	5/55.6	1/11.1			9	10.0
Tertiary Flake			1/100					1	1.1
Shatter									
Uniface			2/50.0	2/50.0				4	4.4
Biface					1/100			1	1.1
Projectile Point									
TOTAL			7	7	2		1	17	18.8

NOTE: Number to left of slash indicates quantity; number to right of slash indicates percentage of the quantity for that particular stage.

TABLE 32A. Arizona CC:3:17

MATERIAL TYPE / STAGE	RHYOLITE	SILICATES	QUARTZ	QUARTZITE	OBSIDIAN	BASALT	ANDESITE	OTHER	TOTALS	PERCENTAGE OF ASSEMBLAGE
Uni-directional Prepared Core		2/66.7						1/33.3	3	2.7
Uni-directional Unprep'd Core		1/100							1	0.9
Bi-directional Prepared Core		2/100							2	1.8
Bi-directional Unprep'd Core										
Multi-directional Prepared Core										
Multi-directional Unprep'd Core										
Primary Cortical Flake		12/100							12	10.7
Secondary Cortical Flake		39/88.6		4/9.1		1/2.3			44	39.2
Tertiary Flakes	5/13.9	26/72.2			1/2.8	1/2.8		3/8.3	36	32.1
Shatter		7/100							7	6.3
Uniface		6/100							6	5.4
Biface					1/100				1	0.9
Projectile Point										
TOTALS	5	95		4	2	2		4	112	
PERCENTAGE OF ASSEMBLAGE	4.4	84.8		3.6	1.8	1.8		3.6		100

NOTE: Number to left of slash indicates quantity; number to right of slash indicates percentage of the quantity for that particular stage.

TABLE 32B. Arizona CC:3:17

STAGE \ WEAR LOCATION	PROXIMAL END	DISTAL END	LATERAL EDGE RIGHT	LATERAL EDGE LEFT	PERIMETER	NOTCH	OTHER	TOTALS	PERCENTAGE OF TOTAL ASSEMBLAGE
Uni-directional Prepared Core									
Uni-directional Unprep'd Core									
Bi-directional Prepared Core									
Bi-directional Unprep'd Core									
Multi-directional Prepared Core									
Primary Cortical Flake				1/50	1/50			2	1.8
Secondary Cortical Flake		1/11.1	4/44.5	3/33.3	1/11.1			9	8.0
Tertiary Flake			1/100					1	0.9
Shatter									
Uniface			1/20	2/40	2/40			5	4.5
Biface		1/100						1	0.9
Projectile Point									
TOTAL		2	6	6	4			18	16.1

NOTE: Number to left of slash indicates quantity; number to right of slash indicates percentage of the quantity for that particular stage.

Arizona CC:3:18. This site yielded 76 chipped stone artifacts. Silicates were the primary material to be exploited with flakes the most common artifact type (Table 33A).

A single biface and a single uniface represented the formal tool types. Only 7.8 percent of the assemblage was utilized (Table 33B). Use analysis revealed light to medium microflaking in the form of round and elongated scars on tool exteriors.

Arizona CC:3:19. This site had an assemblage of 145 chipped stone artifacts. Silicates were the most common material exploited at this site; flakes the most common artifact type. Table 34A summarizes the material type and stage of manufacture of the assemblage.

Unifaces were the only formal tool type present. Four of the seven unifaces were utilized, and one was found to have marginal retouch. Only 13.1 percent of the entire assemblage was utilized. Table 34B summarizes the stage of manufacture and location of edge wear on the utilized pieces.

A use analysis of the tools revealed that light microflaking was present primarily in the form of round and trapezoid bifacial scars.

Arizona CC:3:20. This site produced 275 chipped stone artifacts. Silicates, followed closely by basalt, were the most common materials exploited with flakes the most common artifact type (Table 35A).

A biface was the only formal tool. Only 3.0 percent of the assemblage was utilized including two cores, one secondary and five tertiary flakes. Two of the flakes utilized on the left lateral edge also showed retouch (Table 35B). Use analysis revealed medium to heavy microflaking in the form of round unifacial scars on tool interiors.

Stratum 8. San Francisco River Terraces

Arizona W:15:15. This site yielded 130 chipped stone artifacts. Rhyolite was the most common material exploited and flakes, followed by cores, were the most common artifact type (Table 36A).

Three unifaces represented formal tools at the site, of which two displayed edge wear. Only 6.9 percent of the assemblage was utilized, and the most common artifact utilized was cores (Table 36B). Use analysis revealed no evidence of microflaking on tools.

Arizona CC:W:15:17. This site produced 79 chipped stone artifacts. Silicates, followed closely by rhyolite were the common material types and flakes the most common artifact type (Table 37A).

Two unifaces and a biface represented the formal tool types; both unifaces were utilized. Only 6.4 percent of the 79 artifacts were utilized; including besides the unifaces, one multi-directional prepared core, one

TABLE 33A Arizona CC:3:18

STAGE \ MATERIAL TYPE	RHYOLITE	SILICATES	QUARTZ	QUARTZITE	OBSIDIAN	BASALT	ANDESITE	OTHER	TOTALS	PERCENTAGE OF ASSEMBLAGE
Uni-directional Prepared Core	3/75					1/25			4	5.3
Uni-directional Unprep'd Core	1/100								1	1.3
Bi-directional Prepared Core										
Bi-directional Unprep'd Core										
Multi-directional Prepared Core	1/50	1/50							2	2.6
Multi-directional Unprep'd Core										
Primary Cortical Flake	2/16.7	9/75		1/8.3					12	15.8
Secondary Cortical Flake	1/3.4	27/93.2		1/3.4					29	38.2
Tertiary Flakes	1/4.5	17/77.3		1/4.5	1/4.5	1/4.5		1/4.5	22	28.9
Shatter	2/50	2/50							4	5.3
Uniface		1/100							1	1.3
Biface		1/100							1	1.3
Projectile Point										
TOTALS	11	58		3	1	2		1	76	
PERCENTAGE OF ASSEMBLAGE	14.5	76.3		4	1.3	2.6		1.3		100

NOTE: Number to left of slash indicates quantity; number to right of slash indicates percentage of the quantity for that particular stage.

TABLE 33B. Arizona CC:3:18

STAGE \ WEAR LOCATION	PROXIMAL END	DISTAL END	LATERAL EDGE RIGHT	LATERAL EDGE LEFT	PERIMETER	NOTCH	OTHER	TOTALS	PERCENTAGE OF TOTAL ASSEMBLAGE
Uni-directional Prepared Core									
Uni-directional Unprep'd Core									
Bi-directional Prepared Core									
Bi-directional Unprep'd Core									
Multi-directional Prepared Core									
Primary Cortical Flake									
Secondary Cortical Flake		1/20	1/20	2/40	1/20			5	6.5
Tertiary Flake									
Shatter					1/100			1	1.3
Uniface									
Biface									
Projectile Point									
TOTAL		1	1	2	2			6	7.8

NOTE: Number to left of slash indicates quantity; number to right of slash indicates percentage of the quantity for that particular stage.

TABLE 34A. Arizona CC:3:19

STAGE \ MATERIAL TYPE	RHYOLITE	SILICATES	QUARTZ	QUARTZITE	OBSIDIAN	BASALT	ANDESITE	OTHER	TOTALS	PERCENTAGE OF ASSEMBLAGE
Uni-directional Prepared Core	1/20	4/80							5	3.4
Uni-directional Unprep'd Core		2/66.7						1/33.3	3	2.0
Bi-directional Prepared Core										
Bi-directional Unprep'd Core										
Multi-directional Prepared Core										
Multi-directional Unprep'd Core										
Primary Cortical Flake	1/7.7	10/76.9				1/7.7		1/7.7	13	9.0
Secondary Cortical Flake	6/14.3	36/85.7							42	29.0
Tertiary Flakes	4/6.5	58/93.5							62	42.8
Shatter		13/100							13	9.0
Uniface		6/85.7			1/14.3				7	4.8
Biface										
Projectile Point										
TOTALS	12	129			1	1		2	145	
PERCENTAGE OF ASSEMBLAGE	8.2	89.0			0.7	0.7		1.4		100

NOTE: Number to left of slash indicates quantity; number to right of slash indicates percentage of the quantity for that particular stage.

TABLE 34B. Arizona CC:3:19

STAGE \ WEAR LOCATION	PROXIMAL END	DISTAL END	LATERAL EDGE RIGHT	LATERAL EDGE LEFT	PERIMETER	NOTCH	OTHER	TOTALS	PERCENTAGE OF TOTAL ASSEMBLAGE
Uni-directional Prepared Core							1/100	1	0.7
Uni-directional Unprep'd Core							1/100	1	0.7
Bi-directional Prepared Core									
Bi-directional Unprep'd Core									
Multi-directional Prepared Core									
Primary Cortical Flake			1/100					1	0.7
Secondary Cortical Flake			3/42.9	4/57.1				7	4.8
Tertiary Flake			3/60	2/40				5	3.4
Shatter									
Uniface		1/25	2/50	1/50				4	2.8
Biface									
Projectile Point									
TOTAL		1	9	7			2	19	13.1

NOTE: Number to left of slash indicates quantity; number to right of slash indicates percentage of the quantity for that particular stage.

TABLE 35A. Arizona CC:3:20

MATERIAL TYPE / STAGE	RHYOLITE	SILICATES	QUARTZ	QUARTZITE	OBSIDIAN	BASALT	ANDESITE	OTHER	TOTALS	PERCENTAGE OF ASSEMBLAGE
Uni-directional Prepared Core	2/66.7	1/33.3							3	1.1
Uni-directional Unprep'd Core	1/100								1	0.4
Bi-directional Prepared Core										
Bi-directional Unprep'd Core										
Multi-directional Prepared Core	1/33.3	2/66.7							3	1.1
Multi-directional Unprep'd Core										
Primary Cortical Flake	1/16.7	1/16.7		2/33.3		2/33.3			6	2.2
Secondary Cortical Flake	9/18.8	17/35.4		2/4.2		13/27.1	6/12.5	1/2.1	48	17.4
Tertiary Flakes	17/9.1	57/30.5		38/20.3	2/1.1	56/29.9	17/9.1		187	68.0
Shatter	1/3.85	9/34.6		5/19.2		10/38.5	1/3.8		26	9.4
Uniface										
Biface						1/100			1	0.4
Projectile Point										
TOTALS	32	87		47	2	82	24	1	275	
PERCENTAGE OF ASSEMBLAGE	11.6	31.6		17.1	0.8	29.8	8.7	0.4		100

NOTE: Number to left of slash indicates quantity; number to right of slash indicates percentage of the quantity for that particular stage.

TABLE 35B. Arizona CC:3:20

STAGE \ WEAR LOCATION	PROXIMAL END	DISTAL END	LATERAL EDGE RIGHT	LATERAL EDGE LEFT	PERIMETER	NOTCH	OTHER	TOTALS	PERCENTAGE OF TOTAL ASSEMBLAGE
Uni-directional Prepared Core							1/100	1	0.4
Uni-directional Unprep'd Core									
Bi-directional Prepared Core									
Bi-directional Unprep'd Core									
Multi-directional Prepared Core							1/100	1	0.4
Primary Cortical Flake									
Secondary Cortical Flake		1/100						1	0.4
Tertiary Flake		1/20	2/40	2/40				5	1.8
Shatter									
Uniface									
Biface									
Projectile Point									
TOTAL		2	2	2			2	8	3.0

NOTE: Number to left of slash indicates quantity; number to right of slash indicates percentage of the quantity for that particular stage.

TABLE 36A. Arizona W:15:15

STAGE \ MATERIAL TYPE	RHYOLITE	SILICATES	QUARTZ	QUARTZITE	OBSIDIAN	BASALT	ANDESITE	OTHER	TOTALS	PERCENTAGE OF ASSEMBLAGE
Uni-directional Prepared Core	36/87.8	2/5		1/24		1/2.4		1/2.4	41	31.5
Uni-directional Unprep'd Core	1/100								1	0.8
Bi-directional Prepared Core	9/90					1/10			10	7.7
Bi-directional Unprep'd Core	5/71.4	1/14.3						1/14.3	7	5.4
Multi-directional Prepared Core										
Multi-directional Unprep'd Core										
Primary Cortical Flake	14/87.5					2/12.5			16	12.3
Secondary Cortical Flake	32/86.5	2/5.4				2/5.4		1/2.7	37	28.5
Tertiary Flakes	8/53.3	5/33.3						2/13.3	15	11.5
Shatter										
Uniface	3/100								3	2.3
Biface										
Projectile Point										
TOTALS	108	10		1		6		5	130	
PERCENTAGE OF ASSEMBLAGE	83.1	7.7		0.8		4.6		3.8		100

NOTE: Number to left of slash indicates quantity; number to right of slash indicates percentage of the quantity for that particular stage.

TABLE 36B. Arizona W:15:15

STAGE \ WEAR LOCATION	PROXIMAL END	DISTAL END	LATERAL EDGE RIGHT	LATERAL EDGE LEFT	PERIMETER	NOTCH	OTHER	TOTALS	PERCENTAGE OF TOTAL ASSEMBLAGE
Uni-directional Prepared Core							3/100	3	2.3
Uni-directional Unprep'd Core									
Bi-directional Prepared Core							1/100	1	0.8
Bi-directional Unprep'd Core									
Multi-directional Prepared Core							2/100	2	1.5
Primary Cortical Flake			1/100					1	0.8
Secondary Cortical Flake									
Tertiary Flake									
Shatter									
Uniface			1/50	1/50				2	1.5
Biface									
Projectile Point									
TOTAL			2	1			6	9	6.9

NOTE: Number to left of slash indicates quantity; number to right of slash indicates percentage of the quantity for that particular stage.

TABLE 37A. Arizona W:15:17

STAGE \ MATERIAL TYPE	RHYOLITE	SILICATES	QUARTZ	QUARTZITE	OBSIDIAN	BASALT	ANDESITE	OTHER	TOTALS	PERCENTAGE OF ASSEMBLAGE
Uni-directional Prepared Core	7/70	2/20		1/10					10	12.7
Uni-directional Unprep'd Core										
Bi-directional Prepared Core	7/100								7	8.9
Bi-directional Unprep'd Core										
Multi-directional Prepared Core										
Multi-directional Unprep'd Core		4/100							4	5.0
Primary Cortical Flake	4/44.4	5/55.6							9	11.4
Secondary Cortical Flake	8/32	9/36				8/32			25	31.6
Tertiary Flakes	1/14.3			1/14.3		1/14.3		4/51.1	7	8.9
Shatter		10/71.4				4/28.6			14	17.7
Uniface	1/50	1/50							2	2.5
Biface					1/100				1	1.3
Projectile Point										
TOTALS	28	31		2	1	13		4	79	
PERCENTAGE OF ASSEMBLAGE	35.4	39.3		2.5	1.3	16.5		5.0		100

NOTE: Number to left of slash indicates quantity; number to right of slash indicates percentage of the quantity for that particular stage.

TABLE 37B. Arizona W:15:17

STAGE \ WEAR LOCATION	PROXIMAL END	DISTAL END	LATERAL EDGE RIGHT	LATERAL EDGE LEFT	PERIMETER	NOTCH	OTHER	TOTALS	PERCENTAGE OF TOTAL ASSEMBLAGE
Uni-directional Prepared Core									
Uni-directional Unprep'd Core									
Bi-directional Prepared Core									
Bi-directional Unprep'd Core									
Multi-directional Prepared Core							1/100	1	1.3
Primary Cortical Flake				1/100				1	1.3
Secondary Cortical Flake			1/100					1	1.3
Tertiary Flake									
Shatter									
Uniface			1/50	1/50				2	2.5
Biface									
Projectile Point									
TOTAL			2	2			1	5	6.4

NOTE: Number to left of slash indicates quantity; number to right of slash indicates percentage of the quantity for that particular stage.

primary and one secondary flake (Table 37B). Use analysis indicated medium microflaking in the form of round unifacial scars on tool exteriors.

Stratum 9. Big Lue-Gila River Canyonlands

Arizona CC:4:5. This site yielded 73 chipped stone artifacts. Rhyolite was the most commonly used material with flakes the most common artifact type (Table 38A).

Bifaces and unifaces represented formal tool types, of which only two unifaces were utilized. A Chiricahua stage Cochise point of slightly hydrated obsidian was also found, which displayed marginal retouch. Only 11 percent of the 73 artifacts were utilized, including one core, and four flakes (Table 38B). Use analysis revealed light microflaking in the form of round uniffacial scars on interiors or exteriors of tools.

Arizona CC:4:6. This site provided 253 chipped stone artifacts. Silicates were the most common materials to be exploited and flakes were the most common artifact type. The high frequency of unifaces and the high occurrence of obsidian was also significant for this site. The presence of obsidian was significant because it rarely occurred on project sites (Table 39A).

Formal tools present included unifaces and bifaces. Of these 35 percent of the unifaces and 38 percent of the bifaces were utlized and/or retouched. Also present was one non-diagnostic obsidian projectile point, triangular in shape with a concave base, rounded spurs, and no stem. Of 253 artifacts, 18.1 percent displayed utilization. Of these, secondary and tertiary flakes were most often utilized (Table 39B). Use analysis revealed light microflaking in the form of round and trapezoidal unifacial scars on tool interiors.

TABLE 38A. Arizona CC:4:5

STAGE \ MATERIAL TYPE	RHYOLITE	SILICATES	QUARTZ	QUARTZITE	OBSIDIAN	BASALT	ANDESITE	OTHER	TOTALS	PERCENTAGE OF ASSEMBLAGE
Uni-directional Prepared Core	7/100								7	9.6
Uni-directional Unprep'd Core		1/100							1	1.4
Bi-directional Prepared Core		1/100							1	1.4
Bi-directional Unprep'd Core										
Multi-directional Prepared Core										
Multi-directional Unprep'd Core										
Primary Cortical Flake	3/75					1/25			4	5.5
Secondary Cortical Flake	30/85.7				1/2.9	4/11.4			35	47.9
Tertiary Flakes	3/30				4/40	3/30			10	13.6
Shatter	1/100								1	1.4
Uniface	6/100								6	8.2
Biface					7/100				7	9.6
Projectile Point					1/100				1	1.4
TOTALS	50	2			13	8			73	
PERCENTAGE OF ASSEMBLAGE	68.5	2.7			17.8	11				100

NOTE: Number to left of slash indicates quantity; number to right of slash indicates percentage of the quantity for that particular stage.

TABLE 38B. Arizona CC:4:5

WEAR LOCATION / STAGE	PROXIMAL END	DISTAL END	LATERAL EDGE RIGHT	LATERAL EDGE LEFT	PERIMETER	NOTCH	OTHER	TOTALS	PERCENTAGE OF TOTAL ASSEMBLAGE
Uni-directional Prepared Core							1/100	1	1.4
Uni-directional Unprep'd Core									
Bi-directional Prepared Core									
Bi-directional Unprep'd Core									
Multi-directional Prepared Core									
Primary Cortical Flake									
Secondary Cortical Flake			2/66.6	1/33.3				3	4.1
Tertiary Flake			1/100					1	1.4
Shatter									
Uniface			2/100					2	2.7
Biface									
Projectile Point							1/100	1	1.4
TOTAL			5	1			2	8	11.0

NOTE: Number to left of slash indicates quantity; number to right of slash indicates percentage of the quantity for that particular stage.

TABLE 39A. Arizona CC:4:6

STAGE \ MATERIAL TYPE	RHYOLITE	SILICATES	QUARTZ	QUARTZITE	OBSIDIAN	BASALT	ANDESITE	OTHER	TOTALS	PERCENTAGE OF ASSEMBLAGE
Uni-directional Prepared Core		1/100							1	0.4
Uni-directional Unprep'd Core										
Bi-directional Prepared Core		2/100							2	0.8
Bi-directional Unprep'd Core										
Multi-directional Prepared Core										
Multi-directional Unprep'd Core						1/100			1	0.4
Primary Cortical Flake								1/100	1	0.4
Secondary Cortical Flake	17/27.4	29/46.8			12/19.4	2/3.2		2/3.2	62	24.5
Tertiary Flakes	14/13.2	66/62.3		2/1.9	14/13.2	5/4.7		5/4.7	106	41.9
Shatter	3/12.0	13/52.0			5/20	3/12		1/4.0	25	9.9
Uniface	3/6.5	32/69.6			9/19.6	2/4.3			46	18.2
Biface		3/37.5			5/62.5				8	3.1
Projectile Point					1/100				1	0.4
TOTALS	37	146		2	46	13		9	253	
PERCENTAGE OF ASSEMBLAGE	14.6	57,7		.8	18.2	5.1		3.6		100

NOTE: Number to left of slash indicates quantity; number to right of slash indicates percentage of the quantity for that particular stage.

TABLE 39B. Arizona CC:4:6

STAGE \ WEAR LOCATION	PROXIMAL END	DISTAL END	LATERAL EDGE RIGHT	LATERAL EDGE LEFT	PERIMETER	NOTCH	OTHER	TOTALS	PERCENTAGE OF TOTAL ASSEMBLAGE
Uni-directional Prepared Core									
Uni-directional Unprep'd Core									
Bi-directional Prepared Core									
Bi-directional Unprep'd Core									
Multi-directional Prepared Core									
Primary Cortical Flake									
Secondary Cortical Flake			5/38.5	7/53.8			1/7.7	13	5.1
Tertiary Flake		2/16.7	4/33.3	4/33.3	1/8.3		1/8.3	12	4.7
Shatter							1/100	1	0.4
Uniface		1/6.2	3/18.8	3/18.8	3/18.8		6/37.4	16	6.3
Biface							3/100	3	1.2
Projectile Point							1/100	1	0.4
TOTAL		3	12	14	4		13	46	18.1

NOTE: Number to left of slash indicates quantity; number to right of slash indicates percentage of the quantity for that particular stage.

Table 40. Metric Attributes and Edge Angle Measurements of Tools.

Site Number	Stratum	Mean Length	Mean Width	Mean Thickness	Mean Edge Angle	Mead Edge Length
AZ CC:2:40	2	58.1 mm	45.1 mm	22.2 mm	62°	55.2 mm
AZ CC:2:34	2	59.0 mm	41.0 mm	25.0 mm	65°	18.2 mm
AZ CC:2:33	2	88.5 mm	69.0 mm	55.5 mm		
AZ CC:2:43	3	52.5 mm	46.7 mm	23.7 mm	64°	46.9 mm
AZ CC:2:44	3	51.8 mm	50.6 mm	25.7 mm	41°	45.4 mm
AZ CC:2:46	3	49.7 mm	27.7 mm	12.3 mm	49.7°	27.5 mm
AZ CC:2:58	4					
AZ CC:2:51	5	38.8 mm	35.4 mm	16.0 mm	59°	39.2 mm
AZ CC:2:54	5	54.4 mm	48.7 mm	22.6 mm	58.1°	46.7 mm
AZ CC:2:56	5	48.5 mm	38.3 mm	20.7 mm	59°	32.8 mm
AZ CC:3:26	5	44.4 mm	38.3 mm	20.7 mm	50°	46.7 mm
AZ CC:3:28	5	48.4 mm	50.0 mm	19.5 mm	49°	47.5 mm
AZ CC:3:44	5	49.7 mm	39.0 mm	40.3 mm	59°	40.3 mm
AZ CC:3:24 (Locus 72)	5	53.4 mm	41.8 mm	22.4 mm	60°	44.4 mm
AZ CC:3:24 (Locus 72S)	5	27.1 mm	27.1 mm	4.5 mm	57°	20.7 mm
AZ CC:3:24 (Locus 72X)	5	20.0 mm	15.0 mm	10.1 mm	53°	14.8 mm
AZ CC:3:22	5	41.5 mm	50.0 mm	19.5 mm		
AZ CC:3:4	7	33.0 mm	23.7 mm	9.8 mm	59°	27.8 mm
AZ CC:3:17	7	31.5 mm	23.8 mm	9.1 mm	50.2°	28.1 mm
AZ CC:3:18	7	31.0 mm	22.3 mm	7.5 mm	66°	36.8 mm
AZ CC:3:19	7	28.1 mm	21.9 mm	7.4 mm	66.6°	16.1 mm
AZ CC:3:20	7	39.0 mm	24.1 mm	11.2 mm	55.6°	20.4 mm
AZ W:15:15	8	61.4 mm	60.5 mm	34.8 mm	61.7°	44.7 mm
AZ W:15:17	8	51.0 mm	50.6 mm	19.6 mm		27.2 mm
AZ CC:4:5	9/10	51.0 mm	36.7 mm	16.0 mm	71.7°	28.7 mm
AZ CC:4:6	9/10	24.6 mm	18.8 mm	6.0 mm	57.5°	28.9 mm

APPENDIX II

CERAMICS

by

Deborah A. Westfall

Introduction

Ceramics were recovered from eight sites during the survey and mitigation phases of the AEPCO transmission line R-O-W corridor. Three habitation sites, Arizona CC:2:30, CC:2:31 and CC:2:32, exhibited the greatest variation in types. Ceramics were also found in association with gridded gardens (Arizona CC:2:40) and lithic scatters (Arizona CC:2:34, CC:2:41, CC:2:51 and CC:3:24). Sherds found in association with lithic scatter sites appear to be the remnants of isolated pot breaks; only at Arizona CC:3:24 were ceramics found in direct association with lithic knapping activity.

The different ceramic types with references to published descriptions and known range of dates are presented in the following site-by-site descriptions and tables. It is not the intent of this report to present a detailed analysis of each ceramic type recovered; rather the reader is referred to the sources for full and complete type descriptions.

Sherds were identified with the aid of the ceramic collections at the Arizona State Museum. Dr. Emil Haury assisted in identifying unknown types and his aid is gratefully acknowledged.

The AEPCO Ceramics

One inherent difficulty in analyzing ceramics from a cultural interface area (such as Safford Basin) is their proper cultural and chronological identification. Analysis of the AEPCO ceramics was complicated since the majority were products of the Mogollon, a cultural group that lacks a synthesis of all its myriad components. Mogollon culture has been divided into several branches on the basis of geographical location and local variations in the material culture assemblage. According to Martin and Plog (1973: 90) six regions or branches are recognizable within the Mogollon area: Forestdale, Upper Little Colorado (Cibola), Point of Pines, San Simon, Pine Lawn (Reserve), and Mimbres. A seventh recognized by Wheat (1955: 29) is the Jornada branch, in the vicinity of El Paso, Texas. Each of these branches in turn has its own chronological phase system, separate from but basically correlated to phases of other branches.

Sites in the Safford Basin that were investigated during the AEPCO Phase I survey and data recovery contain ceramics representing several Mogollon branches which may be regarded as intrusive to the study area since they are types known to be produced in areas outside the Safford area. For example, at Arizona CC:2:32, a habitation site, were sherds of Encinas Red-on-brown from the Encinas phase, San Simon branch; Mimbres Bold Face Black-on-white of the Mangus phase, Mimbres branch; and Reserve Smudged of the Reserve phase, Reserve branch. We cannot say at this time whether ceramics of the San Simon and Mimbres branches found at the AEPCO sites represent trade or actual on-site production since no excavation was carried out. Previous investigations into sites in the Safford Basin (Johnson and Wasley 1966; Brown 1973) have not addressed themselves to this problem; hence it is not possible to draw meaningful conclusions regarding the presence of various Mogollon pottery types that occur in the AEPCO sites. For the present, the question of whether the mixture of Mogollon pottery types at the Safford Basin AEPCO sites is intrusive or locally produced must await future research.

Originally, it was the intent of the ceramic analysis to delineate chronological relationships as exemplified by the various Mogollon decorated types. However, since each branch has its own peculiar phase sequence, and these phases are not precisely correlative to each other, and because the sample of diagnostic ceramics was small and biased, it was felt that attempting temporal relationships at the AEPCO sites would not be useful. Sayles (1945) does not assign dates per se to the San Simon branch. Rather, he correlates San Simon phases with phases in the Mimbres branch Mogollon. Due to the insecure position of the Mogollon phases and the lack of stratigraphic control of AEPCO collections salvaged from vandalized features, the AEPCO ceramics are not assigned phase designations; rather the dates for the occurrence of each type are given where known (Table 41). These general problems concerned with chronological and cultural context are discussed further in the conclusions to this appendix.

Prior to a site-by-site description of the recovered pottery types, clarification of two types mentioned in the test is in order. These are "Brown plainware" and Sacaton Red-on-buff: Safford Variety (Gifford 1957; Olson 1959). The former has not been previously described and the latter has only been reported from the Point of Pines area. During the analysis, 42 sherds of a type of brown plainware were isolated from the general collection. Originally, it was thought this type might be a local variant of Alma Plain, the typical Mogollon plainware, but paste and temper attributes were too dissimilar. A thorough review of the literature and other ceramic types housed in the Museum collections revealed no known types similar to the AEPCO examples. Johnson and Wasley (1966: 226) mention a "Plain brownware" recovered from excavations in the vicinity of Bylas, Arizona, "A plain brownware accounted for 54.7 percent of the locally made pottery. This is a heavy, thick type probably used for a wide variety of everyday purposes, such as cooking, storing and carrying." Unfortunately, a detailed description of the physical attributes was lacking. A search of the Museum collections for sample sherds of this type resulted in only a "saver" collection that had a small number of plainware sherds, but which could not be traced to a definite description. An examination of several plainware vessels from the Bylas sites described as "unidentified plainware" revealed a tendency to lump several different plainware types into one

TYPES / PERIOD	MOGOLLON		
	RESERVE-MIMBRES-POINT OF PINES	SAN SIMON	SAFFORD BASIN
	MIMBRES BOLDFACE B/W	GALIURO R/BRN	SACATON R/BF: SAFFORD VARIETY
	RESERVE B/W	ENCINAS R/BRN	TUCSON B/R
	MIMBRES B/W		TUCSON POLYCHROME
	TULAROSA B/W		
	RESERVE SMUDGED		
	SAN FRANCISCO RED		
	PINE FLAT NECK CORR.		
	RESERVE RED		
	RESERVE PLAIN CORR.		
	TULAROSA PATTERNED CORR.		
	RESERVE PLAIN CORR.: SMUDGED		
	TULAROSA FILLET RIM		
	SAN CARLOS R/BRN		

HOHOKAM	ANASAZI	
GILA PLAIN	SNOWFLAKE B/W	PLAYAS RED, INCISED
SANTA CRUZ R/BF	PUERCO B/R	
GILA POLYCHROME	ST. JOHN'S B/R	
	ST. JOHN'S POLYCHROME	
	PINEDALE B/R	

PERIOD: 1400, 1300, 1200, 1100, 1000, 900, 800, 700, 600, 500, 400, 300

Table 41. Diagnostic Ceramic Types by Chronological Association.

category. An effort was made to determine if the brown plainware recovered in the AEPCO investigations would demonstrate affinities with the ceramics at the Bylas sites, but the sample from the latter was too small and tenuous to be used for comparative purposes. It was then decided to describe the unknown AEPCO plainware sherds in terms of physical attributes under the rubric "Brown Plainware." This is not done to establish a new type; rather it is done to set down a description for future research and possible future identification of this pottery type.

Description: Brown Plainware

Number of sherds: 42

Construction: Coiling followed by scraping (?).

Firing: Reducing atmosphere

Paste: Color may range, exterior to interior, from light reddish brown (2.5YR 6/6) to reddish brown (2.5YR 4-5/6). Paste color may also be one of several dark gray tones (2.5YR 5-6/0) with a thin band of reddish brown toward the exterior and interior surfaces. Paste texture is medium to coarse and fracture is clean and straight with a slight tendency to crumble.

Temper: Abundant medium- to coarse-textured angular sand with some gold-colored mica flecks present. Crushed, angular opaque quartz particles are also present. Temper is often exposed on the surface of jar interiors, rarely present on exterior surfaces.

Surface Finish: Interiors scraped and smoothed, with scratch marks usually obliterated. Exterior surfaces smoothed but not polished. Exterior surface color ranges from light reddish brown (5YR 6/4) to dark brown (7.5YR 4/2). Interior surfaces vary from tones of light reddish brown (5YR 6/3-4) to shades of dull gray (10YR 5-4/1). Fire clouds are occasionally present.

Form: No complete or partial vessels have yet been recovered to determine typical forms, although one large thick-walled bowl rim sherd and one recurved jar rim were found. At present, no one distinctive shape is defined. Vessel wall thickness ranges from 0.7 cm to 1.0 cm.

Cultural Affiliation: Unknown

General Comments: This type differs from Alma Plain and other plainwares in the Mogollon tradition in that paste and temper are much coarser. Additionally, only very light polishing is evident on very few sherds, and surface and paste colors tend to be lighter reddish browns, in contrast to the darker grayish and tan colors of the Mogollon wares.

A second type recovered from Arizona CC:2:31 is Sacaton Red-on-buff:Safford Variety, originally reported from the Point of Pines area (Gifford 1957: 296). This type resembles the Gila Basin variety (Gladwin and others, 1937) insofar as design layout, motifs, and vessel forms are considered. According to Gifford (1957: 296):

> There is some feeling that the Point of Pines Sacaton Red-on-buff was made in the Safford Valley and traded northward to the Point of Pines region. If this supposition is true, minor variations from Snaketown Sacaton Red-on-buff in paste, surface color and perhaps design technique, might be expected. Paste is soft and at times crumbly with rough texture; large rounded medium to coarse size particles of quartz and other minerals are frequent but mica is entirely absent.

The samples recovered from Arizona CC:2:31 were collected from the general surface of Feature 6 and from a vandalized area of Feature 7. Two, possibly three, vessel forms are represented: a Gila-shouldered jar and a straight-sided bowl. The bowl specimen exhibits affinities with ceramics of the red-on-brown tradition. That is, the application of the design is executed in a less than precise manner; lines are uneven and lumpy, and the surface color trends to a pale tan color rather than the pinkish buff associated with Gila Basin types (cf. Gifford 1957: 296). The jar sample is heavily eroded and the design is bleached out, yet elements common to Sacaton Red-on-buff are visible; these include scrolls, pendant triangles and parallel lines. The paste and temper composition reflect materials occurring in the vicinity of the site. Paste is extremely fine and crumbly, and temper is extremely fine-grained sharp sand. No mica is present in any of the collected sherds.

Due to the limited nature of data recovery at Arizona CC:2:31 it cannot be substantiated if Sacaton Red-on-buff; Safford Variety actually was made at this site (or in this area) to support Gifford's hypothesis. The jar example is nearer to the typical Gila Basin Hohokam type insofar as design and vessel form are considered. The bowl example exhibits affinities with the San Simon branch (Sayles 1936) or with ceramics of the Tucson area (Hayden 1957) in design characteristics and vessel form (a deep hemisphere). It is unlike the shallow outflaring types typical of Gila Basin forms. Variation in the assemblage is to be expected, however, in this zone of cultural interaction and blending.

Habitation Sites

The three habitation sites exhibited a wide range of ceramic types yet held constant to a dominance of Mogollon types, primarily from the Reserve area. It must be emphasized here that the sampling procedure was biased, due to the fact that the sites were not slated for archaeological data recovery and thus no sampling design for collecting sherds was implemented. Additionally, it was necessary to salvage information from severely vandalized features before all information was lost. Admittedly, in the latter case, data are not always useful, insofar as precise provenience control is needed to delineate cultural processes, yet they can be useful when applied to a very general set of problems. For example, the ceramics can be an aid in defining the limits or extent of interaction between known cultural groups such as the Mimbres branch and San Simon branch Mogollon, as well as the extent of Hohokam and Salado influences.

Arizona CC:2:30. Only two sherds were collected on the survey from this site: one "Brown Plainware" and one Mimbres Black-on-white (Cosgrove and Cosgrove 1932). On the survey it was noted that the majority of sherds were plainwares and redwares. Since only one of these was collected, it is not certain what types are present in this assemblage. Mimbres Black-on-white is a relatively late type, dated at AD 1100-1250 (Breternitz 1966: 86).

Arizona CC:2:31. This site exhibits a ceramic assemblage indicative of a wide range of interaction between cultural spheres in the Safford Basin, particularly during later times. Pottery types typical of the Mimbres-Reserve area are common, with dates ranging from AD 775 to 1400, tending to cluster during the period AD 900-1100.

Collections made from the general surface of the site show the greatest variety of types; those collected from Features 6, 16, and 17 are sensitive enough to make a few general statements regarding cultural affinities.

Ceramics recovered from Feature 5 (Table 42), an almost totally destroyed feature, are all late types (about AD 1150-1300). They are Tularosa Black-on-white (Rinaldo and Bluhm 1956), St. John's Polychrome, and Pinedale Black-on-red (Carlson 1970). It is likely that they represent trade items from the more northerly Mogollon regions.

TYPE	BOWL	JAR	UNIDENT.	TOTAL	DATES (A.D.)
Tularosa Black-on-white		1		1	1150-1300
St. John's Polychrome	1			1	1175-1300
Pinedale Black-on-red	1			1	1275-1325
TOTAL	2	1		3	

Table 42. Arizona CC:2:31, Feature 5, Surface Ceramic Inventory.

Feature 6, a dense artiface scatter indicative of an intensively used activity area, contained sherds indigenous to the Safford Basin, one sherd of Gila Plain, and sherds typical of the Reserve area Mogollon (Table 43).

TYPE	BOWL	JAR	UNIDENT.	TOTAL	DATES (A.D.)
Reserve Smudged	1			1	750-800
Reserve Red		2	1	3	900-1150
Reserve Plain Corrugated	1		8	9	1000-1200
Tularosa Patterned Corr.		1		1	
Mimbres Black-on-white	5			5	1113-1347
Tularosa Black-on-white	1			1	1150-1300
Sacaton R/BF: Safford Variety		1		1	900-1100(?)
"Brown Plainware"			1	1	
Gila Plain		3		3	300-1385
Unident. Smudged Plainware	1			1	
TOTAL	9	7	10	26	

Table 43. Arizona CC:2:31, Feature 6, Surface: Ceramic Inventory.

One sherd of Gila Polychrome (Gladwin and Gladwin 1930) was collected from Feature 11, a small sherd concentration at the extreme eastern edge of the site.

Features 16 and 17 are two architecturally similar rectangular cobble features. The ceramics from these two features lack provenience control as they were retrieved from vandalized areas, yet they do include a dominance of Mogollon types. Feature 16 (Table 44) contained sherds from the Reserve area for the most part, with only one sherd of "Brown Plainware" indicative of local production. The ceramic assemblage from Feature 17 (Table 45) strikes a balance between indigenous Safford Basin types and Reserve area types, with one sherd of Encinas Red-on-brown typical of the San Simon branch (Sayles 1945).

Collections taken from the general surface of the site (Table 46) showed a few trade types in addition to typical Mogollon types: Gila Polychrome (Gladwin and Gladwin 1930), White Mountain redwares (Carlson 1970), and a single sherd of Playas Red, incised from the Chihuahua, Mexico area (Sayles 1936).

Arizona CC:2:32. The ceramic assemblage (Table 47) from this habitation site indicates an earlier chronological context than Arizona CC:2:30 and CC:2:31. Additionally, based on survey observations, plainware

TYPE	BOWL	JAR	UNIDENT.	TOTAL	DATES (A.D.)
Reserve Smudged	1			1	750-800
Mimbres Bold Face B/W	1			1	775-927
Reserve Red	4	3		7	900-1150(?)
Reserve Plain Corrugated		5		5	1000-1200
Mimbres Black-on-white	5			5	1113-1347
San Carlos Red-on-brown	2			2	1345-1385
"Brown Plainware"	1		6	7	
Gila Plain		3		3	300-1385
Plaindale Black-on-red	1			1	1275-1325
Unident. Corrugated		1		1	
Unident. Redware			1	1	
Unident. Black-on-red	1	1		2	
TOTAL	16	13		36	

Table 44. Arizona CC:2:31, Feature 16, Disturbed Area: Ceramic Inventory.

TYPE	BOWL	JAR	UNIDENT.	TOTAL	DATES (A.D.)
Reserve Smudged	1			1	750-800
Mimbres Bold Face B/W	6			6	775-927
Pine Flat Neck Corrugated		1		1	850-1050
Reserve Red		2		2	900-1150
Reserve Black-on-white	2			2	940-1100
Reserve Plain Corrugated		7		7	1000-1200
Reserve Plain Corr.: Smudged	5			5	1050-1200
Mimbres Black-on-white	1			1	1300-1347
Sacaton R/BF: Safford Variety	1	40		41	900-1100(?)
Tucson Black-on-red		1		1	1275-1400
Tucson Polychrome	2	2		4	1275-1400
"Brown Plainware"			4	4	
Encinas Red-on-brown	1			1	950-1200
Gila Plain	2	2		4	300-1385
Unidentified Plainware	2			2	
TOTAL	23	55	4	82	

Table 45. Arizona CC:2:31, Feature 17, Disturbed Area: Ceramic Inventory.

TYPE	BOWL	JAR	UNIDENT.	TOTAL	DATES (A.D.)
Reserve Smudged	7			7	750-800
Reserve Red		1		1	900-1150
Reserve Plain Corrugated	3	7		10	1000-1200
Reserve Plain Corr.: Smudged	4			4	1050-1200
Mimbres Black-on-white	12			12	1113-1347
Tularosa Black-on-white		2		2	1150-1300
Sacaton R/BF: Safford Variety		1		1	900-1100(?)
Tucson Polychrome	1			1	1275-1400
"Brown Plainware"	1		16	17	
Gila Plain		2		2	300-1385
Puerco Black-on-red	1			1	1000-1200
St. John's Black-on-red	1			1	1175-1300
St. John's Polychrome	1			1	1175-1300
Snokeflake Black-on-white	1			1	1100-1200
Playas Red, Incised		1		1	1000-1100(?)
Unidentified Plainware			4	4	
Unident. Polished Brown			1	1	
TOTAL	32	14	21	67	

Table 46. Arizona CC:2:31, General Surface: Ceramic Inventory.

TYPES	BOWL	JAR	UNIDENT.	TOTAL	DATES (A.D.)
Reserve Smudged	1			1	750-800
San Francisco Red	3			3	760-951
Mimbres Bold Face B/W	5			5	775-927
Reserve Red	8	2		10	900-1150
Mimbres Black-on-white	7			7	1113-1347
"Brown Plainware"			2	2	
Galiuro Red-on-brown	1			1	650-850
Encinas Red-on-brown	2			2	950-1200
Santa Cruz Red-on-buff	1			1	700-900
Unidentified Redware	2	1		3	
TOTAL	30	3	2	35	

Table 47. Arizona CC:2:32, General Surface: Ceramic Inventory.

sherds occur in greater abundance at this site than at Arizona CC:2:30 and CC:2:31. Only decorated ceramics were collected for their diagnostic chronological attributes.

Ceramics with a comparatively early temporal occurrence (pre-AD 1000) are Galiuro Red-on-brown (Sayles 1945), San Francisco Red (Haury 1936), Mimbres Bold Face Black-on-white (Cosgrove and Cosgrove 1932), and Santa Cruz Red-on-buff (Gladwin and others 1937). Later types include Encinas Red-on-brown (Sayles 1945) and Mimbres and Tularosa Black-on-white (Rinaldo and Bluhm 1956).

Arizona CC:2:41. This site, situated in the Gila River floodplain, may once have been a habitation site that has since been destroyed by plowing. Abundant plainwares were observed on the surface. A single jar sherd of Reserve Black-on-white (Martin and Rinaldo 1950) was collected from this site and indicates a late (post-AD 1000) occurrence.

Other Sites

Arizona CC:2:34. The single sherd collected from this site is an isolated eroded fragment from an unidentified smudged plainware bowl. It was recovered from the San Simon River channel and evidently was washed downstream from elsewhere.

Arizona CC:2:40. This site, containing agricultural and water control features, had a somewhat mixed assemblage. Ceramics recovered from the surface include one jar sherd of Gila Plain and 32 sherds of a Tularosa Fillet Rim jar (Wendorf 1950). The latter dates during the time period AD 1100-1300 (Breternitz 1966: 99). The remaining sample consists of nine sherds of the locally produced "Brown Plainware." The chronological significance of the sherds at this site is uncertain because of the smallness of the sample.

Arizona CC:2:51. Two sherds were recovered from this site. One sherd of Encinas Red-on-brown (Sayles 1945) was found in the bed of an arroyo running through the site. The second is a sherd of Reserve Red (Gifford 1957) recovered from the surface of Feature 1, a storage pit. Both of these types are tentatively dated between AD 900 and 1200 (Sayles 1945; Gifford 1957). These ceramics are most likely isolated occurrences at this site. They probably are reflective of activities carried out in relation to habitation sites such as Buena Vista, Earven Flat, and Yuma Wash (Brown 1973), and Arizona CC:2:31, which are in the immediate vicinity.

Arizona CC:3:24. This site yielded one sherd each of Mimbres Bold Face Black-on-white and Mimbres Black-on-white (Cosgrove and Cosgrove 1932), both of which are indigenous to the Mimbres Branch Mogollon. Five sherds of an unidentified corrugated type, possibly also of Mogollon, represent remnants of a pot break and were associated with a cluster of lithic thinning flakes. The ceramics can only tentatively suggest this site's affinities with the Mimbres branch.

Summary

Traditionally, decorated ceramics are used to identify cultural groups in time and space. Other studies have focused on interpreting changes in ceramic traditions as a factor of sociocultural behavior. Plainwares are usually recognized as locally produced or imported utility types used for a wide range of everyday subsistence related behavior.

The AEPCO ceramics fall into two basic groups: those collected on survey for cultural identification purposes (Arizona CC:2:30, CC:2:31, CC:2:32, and CC:2:41) and those recovered in the course of mitigation (Arizona CC:2:34, CC:2:40, and CC:2:51 and CC:3:24).

The collections from the three habitation sites reflect a skewed sample that is inappropriate for studies requiring strict provenience and sampling control. Since the original research design did not allow for studies made on sites not slated for mitigation, a few general problems were considered that would apply to the ceramics from these habitation sites.

One problem is the definition of cultural groups in the area. As reflected in the ceramic assemblage in order of dominance, Mogollon, Hohokam, and Salado influences are present. The identification of a local population is not possible at this time, although the ceramics suggest strong similarities with the Point of Pines area (Emil Haury 1977, personal communication). This is borne out by a multiplicity of types representative of groups geographically and culturally surrounding the study area and a comparative absence or scarcity of a recognizable locally produced decorated type. Identification of cultural groups in the Safford Basin was a corrollary study in a project carried out by Brown (1973). Although the major thrust of his work was oriented towards identifying Salado origins, his data indicated a dominant cultural pattern attributed to the Point of Pines-Reserve area Mogollon during the time period AD 1000-1275. Brown postulated an immigration of pre-pueblo groups from the Point of Pines area (1973: 129) although this hypothesis has yet to be confirmed.

The problem of identifying a local indigenous Safford Basin group necessitates isolating traits not typical of other cultures or subcultures. The present sample of sherds and observed surface features from the AEPCO habitation sites do not lend themselves to this type of analysis.

One other problem concerns the designation of certain pottery types as intrusive, particularly when applied to Mogollon types. Since the study area is a zone of interaction between cultures, it is difficult to determine if various types can truly be designated as intrusive. This problem specifically concerns the relationships between pottery of the San Simon branch and that of the Point of Pines-Reserve-Mimbres branches. Sayles (1945: 2, Fig. 1) illustrates San Simon branch sites occurring around Safford, while Brown's research demonstrates a strong Point of Pines presence in the same area. Both branches overlap in time, with the San Simon branch pottery types occurring slightly earlier. Ceramics recovered from the surface of AEPCO habitation sites exhibit a mixture of types typical of both branches. Due to the limited nature of the AEPCO data an attempt to determine the chronological and cultural significance of the collections would not be feasible. Attempts to define these types as intrusive or local requires control over context and time that is possible only with careful excavation.

The entire issue of temporal and spatial aspects of Mogollon culture needs to be better defined and synthesized to understand the processes that lead to intracultural differences. Phase and branch designations often take on an undesirable rigidity and the proliferation of these further complicates efforts to understand processes at sites where mixing and blending of traits occur, as is the case in the Safford Basin. For the present, identification of processes responsible for the development of the Safford Basin culture pattern must await future research.

The ceramics recovered from sites investigated during mitigation represent a very small sample that is useful only for postulating cultural affinities and general activities. Plainware sherds found in association with lithic scatters apparently are remnants of pot breaks, associated with food gathering activities. More simply, they could be the remains of vessels broken in transport. Generally, the sherds recovered from the sampled sites are reflective of activities carried out beyond the habitation sites.

APPENDIX III

POLLEN ANALYSIS OF SELECTED SAMPLES FROM ARIZONA CC:2:40 and CC:2:51

by

Gerald K. Kelso

Objectives

The analysis of the Arizona CC:2:30 (Loci 44/45) and C:2:51 samples was undertaken to determine if the pollen content of the deposits would confirm the prehistoric agricultural use of the rock-bounded areas designated "grid gardens" and would indicate the purpose for which the rock pile at CC:2:40 and the pit (Feature 1) at CC:2:51 were constructed. The pollen spectra of archaeological sites are considerable distorted by human interference with the natural vegetation and it was not anticipated that significant environmental data would be recovered.

Methods

The analysis was conducted at the Laboratory of Paleoenvironmental Studies, University of Arizona. Pollen extraction procedures followed Mehringer (1967). Terminology also followed Mehringer (1967) except that his "low-spine" and "high spine" Compositae categories have been designated "*Ambrosia*-type" and "other Compositae" respectively.

Two hundred pollen grains per sample were tabulated with a compound transmitted-light microscope at 400 power and each side was completely scanned for economic pollen types. Questionable pollen grains were examined under fluid at 1000 power. Identifications are based on the pollen reference collection at the Laboratory of Paleoenvironmental Studies.

Pollen in archaeological sites is especially subject to oxidization due to the loose nature of the deposits and to the presence of decaying organic materials. Absolute pollen sums were computed for all samples (Table 48) using Benninghoff's (1962) exotic pollen addition method. This was done to determine if the quantities of pollen in the prehistoric samples were comparable to those in the surface samples or to those in other archaeological sites and could be confidently interpreted. The pollen grains in each sample that were so degraded as to be unidentifiable (Table 48) were tabulated for the same purpose. These unidentifiable pollen grains were not

Table 48. Arizona CC:2:40 (Loci 44/45) and Arizona CC:2:51: Pollen Sums

SAMPLE	Pinus	Quercus	Juniperus	Prosopis	Tamarix	Alnus	Salix	Compositeae				Cheno-Ams	Tidestromia	Sarcobatus	GRAMINEAE	Plantago	Erigonium	POLYBONACEAE	Euphorbia	NYCTAGINACEAE	UMBELLIFEREAE	LEGUMINOSEAE	ROSACEAE	ONAGRACEAE	CRUCIFERAE	Urtica	C.F. Canotia	Ribes	Larria	Ephedra		Sparganium/ Typha-Monad	CYPERACEAE	Undetermined	Raw Σ	Eucalyptus	Absolute Σ per gram	Undeterminable
								Artemisia	Ambrosia-type	Chichoreae	"Other-Compositeae"																			Torryana-type	Nevadensis-type							
Grid Garden	--	--	--	--	--	--	--	--	--	--	--	--	--	--	--	--	--	--	--	--	--	--	--	--	--	--	--	--	--	--	--	--	--	--	---	--	------	--
PS 44-Surface	7	4	7	--	1	--	--	2	93	--	5	35	1	--	16	--	--	4	3	2	--	4	--	--	1	--	--	1	--	2	--	--	--	12	200	13	32,227	8
10 cm	5	1	3	1	--	--	--	1	101	--	4	49	--	1	9	--	--	8	--	1	--	5	--	--	--	--	--	--	1	2	2	--	1	5	200	33	9,422	20
20 cm	7	1	1	--	--	--	--		94	1	4	50	3	1	7	--	1	3	--	4	1	4	2	1	--	--	--	--	--	5	2	--	--	8	200	20	26,891	20
Rock Pile	--	--	--	--	--	--	--		--	--	--	--	--	--	--	--	--	--	--	--	--	--	--	--	--	--	--	--	--	--	--	--	--	--	---	--	------	--
PS 45-Surface	13	3	5	2	--	--	--	6	52	--	2	67	--	2	12	1	1	--	2	1	3	4	--	--	--	--	--	1	--	1	--	1	--	20	200	5	92,558	6
Interior	7	--	3	--	--	1	--		65	3	--	83	--	1	5	--	--	8	--	7	--	--	1	--	--	--	1	--	3	5	2	--	--	5	200	1	12,464	25
Pit (Feature 1)	--	--	--	--	--	--	--		--	--	--	--	--	--	--	--	--	--	--	--	--	--	--	--	--	--	--	--	--	--	--	--	--	--	---	--	------	--
PS 58-Surface	14	--	8	--	--	--	--		77	--	3	51	--	--	16	--	--	2	2	--	1	5	1	--	--	--	--	--	2	3	--	--	--	15	200	39	13,427	10
13 cm	19	--	4	--	--	--	--	4	91	1	--	48	1	--	1	1	2	5	2	3	1	1	--	--	--	1	--	--	--	9	1	--	--	5	200	48	9,871	35

incorporated in the raw sum and do not appear on the pollen diagram (Figure 123).

Results

The absolute pollen sums of the prehistoric samples (9,422-26,891 pollen grains) were smaller than those of their equivalent surface samples (13,427-92,558 pollen grains) and the quantities of degraded pollen grains in the prehistoric samples were higher. However, the ranges of the absolute pollen sums of the two sample types overlapped, and the quantities of pollen present in the prehistoric samples were equivalent to or higher than those from other southwestern archaeological sites. A certain amount of pollen loss must be accepted in archaeological samples and the preservation of the Arizona CC:2:40 and CC:2:51 pollen spectra is sufficient to permit analysis.

Aboreal Pollen Types

Pinus. All of the pine (*Pinus*) pollen grains present in the Arizona CC:2:40 and CC:2:51 samples were relatively small and fell into the size range (bladder length under 40 microns) which Martin (1963: Fig. 9) defined for the pinyon pines. The majority of the well-preserved pollen grains also displayed the gemmae in the vicinity of the germinal colpus ("belly warts") characteristic of the Haploxlon pine sub-genus to which the pinyon pines belong. The absence of these "belly warts" from a few pollen grains suggests however, that Diploxlon pine species, such as the higher altitude *Pinus ponderosa* and *P. flexilis*, may have contributed to the counts in a small way.

There is little difference between the surface and prehistoric pine pollen frequencies of these two sites; these low counts, 2.5 to 9.5 percent (Figure 123), are consistent with those recorded by Hevly, Mehringer, and Yocum (1963, Fig. 3) for Sonoran Desert Shrub and Grassland in the Tucson Mountain area. Pine pollen can be transported hundreds of miles and all of this pollen type in the Arizona CC:2:40 and CC:2:51 samples was undoubtedly blown in from some distance. Pinyon pines are presently found closer to Arizona CC:2:51 (around 8 km) than to CC:2:40 (around 18 km). This was apparently the case during the occupation period as well, since the pine pollen counts from the prehistoric samples of the latter sites are lower than the pine pollen frequencies from the former site.

Juniperus and *Quercus*. Neither junipers (Juniperus) nor oaks (*Quercus*) grow at present in the vicinity of Arizona CC:2:40 or CC:2:51, and the small quantities of their pollen found in the sites are probably due to long distance wind transport. Both pollen types can be blown considerable distances (Potter and Rowley 1960: 5). Small amounts of wind transported pollen of these types were also found in Hevly, Mehringer, and Yocum's (1964: 130) Sonoran Desert surface samples. The somewhat lesser quantities of juniper pollen found in the Arizona CC:2:40 and CC:2:51 prehistoric samples are more likely due to the degradation of this somewhat delicate pollen type than to lower juniper populations in the past.

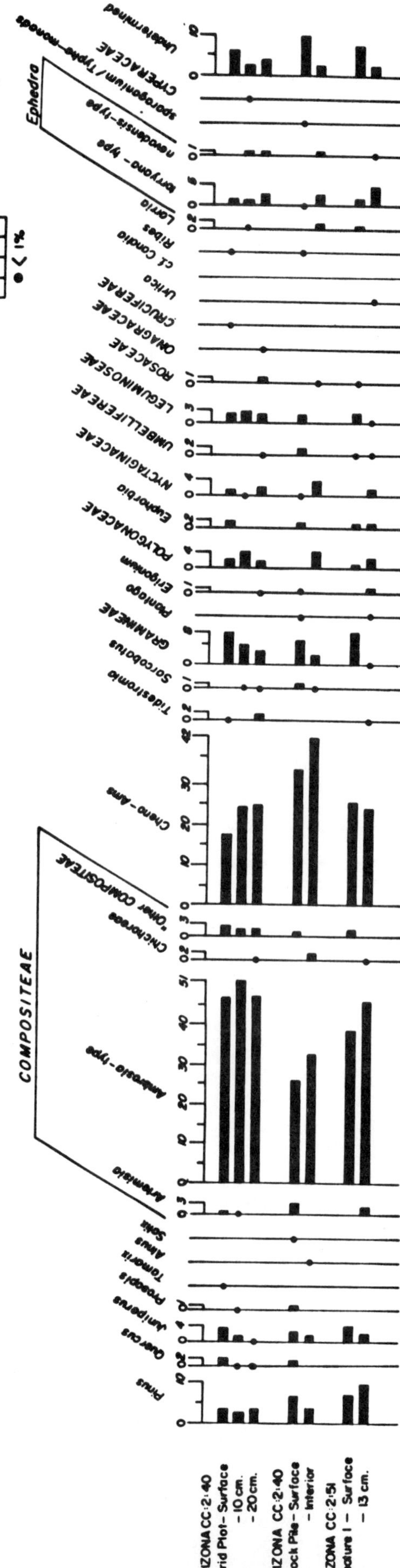

Figure 123. Pollen counts

Minor Arboreal Pollen Types. Occasional pollen grains from mesquite (Prosopis), Tamarisk (Tamarix) alder (Alnus), and willow (Salix) were found scattered through the Arizona CC:2:40 and CC:2:51 pollen spectra. Mesquite and tamarisk are insect pollinated while alder is adapted to wind pollination. Willows disperse their pollen partially by wind and partially by insect. In Arizona all of these trees grow chiefly along streams or where the water table is high (Kearney and Peebles 1951: 211, 215, 401, 557) and their pollen was probably wind transported from the Gila River, about 2.7 km from the sites. Tamarisk was introduced from Eurasia (Kearney and Peebles 1951: 557) and its pollen was seen only in the Arizona CC:2:40 grid garden surface sample.

Non-Arboreal Pollen Types

Ambrosia-type. The pollen contributed by the wind-pollinated members of the Compositae comprises the single most important pollen type in the Arizona CC:2:40 and CC:2:51 samples. The plants producing Ambrosia-type pollen, especially the ragweeds themselves, favor disturbed soils. They are prolific pollen producers and palynologists in Europe (Iverson 1941; Mitchell 1956; Hyde 1959) and eastern North America (Butler 1959; M. B. Davis 1959; R. B. Davis 1967) have interpreted rises in the pollen frequencies of such weedy plants as reflecting the beginnings of agriculture in their study areas. The connection between agriculture and abnormally large quantities of weed pollen in modern soils has been demonstrated in both the eastern United States (Solomon and Kroener 1971) and the southwest (Solomon n. d.).

Samples from southwestern archaeological sites usually contain considerably more pollen from weedy species than do modern soil samples, but this was not the case with Arizona CC:2:40 and CC:2:51. The prehistoric ragweed-type counts from these localities are only slightly higher than those of the modern surface sample and both the prehistoric and modern pollen frequencies fall within the range of the ragweed-type counts from the lower elevations of Hevly, Mehringer, and Yocum's (1963, Table 3) Tucson Mountain and Avra Valley pollen transect. The ragweed-type pollen frequencies from Arizona CC:2:40 and CC:2:51 do not clearly reflect human interference with the natural vegetation.

Some snakeweed (Gutierrezia) is presently growing on Arizona CC:2:40 and most of the ragweed-type pollen in the sites was probably produced quite close by. Some ragweed-type pollen can be wind transported great distances but most of it comes to earth within a few meters of the parent plant (Raynor, Ogden, and Hayes 1973: Figures 6 and 9.

Cheno-Ams. The pollen of the goosefoot family (Chenopodiaceae) and pigweed (Amaranthus), whose pollen cannot be reliably distinguished, constitutes the second most important pollen type in the Arizona CC:2:40 and CC:2:51 pollen spectra. This wind-dispersed pollen type is also a good indicator of disturbed soil conditions and it is prominently represented in samples from almost all southwestern archaeological sites. Plants producing Cheno-am type pollen were also important as gathered food sources to the aborigional inhabitants of the region during the historic period (Stevenson 1915: 66; Robbins and others 1916: 53; Whiting 1939: 73-74; Elmore 1944: 45-46;) and one introduced species, coxcomb (*Amaranthus cruentus*), was treated as a semi-domesticate by the Hopi (Whiting 1939: 16).

The somewhat greater quantitites of Cheno-am pollen in the Arizona CC:2:40 prehistoric samples, when compared to the surface samples, might reflect either soil disturbance attending agriculture or wild resources carried into the site area. The prehistoric Cheno-am count of the Arizona CC:2:51 pit is, on the other hand, somewhat lower than that of the modern sample and comparable quantities of this pollen type are distributed throughout Hevly, Mehringer and Yocum's (1963: Table 3) Sonoran Desert pollen transect. The origin of the Cheno-am pollen in these two sites cannot, therefore, be established.

Gramineae. The gross (Gramineae) pollen frequencies of all three Arizona CC:2:40 and CC:2:51 surface samples are higher than those of their equivalent prehistoric samples and are comparable to the grass pollen frequencies in the Sonoran Desert Shrub segment of Hevly, Mehringer, and Yocum's (1963: Table 3) Tucson Mountain area pollen transect. This suggests that grass populations were depressed during the occupation of the sites. It is possible that the lower prehistoric grass pollen counts were caused by some environmental factor, but none of the other pollen types support such an intrepretation. Human activity of some sort is more likely involved.

Both the Hopi (Whiting 1939: 64-67) and the Zuni (Stevenson 1915: 24) occasionally consumed grass seed and Bohrer (1972: 24) reported indications that grass seed was milled at the Hay Hollow site during prehistoric times. The historic native inhabitants of the Southwest seem, however, to have preferred grass as a raw material rather than as a food. Perhaps the inhabitants of Arizona CC:2:40 and CC:2:51 over-exploited this resource in their vicinity.

Ephedra. Two morphological varieties of Mormom tea (*Ephedra*) pollen were present in the Arizona CC:2:40 and CC:2:51 pollen samples. The *Ephedra torryana*-type, the more prominent of the two, is more common in modern surface samples from the southern portion of Arizona where summer rainfall predominates, while the other morphological variety, the *Ephedra nevadensis*-type, is more frequent in the natural pollen rain of the winter precipitation areas of the northern half of the state. The proportions of these two varieties of Mormon tea pollen in the Arizona CC:2:40 and CC:2:51 pollen spectra suggest that the annual distribution of precipitation during the occupation period was not markedly different from that of the present.

There was slightly more Mormon tea pollen in the prehistoric samples from both sites than in the modern comparative samples but the frequencies involved are rather low and not definitive. Notable quantities of Mormon tea pollen are known to be wind-transported hundreds of kilometers (Maher 1964: 392).

Minor Non-Arboreal Pollen Types. A few of the less prominent non-arboreal pollen types present in the Arizona CC:2:40 and CC:2:51 pollen samples, sagebrush (*Artemisia*), greasewood (*Sarcobatus*), bur-weed/cattail (*Sparganium/Typha*-monads) and sedge (*Cyperaceae*), are wind-dispersed, but the majority are transferred by insect. The wind pollinated types are only sporadically represented and were probably not growing in the immediate vicinity during the occupation.

Some of the insect-adapted pollen types, the buckwheat family (Polygonaceae), the four-o'clock family (Nyctaginaceae) and the pea family (Leguminoseae) for instance, are regular, though low, components in the counts and could not have come from too far away. Such plants do not produce large quantities of pollen and it does not often accidently escape from the flower due to the presence of the resins and sticky oils which cause it to adhere to the insect vectors. Creosotebush (Larrea), for example, dominates the present vegetation of Arizona CC:2:51 but contributed only 1 percent of the pollen grains in the site surface sample.

The only suggestions of trends among the minor non-arboreal pollen types are the slightly higher buckwheat family and four-o'clock family pollen frequencies in the sub-surface samples of both sites. These counts are not, however, sufficiently high to be interpreted as indicating prehistoric utilization of the parent plants.

SUMMARY

None of the pollen frequencies from the Arizona CC:2:40 and CC:2:51 was inconsistent with those recorded by Hevly, Mehringer, and Yocum (1963: Table 3) for the natural pollen rain of Sonoran Desert Shrub in the Tucson Mountain area. No single pollen count stood out sufficiently to imply that the plant that produced it was utilized by the prehistoric inhabitants of the site and no pollen of domesticated plants was found.

There is a suggestion of the kind of soil disturbance that accompanies human activities in the ragweed-type and Cheno-am pollen counts from these two sites, while the grass pollen frequencies may reflect a lower grass population in the vicinity during the occupation period. The proportions of the two morphological varieties of Mormon tea pollen present in the samples imply that the annual distribution of precipitation during the period when the sites were occupied was not greatly different from that of the present.